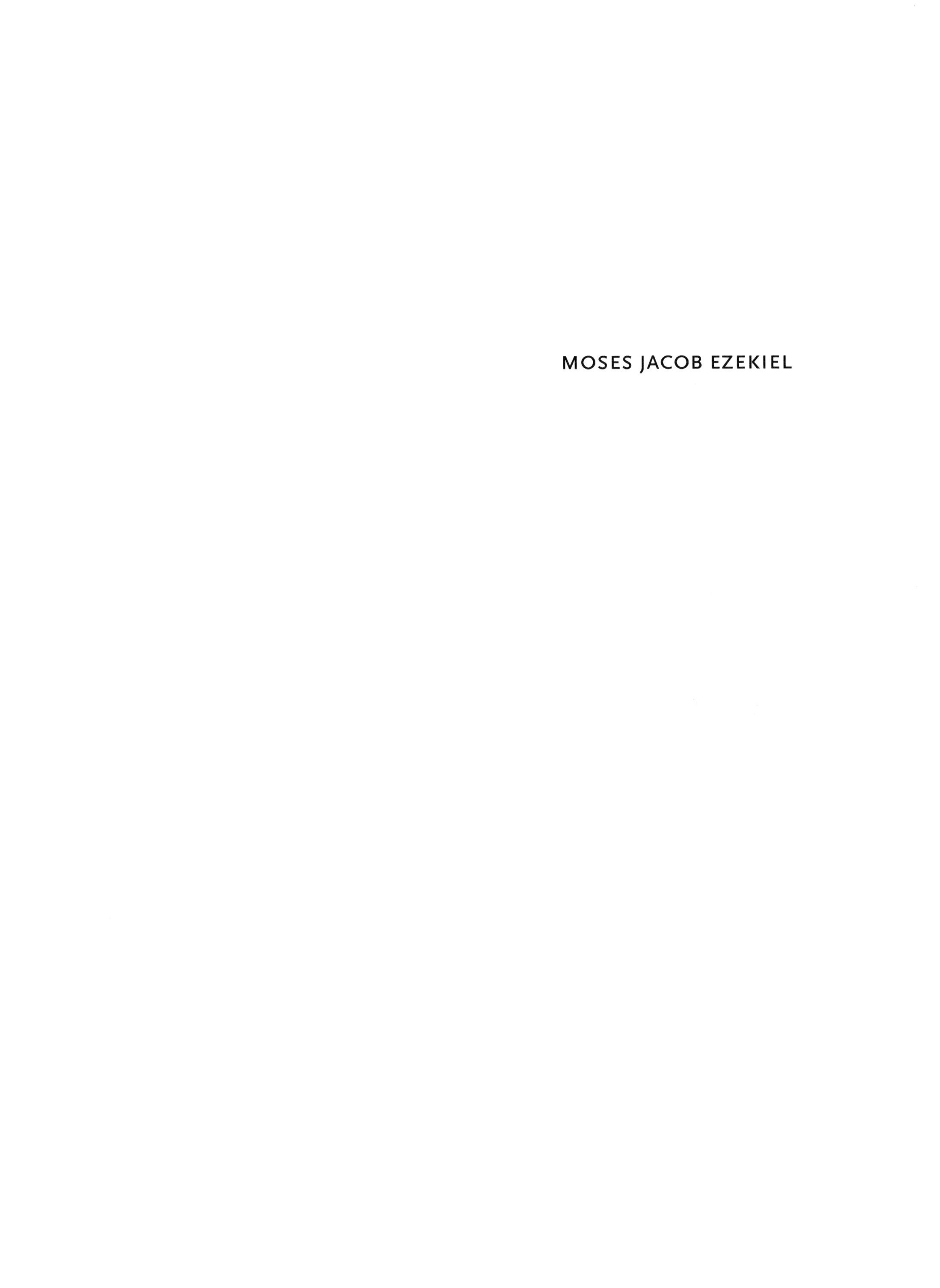

MOSES JACOB EZEKIEL

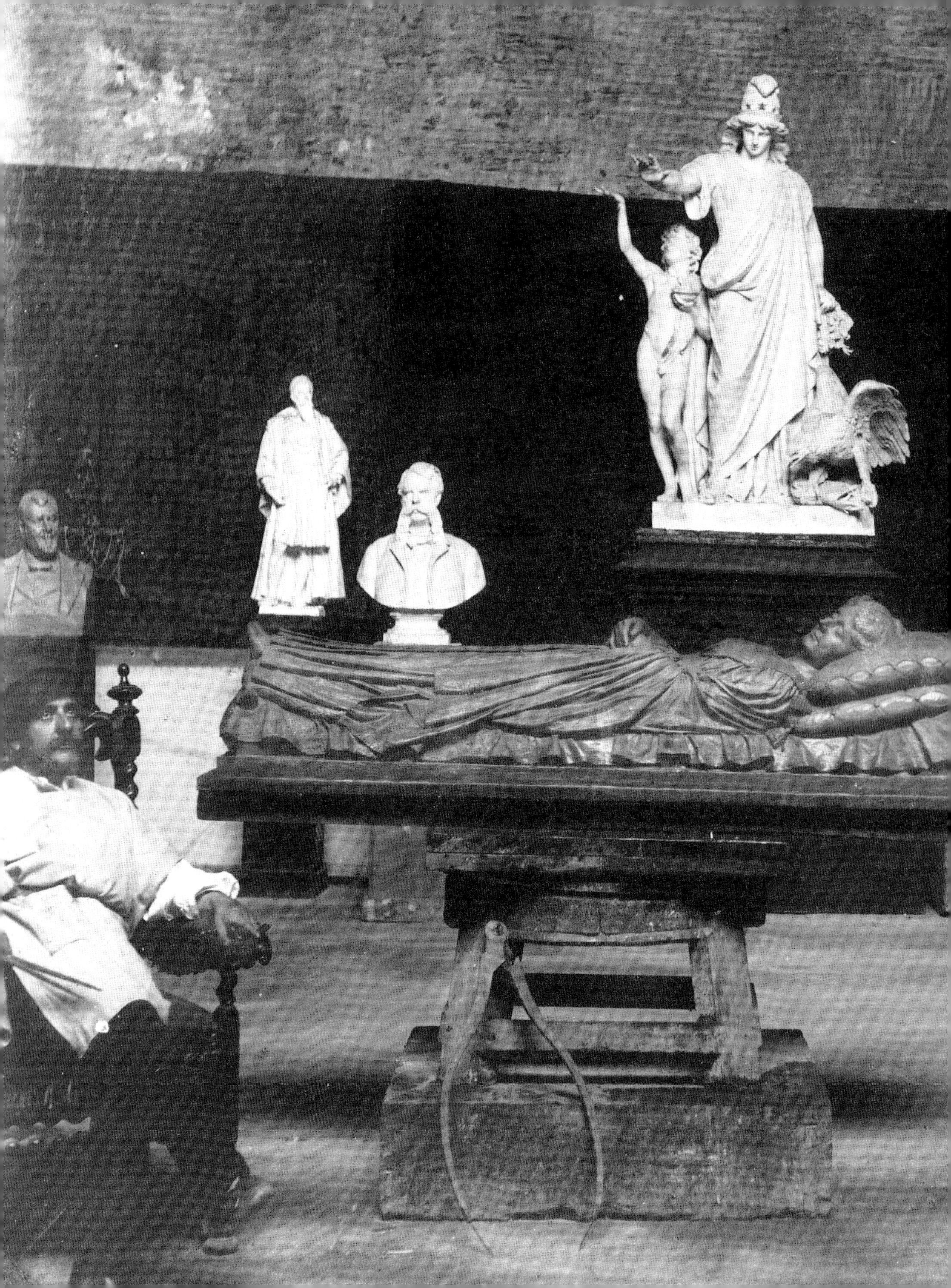

MOSES JACOB EZEKIEL

JEWISH, CONFEDERATE, EXPATRIATE SCULPTOR

SAMANTHA BASKIND

The Pennsylvania State University Press
University Park, Pennsylvania

Library of Congress Cataloging-in-Publication Data

Names: Baskind, Samantha, Author.
Title: Moses Jacob Ezekiel : Jewish, Confederate, expatriate sculptor / Samantha Baskind.
Description: The Pennsylvania State University Press, University Park, Pennsylvania, [2025] | Includes bibliographical references.
Summary: "Examines the life and work of Moses Jacob Ezekiel, exploring how his Jewish, Confederate, and expatriate identities shaped his sculpture. Analyzes his role in the
late-nineteenth-century art market and how his career reflected and challenged American art, history, and cultural values"—Provided by publisher.
Identifiers: LCCN 2025024244 | ISBN 9780271099804 (hardback)
Subjects: LCSH: Ezekiel, Moses Jacob, 1844–1917 | Ezekiel, Moses Jacob, 1844–1917—Criticism and interpretation | Sculptors—United States—Biography | Jewish artists—United States—Biography | Expatriate sculptors—Italy—Rome—Biography | Sculpture, American—19th century | Sculpture, American—20th century | Jewish sculpture—United States.
Classification: LCC NB237.E9 B37 2025 | DDC 730.92
LC record available at https://lccn.loc.gov/2025024244

Printed in the United States of America
Published by The Pennsylvania State University Press,
University Park, PA 16802–1003

The Pennsylvania State University Press is a member of the Association of University Presses.

It is the policy of The Pennsylvania State University Press to use acid-free paper. Publications on uncoated stock satisfy the minimum requirements of American National Standard for Information Sciences—Permanence of Paper for Printed Library Material, ANSI Z39.48–1992.

In memory of
Patrick Alexander,
editor, friend, polymath

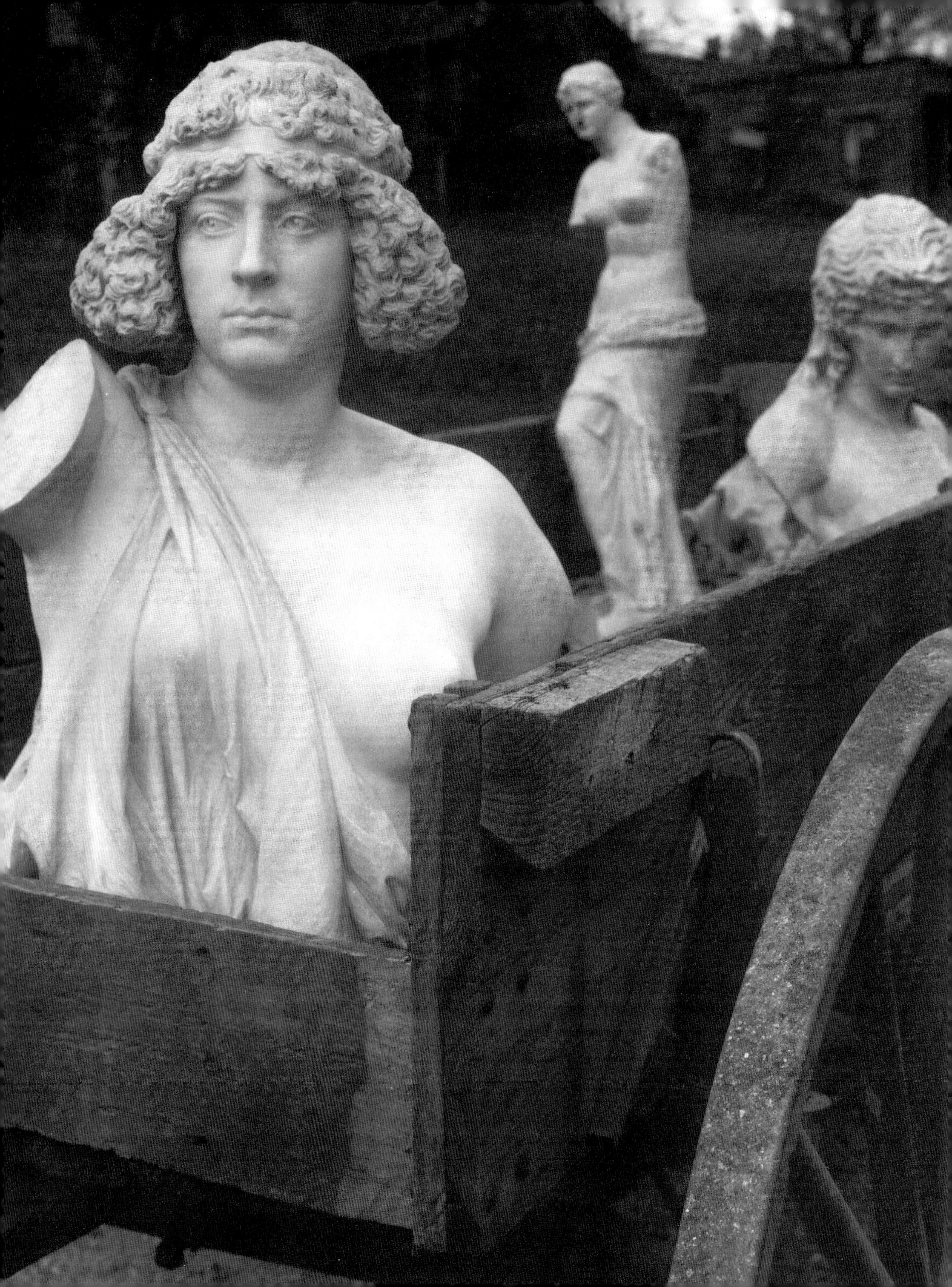

CONTENTS

ILLUSTRATIONS

PREFACE

A Nineteenth-Century American Sculptor and a Twenty-First-Century American Art Historian's Lives Collide

While writing this book, Moses Jacob Ezekiel and I became embroiled in an internationally publicized controversy. Princeton University commissioned me to curate an exhibition of Jewish artists active during the Gilded Age, slated for a September 2022 opening in the Ellen and Leonard Milberg Gallery, located in the university's Firestone Library. The first of its kind, the exhibition broadly intended to demonstrate this understudied group's significant contributions to American art, when newly accorded religious freedoms allowed Jews to participate in larger society and the art world. It would have included approximately fifty objects. Most of the artists' Jewishness had rarely been discussed in conjunction with their artwork. When germane, the show aimed to contextualize this work vis-à-vis Jewish identity, along with nineteenth-century politics and broader creative pursuits.

I selected relevant works around the exhibition's three themes: religion, politics, and art. As the foremost Jewish artist of the period, Ezekiel was to be featured with four sculptures: his busts of Rabbi *Isaac Mayer Wise* and President *Abraham Lincoln*, a half-length bronze of composer *Franz Liszt*, and—the coup of the show—a life-size marble of *Faith*, identical to the same figure in his twenty-four-foot-tall monument *Religious Liberty*.[1] *Faith* was to be positioned at the front of the exhibition, serving as an entry point to the show and demonstrating the religious liberty that allowed Jews, and Jewish artists, to thrive in America. A floor-to-ceiling vinyl of *Religious Liberty* would have been placed on the wall adjacent to *Faith*. To its side, a glass case was meant to display the program for *Religious Liberty*'s unveiling, a photograph of Ezekiel in his studio with the plaster model of the monument, and Simon Wolf's 1895 instrumental book about Jews in the military opened to its frontispiece featuring *Religious Liberty*. This one-two punch at the outset of the show would have been spectacular. After I had already received affirmatives to loan requests from museums and private lenders for more than half the works to be displayed in the show, Princeton officials balked.

Princeton voiced concern about Ezekiel and painter Theodore Moïse, both soldiers in the Confederate army. Worried that students might protest and white supremacists be ennobled, university officials asked me to rewrite the show to omit "Confederate artists," as they put it. Yet there were no works promoting Confederate beliefs in the exhibition, and my carefully crafted wall labels did not elide the artists' Confederate affiliations. More still, the exhibition was being held at an institution of higher learning where students were supposed to learn about the multiplicity of artists' identities—let alone about Jewish American art, culture, and history. They were also meant to enjoy beautiful art born from these multiplicities. The Office of Institutional Equity and Diversity weighed in and the librarians at Princeton censored the show without regard for the signage or the dialogues they sought to foster. After consulting with the show's generous benefactor, Princeton alumni Leonard Milberg, I decided that to display a partial history of nineteenth-century Jewish American art marred the exhibition's narrative and erased history. By canceling the artists, Princeton effectively canceled the show.

Religion News Service first got wind of the cancelation and published an article about the controversy.[2] I, among others, voiced displeasure at the university's sanitizing of history. Jonathan Sarna of Brandeis University, the foremost scholar of Jewish American history, said it best: "One approach is that we have faith in the audience; we display in full complexity the material and talk about it. The other approach is that we cancel it. I'm very reluctant to be part of the woke, cancel everything that doesn't conform to present-day moral standards."[3] Students at Princeton soon heard about the show that was not to be and ran an article addressing the cancelation in their newspaper, the *Daily Princetonian*.[4] These two articles ignited something of a firestorm. Soon, the canceled exhibition became a cause célèbre, discussed by academics on Facebook and Twitter (now X) and more visibly in the national and international press. Reporters called me for several days.

Jewish Telegraph Agency published an article that was picked up by other outlets, including the *Times of Israel*, *Forward*, and the *Jerusalem Post*.[5] Soon the *New York Sun*, *Reason*, *American Thinker*, *College Fix*, the *Princeton Alumni Weekly*, and *Princetonians for Free Speech* covered the "Princeton exhibition debacle," as I termed the incident to my colleagues and friends.[6] *The Hill* even hosted a short episode on YouTube, with three talking heads admonishing Princeton.[7] The statement I generally provided the press, quoted in some of these venues, was the following: "Princeton's effort to avoid any potential controversy was at the expense of a tremendous opportunity to display intriguing and exceptional art to their students, and to open up crucial conversations. A vital learning moment was lost." One article headlined my accusation, when I chastised Princeton for its "anti-intellectual surrender to cancel culture."[8] Indeed, the university's knee-jerk response in pursuit of reputational management superseded interest in knowledge, education, and the enrichment of students and the larger community.

As I see it, historians are tasked to tell the entire story, including those aspects we wish were not there. This book does just that.

ACKNOWLEDGMENTS

The research and writing of this book would not have been possible without the assistance of many institutions and individuals. I wish to thank the staff members at various libraries, museums, and archives, among them Bonnie Eisenman, Beth Ahabah Museum and Archives; Abby Glogower, Filson Historical Society; Will Hopkins, Norfolk Public Library; Cheryl Kempler, B'nai B'rith International Archives; Kelly Kerney, The Valentine Museum; and Mary Laura Kludy, Virginia Military Institute Archives. Special thanks for the extraordinary assistance provided by Dana Herman and her staff at the American Jewish Archives, and Claire Pingel at the Weitzman National Museum of American Jewish History.

I am very fortunate to have received generous funding. The Southern Jewish Historical Society provided a much-needed grant that allowed me to study Ezekiel's Corcoran Gallery sculptures at the Norfolk Botanical Garden. A precious year of quiet research and writing was made possible by a yearlong fellowship from the National Endowment for the Humanities. My most profound thanks are still not enough.

Michelle Facos, Keith Gibson, Ken Koltun-Fromm, Natasha Goldman, Shana Klein, Laura Levitt, Ellen Landau, Adam Mendelsohn, and Andrea Pappas insightfully read and commented on various chapters, and to all of them I convey my most sincere appreciation. Erika Doss, a truly wonderful colleague, offered sage advice and a crucial reading of chapter 6. Larry Silver carefully read the entire manuscript and served as a sounding board throughout the years I worked on the project, which he encouraged me to write. As always, he sharpened my thinking. Jonathan Sarna's scrupulous read of chapter 3 made all the difference, and I am forever grateful for his support here and always. Years of exchange of ideas with Alanna Cooper have enlivened my ideas on this project and so many others. Valuable feedback from audiences at talks in the United States and abroad proved essential to my thinking. I especially thank the Smithsonian American Art Museum fellows and my cohorts convening at the "Uneasy Objects" seminars at Haverford College and Cornell University.

I am endlessly indebted to Colonel Keith Gibson, Director of the Virginia Military Institute Museum System, whose work on Ezekiel paved the way for my own. I have benefited greatly from our many rich conversations. For her graciousness, I extend my very best to Abby Schwartz, Director Emeritus of the Skirball Museum in Cincinnati, who facilitated my examination of Ezekiel's sculptures on more than one occasion and provided unparalleled hospitality. Susanna Gold, Josh Lambert, and Deborah Dash Moore came through in a pinch when COVID-19 hit and I could not access key materials. Thank you to Robert Bagnall, Jonathan Boyarin, Diane Ehrenpreis, Sue Eisenfeld, Audrey Flack, Edward Goldberg, Sean Martin, Leo Mazow, John Miller, Lisa Strong, and Alan Wallach for helping me to piece the puzzle together in various ways.

At Cleveland State University, I am beholden to Catherine Busch for her above-and-beyond administrative help, and my tremendous research assistants, Makialani Kanewa-Mariano, and Elise Provident. Sarah Rutherford's scanning and image expertise is incomparable. To Dean Andrew Kersten and the College of Arts and Sciences, I convey a special thank-you for a publication subvention to ensure the book could be produced as beautifully as possible.

I am privileged to find a home with Penn State University Press and to work with Tristan Bates, Brian Beer, Josie DiKerby, and Jennifer Norton. Nicholas Taylor's copyediting was masterly. But it is to my editor, Director Emeritus Patrick Alexander, that I owe my most heartfelt appreciation for exceptionally wise counsel and yearslong conversations about this book and many other projects. That Patrick will not see this book in print, and to no longer have the gift of his friendship, is a crushing loss. Finally, always and forever, I thank my family: Dan Geller, Asher Solomon Baskind, and Naomi Margalit Baskind.

Portions of chapters 2, 3, and 6 were previously published, respectively, in "Moses Jacob Ezekiel, Eve Hearing the Voice," *MAVCOR Journal* 5, no. 1 (2021): https://mavcor.yale.edu/mavcor-journal/object-narratives/moses-jacob-ezekiel-eve-hearing-voice; "Moses Jacob Ezekiel's Portrait Bust of Rabbi Isaac Mayer Wise, 1899," *American Jewish Archives Journal* 73, no. 2 (2021): 19–30; and "The Jewish Sculptor of the Confederacy," *Tablet Magazine*, January 21, 2021.

INTRODUCTION

Moses Jacob Ezekiel, the Alexander Hamilton of Nineteenth-Century American Art

I live only in the present and think that an artist should represent in his works the philosophic, political, or religious sentiments of the time in which he lives.
—Moses Ezekiel, *Memoirs*

In 1931, the *Richmond Times-Dispatch* ran a contest asking readers whom they regarded as "the ten greatest Virginians." Among those nominated were Presidents George Washington, Thomas Jefferson, James Monroe, John Tyler, Woodrow Wilson, Zachary Taylor, William Henry Harrison, and a host of others—including sculptor Moses Jacob Ezekiel.[1] While this accolade may come as a surprise to readers, during his lifetime, Ezekiel received numerous European honors for his widely admired artistic talent: In 1887, he was bestowed the Cavalier's Cross of Merit for Art and Science by George II, Grand Duke of Saxe-Meiningen. Six years later, Emperor Wilhelm II of Germany presented him the Golden Cross of the House of Hohenzollern, and in 1906, King Victor Emmanuel III of Italy conferred on Ezekiel the honorary title Cavaliere Ufficiale della Corona Italia, making him an officer of the crown of Italy. (Ezekiel co-opted the honorific "sir" on his calling cards, which was repeated in the press for decades because his titles were not easily translatable to Americans.) The man and his art were so venerated that immediately after he died in Rome, a special cable was sent to the *New York Times*: "The death today of Moses Ezekiel, the distinguished and greatly beloved American sculptor, who had lived in Rome for more than forty years, caused universal regret here. . . . No man in Rome was more beloved than Ezekiel."[2] At his American funeral, Ezekiel was honored by a eulogy from President Warren

Harding: "You are gathered to honor the memory of one who was a great Virginian, a great artist, a great American and a great citizen of world fame."[3] Largely forgotten today, Ezekiel (b. Richmond, Virginia, 1844–d. Rome, Italy, 1917), a figure with a life story and body of art holding drama and revelations rivaling those recently brought to light about Alexander Hamilton, was the first Jewish American artist to win international acclaim, a paradigm of the transatlantic artist, and one of the most sought artist-celebrities of his era.

This book thus introduces a sculptor surprisingly lost to the annals of art history.[4] My goals, broadly, are threefold: to resurrect and contextualize Ezekiel's sculptures within the society that initiated them; to explore the business of a late nineteenth-century sculptor and the art market he negotiated; and to examine how Ezekiel's sculpture was influenced by his Jewish, Confederate, and expatriate identities, which necessitates unearthing and narrating his remarkable life. In no way do I only, or mostly, look at Ezekiel's art from a biographical perspective. That is an element of the book, in that he received many commissions because of his distinctive identity, but its larger purpose is an investigation of how Ezekiel's work intertwines with a range of decisive late nineteenth-century topics—the modernization of American Jewry, radical changes in the art world concerning style and patronage, and the aftermath of the Civil War and post-Emancipation race relations—in service to understanding why and how he sculpted what he did.

A study in contradictions, Ezekiel was a patriotic expatriate Italophile for over four decades who never renounced his citizenship because of an exceptionally strong attachment to his Southern and American roots. Ezekiel, from a prominent Sephardic Jewish American family, sculpted both the largest monument to religious liberty and one of the best-known monuments to Thomas Jefferson in the United States. Richmond-born, he was also a teenaged cadet at the Virginia Military Institute (VMI), the first Jewish cadet in the school's history, and engaged in brutal infantry combat at the Battle of New Market. The reverberations of that battle informed several Confederate monuments, including what he viewed as one of his most important works, on commission from the United Daughters of the Confederacy: a thirty-two-foot, highly classical Confederate memorial in Arlington Cemetery, one of the country's most visible monuments to the "Lost Cause." The combination of interlocking and conflicting allegiances that motivated Ezekiel—his conservative Confederate leanings intermingle with his liberal views on peace, Judaism, and religious liberty—make him a compelling case study for understanding nineteenth-century culture and history.

I began writing this book to unravel these intriguing paradoxes, and others, but that incentive evolved halfway through the project when Ezekiel—or at least some of his sculptures—became relevant again for all the wrong reasons. His sculptures were swept up in the country's accelerated moment of decommemoration. Yet, while his monuments have been debated widely, the artist remains nearly invisible. Then this study took on an additional dimension. No longer solely an excavation of a paradoxical and once greatly acclaimed but now overlooked artist, the book additionally became a discussion of the past and its intersection with the present. Ezekiel's *Stonewall Jackson* at VMI, his alma mater, was relocated to a less visible space in 2021; the city of Chicago put his statue of *Christopher Columbus* in storage in 2020; the 2017 Unite the Right rally took place in front of his *Thomas Jefferson* statue at the University of Virginia; and the US government called for the dismantling of his enormous Confederate monument at Arlington Cemetery, a controversy that ended after this book was submitted for copyediting. Rarely was his name mentioned before I, once quietly writing a monograph about a critically neglected artist, stepped in to tell the tale.[5] Ezekiel became a moving target and I was sometimes at the center of it, even beyond the Princeton exhibition debacle.

Accordingly, I am also deeply interested in the commission and reception of Ezekiel's public monuments over time. So, too, I am attentive to shifts in the lives of his sculptures: in their biographies and the transaction of objects whose identities are not fixed. Decades before the country's widespread decommemoration in the 2010s, some of Ezekiel's large figurative marble monuments were improbably relocated and thus displayed in new settings and for unexpected audiences. These include highly prestigious commissions that have nothing to do with the Confederacy. In these other cases, especially, the book explores interactions between object and audience alongside the ideological and cultural assumptions brought to the viewing experience by both period and contemporary beholders.

Ezekiel's Classicism, Illustrious Studio, and Onetime Fame

Ezekiel's work was most often grounded in classicism, a manner in its heyday with American artists and their patrons a few decades before his arrival in Rome.[6] A Virginian through and through, Ezekiel nevertheless was lured abroad by training at a European academy, proximity to marble quarries and skilled stonecutters, and what he understood as the virtue, nobility, and grandeur of his artistic predecessors. Ezekiel saw himself as a descendant of the ancients; Donatello and Michelangelo, whose work he could readily access in Italy; and then an heir to his immediate American expatriate forerunners: Horatio Greenough and Hiram Powers, who settled in Florence, and Thomas Crawford, who lived in Rome.[7] His subjects and allegorical bent were at times motivated by these exemplars, but his artistic choices were often novel, spurred by his chief identity markers—Jew, Virginian, and Confederate veteran. As a second-generation expatriate in Rome, joining sculptors such as Edmonia Lewis and Harriet Hosmer, he arrived at the tail end of a history of American artists enchanted by the aura and classical splendor of Italy. Committed to what he regarded as a timeless style and subjects already regarded by many as outmoded, Ezekiel readily condemned his European contemporaries. "It is no secret that ugliness is fashionable now," he said of the Impressionists. "We must be careful about that."[8] Ezekiel rebuked Auguste Rodin, the most important sculptor of his generation and perhaps of the century: "I saw Rodin's *Victor Hugo* bust which is simply a hurried, pretentious affectation by a talented man. . . . Rodin did some good work in earlier times, but his fragments and sketchy works today show only that he caters to a false taste in art."[9]

He gave American peers little notice in his voluminous writings but did nod favorably to Augustus Saint-Gaudens and Daniel Chester French, whom he described as "the two best sculptors in New York," and would visit with when in the city.[10] Hoping to visit William Wetmore Story's popular salon in the Palazzo Barberini, Ezekiel wrote of reaching out to the established artist during his early years in Rome but did not get a response. Ezekiel did establish close relations with Thomas Crawford's widow and son, celebrated author Francis Marion Crawford, spurred by his unerring admiration of the sculptor.[11] When in Cincinnati, the entrepreneurial Ezekiel made a point to visit with patrons of Hiram Powers. While he much more than once adopted his predecessors' subjects, Ezekiel did not think highly of the best-known sculpture of his day, Hiram Powers's *The Greek Slave* (carved 1844): "[Powers] should not be diving back into mythological ages or representing—in sculpture at least—subjects that mean absolutely nothing in the world we are living in at the present day."[12] Unlike Powers and William Henry Rinehart, Ezekiel never sculpted an idealized female nude and only very early in his career produced on mythological subjects: two marble relief pendants *Confession* and *Consolation* (1873), on commission for a villa when he was studying in Berlin (lost, but recorded in studio photographs), and an 1874 *Pan and Amor* bas-relief (lost, known only through a sketch).

Insight into Ezekiel's passion for the high-minded ideals of classicism can be ferreted out by parsing the world he created in his home and studio in the Baths of Diocletian. Symbolizing his profoundly romantic nature, Ezekiel's home-studio serves as an essential foundation for appreciating the politics of creating and selling art in late nineteenth-century Italy. A brief account of Ezekiel's illustrious home and atelier, likely modeled on the splendor and hospitality enjoyed by myriad visitors to William Wetmore Story's fashionable salon, also introduces his relevance in his day.[13]

Five years after his 1874 expatriation, exactly on the fourth anniversary of the liberation of Rome, Ezekiel moved into the ancient baths, the largest in the city. Situated over thirty acres, the vaulted thermae had long fallen into ruins when Ezekiel rented them for fifty lire a month. With inspiration, he converted the dusty, decrepit baths into a living and working space. There, he carefully cultivated a holistic existence to his liking and purposes, where for three decades his art and life strongly intersected, and within which his own celebrity status rivaled his succeeding twentieth-century American counterparts Georgia O'Keeffe and Andy Warhol.[14] All three artists self-consciously fostered an interrelated manner of living by integrating the decor in their domestic spaces with their larger artistic program.

By day, Ezekiel worked in the lower studio under a half cupola and vaults rising as high as eighty feet, some with green foliage peeking through the cracks. In the upper level, reached by a stairway populated by white pigeons he lovingly nurtured, he lived and entertained countless guests, serving them from his prized antique silver tea service (his will specially indicated who should receive it as a bequest), and a hand-carved table topped by a slab of marble that could accommodate forty, which he often used in full to entertain.[15] Surviving photographs allow an intimate glimpse into the home's elegance, with dark red embroidered draperies accenting ornate black furniture, lighted by candles on tables within walls decorated with festoons of evergreen and garlands (fig. 1).[16] Rare books, various curios, paintings, and statues, and even one antique piece purportedly fished out of the Tiber, surrounded this cavernous space.[17] In a *Lippincott's Magazine* article chronicling artist spaces in Rome, among them Story's au courant studio and that of the aged Randolph Rogers, Ezekiel's comes first. "One of the most delightful evenings I passed last winter," the author wrote,

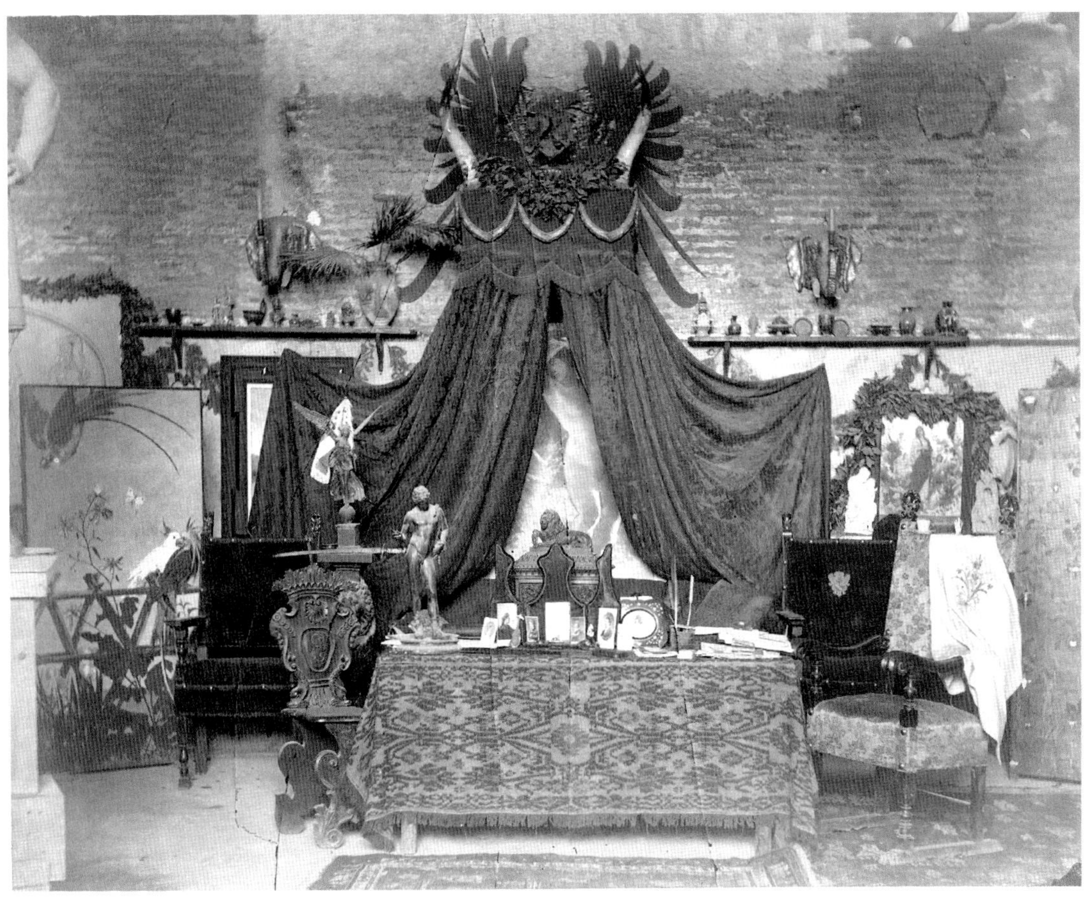

FIG. 1 Ezekiel's studio in the Baths of Diocletian, circa 1900. Photograph. Courtesy of The Jacob Rader Marcus Center of the American Jewish Archives, Cincinnati, Ohio, at americanjewisharchives.org.

"was at a literary and artistic reception given by Mr. Ezekiel, the Virginia sculptor. His studio, where the *soirée* took place, is one of the most picturesque and interesting in Italy." The author exalted the candles, which were held by eight elephants' heads and threw "fitful gleams over the ancient frescoes and modern groups of statuary" by Ezekiel.[18]

Ezekiel saw romance in the decaying ruins that others disregarded, and he encouraged a certain cult around his studio, home, and himself—a nineteenth-century version of the place to be, be seen, and be seen with, akin to the atmosphere that Warhol created at the Factory in 1960s New York. Both self-styled artists, born over eighty years apart, reveled in fame and captured the attention of the press. For Ezekiel, however, his home was a place of gentility and exquisite hospitality, one of beauty, refinement, art, and the finest music. The courtly Ezekiel—who spoke French, German, and Italian—revered art and music almost as much as he worshipped the South, and he lived as a cosmopolitan aesthete in all aspects of his life.

Guidebooks for tourists listed Ezekiel's address, Piazza delle Terme 118, as a destination.[19]

Americans journeying to Europe, a popular pastime in the nineteenth century for the monied class, eagerly toured Rome's ancient ruins, viewed the city's wealth of classical sculpture, and explored museums to see Renaissance masterworks. Visiting artists' studios was also essential to the agenda, and Ezekiel's was a prime stop on that circuit. In variations, the press reported effusively: "It used to be said that no one went to Rome without seeing the Pope, to which may be added now that no Virginian goes to Rome without seeking out Virginia's gifted son, who has added so much to her fame by his devotion to those lofty ideals of art and manhood to which he owes his fame."[20] The *New York Times* wrote about the "magnificent" and "well known" studio, of which "strangers of all nationalities do not consider that they have known the Eternal City until they have seen it."[21] When Corrine Robinson Alsop (niece of Eleanor and Theodore Roosevelt) and her husband traveled to Rome, the same paper covered the trip, noting that Alsop cherished a luncheon given in her honor by Ezekiel as the most excellent experience of her entire vacation. Testament to Ezekiel's renown is that the *Times* found this newsworthy at all, and went out of the way to describe details about lunch in the artist's "unique and picturesque studio," with a headline that only necessitated his last name for reader recognition: "The meal was served on a marble table with lion supports. They sat in old Roman chairs and drank the traditional wine, Castelli Romani, while above them rose the huge bath of Diocletian. The only thing wanting to make it a Roman festival were couches and togas."[22] Novelist and travel writer Caroline Atwater Mason chronicled her visits to the Borghese Gardens and the Fountain of Trevi alongside her stop by the studio, where she effused about Ezekiel's "cordial kindliness of greeting" and "personality [which] commanded instant interest."[23] As Mason walked up an outer stairway to Ezekiel's entertaining space, she was enthralled by "a network of close vines, among which white pigeons flew about with their peaceful, melodious *gurring*. We now entered a vast and vaulted chamber, almost, it seemed to me, as large as the Sistine Chapel and conveying in its proportions an effect of imposing stateliness."[24]

These visitors came to enjoy the company of the feted, genteel Ezekiel as much as to see the plaster and clay models he kept, both past and recent conceptions; some plasters he preserved for years. For Ezekiel, the openness of his studio served a dual purpose: the always financially strapped artist hoped to sell works of art as well as to charm and entertain, one of his truest pleasures. He was a scrappy businessman as much as a creator and curator of pretty things. Yet, while the world saw him as a wealthy and successful artist, in truth he was nearly always beset by fiscal problems, a running theme in his extensive memoir and correspondence. Ezekiel sent copious letters to potential patrons describing works for sale, often including photographs of works in progress, and traveled across the Atlantic to meet with sponsors and sitters, many of whom were influential Americans. Among them were William Corcoran, founder of his eponymous gallery; Isaac Mayer Wise, founder of American Reform Judaism; and Mary Custis Lee, wife of Confederate General Robert E. Lee. According to Ezekiel, post–Civil War he benefited from the counsel and comradeship of General Lee, who urged him to pursue a life as an artist rather than as a soldier or a doctor after he had enrolled for one year at the Medical College of Virginia: "I hope you will be an artist as it seems to me you are cut out for one," Ezekiel remembered Lee advising.

"But whatever you do, try to prove to the world that if we did not succeed in our struggle, we are worthy of success. And do earn a reputation in whatever profession you undertake."[25] He promptly quit medical school, joined his parents in Cincinnati, where they had relocated from war-ravaged Richmond in 1868, and a year later gained admittance to the Royal Academy of Art in Berlin.

The guest of presidents at the White House, Ezekiel welcomed eminent American patriots to his studio, including Ulysses S. Grant, Theodore Roosevelt, and William Taft; among the memorabilia Ezekiel kept until his death was a 1902 personalized invitation to the White House from President Roosevelt.[26] European royalty and immeasurable luminaries visited the atelier as well, seeking out Ezekiel's company and viewing his art. He counted Queen Margherita of Italy, King Victor Emmanuel III, and Kaiser Wilhelm II as visitors. Queen Margherita stopped by more than once and she received him at the palace, where they would talk about his newest commissions. A dear friend was composer Franz Liszt, of whom Ezekiel created one of his most successful portrait sculptures.

Accounts of Ezekiel's life were legion, in over forty different periodicals, proving crucial for this project's stitching together details of Ezekiel's art and life. They covered triumphs and banalities alike. When he crossed the ocean on voyages to America to secure commissions and for unveilings, his comings and goings were covered by the news—from the steamer he was traveling on to the venues he would be visiting. Ezekiel's arrival home, numbering ten stays after his expatriation, some very extended, was always cause for celebration.

Critics in Ezekiel's day, and beyond, included him in the history of that era. *Monumental News* extolled Ezekiel's talents in 1899, and listed over thirty works, with the following commentary: "It is interesting to note the wide range of ability of this American sculptor and the distribution of his work. . . . The above are but a very few of this noted sculptor's works, and he is young yet."[27] Van Wyck Brooks's 1958 narrative of Americans in Italy celebrates a century and a half of his countrymen's travels abroad and the expatriate experience, beginning with familiar names who dominate the canon: Henry James, Washington Allston, Edith Wharton, Hiram Powers, and more. As Brooks's story wanes, he points to Ezekiel: "In Rome, Sir Moses Ezekiel, the last of the old-time expatriate sculptors, the Virginian who had once been a protégé of Robert E. Lee, still carried on his work in the Baths of Diocletian where he had made statues of Poe and Stonewall Jackson."[28] And in Wayne Craven's authoritative 1968 study of American sculpture, he describes Ezekiel's work in some depth at the end of his discussion of second-generation expatriates in Rome.[29] Scattered subsequent scholarship has paid him little attention, with the same few details repeated, sometimes inaccurately; these studies tend to focus on select artworks and, when doing so, rarely from an art historical perspective.[30] A full-length, deeply researched, more comprehensive study is long overdue to fill this lacuna.

A Diversity of Subjects

Ezekiel's sculpture was diverse in subject and media, and those subjects dictate my framework. Because Ezekiel's work is largely unknown, a quick sketch of his themes allows for a general sense to ground readers. His monument to *Religious Liberty* comes at the start for its importance as Ezekiel's first major public commission, the sculpture's unlikely transits, and the audience response in three different venues over its peripatetic history. Standing twenty-four feet, *Religious Liberty* was the first artwork commissioned by a Jewish American fraternal organization to a Jew, B'nai B'rith, and the group's contribution to the 1876 Centennial International Exposition in Philadelphia.

He sculpted biblical works, drawing on sources from both the Hebrew and Christian Bibles, and made what is generally believed to be the first sculpture crafted by a Jewish artist of a living rabbi, the pioneering Isaac Mayer Wise, replicated four times. Companion chapters parse these biblical conceptions, Ezekiel's most overtly Jewish works. In chapter 2, readers learn about ties to his religiocultural heritage and efforts to imbue traditional biblical works with a Jewish identity in Catholic Rome. Chapter 3 explores American Jews' earliest efforts to incorporate art into their institutions by sponsoring the most eminent Jewish American artist of the day, and how Ezekiel's ideological works intersect with the fraught genesis of Zionism.

In 1877, Ezekiel received the prestigious commission to carve eleven larger-than-life sculptures of some of the Western world's best-known artists for the niches of the original building holding William Corcoran's art collection. Made as decoration for the first building established in the United States with the express purpose to serve as an art museum, the unexpected afterlife of these artist sculptures—now all standing among flora in the Norfolk Botanical Garden and including Leonardo, Michelangelo, and Rembrandt—are discussed in chapter 4. Ezekiel's passion for the arts spans other portrait subjects that he hoped would secure his place among the pantheon of great Western artists. At the same time eager to place himself in an American tradition of art, and surely less controversial statuary than his Confederate monuments, are likenesses of three presidents: George Washington, Thomas Jefferson, and Abraham Lincoln. These sculptures, and Ezekiel's interactions with presidents who visited him in Europe and invited him to the White House, are addressed in chapter 5, where I also trace the running theme of religious liberty and its connection to the Jewish American experience.

His monuments to both the Blue and the Gray form the final chapter. Investigation of these outdoor public statues is especially timely considering recent conversations about the illegitimacy of Confederate monuments in the wake of Black Lives Matter and current American conceptions of race. Here, I probe particularly the mutability of his most personal and sentimental monument, *Virginia Mourning Her Dead*, a tribute to the slain corps of underage cadets he fought with during the Civil War. Further, I consider the genesis, commission, deliberations, and reception of Ezekiel's Arlington statue at its dedication to shed light on early twentieth-century race relations, the evolving politics of reconciliation, and how and why Americans remembered a relatively recent, crushing war between compatriots on native soil.

Reconstructing a Life and Oeuvre

Fundamental for this reconstruction of the artist's life and oeuvre are the vast archival materials Ezekiel left behind—his memoir, correspondence, and other documents—along with widespread coverage in the mainstream press. A posthumously published 1975 edited version of his memoir initially piqued my interest, as did its admirable introduction.[31] Through that I came to learn about Ezekiel years ago, and he has returned to my mind again and again, appearing briefly in three earlier books I have written. I sought out the original 638-page, hand-typed manuscript—so famous in his day, the *New York Times* noted that Ezekiel was writing his memoirs.[32] Tucked away in an archive, the memoir was edited mostly for clarity and repetition, and only differs noticeably for its illustrations, among them drawings of his sculptures and friends.[33] This book mostly relies on the published memoir so that future Ezekiel studies can have easy access to the material but occasionally turns to the original when an interesting omitted detail warrants inclusion here. Ezekiel's autobiography, as most, had a certain agenda in its efforts to shape the narrative of his life, which he did not do too much to conceal. He openly extols himself with reviews of his work and quoting accolades, often hearsay, from admirers. Regardless of whether the conversations Ezekiel chronicled took place as he described, the artist's thoughts on sundry subjects come through, and his characterizations are frequently confirmed by primary documents and the historical record. At the same time, he does not shy from lamenting his failures and challenges. His inner turmoil and disappointments are palpable, revealing much about the difficulties Ezekiel faced as a professional artist.

The memoir is also essential to fleshing out what Ezekiel intended his iconography to mean, and to learning how his work was produced, who commissioned it, who bought it, and who viewed it. His discussion of the social, religious, and cultural environments in which he lived and traveled offers insights into the factors that shaped his conceptions. Descriptions of the missing sculptures are indispensable. Arriving in Italy over a decade after its unification, Ezekiel only provides surface commentary on contemporary politics in the Eternal City. His worldview, when addressed, extends more to the goings-on in his native land. Readers learn much about Ezekiel's perceptions of himself, some dictating artistic decisions; his efforts to gain commissions and how they played out; and how in his mind the work was received. His memoir further helped me track the path of lost sculptures. Unlike many artists' autobiographies, because Ezekiel's memoir is heavily based on journals written over several decades, dictated to a scribe who typed them verbatim, much of what he writes is not after-the-fact nostalgia or misremembering. A good portion of material removed from the edited memoir is the minutiae of his everyday activities: the books he read, performances he attended, playing cards with friends, and so forth. Often, his personal letters from years past are repeated in close wording, if not exact, in the memoir the sculptor cobbled together toward the end of life. Notwithstanding, I still remind myself, using the words of autobiographical theorist John Sturrock, to "distinguish the dance from the dancer."[34]

While Ezekiel's memoir has been essential to mapping the chronology of his work, travels, and artistic practice, after exhausting this chief resource, I turned to other writings and archival sources, as much for their content as to substantiate his recollections. Over one hundred letters and postcards he wrote from abroad to his family, friends, and patrons survive. These materials allow access to campaigns for commissions and the working process of a figurative sculptor, and notably one who had to navigate the making of large objects that would eventually travel across the Atlantic—valuable discoveries for future studies on nineteenth-century American expatriate sculptors. A similar number of extraordinary late nineteenth- and early twentieth-century, eight-by-ten-inch albumen photographs of his studio and living space have also been instrumental in establishing his body of work and are enormously helpful in conveying his working method. This rare documentation allows us to see Ezekiel's creative process, expression of his hand, and the changes he made to clay sketches before they were enlarged, plastered, and translated by hired stonecutters into highly finished marble; Ezekiel regularly put the final touches on his work. These photos demonstrate, for example, that Ezekiel modeled his subjects in the nude and dressed them later.

Three additional resources have been invaluable. David Philipson, a rabbi with whom Ezekiel was well acquainted, spoke to him many times about his work and was granted access to the artist's personal correspondence with his brother Henry and father, Jacob (most no longer extant), reproduced at length in a sixty-two-page biographical profile (Philipson also officiated Ezekiel's funeral service at Arlington National Cemetery).[35] A few years after Ezekiel died, family members compiled a list of 117 sculptures made by him, with the following note: "This list is not believed to contain all his works."[36] After five years immersed in Ezekiel's work and life, I can attest that the list is not close to complete; around two hundred seems to be an accurate assessment, and that number is later cited in other primary documents.[37] Letters provide Ezekiel's asides about sculptures, as do passing comments in his memoir. Photographs disclose how many of the prolific artist's sculptures are lost, plus what they looked like. These include a fertile number of portraits busts and reliefs, mostly unlocated because of their personal nature; an astounding number of commissioned portrait busts are described in his unedited memoir. No doubt, unbeknownst to families in Italy, France, and America, a bust made by Ezekiel of a long-lost ancestor is displayed in their home. My research, for example, uncovered a late bronze sculpture of his mother. Another time, a two-by-two-inch note tucked into an archival folder indicated that one of Ezekiel's bronze busts of Lincoln was owned by the Louisville Public Library. It was only after several emails, telephone calls, and prodding on my part that *Lincoln* was discovered at a suburban branch of the city's library system. The piece was perched on a pedestal in a reading room in front of a window, the sun beating on its back. I soon learned that a book about Ezekiel was also a detective hunt, during which I located eleven lost sculptures. Finally, because of his fame, newspapers and magazines constantly reported on him. Especially vital sources are the newspapers the *Cincinnati Enquirer*, the *New York Times*, and the *Richmond Times-Dispatch*, the magazine *Monumental News*, and various Jewish periodicals. I rely on these primary materials, too, to corroborate Ezekiel's assertions. Endnotes throughout this study mention works by Ezekiel not given in-depth discussions in the text, provided for future researchers and to round out a sense of his oeuvre.

Complications of Confederate Ties

Impressionist painter Edgar Degas was an antisemite, postimpressionist painter Paul Gauguin had sexual relations with young girls, German expressionist artist Emile Nolde was a Nazi, and postwar sculptor David Smith was a violent misogynist. Over the centuries, innumerable artists objectify women. Yet, we still teach and study their work.

There would be little left to celebrate in the art world, and beyond, if we only look at art made by perfect individuals. Ezekiel was unquestionably flawed, but he cannot be understood only as a Confederate and consequently excised from scholarly discourse—especially because his Confederate statues are a small portion of his output.

Ezekiel's Confederate ties, certainly damning, are only one aspect of his artistic practice, multidimensional life, and personality—and I urge readers tempted to skip to the chapter discussing his Confederate monuments, not to do so. That final chapter is not the beating heart of this book, even as it is essential. My purpose is to understand Ezekiel's full body of art—portrait sculpture, biblical sculpture, public sculpture (Confederate monuments and otherwise)—in the context of history, as well as to measuredly convey the shades of his life experience, which at no times do I airbrush.[38] I leave it to readers to draw their own conclusions. To that end, Ezekiel cannot be cast entirely as a villain. Ample documents make evident how beloved "Uncle Moie" was by family and friends, and how generous he was, even to strangers. Among many instances demonstrative of his kindness concerns Carlo, Ezekiel's longtime studio assistant. When Carlo's services were no longer needed, Ezekiel suggested they part ways. Carlo worried no one else would hire him, and so Ezekiel kept the man in his employ, remembering, tongue in cheek, "He remained with me until he died. I continued to be the old fellow's servant."[39] After Carlo became ill, Ezekiel had him well cared for in a hospital, paid his debts after he passed, bought mourning garb for Carlo's widow, and paid for Carlo's grave marker.[40] When his widow fell ill, Ezekiel placed her in a woman's home, paid for all expenses, and visited with her when time allowed.[41] To name other occasions: Following a violent 1915 earthquake, Ezekiel was engaging in relief work in devastated villages.[42] Two years later, Ezekiel died of pneumonia, depleted from volunteering for the Italian-American Red Cross Relief Clearing House during World War I. An address at Ezekiel's memorial service in Washington, DC, concluded, "Ezekiel was helpful and generous to the poor, a friend to everyone, and by his works calls all who follow after him to the service of man for better and higher ideals."[43] Obituaries and letters effuse the same. Make no mistake: Ezekiel was a supporter of the Confederacy, and I am in no way defending him. But a fully rounded portrait—to this point unrecovered—is due the artist, just as we study the full oeuvres and lives of Degas, Gauguin, and Nolde.

Because of the weaving together of visual, cultural, historical, religious, and biographical resources, this book should appeal to readers interested in Jewish studies, religious studies, American studies, nineteenth-century history, Civil War history, public monuments, as well as art history. As such, this book recounts the making, history, and context of Ezekiel's diverse monuments—far beyond his work for the Confederacy—and the complex man who sculpted them.

EZEKIEL AND RELIGIOUS LIBERTY

Chapter 1

I feel my inability to express myself fully on this expansive subject, and I must now beg of you to allow my work to speak for itself and for me.
—Ezekiel, speech at the unveiling of *Religious Liberty*, 1876

At the second national convention of the Jewish fraternal organization Independent Order of B'nai B'rith (Sons of the Covenant), held in Chicago in January 1874, chair Simon Wolf proposed that the group commission a statue in recognition of religious liberty. He alone named Ezekiel, a young, untried sculptor, his artist of choice.[1] The monument was to be presented to the United States at the upcoming Centennial International Exhibition, the world's fair in Philadelphia celebrating the one hundredth anniversary of the signing of the Declaration of Independence. Publicity indicates that following the exhibition, B'nai B'rith planned to gift the work to the US government for the Capitol, "to remain as a lasting monument to the great truths it is designed to illustrate," later touted by newspapers across the country.[2] B'nai B'rith brothers were tasked with raising funds to pay for the monument.

The opportunity to sculpt *Religious Liberty* (fig. 2) came as a surprise, with an invitation to submit a design arriving by letter to Ezekiel in Berlin, where he had recently completed his two years at the Royal Academy of Art. Elated to have been offered his first major commission and for a large monument besides, without delay Ezekiel penciled a sketch on the back of the envelope he received, which, he recalled in his memoir, "flashed upon my mind at once."[3] He quickly modeled that ambitious arrangement as a plaster sketch and traveled by steamer to New York to present it to the B'nai B'rith monument committee. Ezekiel's preliminary conception barely changed in the final version, except for a single alteration, suggested by B'nai B'rith: Instead of the figure representing *Faith* extending both hands up to heaven, the monument committee preferred that the boy in the group hold a lamp with the eternal flame in his left hand.

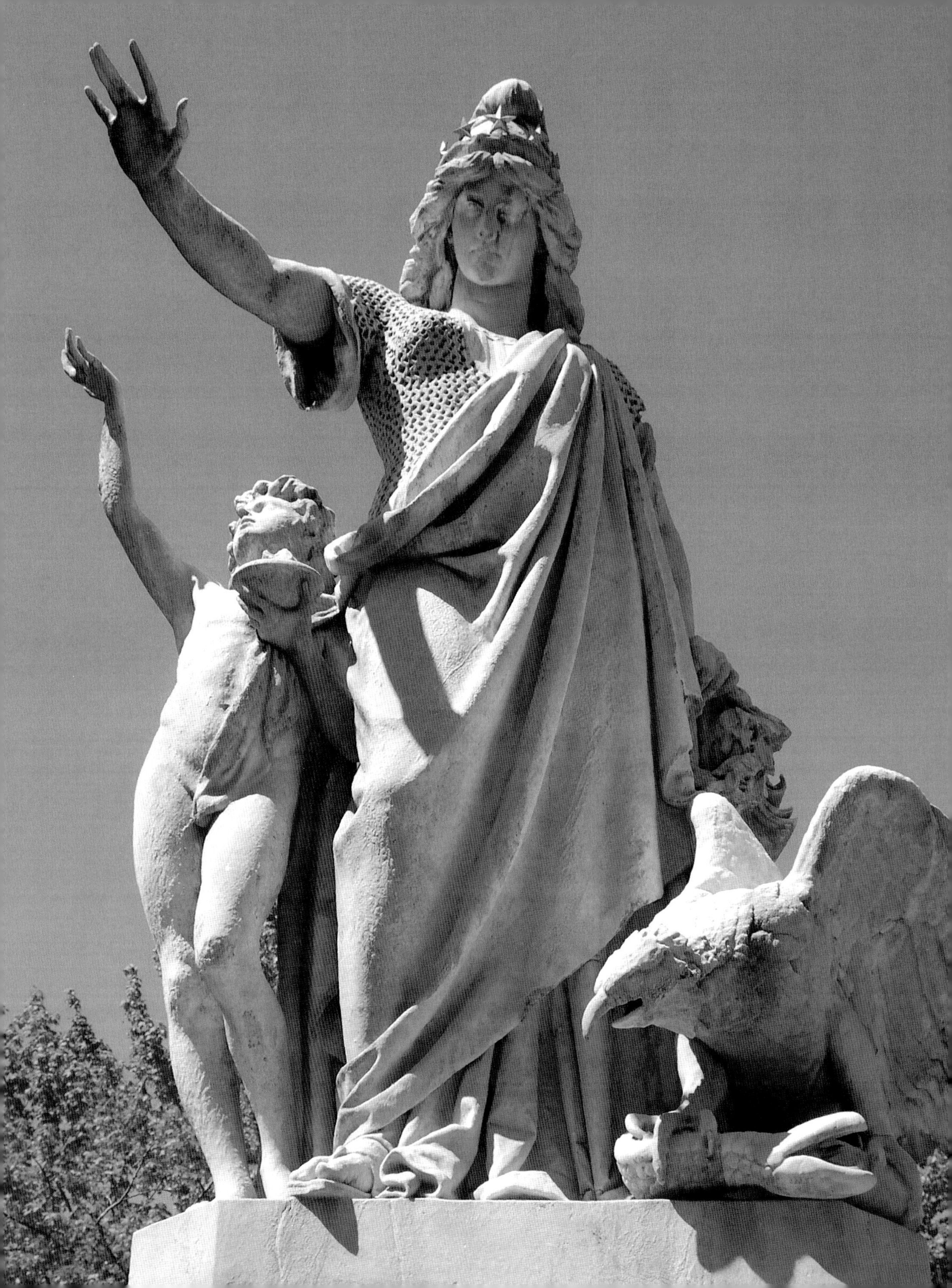

Ceding artistic control on this one detail, Ezekiel returned to Europe with $1,000 and a signed contract, stipulating that he complete and deliver the marble sculpture within two years, on the Fourth of July, for total remuneration of $20,000.[4]

New to Rome, funded by a yearlong Michael Beer Prize—an award he had earned from the Royal Academy for making the most distinguished sculpture among his Jewish peers (chapter 3)—Ezekiel had yet to find a permanent residence and studio. He swiftly rented a space large enough to begin his project, the ground floor of a magazine storehouse. Soon he hired a popular Italian model to pose as *Religious Liberty* and asked the son of a butcher in the Piazza Barberini to pose as *Faith* (the sculpture to be displayed in the censored Princeton exhibition). Working early mornings and late into the night, Ezekiel fashioned a brass band for his forehead with a small lamp in the front to mold the folds of *Liberty*'s dress amid the shadows in his working space. Having completed the clay sketch in spring 1875, Ezekiel traveled to Carrara to choose a block of marble, one and a half times the size of life; by the time he was back in Rome, assistants had plastered the clay. The massive twenty-seven-ton block arrived at the train station in Rome extended on two freight cars. Over several days, a sled operated by twenty men slowly brought the marble to Ezekiel's studio; when the men rested at night from their labors, the sled carrying the marble sank the pavement, forcing Ezekiel to pay for repaving. To block out the statue under tight time constraints, he hired two sets of stonecutters, one group to work at night and the other during the day. Piles of marble chips accumulated at such a pace that Ezekiel regularly had them hauled away by the cartload.

The finished, highly classical, twenty-four-foot-tall allegorical statue presents *Liberty* as a ten-foot woman, wearing a coat of mail partly covered by a toga.[5] *Liberty* dons a Phrygian cap, the *pileus libertatis*, bestowed on freed slaves, with a border of thirteen gilded stars representing the original colonies. She holds a laurel wreath of victory, which also rests on fasces, a bundle of birch rods bound with a ribbon, as a symbol of power and strength in unity. The fasces are covered by an open book, meant to signal the US Constitution. *Liberty* extends her right arm protectively over an idealized, nude boy, standing in classicized contrapposto at her right. That boy, a personification of *Faith*, does indeed grasp a flaming lamp, and he raises his other hand to heaven.[6] At *Liberty*'s feet an eagle, a well-recognized emblem denoting America, attacks a serpent, signifying intolerance. The eagle's sharp, oversized talons grip the serpent, flipped on its back, as the bird quashes its foe. This group stands on a pedestal bearing the inscription "Religious Liberty, Dedicated to the People of the United States by the Order B'nai B'rith and Israelites of America" (fig. 3).

Even though B'nai B'rith, a secular communal organization founded in New York in 1843 by German Jewish immigrants, defaulted on advance payment due to financial difficulties, Ezekiel forged ahead. He wrote of quitting smoking, borrowing money to pay for materials, and living in poverty to conserve his funds. Ezekiel gave up his apartment and moved into his studio, where he slept on a folding chair, remembering these conditions as ones he "would not wish my worst enemy would have to endure."[7] Adolph Sanger, chair of the B'nai

FIG. 2 Moses Jacob Ezekiel, *Religious Liberty*, 1876 (detail). Marble, 10 ft. Weitzman National Museum of American Jewish History, Philadelphia, Pennsylvania. Photo: Samantha Baskind.

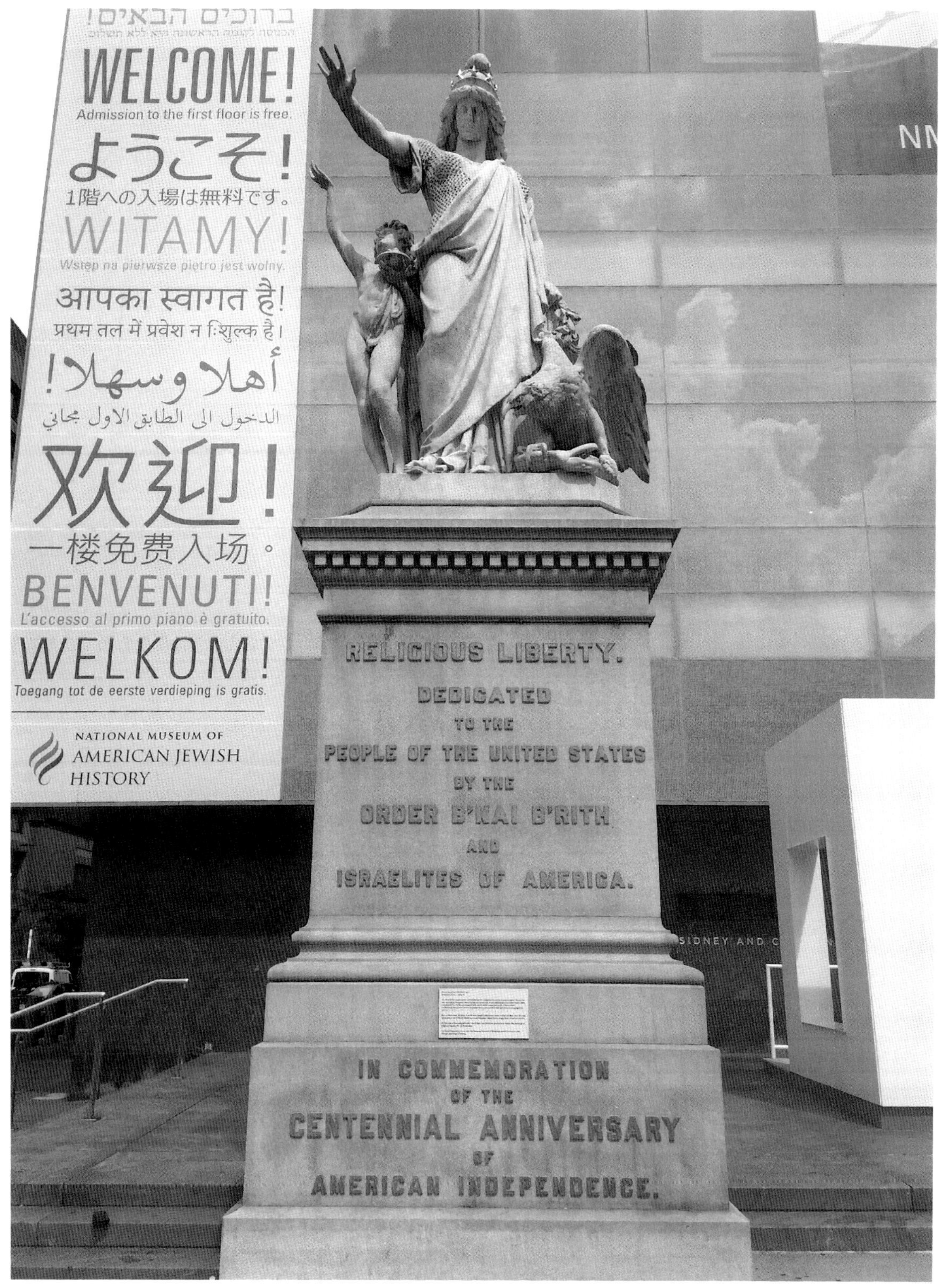

ברוכים הבאים!
WELCOME!
Admission to the first floor is free.
ようこそ!
1階への入場は無料です。
WITAMY!
Wstęp na pierwsze piętro jest wolny.
आपका स्वागत है!
प्रथम तल में प्रवेश निःशुल्क है।
أهلا وسهلا!
الدخول الى الطابق الاول مجاني
欢迎!
一楼免费入场。
BENVENUTI!
L'accesso al primo piano è gratuito.
WELKOM!
Toegang tot de eerste verdieping is gratis.
NATIONAL MUSEUM OF
AMERICAN JEWISH
HISTORY
RELIGIOUS LIBERTY.
DEDICATED
TO THE
PEOPLE OF THE UNITED STATES
BY THE
ORDER B'NAI B'RITH
AND
ISRAELITES OF AMERICA.
IN COMMEMORATION
OF THE
CENTENNIAL ANNIVERSARY
OF
AMERICAN INDEPENDENCE.

B'rith Centennial Committee, even sent a letter to Ezekiel advising him to stop laboring on the sculpture because lodges were having trouble raising money to pay him. Ezekiel, a member of that Order (after expatriating to Italy, he affiliated with an American lodge in Rome) as was his father, Jacob—a charter member of Richmond's chapter of B'nai B'rith—described that letter as "a death blow to me."[8] Nonetheless, Ezekiel persisted because of two core beliefs, both related to his religiocultural heritage: the imperative of the US separation between church and state, and his sense of obligation to the Jewish people: "The work I was doing represented one of the grandest ideas in the world; it was worthy of any little sacrifice I might have to make as far as personal comfort was concerned." Apropos of Ezekiel's obligation to the Jewish people, he keenly wrote—in his memoir and in a letter to Sanger—"It was the first monument that any Jewish body of men had ever wanted to place in the world; the matter had been published to the world, I had received the commission without ever seeking it, and it would have been an eternal disgrace upon every Jewish community in America if the work had been abandoned."[9] Ezekiel was not paid until more than three years after the sculpture was delivered from Rome to Philadelphia, and then not even close to the negotiated amount.[10]

With the monument finally complete, and before it was shipped to the United States, Ezekiel opened his Roman studio for public viewing; the final plaster remained on display there for decades after its completion (fig. 4). The newspaper *Il popolo romano* described the work in some detail and in glowing terms: "The idea of grappling with such a subject as Ezekiel has so successfully mastered, challenges a world's admiration and stamps him a true genius." Further lauding *Religious Liberty*'s classicism, the paper's critic hyperbolically compared Ezekiel to his artistic idol and indicated the sculpture was the first "since the advent of Michel Angelo [*sic*] which has [garnered] such universal respect and admiration."[11] Another Italian newspaper, *Publica opinione*, praised the sculpture: "Usually abstract ideas incarnated in marble or on canvas are mute. Ezekiel gives them speech. Modern sentiments of a philosophico-religious character utter audible words in his marble."[12] The German art magazine *Leipziger Zeitschrift für Bildende Kunst* characterized the effort as "a really glorious one," singling out "the first gratifying realism we have ever seen in a plastic representation of the 'King of Birds.'"[13]

Individuals were impressed as well. Giuseppe Garibaldi, the distinguished general of the Risorgimento, remarked, according to a contemporary observer, "To know that a work of art representing the separation of church and state could have been conceived and carried out under the shadow of the Vatican itself is solace indeed."[14] Ezekiel recounted the general as saying, "There can be no peace on earth as long as any church is connected with the political government of any country."[15] When Ezekiel himself characterized the sculpture as depicting "the separation of church and state" to an Italian visitor in his studio, she was not as impressed as Garibaldi and the press. Describing her reaction as "horrified," Ezekiel quoted her as follows: "How can you come and make a work like that here in Rome under the shadow of the Vatican? It's a horrible thing to do!"[16]

In the end, what really mattered was that Ezekiel's patrons were pleased with the monument, and

FIG. 3 Moses Jacob Ezekiel, *Religious Liberty*, 1876. Marble, 24 ft. with pedestal. Weitzman National Museum of American Jewish History, Philadelphia, Pennsylvania. Photo: Samantha Baskind.

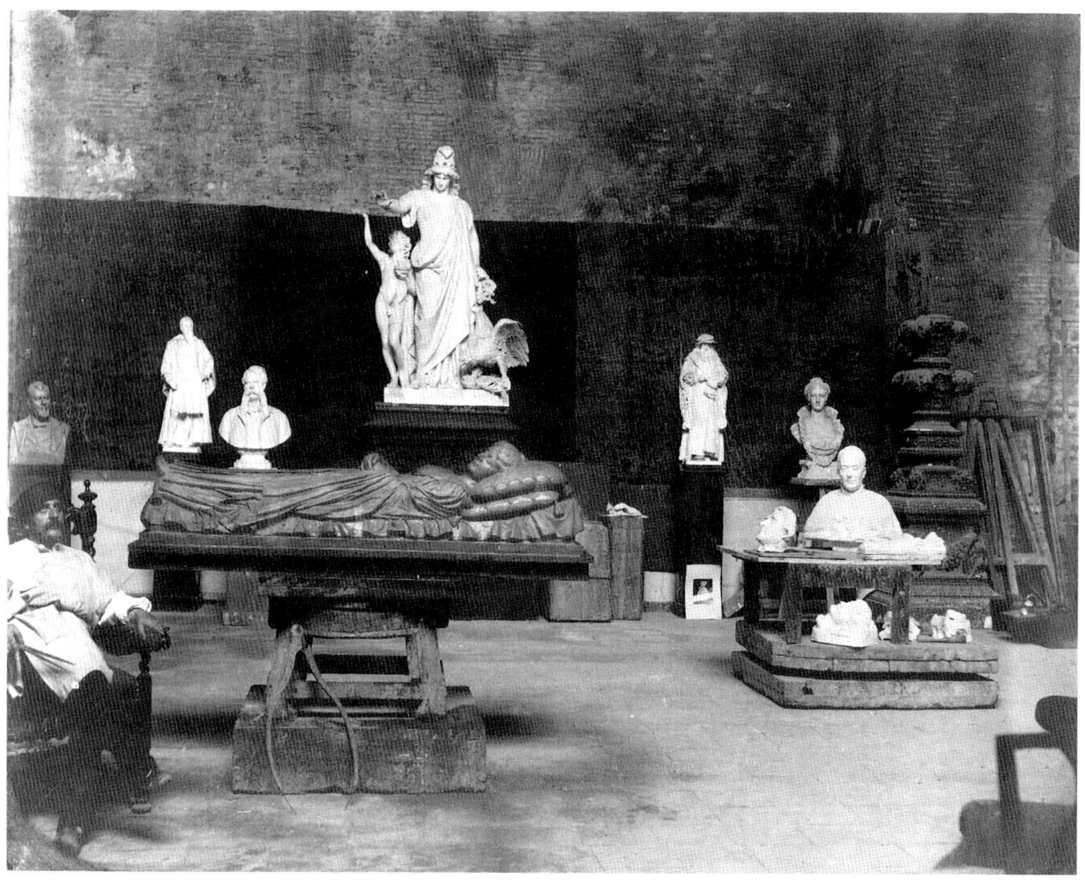

indeed they were. B'nai B'rith as well as the American Jewish community have publicly acclaimed the monument for over a century, satisfied that Ezekiel ably fulfilled his task of embodying religious freedom. The enormous sculpture stood in Philadelphia's Fairmount Park for 108 years, until it was relocated to the front of the National Museum of American Jewish History (known since 2021 as the Weitzman National Museum of American Jewish History), beside Independence Mall. There, *Religious Liberty* offers a towering prelude to the message of freedom and the opportunities that freedom enables, ardently touted within the museum's walls. But for Ezekiel, the monument was more than the excitement of his first major commission, more than a paean to religious liberty, and more than the first of a lifetime of disappointments and failures by patrons. For even as *Religious Liberty* is outwardly universal in theme and adopts standard "American" iconography, Ezekiel subtly nodded to Jewish tradition beyond his celebration of religious liberties in his homeland. So, too, documentation about *Religious Liberty*'s commission, celebrations of the statue, and the monument's subsequent relocations to its decidedly visible new homes is quite telling about how Jews frame their Americanization experience, heightened in dialogue with the Weitzman's permanent exhibition.

Lady Liberty

The statue's message would have been easily understood by nineteenth-century viewers, even without an inscription, because Ezekiel used a common trope of the moment: Lady Liberty.[17] European female national personifications also preceded Lady Liberty with Marianne as the French national icon and Britannia standing as the United Kingdom (often referred to as the Mother Country), and the ubiquitous allusion to Russia as Mother Russia.[18] Thomas Crawford's bronze *Statue of Freedom* (1863; fig. 5), a female personification of Liberty, crowns the Capitol dome in Washington. Inside the Capitol building, Constantino Brumidi's illusionistic fresco in the cupola of the dome, *The Apotheosis of Washington* (1865), features the father of the country ascending to heaven, flanked by two female allegories: Liberty and Victory/Fame. During the Revolutionary era, America was also personified as a female virtue, such as Freedom or Liberty.

Images of Liberty, as far back as the third century BCE in Rome, show her akin to Ezekiel's conception, dressed in a draped robe but alternatively with other attributes: a scepter, symbolizing sovereignty; a cat, an animal with no master, at her feet; and a shattered pitcher, signifying freedom from confinement, or the obvious broken chains. A key attribute of Liberty is her Phrygian cap. In Cesare Ripa's landmark emblem guide *Iconologia* (1603; fig. 6), Liberty appears as a middle-aged woman wearing classical robes and a helmet, with her Phrygian cap hanging atop a scepter, sometimes termed a "liberty pole," and a cat at her feet.[19] Edward Savage's oft-reproduced engraving *Liberty in the Form of the Goddess of Youth, Giving Support to the Bald Eagle* (1796) presents a comely young woman in a flowing dress as Liberty tramping on

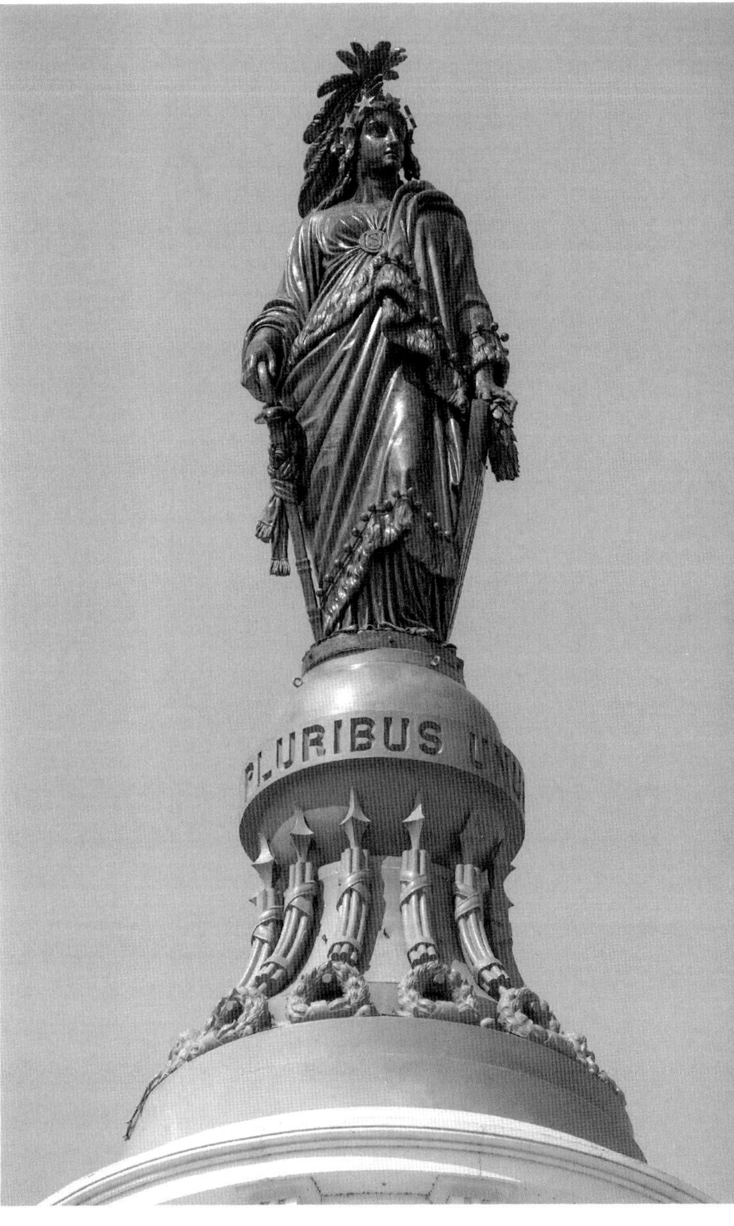

FIG. 4 (OPPOSITE) Moses Jacob Ezekiel in his studio with the plaster model of *Religious Liberty*, circa 1890. Photograph. Courtesy of The Jacob Rader Marcus Center of the American Jewish Archives, Cincinnati, Ohio, at americanjewisharchives.org.

FIG. 5 Thomas Crawford, *Statue of Freedom*, 1863. Bronze, 19 ½ ft., pedestal 18 ½ ft. US Capitol dome, Washington, DC. Courtesy of Architect of the Capitol.

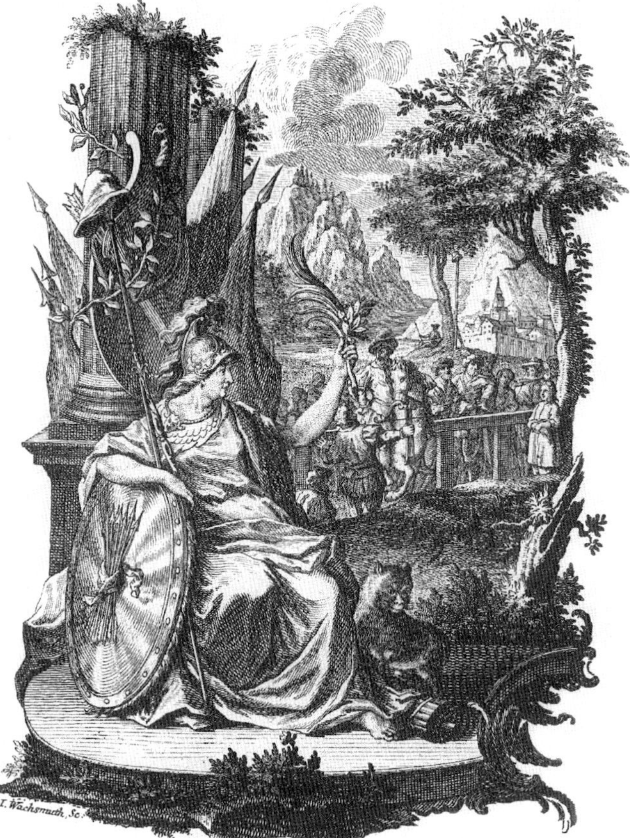

FIG. 6 Cesare Ripa, *Liberté*, circa 1758–60. Woodcut illustration in *Iconologia* (Hertel edition).

a scepter and the chains of tyranny as she offers sustenance to a bald eagle. An American flag floats behind her, topped by a Phrygian cap.[20]

Liberty took on several guises in her American incarnations, with amendments based on either an artist's desire or a sponsor's request, as in the case of Crawford's *Statue of Freedom* atop the Capitol dome. Crawford deviated from typical Liberty imagery because one of his designs, which incorporated a shield, a sword, and stars around a liberty cap, was opposed by slave owner Jefferson Davis. When serving as US secretary of war, Davis—who was eventually president of the Confederacy—requested the elimination of the customary liberty cap because of its status as a symbol of freed slaves. Crawford replaced the liberty cap with a helmet surmounted by an eagle headdress. His final, militant 19 1/2-foot Liberty grasps the hilt of a sheathed sword in her right hand, and in her left, she holds a laurel wreath and the shield of the United States with thirteen stripes. Dressed in classical drapery, she stands on a globe encircled with the national motto, *E pluribus unum*, and both fasces and wreaths decorate the lower part of her base.[21] Ezekiel's sculpture is not armed and bellicose like Crawford's, but she still wears chain mail, ever prepared to defend her Liberty role, even while wearing a peacetime toga. *Religious Liberty* resolutely and peacefully strides forward with the common Liberty trappings of fasces, a Phrygian cap, and the bald eagle.

Mindful of the gravity of his task and of the weight of the word "liberty" for his nation, conceived in liberty, Ezekiel researched his subject before embarking on its making. After receiving the commission, he set sail from Europe to Cincinnati, to visit his parents and other relatives; to Richmond, to see his old home and some of his thirteen siblings who remained behind after the Civil War; and to Philadelphia, his father's birth city. There he saw the Liberty Bell and purchased a small replica. Ezekiel intended to recreate the bell as the base for *Religious Liberty*, an idea soon rejected but ultimately adopted decades later for his Thomas Jefferson monument (chapter 5). Back in Italy, he stopped in Turin to examine and sketch chain armor to ensure its accuracy for his Centennial sculpture. Authenticity, as the following pages will show, was paramount for Ezekiel.[22]

In telling ways, Ezekiel's *Liberty* strays from these common precedents. She leans on the traditional Roman fasces, an emblem most associated with Republican Rome, although in Roman art an ax typically accompanies the fasces. Liberty was also shown with fasces on the first and second seals of the French Republic when she served as its emblem. Fasces, though, do function as an official symbol in several US government venues. Among others: two fasces are pictured on either side of the US flag in the House of Representatives; the seal of the Senate features a pair of crossed fasces at bottom; fasces ring the base of Crawford's *Statue of Freedom*; and Brumidi's Liberty in the Capitol dome carries fasces. Italian sculptor Enrico Causici's 13 1/2-foot neoclassical plaster *Liberty and the Eagle* (1817–19; fig. 7), ensconced in a high niche at the Capitol building, seems a fitting model for Ezekiel on this front and others. Fasces entwined by a serpent stand on her left side and an eagle to her right, although she is devoid of a Phrygian cap. However, Causici's sculpture was not intended to depict Liberty but rather the "genius of the constitution," hence the scroll she proudly extends.[23] Despite this long-held misinterpretation, the eagle and entwined serpent, and absence of a cat, chains, or a scepter, easily allow for its influence on Ezekiel.

Most prominent for Ezekiel would have been Jean-Antoine Houdon's statue in the Rotunda of the Virginia State Capitol (1788–92; see fig. 69), where George Washington leans on fasces. Houdon's Washington was known to Ezekiel, a native of Richmond, but he remembered most clearly a bronze copy at the Virginia Military Institute from his cadet days. Ezekiel's invention was to add the Constitution, lying open and covering the fasces. Inclusion of the Constitution atop the fasces reinforces the importance of the individual and the freedoms accorded to them through this founding document. In regard to religion, Ezekiel's preeminent constitutional concern, the First Amendment states, in a phrase

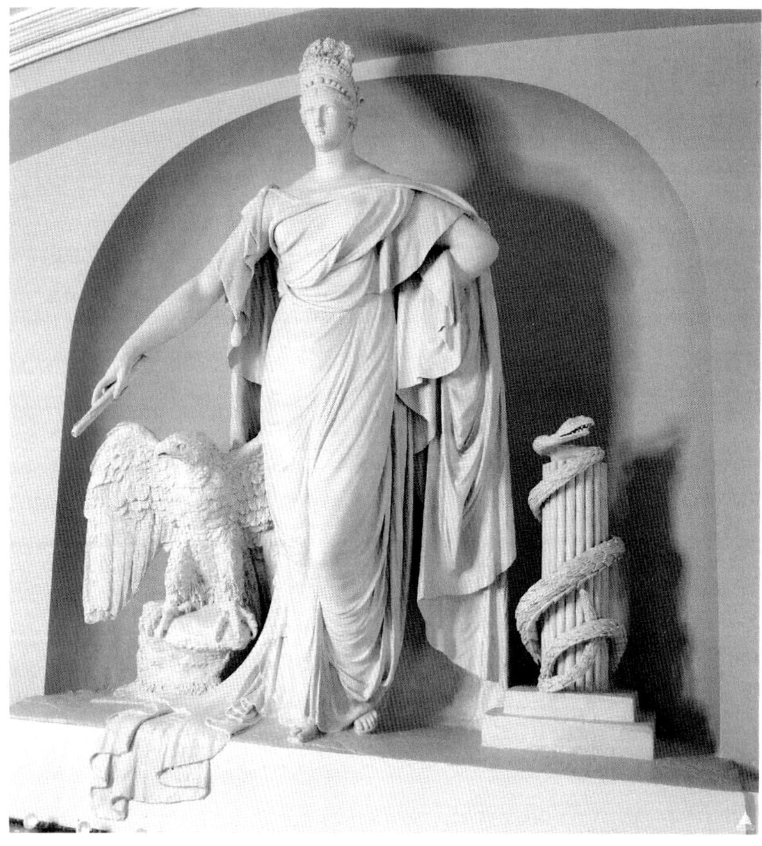

FIG. 7 Enrico Causici, *Liberty and the Eagle*, 1817–19. Plaster, 13 ft., 7 in. US Capitol, National Statuary Hall, Washington, DC. Courtesy of Architect of the Capitol.

that the artist partially quotes in his autobiography when reflecting on *Religious Liberty*, "Congress shall make no law respecting an establishment of religion, or prohibiting the free exercise thereof."[24] When *Religious Liberty* arrived in Philadelphia from Leghorn, after two months at sea, she was placed on a temporary pedestal that bore these words, before her permanent base could be installed.

The Centennial Exhibition and a Belated Unveiling

Established by an act of Congress in March 1871, the Centennial International Exhibition took four years to plan. From May 10 to November 10, 1876, nearly ten million visitors flocked to 236 acres of fairgrounds in Philadelphia to celebrate the great achievements of a young country alongside thirty-six foreign nations participating in the exhibition. Fairmount Park was transformed into a beacon of American industriousness and success since the nation's founding and a demonstration of national unity in the aftermath of the Civil War. Five principal buildings along with over two hundred smaller constructions presented advances in technology, agriculture, science, industry, and the arts. One of the largest buildings, Memorial Hall, showcased art from the Western world, including Ezekiel's now-lost plaster bas-relief of Jesus, in Gallery J for German art. Works by artists in Europe were submitted for approval to committees composed of Americans living abroad.

Three marble busts by Ezekiel—*Grace Darling* (ca. 1874; lost), *Sailor Boy* (1874; lost), and *Infant Mercury* (1876; Virginia Military Institute)—were on view in a smaller, separate Art Annex erected a short distance north of Memorial Hall.[25] Even with seventy-five thousand square feet of wall space for hanging and twenty thousand square feet of floor space for sculpture, Memorial Hall was woefully insufficient to display all the art chosen for the celebration. The Art Annex was constructed to accommodate the overflow, with sixty thousand additional square feet of wall space. (There was a separate Photographic Hall, measuring 258 by 107 feet with twenty-foot walls and divided into sections with twenty-eight partitions.) Ezekiel's marble statues were placed in Gallery 10 of the Art Annex, one of fifteen galleries slated for American art.[26] Gallery 10 mostly exhibited paintings and some sculpture by expatriate Americans in Paris, Munich, and Rome, many on loan from American collections. Ezekiel's sculptures were loaned by his brother-in-law, Levi Jacob Workum of Cincinnati, who married Ezekiel's oldest sister, Hannah. Executed by Ezekiel in Berlin around 1872 or 1873, a colossal bust of George Washington was also to show at the fair, but it was miscarried and never exhibited (see fig. 68). A catalog for the Centennial hails Ezekiel as "one of the ablest and withal most modest artists of whom sculpture in our days can boast."[27] Be that as it may, although *Religious Liberty* was intended to be Ezekiel's magnum opus and grand introduction to the art world, it did not touch US soil until the Centennial had ended its six-month run, delayed by both Ezekiel's perfectionism and the challenges he incurred because of B'nai B'rith's failure to provide timely payment.

The unrealistic schedule laid out by B'nai B'rith, coupled with the slow disbursement of funds to help assuage the costs of material, hired labor, and shipping, caused Ezekiel great consternation as did the pressure of his own ambitions. He wrote to fellow sculptor and Southerner Edward Valentine, "I cannot get such an enormous marble work properly finished and in such a short space of time as [been] allotted to me, and I do not care to hurry a work at the expense of its perfection."[28] The press closely followed the progression of Ezekiel's undertaking. A French-language paper published in Rome, *L'italie*, defended the extended time it was taking Ezekiel to finish, commenting on the ardor by which he was laboring, noting that he employed six assistants to aid him in meeting a difficult deadline, and chastising the Americans' impracticable expectations. This article refers to a dagger by *Liberty*'s side, an iconographic element discarded by the artist. The author interprets the dagger, in conjunction with *Liberty*'s coat of mail, as indicative of the sort of fate that would befall any who dared to injure what lies in her care: faith, or *Faith*.[29] *Il cosmopolita* described the model for the sculpture in depth, although not mentioning the dagger, and concluded that Ezekiel "has most successfully accomplished the arduous task allotted to him."[30]

The official guide for the exhibition, the only one allowed to be sold on the fairgrounds, indicates that the intended location of the monument would have been a prime spot near Memorial Hall.[31] *Religious Liberty* received mention in a prepublished, book-length guide to the event, for the most part described accurately, except for one interpretation: that the eagle's talons gripping the snake signified the destruction of slavery.[32] An index for this same guide provides a listing of "all places of interest, and how to reach them," including a synagogue on the corner of Broad and Mount Vernon Streets, with the names of which streetcars to take to get there.[33] Although not mentioned by name, that synagogue, Rodepf Shalom, was founded in 1795 and is the oldest Ashkenazi congregation in the Western Hemisphere. (Ezekiel's father, Jacob Ezekiel, wrote a history of Rodepf Shalom for the Centennial.) A different guide for the exposition describes *Religious Liberty*, concluding that the monument "typif[ies] the glory and power of the country of Washington."[34]

It was a difficult journey for the enormous sculpture, which could only be removed from Ezekiel's studio when a wall was knocked down, just as a portion of the facade of the building had been removed when the block of Carrara marble arrived. So large that the sculpture could not fit in the steamer's hold, *Religious Liberty* sailed across the Atlantic on the deck, covered by a tarp. Because its protective double box was too big to fit through tunnels from Rome to Leghorn, the outer box was removed for that initial leg of travel. Another setback ensued when the boat anchored in New York; during the sculpture's unloading, the outermost of its two protective crates broke, weakened by ocean waves splashing on the ship's deck.[35] Fortunately, the sculpture remained intact, but Ezekiel, stressed and still largely unpaid by B'nai B'rith, discovered that the brotherhood did not have funds to transport the sculpture from New York to Philadelphia. Once again, Ezekiel scrambled, borrowing money to bring his thirteen-ton monument to its final resting place, twenty days after the Centennial world's fair had ended. (He also had to borrow to pay for the temporary pedestal, which B'nai B'rith had not provided for either.) Before its dedication, Ezekiel had one last preparatory task: to cut the marble supports between the fingers of *Liberty* and *Faith*, and a support from *Liberty*'s thigh to the wrist of her uplifted arm, then to finish those areas of marble.

On a cold Thanksgiving Day, Jews and non-Jews stood together—along with Ezekiel, members of his family, and representatives from B'nai B'rith—as *Religious Liberty* was finally and triumphantly unveiled in Philadelphia's Fairmount Park, in front of Horticultural Hall and positioned across from a statue of Christopher Columbus. (Ezekiel would later sculpt his own *Christopher Columbus*; conclusion.) About 250 dignitaries processed to a platform impressively decorated in American bunting, accompanied by music from McClurg's Cornet Band, which played patriotic songs throughout the elaborate ceremony: "The Star-Spangled Banner," "Home Sweet Home," and "Yankee Doodle Dandy." When the initial pomp ended, Rabbi George Jacobs addressed approximately 1,500 spectators. Jacobs, who had served as a rabbi in Ezekiel's hometown of Richmond, carefully mentioned God but avoided Hebrew or specific Hebrew prayers. Instead, he spoke in large part about the good fortune of American Jews, thus implying their misfortune elsewhere: "Almighty God, Sovereign of the Universe, who art enthroned high above all mortals and rulest the destinies of all nations, we approach Thee this day with thankful spirits for having preserved us alive and sustained us to behold the advent of this joyous occasion to which every Hebrew heart, as well as the heart of every lover of religious liberty, has looked forward to with anxious and blissful expectation . . . to unveil a precious monument—one that belongs not to any creed or sect, but which interests the good and the true of all denominations."[36]

Considering some of the major goals of B'nai B'rith, the rabbi's inclusive word choice makes sense. Later in the ceremony, chair Adolph Sanger recited verbatim a portion of the Order's preamble in its most recent mandate: "To develop and elevate the mental and moral character of our race, by a liberal support of science and art, and the inculcation of the holiest and purest principles of philanthropy, honor and patriotism."[37] Sanger's broad statement focused on philanthropy and personal growth rather than on promoting religious Judaism. And, to be sure, the organization has primarily been secular and unifying, committed, as the opening sentence of their then-current constitution, from 1868, expansively indicated, to "the highest interests of humanity."[38] The Order's mission explicitly advocated patriotism—in other words, becoming one with the nation in which Jews reside—in line with the sculpture's expressly Americanized conception.

Antisemitic Views on Jewish Patriotism

Simon Wolf, chair of the *Religious Liberty* monument committee, and a lawyer and activist who had the ear of presidents, was a vehement promotor of "patriotic citizenship," which for him markedly centered on military service.[39] In 1895, Wolf, who served as lodge president of the B'nai B'rith Washington, DC, chapter and eventually led the national organization (1904–5), published *The American Jew as Patriot, Soldier and Citizen*, with Ezekiel's *Religious Liberty* featured as the cover image, repeated inside as the frontispiece (fig. 8; the volume to be displayed in the censored Princeton exhibition). The book aimed to dispel antisemitic claims that Jews avoided military service in American wars, especially the Civil War. One of the arguments Wolf tendered is that Jewish soldiers in both the Union and Confederacy exceeded their proportions in the general population.[40] Doubtless, Ezekiel would have proudly agreed to have his sculpture on the cover of a book about Jewish military service and contributions to American freedom. Not a sculpture about war but about religious liberty, this opening image reinforces Wolf's goal as well as that of Ezekiel's work. Wolf's book aimed to prove that Jews were very much American, participating in American life, and consequently deserving of religious equality, considering how they fought side by side with their gentile neighbors. Further impetus for Wolf was to rebut journalist and historian Goldwin Smith's well-read and virulently antisemitic writings proclaiming that Jews were unpatriotic and did not fight in the Civil War. (Ezekiel executed a marble bust of Smith for Cornell University in 1906, unveiled at that year's commencement; now in storage.)

Smith wrote extensively on the "Jewish Question," naming Jews a "parasitic race" with "a marked and repellent nationality of their own," and regurgitated slurs about Jews as money hungry.[41] Most offense to Wolf (and Ezekiel), and iterated in variations, would be Smith's tribalism and disparagement of Jews in the military: "They [the Jews] have now been everywhere made voters; to make them patriots, while they remain genuine Jews, is beyond the legislator's power. Benevolent and munificent they often are in the highest degree, patriots they cannot be; their only country is their race, which is one with their religion."[42] This shibboleth persisted before and after Wolf's publication. A late nineteenth-century volume on diseases chronicled the Jewish failure to fight: "Since they were conquered they have never

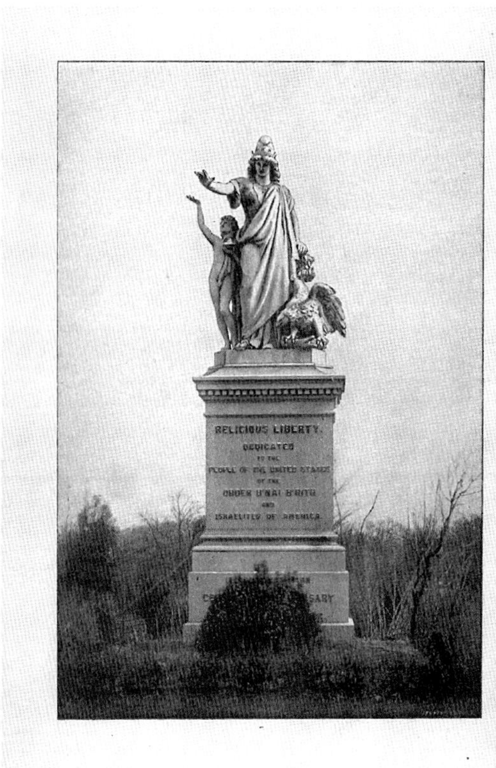

STATUE OF RELIGIOUS LIBERTY,
Fairmount Park, Philadelphia.

THE

AMERICAN JEW

AS

PATRIOT, SOLDIER AND CITIZEN

BY

SIMON WOLF

EDITED BY

LOUIS EDWARD LEVY

PHILADELPHIA
THE LEVYTYPE COMPANY
PUBLISHERS

NEW YORK—CHICAGO—WASHINGTON
BRENTANO'S
1895

FIG. 8 Frontispiece for book by Simon Wolf, *The American Jew as Patriot, Soldier and Citizen*, 1895. Photo: Samantha Baskind.

from choice borne arms nor sought distinction in military prowess. . . . To be plain, during their most severe persecutions nothing told so strongly against them as their apparent feebleness of body."[43] A turn-of-the century article in *Popular Science Monthly* perpetuated the canard: "Jewish immigrants of a military age who could pass our army requirements for recruits are comparatively rare."[44] Artists of the time decried the same. As recorded in the teenage diary of Julie Manet, daughter of painter Berthe Morisot and niece of Édouard Manet, French Impressionist Pierre-Auguste Renoir railed, "They come to France to make money and then when there is fighting they go and hide behind a tree. . . . [Jews] are of no country and don't do their military service anywhere."[45]

Alongside Wolf and across borders, other nineteenth-century Jews aimed to question and disprove Smith. Chief rabbi of the United Hebrew Congregations of the British Empire, Herman Adler, refuted him as follows: "The time was when, on being reproached and reviled, we had no alternative but to muffle our faces in our gaberdines and meekly to hold our peace. Those times, it is to be hoped, have gone for ever. . . . The interests of truth, the sacred cause of civil and religious freedom, demand that we should repel with indignation charges against our faith and our race—charges which I cannot characterise otherwise than cruel and gratuitous calumnies."[46] Several outlying publications accessible to a large audience, penned by pastor Madison Peters, praised Jewish patriotism and larger Jewish contributions to the world. In *The Jew as a Patriot*, Peters does much of the same work as Wolf, to whom he acknowledges his indebtedness.[47] The book's lengthy introduction by Oscar Straus, a Bavarian immigrant and son of slaveholders, who was the first Jew to serve in the US Cabinet, explicated how the Mosaic Code served as a model for democratic ideals laid out by Puritans in colonial America and their "heroic struggle for civil and religious liberty."[48] As interesting as the self-explanatory rebuttals is the newfound freedom Jews finally enjoyed to write in defense of themselves.

With the date for the installation ceremony of *Religious Liberty* finally firm, Wolf sent a letter to President Ulysses S. Grant, inviting him to attend, using vernacular akin to that found in *The American Jew as Patriot, Soldier and Citizen*: "This evidence of patriotism and love of liberty on the part of American citizens of Jewish faith is in keeping with their history and their lofty ideals and conception of duty. No class of citizenship has been made happier by religious liberty than the Jew, for the denial of that liberty in other lands has been the cause of endless persecution and misery." President Grant declined, citing a schedule busy with other official duties, but his history of antisemitism, as evidenced by his issuing of General Orders No. 11 on December 17, 1862—expelling all Jews "as a class" within twenty-four hours from districts occupied by the Union army in Kentucky, Mississippi, and Tennessee—may have been another factor (chapter 5).[49]

A Universal Meaning and a Particularized Meaning

Centennial Committee Chair Sanger, during his lengthy remarks at the unveiling, impartially presented the sculpture to the nation: "It is not in our special character of Jews that we offer this tribute, for we do not conceive that it is strictly as Jews that we enjoy Religious Liberty, that being a blessing which is offered freely to all."[50] Richard Magee's popular guide to the Centennial similarly framed the sculpture in broad terms: "Liberty protecting Religion, and in the idea, personified by religion, it is intended to express in a universal sense the reliance on a divine power common to humanity."[51] B'nai B'rith and Ezekiel's neutral approach differed from the other American religious or ethnic parties' contributions to the Centennial celebrations, including Italian Americans, German Americans, Catholics, Presbyterians, and "colored citizens," in that these groups represented their own history and historical personages.[52] To name two instances, Italian Americans presented a marble portrait sculpture of Christopher Columbus (1876), who wears a tunic and cape, with an anchor at his feet and his hand resting on a globe atop a column. A relief on the base portrays Columbus approaching the coast, his landing, and the coat of arms of the United States and Italy. The German American sculpture by Friedrich Drake (1871) depicts geographer, explorer, and diplomat Alexander von Humboldt in bronze, solemnly holding a scroll with his right hand as his other hand lightly touches a globe.

Other religious groups commissioned conventional monuments of religious men relevant to their church history. The Catholic coalition erected a grandiose sculpture, titled the *Catholic Total Abstinence Union Fountain* (1876), designed by architect Herman Kirn.[53] Statues on separate pedestals present four eighteenth-century American Catholic figures—Father Theobald Mathew, Charles Carroll, Archbishop John Carroll, and Commodore John Barry—along with the biblical Moses, imposingly at the center, grasping the Tablets of the Law at his chest. The Presbyterians' sculpture also featured a member of the clergy, a straightforward bronze likeness by Joseph Bailly of *Reverend John Witherspoon* (1876), a signer of the Declaration of Independence.

Religious Liberty, however, deviated from this norm of mostly portrait monuments. B'nai B'rith's comments make clear that the sculpture was meant to resonate widely. Jews, still tentative about the freedoms they had been accorded, as an oppressed minority understood as a race—the race of Israelites, a term used by Jews and non-Jews in Ezekiel's day—treaded lightly. B'nai B'rith recognized that an enormous, permanent, highly publicized marble monument calling attention to Jewish "otherness" or the "foreign" aspects of their religion would not benefit their still fragile place in American society. An 1873 proposal by the National Reform Association, advocating a constitutional amendment pointing to the Christian foundation of the country and "the Lord Jesus Christ as the ruler of nations," probably reinforced B'nai B'rith's desire to tout religious freedom as well.[54] Moreover, who would the Order have chosen to depict in a portrait monument for the Centennial? With such a short history in the United States, Jews had no signer of the Declaration of the Independence of which to boast. A request for a large public monument of an ancient Torah scholar such as Moses Maimonides would raise questions and only highlight Jewish difference.

For the average viewer, Ezekiel's sculpture was a classical rendition of a key democratic ideal, fully in line with the Order's stated motives; thus far, *Religious Liberty* has been understood in its American context and its common "American" iconography fleshed out. Yet, close looking at Ezekiel's sculpture reveals two distinctive variations indicating that the sculpture held a larger message, although likely too subtle to even be fully understood for much of its contemporary Jewish American audience. These two iconographic divergences suggest that as much as the statue was being presented "universally" to American viewers, B'nai B'rith and Ezekiel still imbued the monument with subtle, distinctly Jewish symbols, recognizable to attuned Jews, although not all, and almost certainly beyond a non-Jew's understanding.

B'nai B'rith's request for Ezekiel to place the eternal flame in *Faith*'s hand indicates that although the Order was service-based, not religious, it still acknowledged that components of traditional Judaism formed the group's essence and had to be maintained for Jewish continuity. Early projects sponsored by the fraternal lodge involved funding the first Jewish community center in the United States, in New York City in 1851. The following year, B'nai B'rith dedicated the first Jewish public library in the United States, also located in the same city. Nineteenth-century humanitarian work included disaster relief in 1868 in response to a severe flood in Baltimore. Still, B'nai B'rith valued the eternal flame as critical to *Faith*'s conception. The eternal flame, or eternal light (Ner Tamid), hangs near the Torah ark in all synagogues. As written in Exodus, "And thou shalt command the children of Israel, that they bring unto thee pure olive oil beaten for the light, to cause a lamp to burn continually. In the tent of meeting, without the veil which is before the testimony, Aaron and his sons shall set it in order, to burn from evening to morning before the LORD; it shall be a statute for ever throughout their generations on the behalf of the children of Israel."[55] The eternal light functions as a reminder of God's eternal presence, a principal representation recognizable by most Jews.

Later and more famously, the Statue of Liberty (1875–84; officially *Liberty Enlightening the World*), a gift from France to America to honor the friendship between the two countries, likewise featured a classically rendered, crowned female personification of freedom rising high on a tall pedestal. In this case, she stands alone and holds the flame herself. Nearly twenty years in the making, Frédéric Auguste Bartholdi's statue stands for broader democratic freedoms than *Religious Liberty*. Part of the Statue of Liberty's colossal arm holding the torch of enlightenment was debuted for Americans at the Centennial. Like Ezekiel's *Religious Liberty*, Bartholdi's *Liberty* arrived late from Europe to its destination, in this case a month before the fair ended. Raising funds for the statue's pedestal, which fell on Americans through public subscription, was also a challenging task for Bartholdi, and he, too, ended up with little pecuniary reward for his protracted labors. The Statue of Liberty's torch, meant to symbolize the enlightenment of freedom, offers a powerful icon that carries no alternate meaning.[56]

The most obvious example that Ezekiel's sculpture was meant to hold an alternate meaning for Jewish viewers can be discerned by another iconographical invention: the striking and peculiar manner by which the artist conceived *Liberty*'s right hand. *Liberty*'s elongated gesture, which extends over the barely draped *Faith*, at the same time reaches over spectators of the sculpture, offering them a protective blessing of freedom as well. Her fingers spread unnaturally, with two middle fingers connected, separated from her pinkie and index finger. That gesture insinuates the priestly blessing, decreed in Numbers: "The LORD bless thee, and keep thee; The LORD make His face to shine upon thee, and be gracious unto thee; The LORD lift up His countenance upon thee, and give thee peace. So shall they put MY name upon the children of Israel, and I will bless them."[57] Kohanim (descendants of Moses's brother, Aaron) in Jerusalem's ancient temple blessed the Jewish people this way daily, while in its modern, American context the blessing is bestowed on congregants near the end of prayer services at major Jewish holidays in traditional synagogues. A Kohen raises his hands with palms facing downward and forward, and the four fingers separate into two groups with thumbs touching, a gesture sometimes reproduced on Jewish ritual objects and gravestones (fig. 9). *Liberty*'s fingers are thus deliberately split into the twenty-first letter of the Hebrew alphabet, shin, which comprises three pronged lines and looks like a crown (ש). A shin symbolizes Shaddai, one of several Hebrew names for God. Traditionally, congregants avert their eyes as this blessing is made, because the divine presence is said to shine through the open fingers, which have formed "windows" to let light in.

Compositionally, it would have been awkward for Ezekiel to have *Liberty* give this exact, uniquely Jewish blessing, and such an arrangement may have also raised questions about its connotation, thereby overtly linking what B'nai B'rith intended to be a universal allegory of freedom to religious

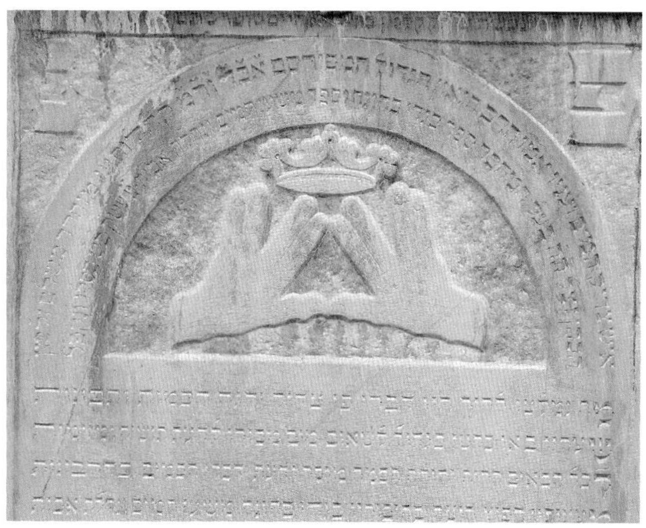

FIG. 9 Gravestone of Rabbi Meschullam Kohn, 1819. Fürth, Germany. Photo: Wikimedia Commons / Alexander Mayer. CC BY-SA 3.0. Cropped.

Jewish practice. With the sculpture in progress in Rome, the *Jewish Record* reported, "There will be no emblem either sectarian or denominational in its character to adorn this structure; it is contemplated as a '*freewill offering of the Israelites*' to the cause of '*Religious freedom*' and '*National Equality*,' a blessing which has been enjoyed by the Israelites in common with all other sects and creeds during the past century."[58] Instead, Ezekiel shows *Liberty* delivering a variation of the priestly blessing with a single hand creating a shin pattern. *Faith*'s hand nearly mirrors his guardian's. His palm raises upward in the other direction, to God and heaven, with his fingers forming the same shin arrangement. Moreover, when the two figures' hands are looked at together, they form a modified two-handed priestly blessing.

Ezekiel well knew the form and meaning of the blessing and used it in his art before and after *Religious Liberty*. For example, Ezekiel's bas-relief *Israel* shows Jesus offering the blessing at center (see fig. 34). Two decades later, Ezekiel employed the same gesture for his recumbent *Christ in the Tomb* (see figs. 27 and 31). Ezekiel claimed that when Queen Margherita visited his studio to see *Christ in the Tomb*, she asked about Jesus's gesture. He replied, "I had to tell her the meaning of the divided fingers, how they meant the ineffable name of God. She wanted to know if the priests give blessings with their fingers separated today." Open about his Jewishness to all, he also explained the meaning of the holiday Yom Kippur (Day of Atonement) to the royal vis-à-vis the priestly blessing.[59]

The letter shin itself is so central in Judaism that it is replicated in another chief ritual, performed every weekday morning by observant Jewish men: the wearing of tefillin. Special boxes and straps wrapped on one's head and arm, tefillin serves as a symbolic connection to God. Considered one of the primary mitzvot (commandments), the wrapping of tefillin is commanded in the Oral Law and four times in the Bible, first in Exodus: "And it shall be for a sign unto thee upon thy hand, and for a memorial between thine eyes, that the law of the LORD may be in thy mouth; for with a strong hand hath the LORD brought thee out of Egypt."[60] The arrangement of straps on one's hand purposefully forms a shin, and on the four-sided box attached to one's head, two of the four sides display the letter shin as a reference to Shaddai. The box itself holds parchments inscribed with verses from the Bible, including the oldest and foremost daily prayer in the Jewish religion: the Shema. Recited every morning and evening, the Shema proclaims God's oneness as the most basic Jewish profession of faith (Deut. 6:4–9). Mezuzahs are often ornamented with a decorative shin for Shaddai.

Crucially, in a less commanding clay sketch, *Liberty* tepidly extends her left hand, not her right, with her fingers fully connected (fig. 10). *Faith* mostly conforms to the final sculpture except that his fingers, too, remain connected. In this discarded composition, a smaller, hardly majestic *Liberty* wears an awkward crown. *Liberty* and *Faith* look in separate directions rather than in tandem, working together to ensure religious freedom, as in the monument eventually erected in Philadelphia. The fasces appear between the pair, not at *Liberty*'s side, and Ezekiel had placed a round shield at their feet. No allegorical eagle or serpent had been introduced. Ezekiel's decision to rework his original idea in favor of the all-important priestly blessing—which complicated shipping of the sculpture because of the fingers' fragility, consequently requiring extra supports the artist was forced to design for safe shipping—evinces his continuing commitment to the Jewish religion and desire, like his B'nai B'rith brothers, to have aspects of Judaism encoded in the sculpture.

It is essential to point out that there are no extant documents to substantiate how much of Ezekiel's nineteenth-century Jewish audience received the sculpture's implied message as the artist intended. As Michele Bogart observes in her fundamental study on early modern American public sculpture, however attuned an informed viewer may be to certain representations, allegorical sculpture can still be challenging to decode, and the same can be said for the out-of-context Jewish symbolism of *Religious Liberty*.[61] Yet, as difficult as it is to trace the reception of large-scale civic works from centuries past, it is still instructive to clarify the intended meaning of *Religious Liberty* to see how the statue's multilayered message may have resonated in its own time and place. Ezekiel was versed in the symbols and conventions familiar to his Jewish audience, and, not least, to the values held dear by Jews. Surely, this is the reason B'nai B'rith gave him the commission for *Religious Liberty*, even though he was an impractical choice to sculpt the monument, considering that he lived across the ocean.

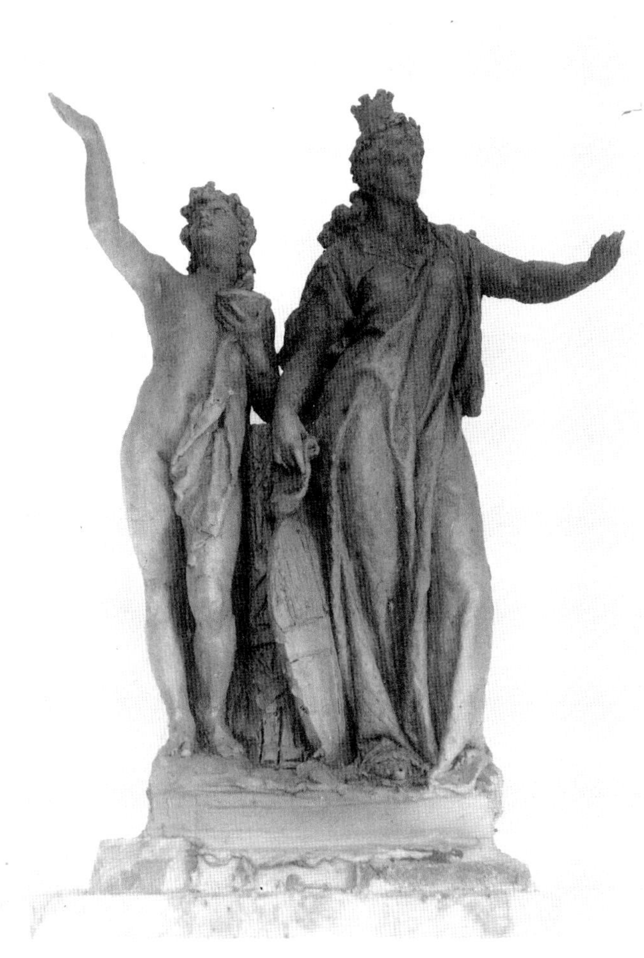

FIG. 10 Moses Jacob Ezekiel, clay sketch of *Religious Liberty*, 1875. Courtesy of The Jacob Rader Marcus Center of the American Jewish Archives, Cincinnati, Ohio, at americanjewisharchives.org.

There is one last point of consideration: Ezekiel's father, B'nai B'rith member Jacob Ezekiel, had his own very public link to religious liberty, which may have played a further role in the younger Ezekiel receiving the prestigious assignment, beyond the sculptor's Jewish heritage. At the very least, Jacob Ezekiel's connection to religious freedom played a part in Ezekiel's push to finish his sculpture in the face of tremendous difficulties. Years earlier, in defense of the separation of church and state, the elder Ezekiel felt compelled to write, from Richmond, to the newly inaugurated President John Tyler. In the wake of William Henry Harrison's untimely death in 1841 from pneumonia, a bare month into his presidency, Tyler issued a proclamation urging Americans to visit houses of worship and observe a day of fasting. While Jacob Ezekiel supported such mourning practices, he objected to the specific language that Tyler had used at the start of his proclamation: "When a Christian people feel themselves to be overtaken by a great public calamity . . ." In response, Jacob Ezekiel penned a long, thoughtful letter to the new president, pointing out the exclusionary nature of his language: "I am fully conscious that a denomination of 'Christian People' exists in this country as in other[s], and no doubt you are aware that there exists a *Jewish People also* 'that have been overtaken by this great calamity' which has befallen our country, as well as a *People who neither profess Judaism or Christianity* but believes in a Supreme Being and Creator of the universe whom they adore." Tyler promptly and apologetically wrote back, clarifying that he did not mean to be exclusionary and extending his "profound respect" for the Jewish people.[62]

Perhaps Ezekiel told his patrons about his iconographic particularism once the sculpture arrived in the United States, perhaps he waited for the brothers or others to notice that the sculpture was not entirely neutral, or maybe *Liberty*'s priestly blessing was a secret nod to the Jewishness that Ezekiel always held dear. Regardless, Ezekiel's variation of a greatly recognizable sign, or ritual, adapted in the context of a different, "secular" kind of blessing opens a tripartite understanding of the artist, his work, and Jewish life in late nineteenth-century America.

"The Tragedy of My Life"

Ezekiel considered his trouble with B'nai B'rith and his travails in getting *Religious Liberty* paid for, finished, and delivered as "the tragedy of my life." Bereft by all the obstacles to the statue's completion and the Order's financial shortcomings, he further wrote, "I do not refer to it without pain because it cost me too much moral and physical suffering ever to be forgotten by a human being."[63] The Order tried to rectify those obstacles at the onset but to no avail. One year after the Order sanctioned the sculpture, a frustrated Centennial Committee implored the brothers in a memo, "Your *faith and honor are pledged to the fulfillment of this task* and we simply ask you to stand by the action of your own representatives, and to use every effort to provide a sufficient contribution to liquidate the obligations this Committee has assumed. . . . Brethren! We expect your united support and sympathy!"[64]

With the sculpture unveiled, B'nai B'rith leaders were still desperately exhorting members to find the funds to fully compensate Ezekiel for *Religious Liberty*. At the twenty-fifth annual convention of the B'nai B'rith in Cincinnati (1877), the chapter president devoted a portion of his address to the tardy payment. He lauds *Religious Liberty* for shedding "luster" on Ezekiel and the Order in general, and he asks the brothers to exert themselves to liquidate the debt incurred from such a

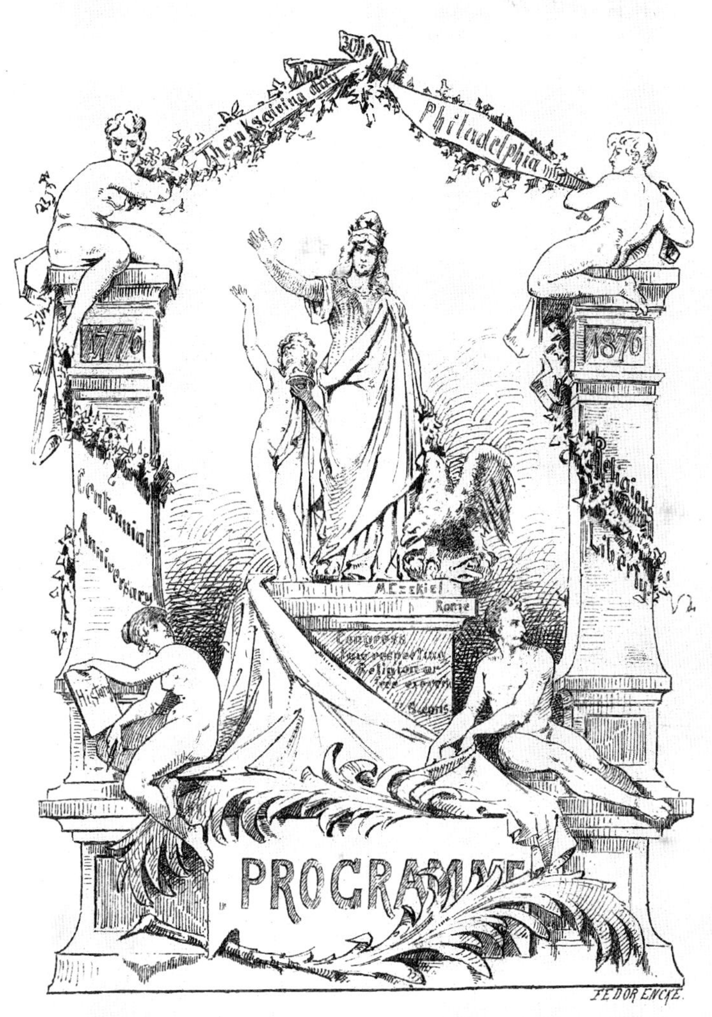

FIG. 11 Fedor Encke, program cover for unveiling of *Religious Liberty*, 1876. Courtesy of Weitzman National Museum of American Jewish History, Philadelphia, Pennsylvania. 1998.33.1. Gift of Garry G. Greenstein.

commendable undertaking. Until then, the artist had been provided only with a meager fee for his labors, $4,500 (after expenses paid); in all, costs for materials, freight, labor, and other fees came to around $40,000.[65] Individuals attempted to procure monies as well. Three months following the dedication and with Ezekiel still awaiting remuneration, one B'nai B'rith member wrote a letter to the editor of the *American Israelite* recommending that a small fee be assessed from members to fulfill the contract, considering that brothers, numbering around twenty thousand, were not fund-raising or donating as expected.[66] Simon Wolf submitted a letter to the editor of a different Jewish newspaper, the *Jewish Record*, praising the sculpture and appealing to his B'nai B'rith brethren to donate toward Ezekiel's payment.[67] It took over three years of urgent memos and direct personal solicitation to pay off the sculpture and to provide Ezekiel with some compensation. B'nai B'rith documents indicate that in January 1879, $13,963.10 was still due to the artist.[68] Ezekiel finally used the little money he received to pay off his creditors for the statue.

The artist still graciously handed over his sculpture at the dedication ceremony to members of B'nai B'rith, whose mission he extolled as "a sacred charge."[69] He also fondly recalled the fanfare of that day, with speeches to the large crowd, and then, of course, the climactic moment "when the veil fell off, [and] hundreds of small American flags, with *Religious Liberty* stamped on them, fluttered around and were gathered by the spectators."[70] As punctuation, the band played the American hymn "Hail, Columbia" and the German patriotic anthem "German Fatherland." Spectators could take home the specially designed flags along with the ceremony's program, whose cover was designed by Ezekiel's close friend, German painter Fedor Encke, who traveled with him to America during the transport of *Religious Liberty* (fig. 11; the program to be displayed in the censored Princeton exhibition). Four nudes lounging on a loose approximation of ancient Greek architecture decorated the border of the cover to complement Ezekiel's classically inspired sculpture at center.

Religious Liberty / Religious Liberty and the National Museum of American Jewish History

Over the years, *Religious Liberty* has served as the focal point for several celebrations orchestrated by B'nai B'rith.[71] During the Great Depression, in October 1936, nearly six decades after the monument was erected in Fairmount Park, the Order rededicated the sculpture in conjunction with the tercentenary of the banishment of Roger Williams from Massachusetts Bay Colony for his advocacy of religious freedom. The timing was no accident: with the rise of Nazi persecution in Europe, Jews would especially want to remind America of the importance of religious liberty. More than 2,500 attended the event, with addresses delivered by figures associated with the three major religious affiliations in the United States: Catholicism, Protestantism, and Judaism. Immediately before the ceremony, the speakers' remarks were broadcast across the nation by NBC radio, heard by millions. Alfred Cohen, president of B'nai B'rith and the Jewish speaker at the event (he briefly mentioned Ezekiel), made certain that invitations were sent to Jewish organizations across the country in the spirit of uniting Jewry. Musical selections were played by the Works Progress Administration band and the ceremony started and ended by nodding to the statue's Jewish origins: The ceremony began with a prayer delivered by Rabbi William H. Fineshriber and concluded with a choir of two hundred children from the Associated Talmud Torahs singing "America the Beautiful," along with a final prayer delivered by a second rabbi.[72] In May 1954, the statue was rededicated in a less elaborate ceremony but still with addresses from representatives of the three major American religious affiliations. The rededication coincided with B'nai B'rith's first "Annual Pilgrimage" to the sculpture. After some unspecified repairs, funded by the Philadelphia lodge of B'nai B'rith, the statue was quietly rededicated in 1964.

The sculpture was rededicated for a fourth time as part of the yearlong series of bicentennial observances by the Order during the US bicentennial celebrations in 1976. Among the speakers were, once more, a cross section from the Jewish, Protestant, and Catholic faiths. The last page of the event's program reproduced an image of George Washington and quoted an excerpt from his letter to the Hebrew Congregation of Newport, advocating religious equality (chapter 5). In an article published by the *National Jewish Monthly*, B'nai B'rith President David Blumberg celebrated *Religious Liberty*, mentioning Ezekiel's name as the sculptor of the monument (as do most documents regarding all the rededications), and he concluded by encouraging American Jews to savor religious liberty but not to be so seduced by it that they discard their faith: "Let me therefore suggest that the Jew who fails to exercise his freedom to be affirmatively Jewish—who treats it passively—is denying, not defending, religious freedom."[73] This line of thinking carries forward from Ezekiel's day; Simon Wolf, too, understood the importance of religious observance to sustain Jewish continuity, maintaining that while Jews must always be inspired by duty to one's country, they must concurrently "be willing to die for one's religion, and to uphold at whatever sacrifice its tenets and teachings. . . . I claim that no man can be a good citizen without being true to the highest teachings of his faith."[74]

In August 1985, after more than a century in Fairmount Park, *Religious Liberty*, wrapped in packing blankets and tied with rigging, journeyed seven miles to the grounds of the National Museum of American Jewish History, with the financial assistance of B'nai B'rith International and several individual benefactors. Three considerations shaped the decision to relocate the statue: its theme is well suited for Independence Mall; more people could see the monument in such a conspicuous location; and its message of freedom coincides with that of the museum. Indeed, prominent signage for the museum's permanent exhibition marks each of the three floors: "Foundations of Freedom: 1654–1880," "Dreams of Freedom, 1880–1945," and "Choices and Challenges of Freedom." A press release about the relocation reiterated the endurance of the weighty principles imparted by Ezekiel's sculpture: "The historical monument, *Religious Liberty*, symbolizes the commitment to the ideal of freedom which has made America the great nation that it is. Relocating the sculpture to the Museum to a site on Independence Mall facing the Liberty Bell puts this national treasure in the birthplace of our nation's freedom and places the symbol of a fundamental civil liberty in proximity to the emblem of American independence. . . . Underscoring our nation's commitment to freedom and equality, the relocation project will affirm the continued dedication of B'nai B'rith and the Jewish community to this cherished ideal."[75]

That relocation occasioned another rededication event in 1986, before which the sculpture underwent conservation, including replacing some of *Liberty*'s missing fingers and the eagle's beak. (In 1987, the statue was vandalized and underwent further conservation.) Once more, a full page of the event's program reproduced an image of George Washington along with his letter in support of religious equality. A time capsule was buried beneath the sculpture, by then on long-term loan to the museum from the city of Philadelphia, to be opened during the nation's tricentennial in 2076.

Ezekiel's tribute to religious tolerance was relocated again, in 2010, to the front of the museum's new, enlarged building, a major upgrade from the former museum space, housed inside a synagogue. Only transported some five hundred feet, *Religious Liberty* fittingly remains on Independence Mall—mere steps from the Liberty Bell, a block south of the National Constitution Center, and a block north of Independence Hall, where American liberty was born—thus still serving as a proud reminder of the liberties that have allowed Jews to thrive, finally in freedom, in America (the very theme of the museum). These two moves, from a civic space in Fairmount Park to markedly "Jewish" spaces, reshape the meaning of Ezekiel's monument, now overtly connecting it to a Jewish history within a broader American history. Essentially, the statue currently embodies the same dual dialogue that Ezekiel envisioned for his towering sculpture, which rises high before the museum's dramatic glass facade. As the twofold mission statement for the museum currently reads, in part, "Its purpose is to connect Jews more closely to their heritage and to inspire in people of all backgrounds a greater appreciation for the diversity of the American Jewish experience and the freedoms to which Americans aspire."[76]

Because of the liberty afforded American Jews, they could contribute to American life and culture, a theme emphatically underscored within the museum's permanent exhibition, whose predominant message echoes that of *Religious Liberty*. To be sure, *Religious Liberty* boldly announces its purpose, which the museum slowly but forcefully unfolds. A museum brochure for visitors communicates this very idea: "NMAJH brings to life a story of transformation that could only happen in America."[77] At the end of the museum's installation, a quote from Jewish poet Emma Lazarus—best known for her poem "The New Colossus" inscribed on the base of the Statue of Liberty—sums up the overriding point: "Until we are all free, we are none of us free." The museum asks a final question beneath that essential imperative: "What does freedom mean to you?"

And when visitors emerge from the building, they encounter Ezekiel's stately sculpture anew, which he more affirmatively remembered in 1906, in a letter to Simon Wolf on the occasion of his seventieth birthday:

> I, who have been the humble instrument of carrying out in enduring stone the fundamental idea of that which alone can give peace on earth and good will towards all men, owe the initial steps to you and . . . your most noble desire to reflect honor upon our race. The placing of an enduring record of the one principle of our government which alone prevents the recurrence of oppression, of religious fanaticism and intolerance, and makes our country the most civilized one on the face of the earth. I come to you, therefore, today with feelings of deep reverence and gratitude.[78]

In 1876, Ezekiel's *Religious Liberty* and its surrounding fanfare simultaneously reminded Jews about their good fortune and alerted Americans to their democratic lineage. By crafting a large, public, sculpted testimonial in support of democratic principles, Ezekiel elicited a dual sense of national and Jewish pride. Concurrently, Ezekiel aimed to convey the particularism of his faith in an unobtrusive fashion during a still uncertain moment in American Jewish history. Today, *Religious Liberty*—the very fact of its making, as well as its subject—still serves as a highly visible reminder of the rights granted Jews by the First Amendment in multicultural America.

EZEKIEL, JUDAISM, AND THE BIBLE

Chapter 2

My relief *Israel*, my *Judith*, *David*, and *Christ in the Tomb* show that my ideals have always been deeply connected with Jewish traditions and ideals.
—Ezekiel, letter to his brother Henry, 1903

When a young man, Ezekiel dreamed he was walking along Main Street in his native city of Richmond and looked up to the sky. He wrote of seeing a bright cloud that transformed into a face soon speaking to him: "If you will lead a virtuous life and observe the Sabbath day, you will finally be able to go across the Ocean and work as an artist."[1] That dream, a product of Ezekiel's mythmaking or perhaps the kind of wishful bargain children sometimes make with a higher power, came to permanent fruition soon after the dedication of *Religious Liberty*. Once *Religious Liberty* found her new home on American soil, Ezekiel found his new home when he set down permanent roots in Rome. He continued to observe the Sabbath day in the faraway land of his dream. Even in Catholic Rome, the epicenter of a complicated history between the church and the Jews, Ezekiel's deep bond with the Jewish people and profound interest in Jewish history and religion would openly and profoundly manifest in his life and art.

Most obviously, Ezekiel's Jewish heritage finds form in his biblical works.[2] While Ezekiel received commissions from Jews—*Religious Liberty* and later the *Thomas Jefferson* monument (chapter 5), to name two major instances—that engaged aspects of the Jewish secular experience, expressly religious freedom, he also executed works with biblical subjects, the focus of this chapter and the next. Viewed together, Ezekiel's biblical works demonstrate his deep knowledge of the Hebrew Bible and are distinctive for his amalgamation of various sources. Perhaps unexpected is Ezekiel's ongoing interest in the Christian Bible, namely a handful of sculptures portraying Jesus as Jewish. Ezekiel's subjects were frequently like those adopted by some of his non-Jewish peers, but their mold-breaking final conception demonstrate the influence of his

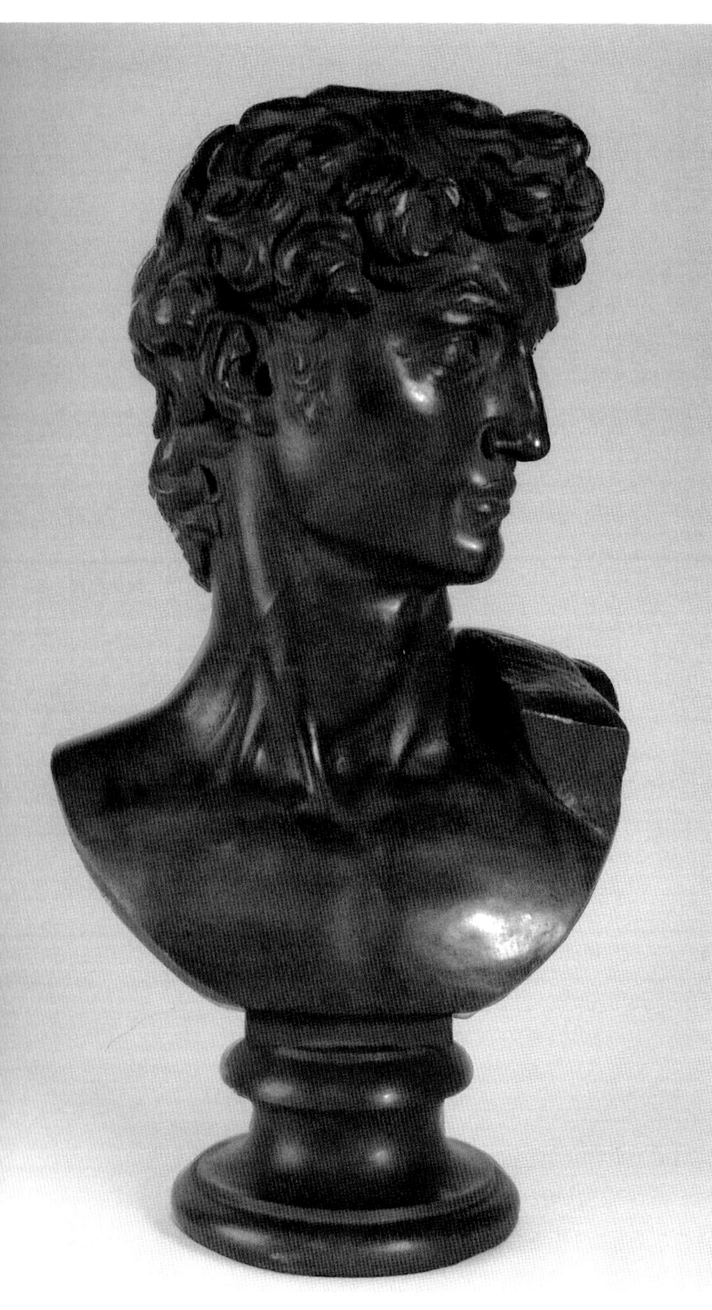

FIG. 12 Moses Jacob Ezekiel, *David*, 1893. Bronze, 25 × 14 × 9 in. Collection of Skirball Museum, Skirball Cultural Center, Los Angeles, California. SCC 2012.3430. Photography by KeAnne Langford.

religiocultural upbringing, which led to his inventiveness. This chapter focuses on those sculptures depicting individual figures from the Bible, all noncommissioned and initiated by Ezekiel's private passions. Chapter 3 looks at commissioned biblical works with Zionist implications.

That Ezekiel would be attracted to biblical matter is unsurprising. Practically, biblical subjects are a staple in the history of art. Art with biblical themes could be seen throughout Europe, which Ezekiel traveled widely, and they are especially pervasive in his adopted city. Michelangelo was his professed artistic idol; Ezekiel fashioned a bronze replica of the head of Michelangelo's *David* (1893; fig. 12).[3] Successful nineteenth-century American sculptors also gravitated to the Hebrew Bible. Randolph Rogers's crouching *Ruth Gleaning* (after 1853; Newark Museum, NJ) and Edmonia Lewis's *Hagar in the Wilderness* (1875; Smithsonian American Art Museum, Washington, DC) offer two particularly potent examples, although much more idealized than Ezekiel's sculptures. Ezekiel's penchant for time-honored subjects and his desire to be ranked in the pantheon of great artists—one reason that he lived as an expatriate while he remained a staunch Virginian—likewise stimulated his biblical work.

Just as crucial to his choice of subject matter is Ezekiel's upbringing and deep familiarity with the Holy Writ. His memoir and other documents record a childhood suffused with Jewish thinking and holidays. Ezekiel's grandfather petitioned the Virginia Military Institute to grant his grandson a furlough to come home for the High Holidays (Rosh Hashanah and Yom Kippur) and Passover, unprecedented requests that were approved. (One of fourteen children, Ezekiel lived with his maternal grandparents as a child for financial reasons but always remained close to his parents, whose

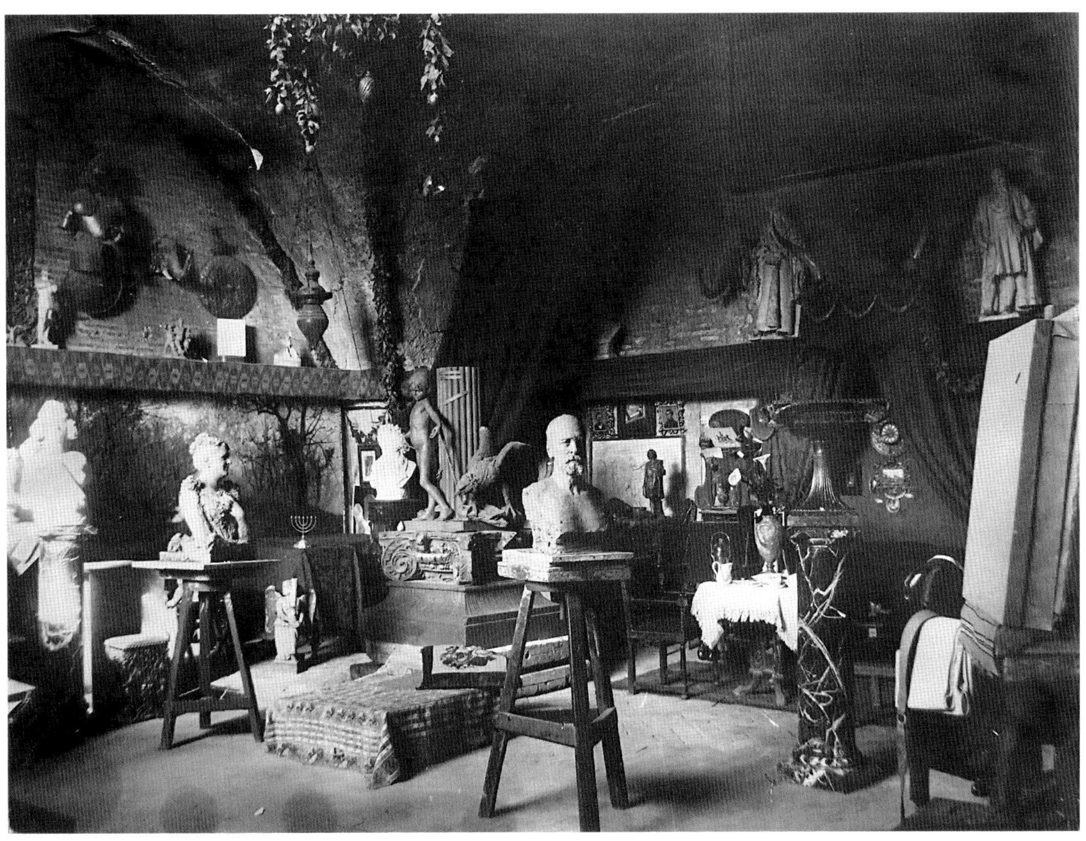

FIG. 13 Moses Jacob Ezekiel's studio, circa 1890. Photo: Virginia Military Institute Archives, Lexington.

home was nearby.)[4] In an 1869 letter to his mother from Berlin while studying at the Royal Academy, the young sculptor wrote about missing his family during the High Holidays.[5] His father, Jacob Ezekiel, served as secretary of Richmond's first synagogue and was a scholar of Jewish theology. The elder Ezekiel owned all the writings by Moses Maimonides, a principal medieval Jewish scholar and philosopher, a fact that Ezekiel mentioned with pride.[6] Ezekiel made a point to describe at length an observant Jewish neighbor's use of tefillin (two leather boxes worn by Jewish men during morning prayers that contain the shin; chapter 1), explaining their use to his memoir's readers "to give an idea of what my surroundings were in the early days of my life."[7] This background provided Ezekiel with intimate knowledge of the Bible and Jewish thought and practice, as well as an enduring commitment to his coreligionists. Despite crushing frustrations over the years, that commitment spurred him on: "The race to which I belong had been oppressed and looked down upon through so many ages, I felt that I had a mission to perform. That mission was to show that, as the only Jew born in America up to that time who had dedicated himself to sculpture, I owed it to myself to succeed in doing something worthy in spite of all the difficulties and trials to which I was subjected."[8]

Even after his parents moved from Richmond to Cincinnati following the Civil War, where they affiliated with Reform Judaism (a modernized form of Judaism), Ezekiel practiced some traditional customs. Living in Italy, he still observed the Sabbath, fasted during Yom Kippur, and attended synagogue.[9] He noticeably displayed a menorah in his greatly visited studio in the heart of Christendom, as evidenced by a photograph of that storied space (fig. 13). One's eye is immediately drawn to the menorah at left; most of the other objects are crowded by bric-a-brac, but the menorah sits on a conspicuously empty table. It is as if, in this photograph that Ezekiel knew was being taken, he wanted viewers to notice the Jewish ritual object among all the items in his cluttered studio. In correspondence home to his father, Ezekiel mentioned studying Kabbalah (medieval Jewish mysticism) and reading the Zohar (a foundational Kabbalistic text), and other materials demonstrate his command of the Hebrew language and the Bible. He opined on his regard for Jewish texts, apropos their wisdom "to solve many problems that concern us intellectually and spiritually in our pilgrimage on earth."[10] When news of his mother's death reached him in Rome, he sat shiva (a weeklong mourning period after burial) in his studio; and throughout the year following her burial, he attended requisite religious services to recite the Mourner's Kaddish (a Jewish prayer for the dead) each morning and evening. Upon Ezekiel's own death, his closest friends arranged a funeral in Rome according to what they believed to be "the true spirit of his religious feeling essentially Jewish [*sic*]" and had a rabbi recite ritual prayers.[11] Mary Argyle Taylor, the daughter of a Baptist minister from Richmond who lived in Rome with her family for years, was close with Ezekiel, and she remembered him in an appreciation written soon after his death: "Though possessed of a singularly wide humanity, he was intensely proud of, and loyal to, his family and race."[12]

The Origins and Trials of a Jewish Artist

As a boy in Richmond, Ezekiel's subjects featured the biblical narratives he knew best. A large drawing in crayon, titled *The Revolt of the Children of Israel in the Desert and the Stoning of Moses* (ca. 1857; lost), is one of a few childhood works mentioned in his memoir. In this early stage, Ezekiel explored oil painting and created two canvases that still remain.[13] His first efforts as a sculptor include *Cain Receiving the Curse of the Almighty* (ca. 1860; lost) and *Moses Receiving the Law on Mount Sinai* (ca. 1860; lost). The latter dismayed his maternal grandmother, Hannah Waterman. When the plaster model collapsed because Ezekiel failed to provide proper supports, Waterman understood that failure as an omen from God that her grandson should abandon sculpting. Her reaction can be attributed both to a misunderstanding of the Second Commandment, which when interpreted strictly prohibits the making of images, and her unease that Ezekiel would choose a profession that might disallow him from earning a proper living, both subjects addressed in his memoir.[14] As a young man, Ezekiel spent a year at the Medical College of Virginia, he wrote, only because he felt that a career in art was unrealistic and medicine would provide financial security.[15] At the least, his study of anatomy at medical school, where he performed dissections, helped him gain knowledge of the human form for his art.

But once Ezekiel arrived in Cincinnati following his year studying medicine, his desire to pursue a career in the arts was secured. His father's dry goods business had burned to the ground during the Civil War, and the family's attempt to rebuild in Virginia was fruitless. The Queen City seemed hospitable because of its large, vibrant Jewish presence, including his sister Hannah, who had married into the well-established Cincinnati Workum family, among the first Jews to arrive in the city (in 1825). By 1870, it was estimated that between eight thousand and twelve thousand Jews lived in Cincinnati. Further, 13 percent of the working Jewish population worked in the dry goods trade.[16]

Coincidentally, for an aspiring artist, Cincinnati held promise as an artistic center; among others, sculptors Henry Kirke Brown and Hiram Powers were once based there, as were painters John Henry Twachtman, Robert Duncanson, and Henry Mosler, a Jewish American and Ezekiel's exact contemporary.[17] By then, his grandmother's concerns had abated. She had decorated her grandson's new room in the Queen City with four plaster statues of Venus: *Venus de Milo*, *Medici Venus*, *Capitoline Venus*, and the more contemporary neoclassicist Bertel Thorvaldsen's *Venus* (1821; Chatsworth House, Derbyshire). Over the family fireplace, she also placed a plaster relief head of *Napoleon*, a subject he adopted in the round late in his career.[18] Emboldened by the thriving arts community in Cincinnati, Ezekiel forged ahead as a sculptor. In Cincinnati, he took classes with stonemason Thomas Dow Jones, who had achieved some success sculpting portrait busts, among them several copies in various mediums of an *Abraham Lincoln* (1861; National Portrait Gallery, Washington, DC).[19] There Ezekiel completed his first sculpture, a small plaster statuette painted bronze, titled *Industry* (1869; lost). It depicts a young girl sitting on a barrel, knitting socks while studying from a book, for which his youngest sister Sally (Sarah) modeled. The sculpture was displayed in the window of a local gallery and received notice in a local paper. That acknowledgment, Ezekiel wrote, spurred him to continue his nascent art efforts.[20]

Like Ezekiel, Mosler was involved in Civil War efforts, not as a soldier but as an artist–correspondent for *Harper's Weekly*, joining the ranks of other artists such as Winslow Homer. In the mid-1860s, Mosler studied at the Düsseldorf Academy, before returning to Cincinnati for eight years. There, he painted *Plum Street Temple* (ca. 1866; Skirball Museum, Cincinnati), detailing the exterior of Rabbi Isaac Mayer Wise's newly built temple, B'nai Yeshurun, and a canvas considered essential to the canon of Jewish American art. Mosler's portrait commissions include a likeness of Wise's wife, Therese Bloch Wise (ca. 1867; Skirball Museum, Cincinnati). As artists and Jews in Cincinnati, Mosler and Ezekiel became acquainted. The two artists' fates could very well have been intertwined had Ezekiel taken up Mosler's offer to go with him to Paris.[21] An expatriate for two decades, Mosler ran a Parisian studio, where students took private lessons and artists visited him, including Ezekiel. The *American Israelite* hailed Ezekiel and Mosler together in a single headline: "Two Israelites in Cincinnati Have Recently Attained High Distinction in Fine Arts." Almost twenty years later, the Jewish community again paired the artists together with pride in a brief *American Israelite* article: "Ezekiel-Mosler: Two Famous Cincinnatians."[22] As for Ezekiel, encouraged by artists he met in Cincinnati and eager for more intensive education, the fledgling sculptor crossed the Atlantic to study at the Royal Academy of Art in Berlin.[23] His training there, from 1869 to 1871, and study with sculptors Albert Wolff and Rudolf Siemering, shaped his academic style, a propensity for allegory and historical subject matter, and his belief in the central role of the human figure, faithfully rendered, in art.

Eve's Belly Button

Ezekiel turned to the holy book from the start of his professional career, before he became celebrated for portrait busts and large public monuments, starting with *Religious Liberty*. While working on *Religious Liberty*, Ezekiel sculpted the world's first woman, which he gave the unconventional title *Eve Hearing the Voice* (fig. 14). This life-size conception, completed in clay in 1876 as evidence to the Michael Beer Prize committee of what he did during his awarded year in Rome, was not bronzed until around 1904.[24] Ezekiel portrays a naked Eve after she has been tempted by the serpent and eaten from the Tree of Knowledge, at the moment she suffers God's rebuke (Gen. 3–13). The naturalistically modeled Eve theatrically averts her head and painfully attempts to hide her face in the crook of her left arm, which partially covers her bare chest. She crosses her legs awkwardly, attempting to conceal her nudity. At her feet, the serpent coils menacingly around the tree stump on which she cowers, and Eve's bowed head looks downward at her tempter. Ezekiel took great care to delineate the textures of the serpent's scales, just as he lavished attention on the thick hair that cascades gracefully down Eve's muscled back and spirals over her face, down to her left breast (fig. 15). These details, and Eve's palpable despair, obscure the most unusual feature of the sculpture: Ezekiel fashioned Eve, the only full nude that he ever produced, without a navel.

To convey Eve's distress in the once blissful garden when her sinful act was revealed before God, Ezekiel enlists her entire body. Less interested in classical stillness and more in the emotional and physical implications of Eve's fateful choice, Ezekiel's sculpture engages viewers, asking them to put themselves in her place, to imagine the unbearable regret of her impulsive act, and to suffer its consequences. Ashamed, she collapses into herself, unable to look toward the heavens. And then there is the missing navel. While conceiving *Eve*, Ezekiel carefully read the biblical text, which states that God created Eve from one of Adam's ribs. In his memoir, Ezekiel deliberately chronicles a conversation with a visitor to his studio about why he sculpted Eve as such: "I had made my Eve without an umbilicus. . . . It was very natural to do so since Eve wasn't born, but created directly from one of Adam's spare ribs."[25] A clay model in Ezekiel's studio shows her with a navel, the pivotal element that he eliminated (fig. 16). The absence of the navel reminds the viewer that Eve is unlike us. She is the first woman, and she has no parents. All that Eve has is Adam and God, both of whom she betrayed, and the serpent whom she trusted, but whom she now realizes has betrayed her as well. The absent umbilicus is part of the dramatic story that Ezekiel tells in bronze.

Nineteenth-century sculptors, American and others, also favored Eve as a subject, for the emotional possibilities of her story and the freedom to depict a female nude in a socially acceptable way. Inevitably, these sculptors included her navel, as

FIG. 14 Moses Jacob Ezekiel, *Eve Hearing the Voice*, modeled 1876, cast 1904. Bronze, 55 7/8 × 40 7/16 × 33 9/16 in. Cincinnati Art Museum, Ohio. Gift of Dr. Merlyn McClure and the Family of Dr. George W. McClure. Photo: Samantha Baskind.

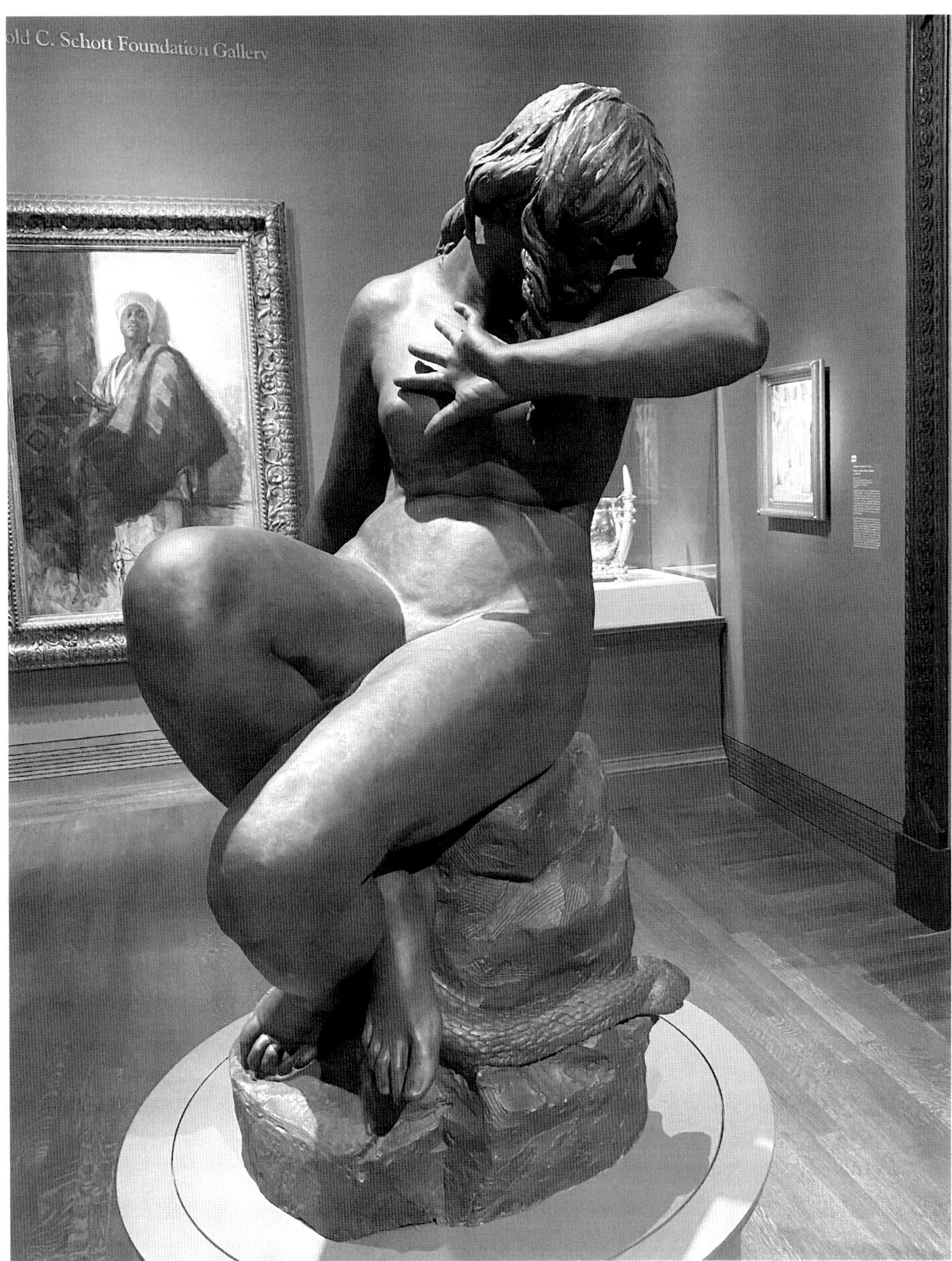
old C. Schott Foundation Gallery

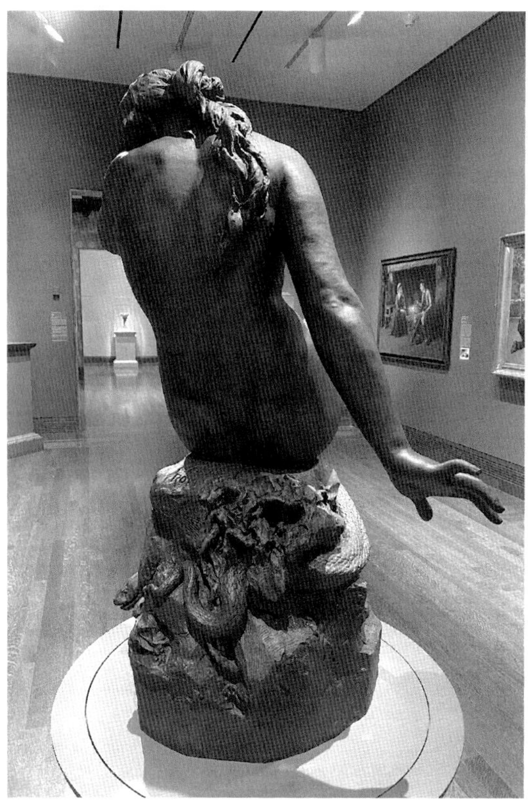

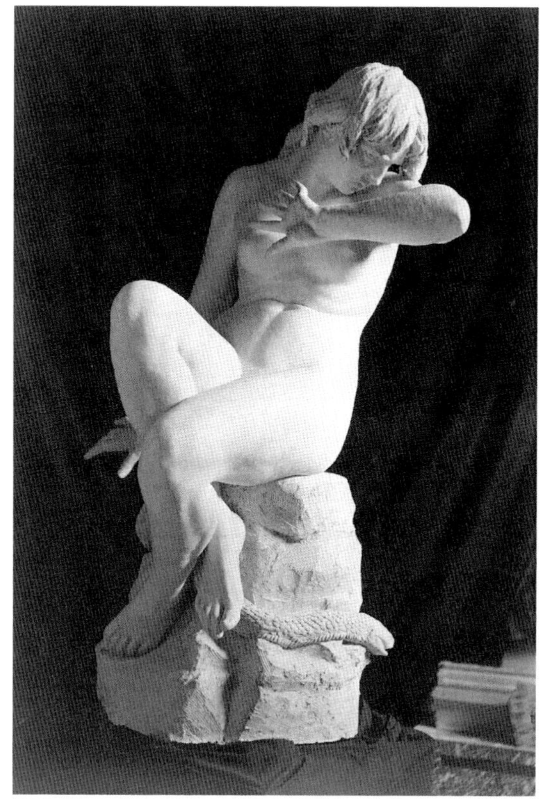

FIG. 15 Moses Jacob Ezekiel, *Eve Hearing the Voice*, modeled 1876, cast 1904. Back view. Photo: Samantha Baskind.

FIG. 16 Moses Jacob Ezekiel, *Eve Hearing the Voice*, 1876. Clay sketch. Courtesy of The Jacob Rader Marcus Center of the American Jewish Archives, Cincinnati, Ohio, at americanjewisharchives.org.

did most painters. Hiram Powers reworked his marble, neoclassical Eves for several years.[26] *Eve Tempted* (modeled 1839–42, carved 1873–77; Smithsonian American Art Museum, Washington, DC) and *Eve Disconsolate* (1858–60, carved 1872–77; fig. 17) show Eve at two pivotal moments: as she prepares to eat the forbidden fruit and reacting after she has been castigated by God. Powers's delicate *Eve Disconsolate* is quiet in its reflective sorrow when compared to Ezekiel's dramatic, less idealized bronze—in part, a function of the differing medium and of its representation. To be sure, Powers's sculptures of women were idealized, an interpretation that Ezekiel resisted for one he hoped would show Eve, he wrote, as "perfectly human."[27] In contrast, Ezekiel's other sculptures of biblical figures are imbued with divinely inspired, uncommon strength or faith.

As a fellow American expatriate, Ezekiel may have visited Powers's Florence studio, which remained open after he died, and viewed versions of *Eve* there. At least, he was likely to have seen photographs of them, and perhaps had heard about the sculptures from friends in Cincinnati, the city from which Powers expatriated and where Ezekiel retained close ties. Always aiming for originality and authenticity (at least as he perceived it, and here based on a precise reading of the Hebrew Bible), Ezekiel departed from those norms by fashioning an agonized Eve without a navel. In a letter to sculptor Edward Valentine, Ezekiel modestly pointed to Eve's novelty: "It has at least the merit of originality among its many faults."[28]

Ezekiel briefly indicated in his memoir the moment that he chose to represent, "When she hears the voice of God in the garden and is ashamed," a description that closely echoes the work's title, *Eve Hearing the Voice*.[29] Accordingly, Ezekiel did not name his bronze with a standard, identificatory title like his nineteenth-century American contemporaries: the aforementioned Powers's *Eve Tempted* and *Eve Disconsolate*, and Edward Sheffield Bartholomew's *Eve Repentant* (1858–59; Wadsworth Atheneum, Hartford). Nineteenth-century Europeans also employed terse, broad titles; for instance, Eugène Delaplanche's *Eve After the Fall* (1869; Musée d'Orsay, Paris; followed much later by *Eve Before the Fall*, 1891) and Jean-Baptiste Carpeaux's *Eve Tempted* (1871; Musée des Beaux-Arts, Valenciennes), all stemming from France and carved in marble. Ezekiel originally titled his sculpture *Eve After the Fall*, which represents a decidedly Christian theological interpretation of the creation story that he purposefully changed.[30] He may also have been initially drawn to this title because his *Eve* much resembles Delaplanche's marble, with the first woman sitting on a rock wrapped by a serpent. Instead, Ezekiel settled on a title that hewed to the biblical verse: "And they *heard the voice* of the LORD God walking in the garden toward the cool of day; and the man and his wife hid themselves from the presence of the LORD God amongst the trees of the garden."[31]

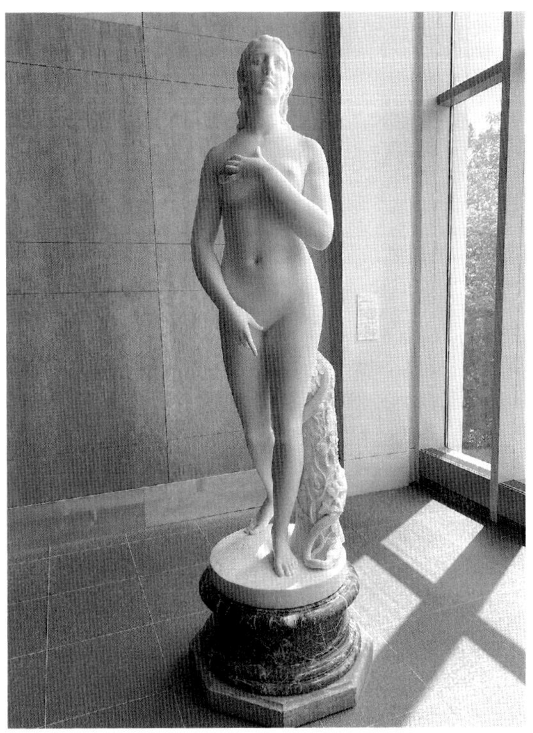

FIG. 17 Hiram Powers, *Eve Disconsolate*, modeled 1858–60, carved 1872–77. Marble, 78 1/16 × 22 5/8 × 25 15/16 in. Cincinnati Art Museum, Ohio. Gift of Nicholas Longworth. Photo: Samantha Baskind.

By choosing such a specific title, directly associating the sculpture with its textual source, Ezekiel aimed to shape viewers' experience of, and response to, the work. He narrowed the interpretive possibilities to one exact moment. Eve is tempted over the course of several verses, and she remains fallen or disconsolate over a number more. But she only first hears the voice in a few words, experiencing that initial horror of God chastising her disobedience. Eve urgently tries to muffle what Ezekiel imagined as God's thunderous reproach, her hair covering her right ear almost entirely and her left nearly pressed on her shoulder. She cannot escape the Lord's wrath. Ezekiel's *Eve* calls attention to that very instant by the form he modeled, and ensuring so by the title. As John Fisher aptly observes, "When an artwork is titled, for better or for worse, a process of interpretation has inexorably begun."[32] Likewise, the title opened up a conversation to curious visitors, which allowed Ezekiel to explicate his sculpture, to offer a "lesson" in a very public space, his studio in the Baths of Diocletian where artists, musicians, politicians, and tourists from the Western world came to see his art. Powers, too, labored over the names of his sculptures, indicating the importance of titling in the day. Before settling on *Eve Tempted*, he called the piece *Temptation of Eve* and *Eve Before the Fall. Eve Disconsolate* was once poetically titled *Paradise Lost*, the more standard *Repentant Eve*, and *Eve After the Fall.*[33]

Eve was crafted in Ezekiel's initial Roman studio and then moved to his atelier in the Baths of Diocletian, where it remained on view for decades, with a constant stream of visitors voicing their admiration. Ezekiel once wrote of "turn[ing] my statue of *Eve* for my visitors to see" during a concert by Franz Liszt in his workspace.[34] His deliberate title is fundamental to the work in a way that a generic title would not be. It provides a point of entry into the sculpture by directing viewers to the foundational words of the biblical text that served as Ezekiel's springboard rather than broadly referencing Eve's powerful but well-worn story. Unquestionably, Eve's lack of an umbilicus was informed by Ezekiel's Jewish heritage, which the sculptor readily acknowledged was influential on his art: "My relief *Israel*, my *Judith*, *David*, and *Christ in the Tomb* show that my ideals have always been deeply connected with Jewish traditions and ideals."[35] To which could be added, Eve without her belly button.

No doubt, Ezekiel's Jewish identity inflected his art. But he did not see Jewishness as the sum of his parts. The first Jewish American artist to address seriously his feelings about art and his obligations as a Jew in the field, Ezekiel frankly discussed his opinion on Jewish art and the category of "Jewish artist":

> I must acknowledge that the tendency of the Israelites to stamp everything they undertake with such an emphasis [Jewish art] is not sympathetic with my taste. *Artists* belong to no country and to no sect—their individual religious opinions are matters of conscience and belong to their households and not to the public. . . . Everybody who knows me knows that I am a Jew—I never wanted it otherwise. But I would prefer as an artist to gain first a name and reputation upon an equal footing with all others in art circles. It is a matter of absolute indifference to the world whether a *good artist* is a Jew or a Gentile and in my career I do not want to be stamped with the title of "Jewish sculptor."[36]

Ezekiel rightly assessed that Jews of his age embraced him with pride as a "Jewish sculptor." At the same time, Southern Americans considered him a "Southern sculptor." Beyond portrait busts, he received few commissions from Europeans, and in Italy, he was regarded as an "American sculptor." The ambitious Ezekiel saw himself as an artist of the world.

Eve Hearing the Voice was greatly appreciated in its own day. So pleased with his conception, Ezekiel intended to send the plaster sculpture to an exposition in Berlin in 1876, but for reasons unknown he never did.[37] In 1904, *Eve* was finally bronzed for exhibition at the St. Louis World's Fair, where it won a silver medal, and in 1907, the sculpture showed in the Cincinnati Art Museum's Fourteenth

Annual Exhibition of American Art.[38] A smaller replica in marble had much earlier been ordered, in 1884, by John H. Harjes (partner of John Pierpont Morgan), who gifted it to Wilhelm II, Emperor of Germany in 1902.[39] Soon after, the emperor placed *Eve* in the Sanssouci Picture Gallery in Potsdam.[40] In 1929, the marble *Eve* was moved to a theater in Potsdam, which was destroyed in the last days of World War II, along with everything in it. A different patron, a banker named M. M. Lowenstein, purchased another marble *Eve*.[41] Cast in gold bronze, a small statuette of *Eve* was modeled at some point; this may be an *Eve* that Ezekiel gifted to his friend, physicist Alfonso Sella, on the occasion of his marriage.[42]

American Mary Agnes Tincker based a character on Ezekiel in her novel *The Jewel in the Lotos* (1884), in which a fictional sculptor lived in the ancient Roman thermae and was laboring on sculptures of *Judith* and "a large pallid Eve [who] shrank away from the curse, one perfect hand pushed out."[43] Dutch author Carel Vosmaer also based a character in his novel *The Amazon* (1881; English ed., 1884) on Ezekiel. The sculptor in that story similarly lived in the Baths of Diocletian and was hard at work on a sculpture of Eve "crouching on the ground in shame, and huddling herself together as if to hide her figure, her one hand seeming to ward off Adonai, who has come to demand an account of her deed."[44] Vosmaer, a non-Jew, almost surely learned the word "Adonai," one of the Hebrew words for God, from Ezekiel during his visit to the artist's studio. Again, Ezekiel demonstrates his Jewish perspective and unabashedly exposes it in Rome, despite possible antisemitic repercussions. Additionally, he showcases his knowledge of the Hebrew Bible, in which God is referred to over four hundred times as Adonai.

The sculpture's peregrinations are a story unto itself. Ezekiel's will bequeathed the unsold bronze *Eve Hearing the Voice*, which had been in storage in New York City for many years, to his brother Henry, who unsuccessfully tried to sell it at an estate sale. In turn, Henry willed the sculpture to his son-in-law Simeon Johnson. The weight of the sculpture was so great that Johnson's floors were unable to sustain it, and so he was forced to move *Eve* outside to his yard. The sculpture left the family when Johnson gave *Eve* to his doctor in the early 1950s, and the doctor eventually willed it to his daughter, Merlyn McClure. When moving homes in 1997, McClure donated the bronze to the Cincinnati Art Museum. Because the sculpture had been outdoors for over sixty years, it required extensive conservation efforts.[45]

By all accounts, *Eve Hearing the Voice* is the earliest known sculpture of Eve by a Jewish artist, and in both iconography and name it deviates significantly from the standard produced by Christian artists. Eve's nonexistent navel and the sculpture's inventive title shed light on Ezekiel's sui generis variation of an oft-attended theme in the history of Western art, precipitated by his engaged reading of the original source and different world view.

Antisemitism and That Old Canard About Jews and the Arts

To evoke a sense of the environs in which Ezekiel lived—as a Jew who openly worshipped and an artist who crafted interpretations of the Bible from a Jewish perspective in Catholic Rome—one must look at the position of Jews in the three countries he resided, and the disgraceful, divisive, antisemitic Dreyfus affair, which stretched from 1894 to 1906.

Accounts demonstrate that during the Civil War, some residents of Richmond denigrated Jews. An article in the *Richmond Examiner* connected Jews to the fight at hand: "One has but to walk through the streets and stores of Richmond, to get an impression of the vast number of unkempt Israelites in our marts. . . . Every auction room is packed with greasy Jews. . . . Let one observe the number of wheezing Jewish matrons . . . elbowing out of the way soldiers' families and the more respectable people in the community."[46] The weekly periodical *Southern Punch* was equally derogatory, criticizing the upward status of Jewish merchants during the war years: "The dirty greasy Jew pedlar, who might be seen, with a pack on his back, a year or two since, bowing and cringing even to negro servants, now struts by with the air of a millionaire."[47] Ezekiel does not refer to any such incidents and waxed nostalgically about his life in Richmond and childhood neighborhood, which was populated amicably by Jews and Christians.

Yet, the second paragraph of Ezekiel's lengthy memoir is out of tune with the rest of his narrative, and its conspicuous positioning curious: "Although the Declaration of Independence of the United States begins with the statement that all men are created equal, I do not know a phrase that contains a more seeming falsehood than this famous one. For, albeit that my ancestors were men who played no inconsiderable part in that portion of the world's history which brought forth the blessings of political and religious liberty to mankind, I myself was born in a very lowly position, and by no means free, and by no means equal to scores of other children I happened to know."[48] Here, Ezekiel returns to the theme of religious liberty and his status as a member of a religious minority; the issue was on his mind more than just as a subject of a commissioned monument for B'nai B'rith and later his monumental *Thomas Jefferson*, memorializing the author of the Virginia Statute for Religious Freedom (chapter 5).

During his student days in Germany, an 1873 newspaper article mentioned the young artist's promise and his opportunity "to disprove by other works the prevailing notion that the race of Shem has no notion for the plastic arts."[49] The old antisemitic canard about Jewish imagephobia was then widespread and has since died hard. Immanuel Kant and Georg Hegel in wellspring remarks regarded Jews as a verbal people who preferred abstraction and monotheism to the materiality and potential idolatry of art objects; hearing and the word were more significant than sight and the body. Closer to home for Ezekiel, German composer Richard Wagner—the son-in-law of Ezekiel's dear friend Franz Liszt—tarred Jews with this limitation in an 1850 essay, "Jews in Music." Wagner's condemnation asserts that Jews cannot excel in music, or the arts in general, because to do so means to give expression to the spirit of the people. Being a wandering people, Jews will be ill-suited to express the true sentiments of their homeland, wherever they settle.[50]

An 1899 sermon by New York–based Christian pastor Madison Peters, titled "Justice to the Jew" and described at length in the *New York Times*, also took up the issue of Jews in the arts. Defending aspersions against Jews, Peters pointed with admiration to Jewish military service, aptitude for the law, and contributions to the sciences and arts. (He wrote an entire book on the wider subject with the same title; see chapter 1.)[51] More interesting than Peters's apologetic are letters to the editor in response to his sermon. A Jew from England wrote a long letter admonishing Peters for his "falsehoods": "Such twistings and turnings of history to wring us for credit which we do not deserve is not flattering to our people." Surprisingly, the letter's Jewish author then tendered the shibboleth that Jews are not an art-making people: "In painting and sculpture we have, indeed, until the very latest days, had no artists whatever, for the reason that our religious traditions made it sinful to make an image of anything. The few Jews who now practice either art have yet to show whether they can excel."[52] Clergyman Peters took exception to that letter and sent a rebuttal to the paper, naming Ezekiel and painter Henry Mosler as American artists who have ably "shown that they 'can excel.'"[53] Ezekiel makes no mention of the German review or the *New York Times* exchange about Jewish artistic abilities and the praise extended to him. Notwithstanding Peters's compliment, it was against these kinds of pervasive falsehoods about Jews and art-making that Ezekiel worked.

Nor does Ezekiel describe Catholic antisemitism during his years in Rome, historically a city inhospitable to Jews. They were subjected to forced baptisms and compulsory Christian sermons. Jews were further sanctioned to wear identificatory clothing, accused of blood libel (the charge that Jews sought the blood of young Christians for their rituals), disallowed to own property and practice certain professions, and, most vividly, constrained inside a small, poverty-stricken ghetto. The establishment of the Roman ghetto in 1555 by Pope Paul IV confined Jews to live in crowded squalor and locked at night behind walls, for which they were forced to pay the construction. Until 1870, the execrable ghetto remained under papal control, save for a few respites (e.g., during the Napoleonic Wars), and was finally abolished with the reunification of Rome.[54] At the turn of the twentieth century, Ezekiel penned an account about the laying of the cornerstone of the new Jewish temple in the old Roman ghetto, which ran in the *Cincinnati Enquirer*. Ezekiel described thousands of spectators joining together to sing a Hebrew psalm as the cornerstone was placed, and he extolled the moment as "the most impressive and spontaneous demonstration it has ever been my good fortune to witness."[55] During travels to central Europe on business, Ezekiel made it a priority to visit Prague's Jewish ghetto, cemetery, and six-hundred-year-old synagogue. He described the decoration of the synagogue and marveled at "the scenes of day-to-day work of these poor descendants of the first wanderers of the Holy Land to this Prague, one of the oldest spots of their worship in this part of the world!"[56]

Ezekiel intently followed all details of the Dreyfus affair, the scandalous case that served as a lightning rod for antisemitic impulses within powerful rival nationalisms at the century's end.[57] Bleak, sensationalized, and one of the most debated news stories at the end of the nineteenth century, the Dreyfus affair concerned Alfred Dreyfus, an Alsatian Jew and officer in the French army falsely accused of treason.[58] His arrest in 1894 and dismissal the next year was appealed in an 1899 retrial, provoking a fervent broadside by critic–novelist Émile Zola, "J'accuse . . . !" ("I Accuse . . . !"). Dreyfus was eventually exonerated after his renewed court-martial but only reinstated six years later. While Ezekiel maintained that he did not personally experience antisemitism in his adopted country, history demonstrates that the Vatican still openly propagated such beliefs, which were especially virulent after the onset of the Dreyfus case. In late 1897, the Vatican's daily newspaper *L'osservatore romano* saw Dreyfus's alleged disloyalty as a fait accompli: "The Jewish race, the deicide people, wandering throughout the world, brings with it everywhere the pestiferous breath of treason."[59] Antisemitism was growing "among the masses," the paper noted in a different article, "who are being excessively oppressed by the Judaic spirit, a spirit which is the opposite of the Christian spirit."[60] Indeed, antisemitism surged in Italy with the Dreyfus affair. The Vatican's paper unequivocally condemned Dreyfus because of his Jewish heritage: "It is hardly surprising if we again find the Jew in the front ranks, or if we find that the betrayal of one's country has been Jewishly conspired and Jewishly executed."[61] Another periodical tarred Jews as financial fiends and with other sinister aspersions: Jews are "a foreign race, camped among us, a race that has neither our blood, nor our instincts, nor our ideals . . . a race without a country, an intransigent, usurious race, lacking a moral sense, a race capable of selling and buying anything."[62]

Artists in France—where Jews were first emancipated in Europe—split along political lines, leading to a polarized culture war.[63] Impressionists Claude Monet and the Jewish Camille Pissarro joined Zola in the pro-Dreyfus camp, whereas Paul Cézanne, Mary Cassatt, Edgar Degas, Auguste Rodin, and Pierre-Auguste Renoir were anti-Dreyfus.[64] More than once, Renoir gave voice to his anti-Jewish stance: "If they [Jews] get kicked out of all countries, there is a reason for it, and they shouldn't be allowed to become so important in France."[65] Renoir protested against being associated with Pissarro (born Jacob Abraham Camille Pissarro) because "to exhibit with the Jew Pissarro means revolution."[66] Degas was venomously antisemitic in word and image. After the death of a Jewish military officer with whom Degas was acquainted, he penned a malicious letter: "So he is gone, the poor Wandering Jew. . . . What did he think since the dirty [Dreyfus] Affair began? What did he think of the awkwardness one felt with him, in spite of oneself? Was he suffering from it? . . . What was going on in his old Israelite head? Did he ever think back to the time when we more or less overlooked his terrible race?"[67] Art critic Jean Ajalbert reported that when a model indicated Dreyfus might not be guilty, Degas furiously instructed her to put her clothes on while screaming, "You are Jewish . . . you are Jewish," although he knew that was not the case.[68] While no record exists of such overt hostility toward Ezekiel as a man or an artist, this fraught environment and such comments by others indicate that in Europe, he must have experienced history's longest hatred.

In her appreciation, Mary Argyle Taylor meant to extend a compliment but instead offered a revealing look into Ezekiel's character as well as general thinking about Jews at the time: "Once when I said I could not understand prejudices against Jews, someone retorted: 'Pshaw! That is because you never knew any but Ezekiel!' Indeed, he was a 'living epistle' of the nobler, more magnanimous side of his race, and interpreted the thirteenth chapter of Corinthians by his own life and spirit."[69] Taylor refers to the well-known opening of Corinthians about love, which weaves through the chapter, and presents Ezekiel as an exemplar of this virtue. Yet, that she even had such a conversation about Ezekiel's deviation from the "standard Jew"—and so casually summons it in a tribute to the artist—indicates this normative perspective.

Taylor also remembered an evening when Ezekiel read *The Merchant of Venice* aloud to a group gathered in his studio: "He was able to invest the part of Shylock with a vindication and a certain dignity, which I had never seen before. I remember the sense of shame, of my own people, I felt as the words: 'Hath not a Jew eyes? Hath not a Jew hands, organs, dimensions, senses, affections, passions?' fell from the lips of one who had such a Christian heart of compassion himself."[70] In two instances, Taylor compares Ezekiel's goodness to Christian goodness, as if goodness were not inherent to humankind but an aberration when a Jew embodied qualities such as love and compassion. As for Ezekiel, he unabashedly chose to read the famous words of Shylock, the moneylender in *The Merchant of Venice* who was denied citizenship in Italy because of his Jewish heritage. Reading from Shakespeare's play to an audience could have resulted in two outcomes: either stereotyping the Jew who read the Jewish role, or else creating sympathy for Jews because of Shakespeare's powerful language.[71]

The Power of Right over Might

Ezekiel's interest in sculpting individuals from the Hebrew Bible and Apocrypha extends to four other figures—Judith, David, Judah Maccabee, and Esther—all of whom demonstrate the prominence in his mind of the power of right over might. For those extant sculptures, one can again discern his original "Jewish" takes on familiar themes. The first was a marble torso of *Judith* (fig. 18), also started in 1875, while Ezekiel was working on *Religious Liberty*. It was intended to be full-length, with the heroine brandishing a sword in her right hand. Regrettably, the fragile clay collapsed before Ezekiel had time to replicate the model in plaster. In correspondence with Edward Valentine, Ezekiel humorously recalled returning from Rome after a visit to Florence and discovering that his assistant had overwatered the clay, leaving Judith "as headless as Holofernes."[72] Ezekiel was able to salvage Judith's head and torso.

Judith, her face rounded, expression severe, and physique solid, stares resolutely into the distance. Her hair, a mass of heavy, tightly wound curls topped by a diadem, contrasts with the loosely falling drapery that is cinched over a strong shoulder, exposes one breast, and wraps around her waist. At a glance, finely chiseled decorations on the material winding around her waist approximate embroidery, a delicate touch on this otherwise stark torso. But Ezekiel again adds a subtle Jewish reference, likely only recognizable to Jewish viewers, much as the priestly blessing extended by *Religious Liberty* would only be comprehended by Jews. What appears to be embroidery is actually a tallit (Jewish prayer shawl), worn for centuries to remind wearers of the Commandments as decreed in Numbers (15:38) and Deuteronomy (22:12). The shawl is accurately rendered with its specially twinned and knotted fringes, to which he added three decorative Stars of David. Dressing *Judith* with a tallit is quite significant both for its Jewish iconography and because traditionally only men wore prayer shawls until the late twentieth century. By bestowing Judith the honor of wearing the sacrosanct garment, Ezekiel emphasizes her position as a savior of the Jewish people. American writer Eugene Didier described *Judith* in *Lippincott's Magazine* as "a striking Semitic type" and the tallit as an "Oriental scarf."[73] Ezekiel purposefully gave his biblical subjects fuller features, even more pronounced for his Jesus figures, but Didier was the only critic in his day to take notice.

Judith, who coolly decapitated General Holofernes with his own sword by way of her

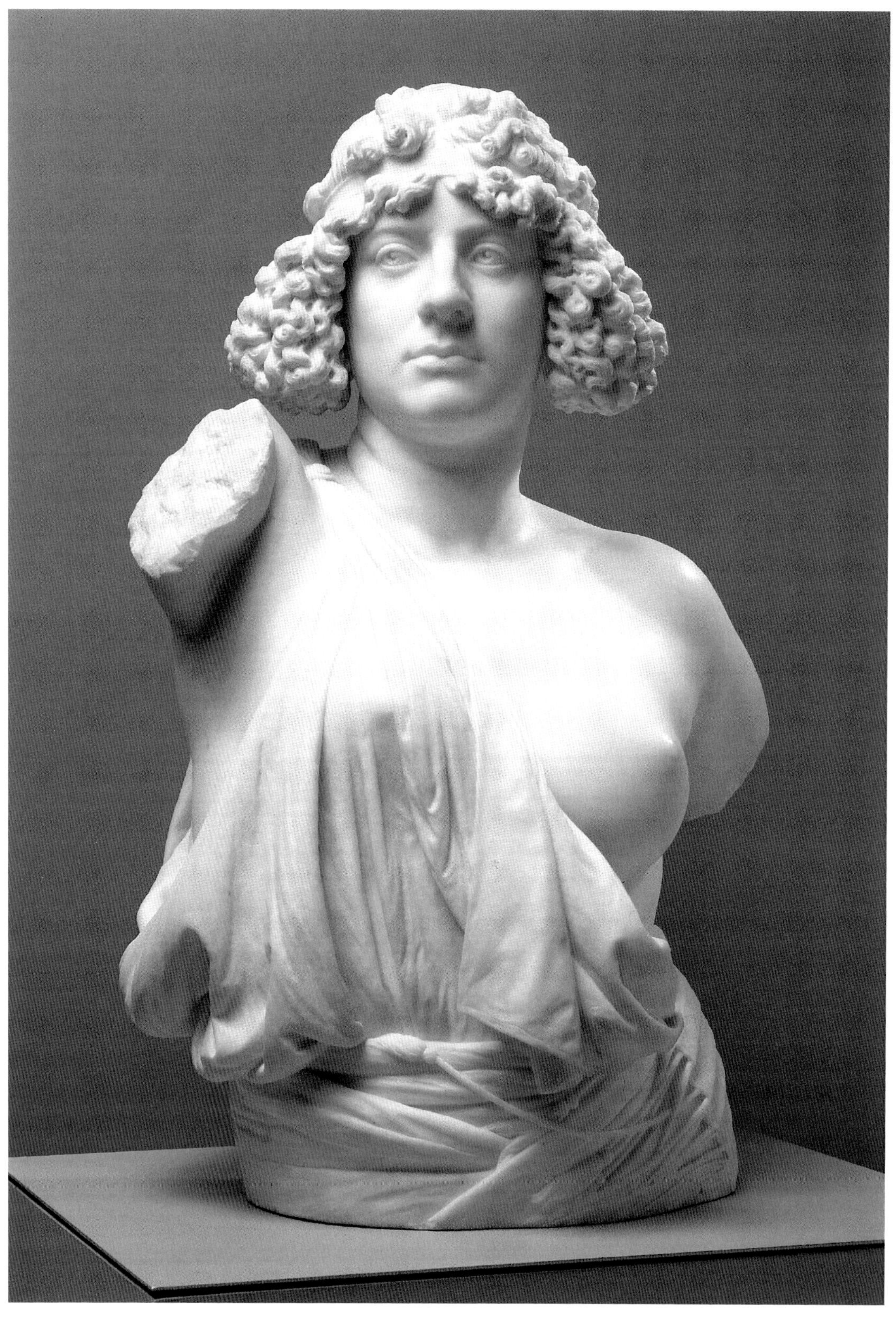

single-handed plan and who thereby quashed the Assyrian siege of her people, is the epitome of right over might. This feat brought her to the attention of artists across the ages, among them Donatello, Caravaggio, Artemisia Gentileschi, and Francisco Goya. Works by these earlier artists focus on the drama inherent in the most iconic moment from Judith's story, stressing her bloody beheading of Holofernes. At times, artists also render Judith's triumphant declaration of victory, showing her holding the general's severed head with his sword nearby. Considering Ezekiel's reverence for Donatello, it is possible that the pose of his collapsed, full-scale clay Judith was influenced by the fifteenth-century artist's depiction of the same theme (1455–60; Palazzo Vecchio, Florence); Donatello's Judith raises her sword, prepared to slay her foe. It can be surmised that Ezekiel intended to portray Judith in victory as he would later conceive *Judah Maccabee* (ca. 1909; see fig. 44), a defiant, armored, full-length figure wielding a sword in his right hand and proudly presenting a banner with the word "Maccabee" in bold Hebrew relief.[74]

This latter supposition is bolstered by Judith's positioning as the female counterpart to Judah Maccabee, a leader of the Maccabean Revolt—and the name "Judith" serves as the feminine form of the masculine name "Judah." Judith's tale has long been invoked at the annual festival of Hanukkah. Her deeds are celebrated during the festival of lights, a holiday not folded into the Jewish biblical canon. Hanukkah remembers the valiant second-century BCE Maccabean Revolt and subsequent rededication of the Temple in Jerusalem. As chronicled in the apocryphal book that bears her name, Judith presciently announced, "I am about to do something that will go down through all generations of our descendants."[75]

FIG. 18 Moses Jacob Ezekiel, *Judith*, modeled 1875, carved circa 1880. Marble, 30 7/8 × 18 5/16 × 15 9/16 in. Cincinnati Art Museum, Ohio. Bequest of Margaret Rives Nichols, Marquise de Chambrun, 1952.66. Photo: Cincinnati Art Museum.

Exhibited at the French Salon in 1881 and the Roman Exposition on the Via Nazionale, *Judith* still sat unpurchased in Ezekiel's studio.[76] Never hesitant to flatter himself, Ezekiel was surprised by disinterest in *Judith*, of which he immodestly assessed, "It was then and is now one of the most original works of modern art."[77] Obviously, Ezekiel exaggerated a bit here. *Judith* is Ezekiel's most modern conception, but his oeuvre never resembles anything avant-garde, and in general, he found modernism distasteful. This early period has him briefly exploring styles beyond the confines of classicism, as seen with *Eve* and *Judith*. Nonetheless, while Ezekiel destroyed many plaster models for a lack of room, he kept the model for *Judith* until at least 1909.[78]

Around five years after *Judith* was finished in clay, Ezekiel finally sold the torso to a patron—artist, avid art connoisseur, and Cincinnatian Maria Longworth Nichols Storer—allowing the financially strained artist to repay a bank loan. (A few years after, he modeled a bust of Storer's husband, US Congressman Bellamy Storer [ca. 1890; Cincinnati Art Museum]).[79] As always, those debts were the result of Ezekiel's efforts to pay for materials and make sculptures on speculation, his extravagant taste, and a byproduct of his tremendous generosity. Later, his financial instability stemmed from his donation of Confederate sculptures. One example of his generosity concerns the model for *Judith*, a mother of three named Vittoria Giulianelli, who was considered, Ezekiel claimed, the handsomest woman in Rome. When Giulianelli

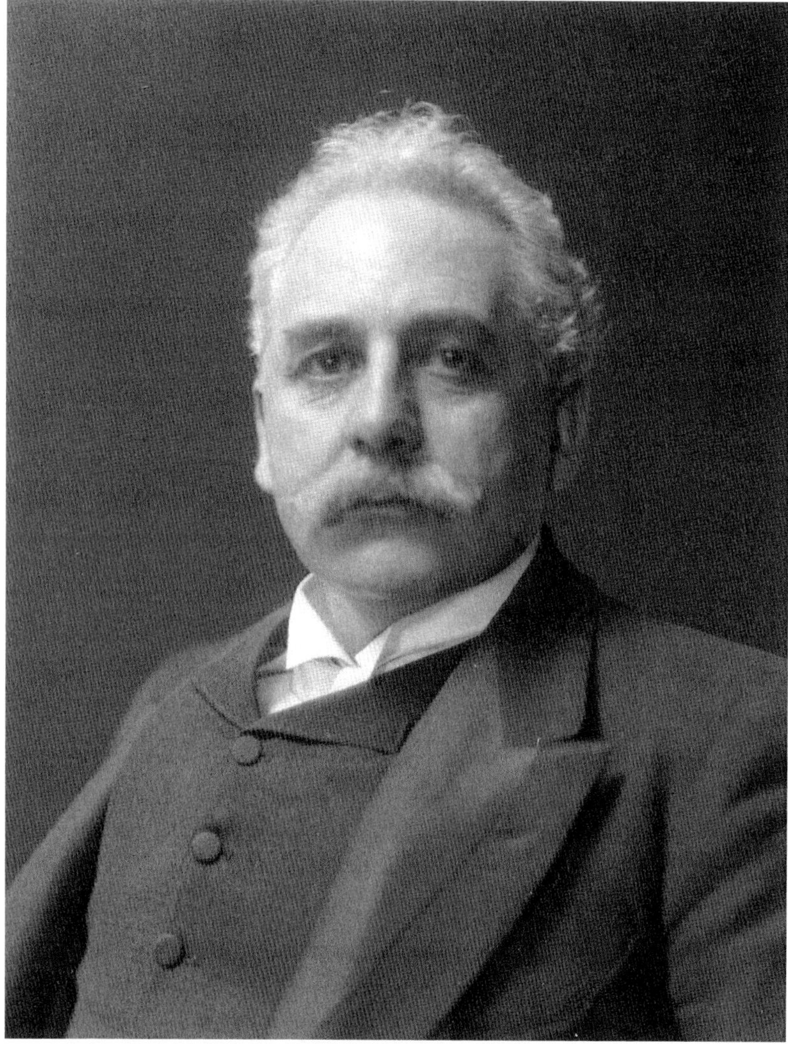

FIG. 19 Alfred Stieglitz, *Moses Jacob Ezekiel*, 1894, printed 1895–96. Platinum print, 7 1/16 × 5 1/2 in. National Gallery of Art, Washington, DC. Alfred Stieglitz Collection. 1949.2.222.

suffered hardship, Ezekiel gave her money at different times to help feed her children and provide needed medicine for her son, and to fund a stand for her to sell roasted chestnuts and make a proper living. After Giulianelli's untimely death, Ezekiel arranged for her burial.[80] Ezekiel very much adhered to the key Jewish principle of tzedakah (charity) through his unfailing generosity to the sick and needy. Jews are commanded to donate at least 10 percent of their income to assist worthy causes, and for Ezekiel that translated to giving money to suffering friends, a quality exceedingly celebrated in the many tributes after his death.

Judith's afterlife surpasses *Eve*'s serpentine journey. A marble copy of *Judith* was once in the collection of Edward Stieglitz, Ezekiel's staunch patron and friend, for whom Ezekiel crafted a marble bas-relief portrait in the vein of a Roman portrait medallion (ca. 1885; private collection) during one of several visits to the family home.

Ezekiel even stayed with the Stieglitz family for an extended time during a trip to the United States, living in their apartment on the Upper East Side of Manhattan for several months in 1878 and vacationing at their country home. Edward Stieglitz was the father of pioneering photographer Alfred Stieglitz, himself a patron of the arts, who garnered much more attention and lasting fame than Ezekiel ever did. On Stieglitz, whom he met as a teenager, Ezekiel only wrote, "The eldest son, Alfred, never spoke a word to my knowledge, but he was deeply interested in making photographs. He finally became so proficient in photography that he won all the prizes of the world in that art."[81] Ezekiel helped Stieglitz gain commissions to take photographs of his friends' paintings and drawings, and Stieglitz photographed Ezekiel in 1894, on a different visit with the Stieglitz family (fig. 19).[82]

The elder Stieglitz kept the bust at his summer residence in Oaklawn, New York, on Lake George, where Ezekiel vacationed with the family on at least one occasion. Stieglitz so admired *Judith* that he had plaster copies made for all his children.[83] When objects were moved from Oaklawn to a nearby farmhouse known as the Hill, Alfred Stieglitz took a photograph of a few works being transported in a wooden cart, among them the marble *Judith* (1920; fig. 20). Stieglitz's goal was not to immortalize Ezekiel's sculpture, which was the subject of derision among the younger Stieglitz clan. Subject choice mattered less than pictorial form in Stieglitz's cheekily titled photograph *The Way Art Moves*, as with his other output from this time. *The Way Art Moves* was exhibited in Stieglitz's 1923 show at the Anderson Galleries in New York City.

A different photograph of *Judith* (1922) by Stieglitz shows her crowded into a corner of a room at the Hill, with a dried-out vine unceremoniously thrown over her shoulder.[84] This was the least of the indignities to which *Judith* was subjected. Other gestures of ill will included wearing Stieglitz's hernia truss on her head, and a makeover with lipstick and eye shadow, topped by a crayoned black mustache for extra effect.[85] Stieglitz called *Judith* "the marble heroine with busts to bust."[86] According to family lore, Stieglitz's wife, painter Georgia O'Keeffe, so vehemently disliked the marble bust that she surreptitiously disposed of *Judith* after the move to the Hill, allegedly burying the bust near the farmhouse because she deemed it ugly and inauthentic.[87] The sculpture has never been found.

Ezekiel's attraction to biblical figures unlikely to vanquish the strong continued in subsequent pieces instigated by the Holy Writ. He fashioned a torso of another major female figure from the Hebrew canon and improbable heroine, *Esther* (ca. 1891), the biblical queen who saved her people from annihilation. Lost and with no visual evidence, all we know is that the sculpture was never purchased.[88] Also lost, *David Returning from Victory* (1886) offers one other potent example of right over might. A critic described the piece in its day: "He is there nude, savage, the sword of the Philistine in his hand for he is exalting the God who made his arm victorious. . . . The beholder cannot but be struck by the expression on the lad's face. Sculptors in modeling David in his contest with Goliath usually depict him as the triumphant hero glorying in his victory; Ezekiel on the other hand makes the face express the religious transport, the gratitude to God for having been with him in the unequal contest and having given him victory."[89] Further testimony indicating the effect of *David Returning from Victory* beyond a single surviving, blurry photograph comes from an 1887 poem by Gabriele D'Annunzio, whom Ezekiel knew from

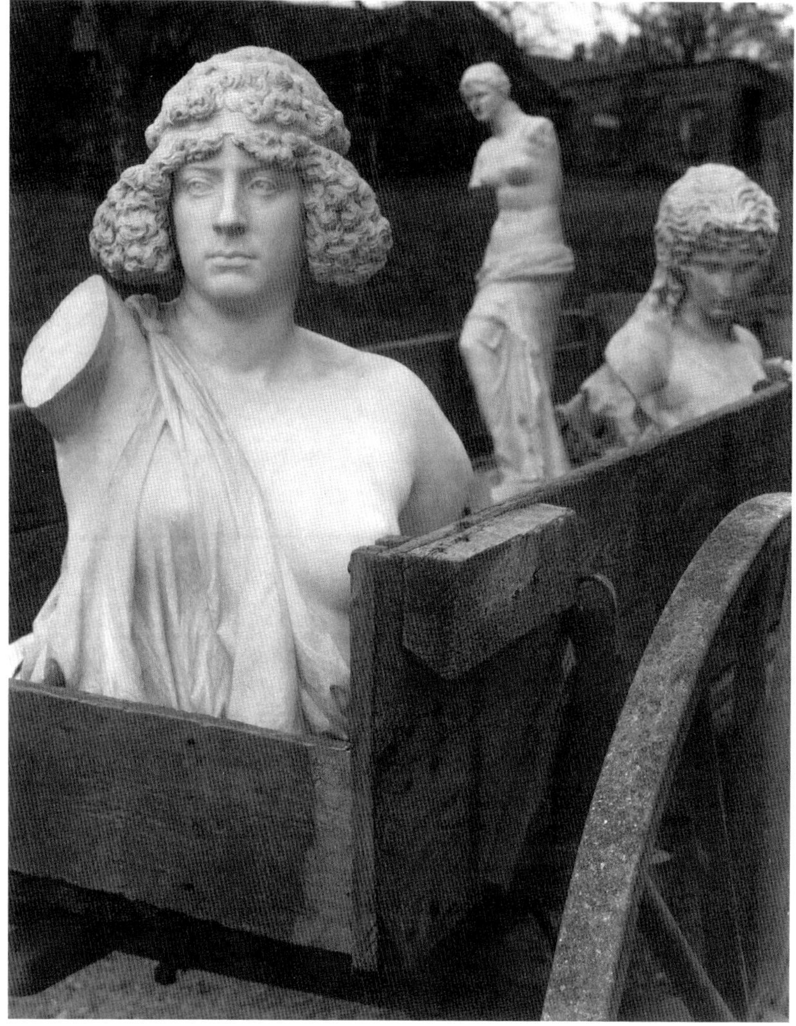

FIG. 20 Alfred Stieglitz, *Judith Being Carted from Oaklawn to the Hill or The Way Art Moves*, 1920. Gelatin silver print, 9 ½ × 7 ⅜ in. National Gallery of Art, Washington, DC. Alfred Stieglitz Collection, 1949.2.441.

the International Art Club in Rome. D'Annunzio, later bestowed with the title of "prince" for his contributions to Italian culture (but sadly later a fascist), eulogized *Judith* in verse as well (translated by Ezekiel from Italian):

> "David" lifts up to God his hand victorious
> Singing; and on his divine shoulder swings—
> And crescent-like glistens, his mighty steel.
> "Judith" looks down placid in scorn and glorious;
> And from her temples, tresses of wavy rings
> Descend, a heavy clustering grape-like weal.[90]

David's left hand reaches up to God, and his right rests Goliath's sword on his shoulder blade. The future king of Israel's face displays the rapture of a boy grateful to God, who spared his life. Michelangelo showed a muscular David anticipating the fight with his enemy—perhaps unsure of God's divine intervention—and Donatello portrayed David as an adolescent, contemplative victor. But Ezekiel was more interested in David's relationship with God after his improbable defeat of Goliath, much as he explored the dynamic between Eve and God at the moment of her betrayal.

The youthful, inexperienced shepherd, who beat the giant Goliath against all odds with an inferior weapon, wears a fringed loincloth. Because the sole photograph is of poor quality, one must infer its true form. However, considering Ezekiel's use of a tallit wrapped around *Judith*, David may wear the same. If this is the case, Ezekiel's conception predates Marc Chagall's use of a tallit as Jesus's loincloth in his painting *White Crucifixion* (1938; Art Institute of Chicago), a lament on the persecution of Jews over time but particularly in conjunction with increased antisemitism in the years just before the Holocaust.[91] Ezekiel never found a buyer for *David Returning from Victory*, and it remained in his studio for years.[92] By 1909, the sculpture still stood in his studio but in a revised state. One written account describes Goliath's head at David's feet, in the manner that Donatello sculpted the surprising hero.[93]

In addition to Ezekiel's copy of the head of Michelangelo's *David* and *David Returning from Victory*, he executed an expressive marble head titled *David Singing His Song of Glory* (1903; fig. 21), which shows the psalmist and future king with his eyes raised to heaven and his mouth open in a song of gratitude to God above for helping him conquer Goliath. His thick curls and symmetrical features conspicuously educe Michelangelo's *David* and resemble the wide curls, parted lips, upward gaze, and protruding chin of *The Dying Alexander* (late

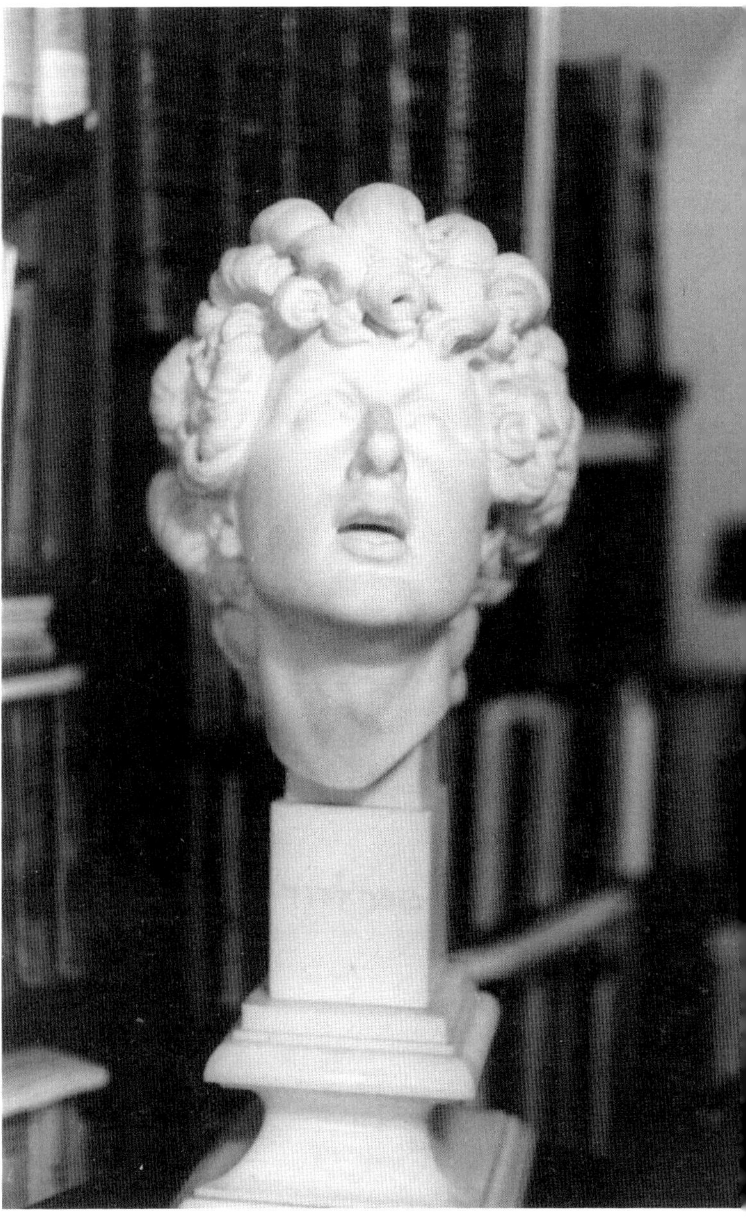

FIG. 21 Moses Jacob Ezekiel, *David Singing His Song of Glory*, 1903. Marble, 22 × 10 × 9 in. Lost. Courtesy of The Jacob Rader Marcus Center of the American Jewish Archives, Cincinnati, Ohio, at americanjewisharchives.org.

second century BCE), a Greek marble in the Uffizi of which Ezekiel made a marble copy in 1906.[94] These obvious quotations of the classical endow the head with heroic authority. Even as he deeply admired Michelangelo and Donatello's *Davids*, and at the very least had knowledge of Crawford's earliest ideal work *Orpheus and Cerberus* (1839–43; Museum of Fine Arts, Boston) and perhaps Rinehart's *Leander* (1859, carved 1875; Chrysler Museum of Art, Norfolk), he was never interested in chiseling a standing male nude.

At the center of the sculpture's pedestal, Ezekiel engraved "Song of David" in Hebrew (*Mismor le David*). In the Hebrew Bible, several psalms are titled "Mismor," indicating those hymns for which David's authorship is attributed. While the tallit around Judith's waist is a subtle Jewish nod, Ezekiel marked his sculpture of *David* as undeniably Jewish in the making by including Hebrew—which his gentile audience would at least recognize as a Jewish language while probably not understanding the meaning. With no precedent in American or western European art for a sculpture of David accompanied by a Hebrew inscription, one wonders whom Ezekiel envisioned his patron to be and how his aspirations for widespread appeal might be hindered by such a "Jewish" signifier. The same, too, could be said for his *Judah Maccabee* holding a banner inscribed with Hebrew, although there is no evidence that the sculpture ever was produced in marble or bronze. One can only surmise that, however imprudently, some of these biblical sculptures were made for his own fulfillment, further contributing to his financial woes.

Judith, David, Judah Maccabee, and Esther offer the very best of Judaism's courageous spirit, figures fearlessly standing up for their people even at the risk of their lives. Ezekiel—unafraid to worship as a Jew in Catholic Rome, a young soldier on the side of the Confederate secession, and a sculptor creating in increasingly outmoded styles and subjects, and sometimes with obvious Jewish signs—was of the same mind. So, too, Ezekiel exhibited his own courageous spirit when bucking against prevailing thinking about the modernization of American Judaism in both word and image, the theme of his other sculptures inspired by the Bible (chapter 3).

Jesus as Jewish

In Rome, Ezekiel was regularly exposed to art portraying figures and stories from the Christian Bible, especially the life of Jesus. Various documents, letters, and Ezekiel's memoirs mention several works he made depicting Jesus, and it is unclear whether some titles indicate different sculptures or else different names for the same sculptures. Six sculptures of Jesus can be identified with certainty, and three can be located. The earliest is Ezekiel's lost plaster bas-relief of Jesus, which was exhibited at the Centennial Exposition. A list of works compiled by Ezekiel's family after his death notes a bronze Jesus on the cross, which the artist mentions in passing in his memoir, but there is no sense of scale or what it may have looked like.[95]

A surviving marble torso made in 1876, likely based on the exposition plaster and which is probably the Jesus once part of the Peabody Institute's art collection, is titled *The Martyr* and at times referred to as *Christ Bound* (fig. 22).[96] *The Martyr* shows Jesus with a rope wrapped twice around his classically draped body, a mass of tight corkscrew curls chiseled akin to Judith's hair, and a split beard. He cocks his head awkwardly over his left shoulder, and his eyes are absently directed upward. Most apparent, like his portrayal of *Judith*, Ezekiel stressed Jesus's Semitic features and included other Jewish markers; he hints at *payot* (side curls) hanging straight over Jesus's ears, and more explicitly he wears a kippah (skullcap). Critics did not mention these Jewish signs. Rather, they admired *The Martyr* on its formal merits and convincing representation of quiet sorrow. A Roman newspaper cited the piece as evidence of Ezekiel's ability "to breathe life into marble."[97] Critic Lorado Taft found the sculpture's pose and treatment "striking": "A rope passes twice about the body, and the drapery and hair are remarkable for their clever workmanship—so clever, indeed, are they that one quite forgets the intention of the bust while studying its surface."[98] Another contemporary figure extolled, "As a marble rendition of physical and mental suffering, it is matchless."[99]

The design came to Ezekiel by way of his acquaintance with sculptor Mark Antokolsky, who worked next door to the American when he kept an early studio on the Via Torino. Born in the Pale of Settlement in Vilna, Antokolsky, the foremost nineteenth-century Russian Jewish sculptor, was crafting a full-length, standing, bound image titled *Christ Before the People* (1876; fig. 23). Antokolsky's sculpture, exhibited at the 1878 Paris World's Fair, accentuated a Jewish countenance, and showed Jesus with *payot* and a kippah. Ezekiel saw Antokolsky's Jesus when still in clay, which he well-liked, and soon set out to make his own Christ bound.[100] Contemporaneously in Europe, Jewish artists—Polish painter Maurycy Gottlieb, German painter Max Liebermann, and Galacian Zionist graphic artist Ephraim Moses Lilien—were producing daring imagery that interpreted Jesus very much as a Jew.[101]

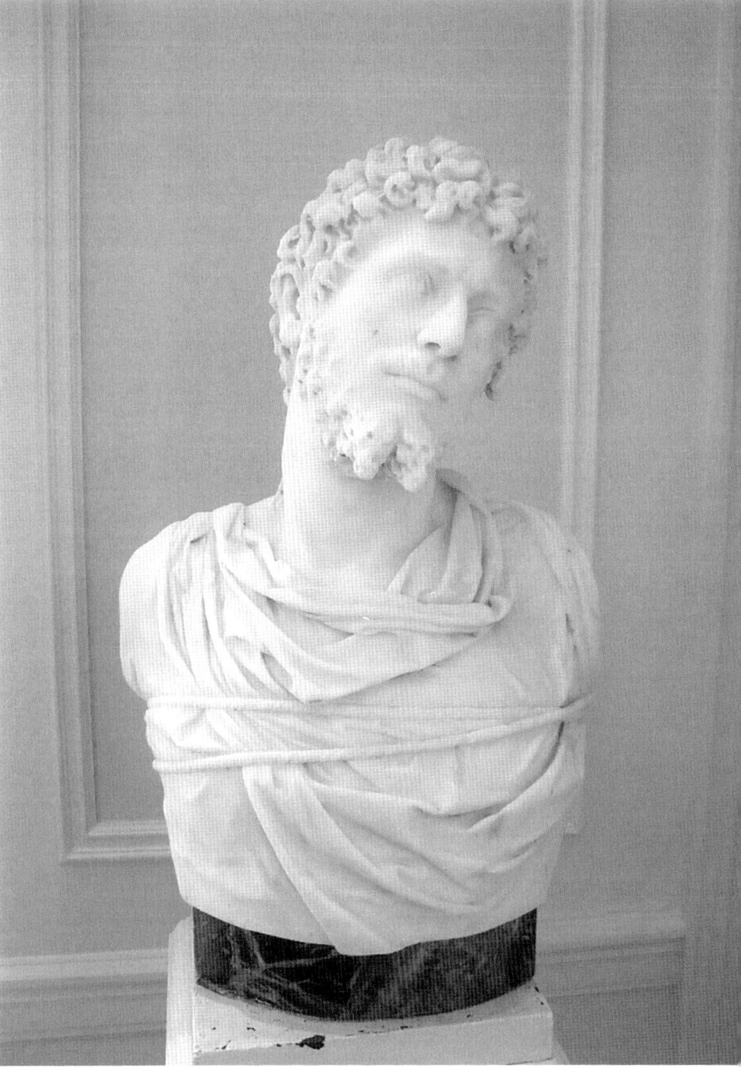

FIG. 22 Moses Jacob Ezekiel, *The Martyr*, 1876. Marble, dimensions unknown. Archdiocese of Baltimore, Maryland. Photo: Robert Simon Fine Art.

Ezekiel presented Jesus as a martyr because such imagery was pervasive in Rome, but he also had his mind on Jesus as a suffering Jew because of the Jewish Jesus imagery he had adopted in his recently completed relief bas-relief *Israel* (see fig. 34). *The Martyr* and the two other Jesus

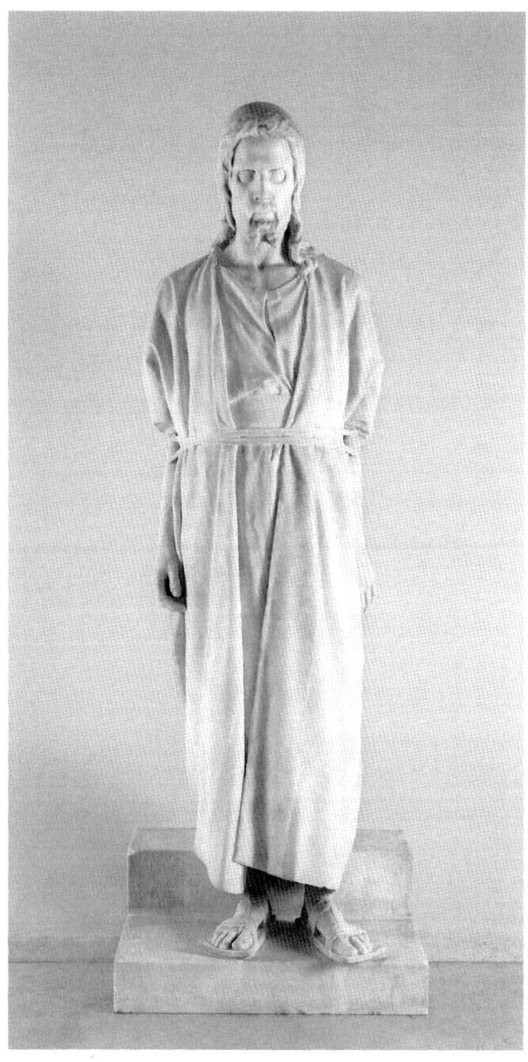

FIG. 23 Mark Antokolsky, *Christ Before the People*, 1876. Marble, 76 ½ in. State Tretyakov Gallery, Moscow. Photo: Wikimedia Commons / Shakko, CC BY-SA 3.0.

FIG. 24 (OPPOSITE) Hiram Powers, *Ideal Christ*, 1864. Marble, 31 in. Private collection. Photo courtesy of Brigham Young University Museum of Art, Provo, Utah.

FIG. 25 (OPPOSITE) Max Rosenthal, *Jesus at Prayer*, 1904. Oil on canvas. Lost, reproduction from "A Jewish Painter's Idea of Jesus." *New Era Illustrated Magazine* 5, no. 1 (1904): 75. Courtesy of the Klau Library, Cincinnati, Ohio, Hebrew Union College–Jewish Institute of Religion.

sculptures for which we have visual evidence expressly show him with curly hair and a full mouth and nose (with Ezekiel's final Jesus taking Jewish symbolism considerably further). Ezekiel very purposely conceived an afflicted Jesus with Semitic features, a far cry from serene renditions by his non-Jewish contemporaries.

The novelty of how Ezekiel presented Jesus can be appreciated in reference to Hiram Powers's *Ideal Christ* (fig. 24), for example. That 1864 marble sculpture presents Jesus as commonly shown in both sculpture and paintings over the ages—a placid figure with a delicate nose, straight flowing hair, and thin lips. In fact, when Powers sent a model to a prospective buyer, he requested that the sculptor make Jesus's lips more slender.[102] Horatio Greenough rightly understood his *Christ* (ca. 1845; Boston Public Library), the first American sculpture in the round on this subject, as an aberration in Protestant America: "I am not aware that any American has, until now, risked the placing before his countrymen a representation of Our Savior. The strong prejudice, or rather conviction of the Protestant mind has, perhaps, deterred many."[103] As a Jewish American artist working outside his homeland, Ezekiel was not impacted by these concerns. Nor is it likely they would have affected Ezekiel if he remained at home. His nonconformist spirit kept him true to his artistic muse.

A few decades later, Jewish American artist Max Rosenthal attained notoriety for daring to show Jesus as a Jew with Semitic features, and even more openly identifying him as Jewish by his tallit and phylacteries (fig. 25). In the bottom right corner of that lost 1904 painting, *Jesus at Prayer*, a thorny bush presages Jesus's fate. Each corner of the specially designed ornate frame featured plentiful grapes, a symbol of the Eucharist or, as mistakenly

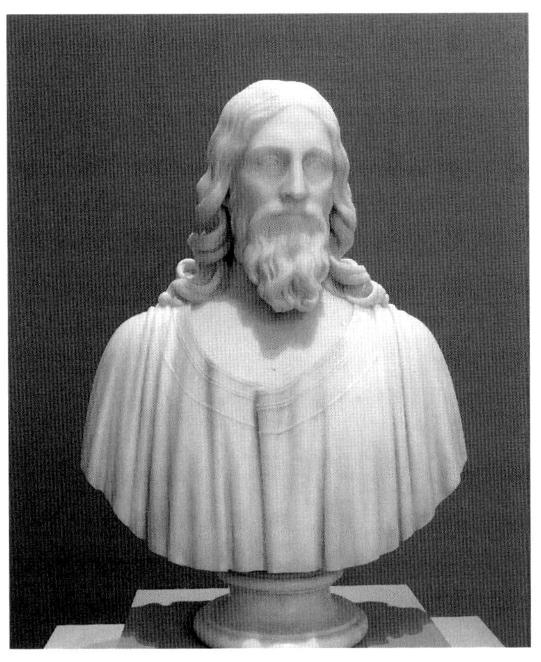

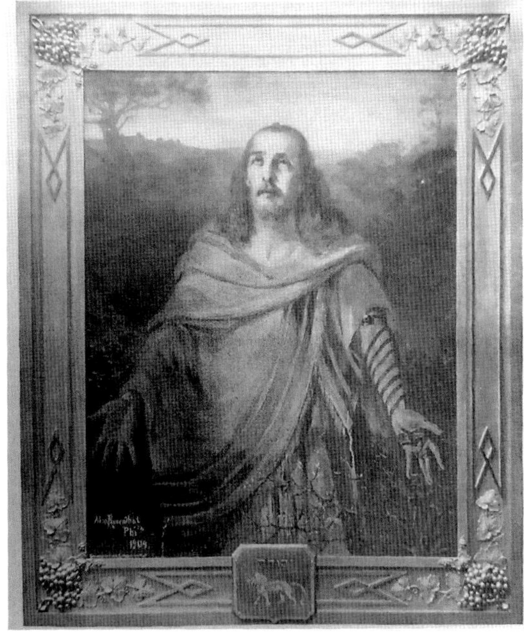

described by the Jewish press, a symbol of Judah.[104] More easily identified is the lion carved at bottom center, symbolizing the Tribe of Judah, with Judah's name printed in Hebrew. Created on commission for a Protestant church in Baltimore, the painting was promptly rejected by its Christian patrons. Baltimore's Cardinal Gibbons was understandably taken aback, even as he admired the canvas: "I was a little surprised at Mr. Rosenthal's use of the phylacteries, because our Lord condemned the wearing of them and said that the truth should be found in our hearts, not worn on the outside. But I am very glad to have seen the painting. It is a very striking picture."[105] In defense of *Jesus at Prayer*, one writer countered that in art, over the ages, "Jesus has been everything, except what he was—a Jew. . . . [Rosenthal's] readings in the New Testament have given him no reason to believe that all the Jewish customs in regard to prayer were not observed by Jesus. . . . Mr. Rosenthal has, therefore, painted Jesus standing erect and open-eyed, instead of kneeling with bowed head, as Christian painters have been accustomed to represent him, an attitude unknown among Jews, and therefore unlikely to have been assumed by Jesus."[106] Rosenthal himself understood the painting, which he said was the dream of his life to paint, not "as a religious, but distinctly as an historic picture, aiming at conscientious accuracy."[107]

Ezekiel also created a forceful, realistic bronze Jesus with an overt Christological reference. Now titled by museum officials *Ecce Homo* (fig. 26), Ezekiel called the sculpture *Christ Represented as a Jewish Martyr*.[108] *Ecce Homo* is a powerfully built bronze torso with a heavy beard and a pronounced crown of thorns. The textured thorns are markedly conspicuous because the suffering Jesus bows his head to show them cutting into his scalp, while *The Martyr* has Jesus cocking his head upward in quiet reflection. Ecce Homo (Behold the man) is an episode represented in traditional devotional paintings about Jesus's Passion, showing him shortly before the Crucifixion, as related by John (19:1–8). Ezekiel boasted that some admirers mistook *Ecce Homo* (here, he refers to the sculpture as *Christ Bound*), which he had buried for over a year to give it an aged patina, as a Donatello.[109] A bronze copy of *Ecce Homo* (after 1895; lost) was made as a gift for Lady Sherbrooke, wife of British politician Robert Lowe (Lord Sherbrooke), who placed it in her home in Surrey.[110] That sculpture served as a thank-you both for her gracious patronage, including two commissioned busts of her husband—one in a niche at St. Margaret's Church on Parliament Square next to Westminster Abbey (1895)—and for her hospitality over the years, when she entertained Ezekiel in London and Surrey.

Most venerated in its day but now hidden in Chapelle Notre Dame de Consolation, an obscure church in Paris, is Ezekiel's 1896 *Christ in the Tomb* (fig. 27). The marble sculpture offers a life-size, recumbent Jesus encased in a twisted sheet of drapery. To aid his thinking, Ezekiel read the book of John, which describes Jesus wrapped in a winding sheet with a cloth on his head (20:5–7).[111] That careful consultation of the Bible harks back to his fastidious textual conception of *Eve Hearing the Voice*. Ezekiel had been interested in this presentation for some time, irrespective of a sponsor: "In 1889, I made up my mind to model a statue of Christ in the Tomb. I had seen him in my dreams three times." Although his good friend Adolfo de Bosis warned that he would not be able to sell such a piece, Ezekiel was undeterred: "I wanted to make a statue of the greatest Jew and the greatest reformer of millions of people, a sufferer who had been crucified and deified."[112] Ezekiel considered Moses, Napoleon, and Jesus "the three greatest men that had ever lived."[113] He hired a male model to lay in repose, and promptly began to achieve his vision.

Two vastly divergent sculptures seem probable precedents. Giuseppe Sanmartino's 1753 virtuoso *Veiled Christ* in the nave of Sansevero Chapel in Naples, a city Ezekiel visited many times, presents Jesus delicately covered in a transparent shroud with the crown of thorns at his feet (fig. 28). Jesus seems to melt underneath the transparent drapery. Across the ocean, Edward Valentine had sculpted in 1875 a recumbent statue of a uniformed Robert E. Lee (fig. 29) wrapped in drapery that falls over his body. Although General Lee appears to be lying atop a sarcophagus and is situated in the chapel at Washington and Lee University, he is meant to be seen as sleeping on the battlefield rather than as part of a funerary monument. Envious that Valentine received the Lee commission, Ezekiel may have chiseled *Christ in the Tomb* as a rejoinder to his rival. The artistic quotation in *Christ in the Tomb* could also be a comment on Lee's status, in Ezekiel's mind, as a divine martyr (chapter 6). *Christ in the Tomb* resembles Ezekiel's recumbent monuments for contemporary individuals in eternal sleep, heads resting peacefully on tasseled cushions. Cornell's Sage Chapel houses the heavily draped *Mary Outwater White* (1889; fig. 30), wife of University President Andrew D. White, and *Jennie McGraw Fiske* (1908), who donated generously to the university.

Lilian Vernon de Bosis, wife of Adolfo de Bosis, published an article in the *Cincinnati Enquirer*

FIG. 26 Moses Jacob Ezekiel, *Ecce Homo*, circa 1886–89. Bronze, 21 3/4 × 17 15/16 × 18 1/16 in. Cincinnati Art Museum, Ohio. Gift of Harry W. Levy and George W. Harris, 1902.6. Photo: Cincinnati Art Museum.

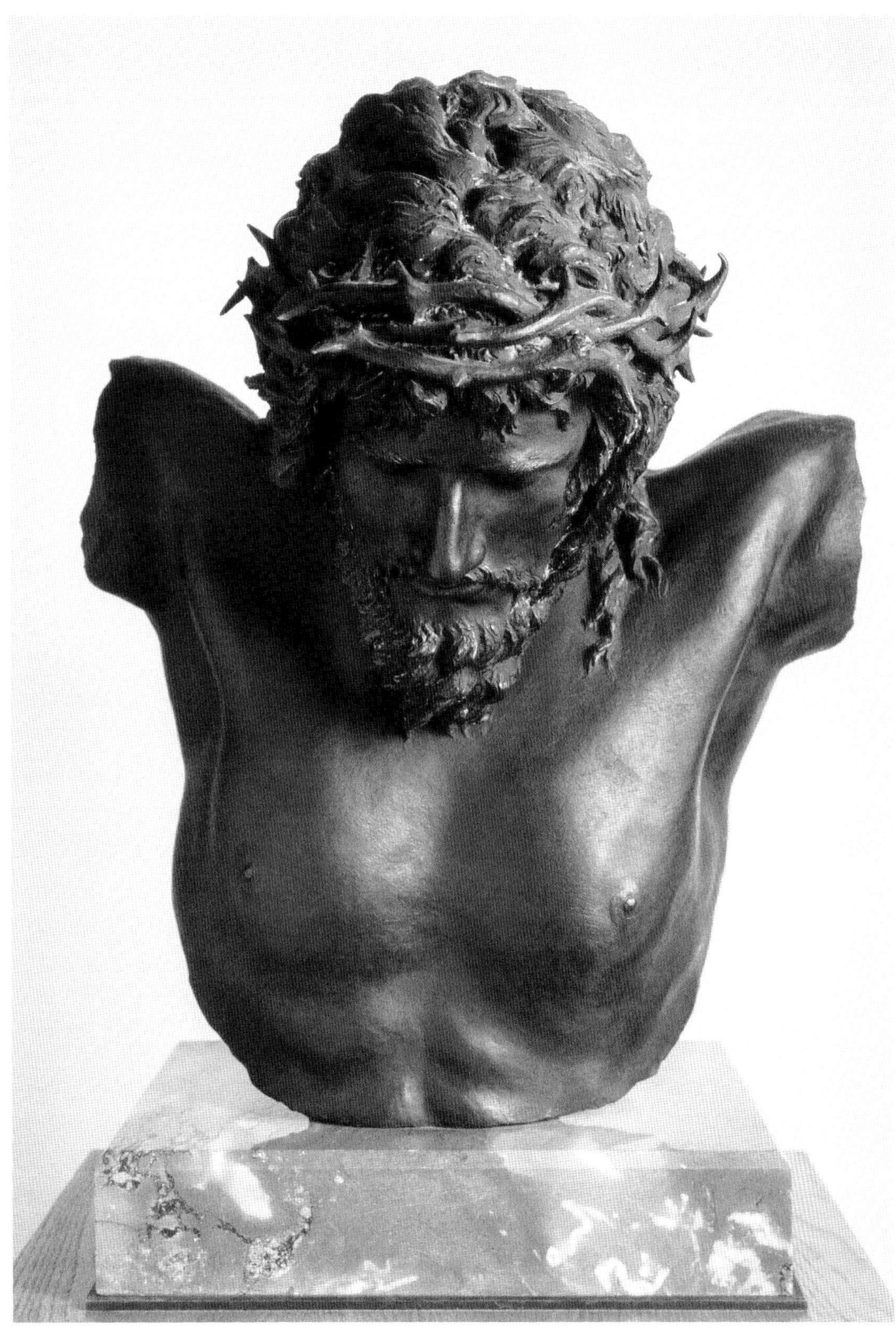

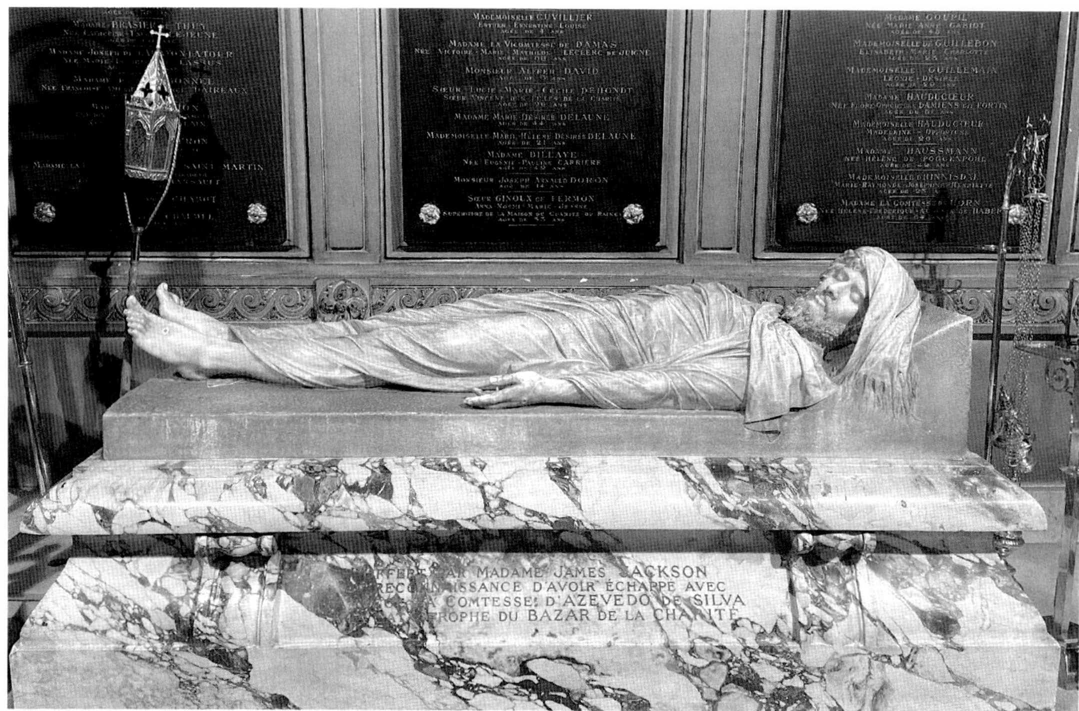

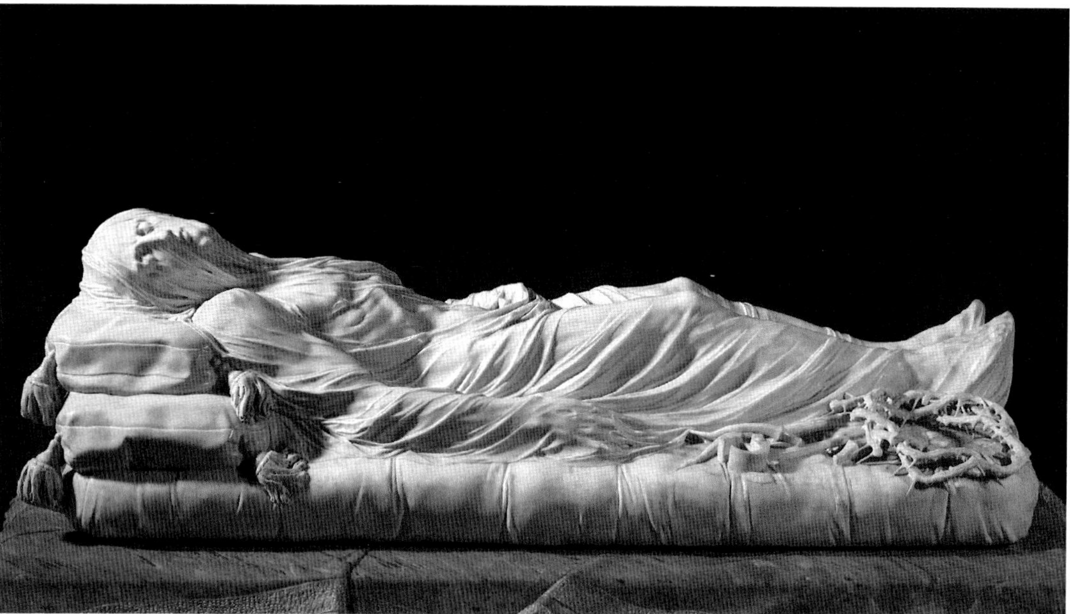

FIG. 27 Moses Jacob Ezekiel, *Christ in the Tomb*, 1896. Marble, life-size. Chapelle Notre Dame de Consolation, Mémorial du Bazar de la Charité, Paris. Photo: Samantha Baskind.

FIG. 28 Giuseppe Sanmartino, *Veiled Christ*, 1753. Marble, 20 × 31 × 71 in. Sansevero Chapel Museum, Naples. Photo: Marco Ghidelli © Archivio Museo Cappella Sansevero.

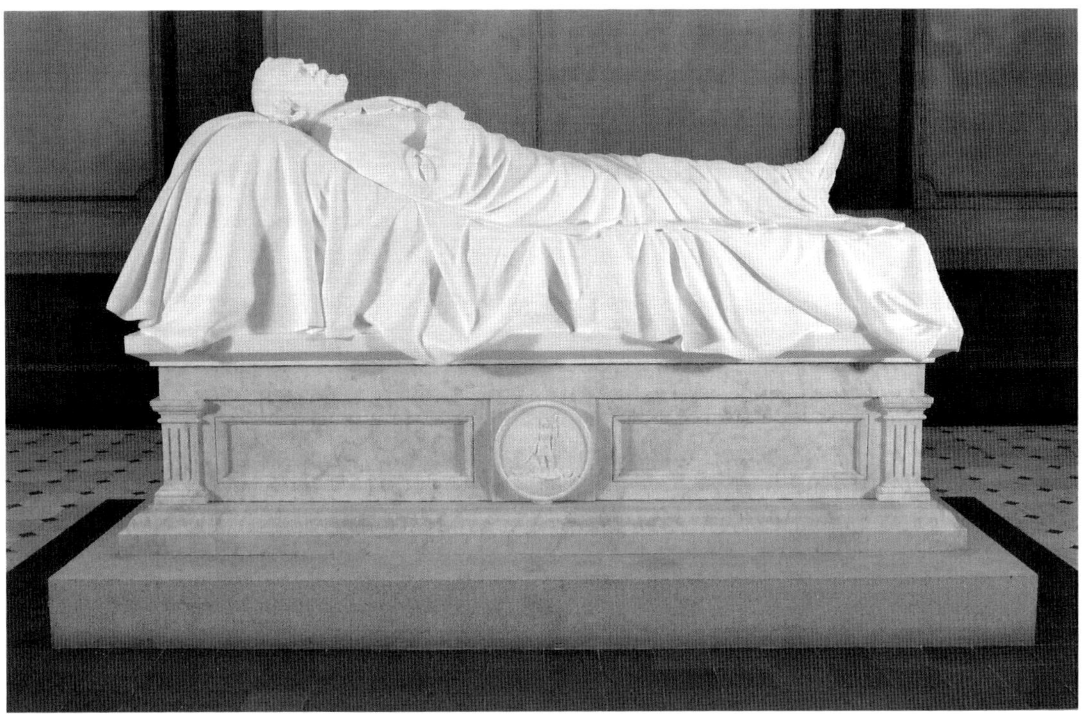

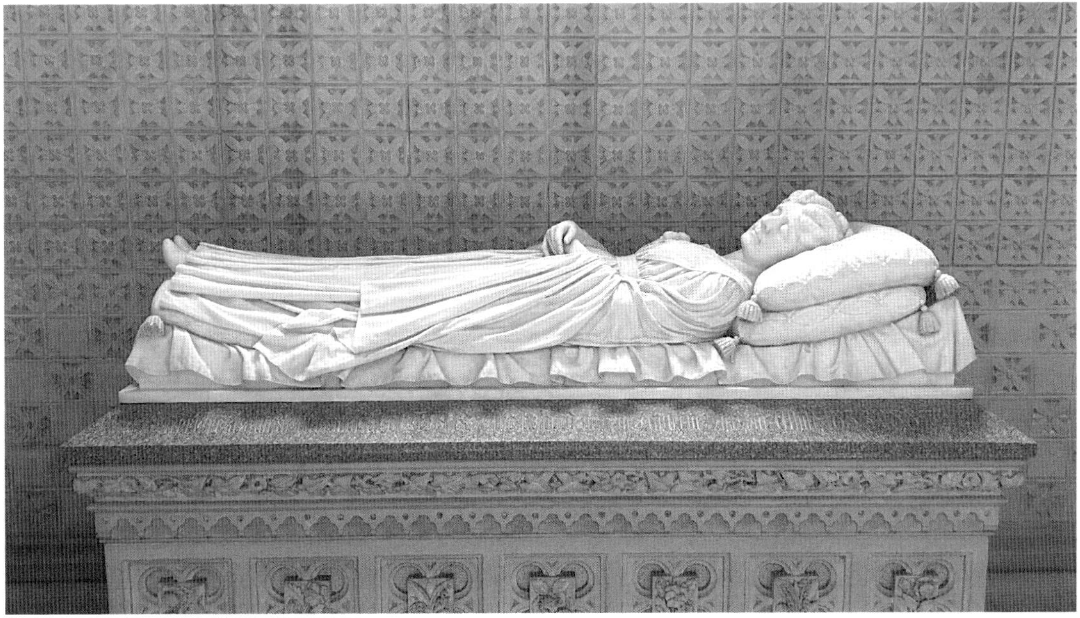

FIG. 29 Edward V. Valentine, *Recumbent Lee*, 1875. Marble, 41 ½ × 54 ½ × 96 ½ in. Washington and Lee University, Lexington, Virginia. Courtesy of Washington and Lee University, University Collections of Art and History.

FIG. 30 Moses Jacob Ezekiel, *Mary Outwater White*, 1889. Marble, life-size. Sage Chapel, Cornell University, Ithaca, New York. Photo: Clare A. Weislogel.

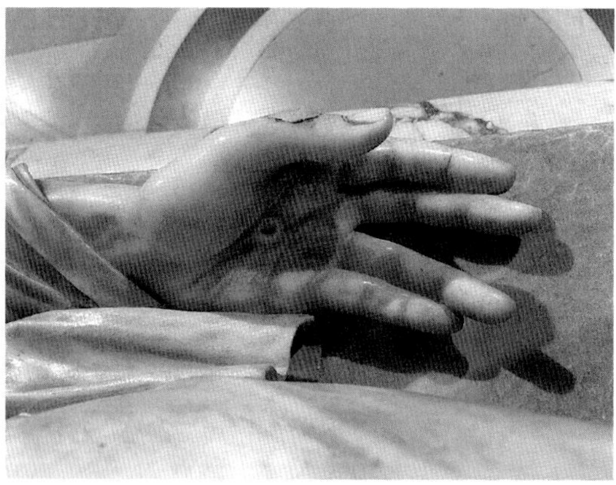

FIG. 31 Moses Jacob Ezekiel, *Christ in the Tomb*, 1896 (detail). Photo: Samantha Baskind.

about Ezekiel's studio. There, she judged *Christ in the Tomb* as the most beautiful of Ezekiel's work, supplanting his lauded funerary monument of Mary White, which "faded [in comparison], as the human must before the divine. [Christ] is at the moment when life commences to reawaken in the cold body. The limbs are still rigid under the severe winding sheet; but the noble conscious head and the hand are full of life, triumphant over death, the flesh and all of the dross of humanity. This is the artist's greatest work."[114] De Bosis was not alone in her adulation of *Christ in the Tomb*. According to Ezekiel, visitors purposely came to see the sculpture and lavishly applauded the piece. One admirer, Ezekiel claimed, fainted after encountering it and had to be carried outside for fresh air.[115] A verifiable appraisal comes from American tourist Pauline Stiles. During her nine-month excursion through Europe, mostly in Italy, she visited Ezekiel's studio and saw *Christ in the Tomb*, which she wrote about in her travel diary: "[I] looked down at the swathed figure of a tall, splendid man, lying in perfect repose. The face seemed inspired. . . . It was the face of a Man who had suffered for all the world. It inspired one with awe rather than pity."[116] Another observer glorified the work likewise: "It is usual that an utter silence will seize the most thoughtless person present, and some will even step back as before a mighty presence; the impression produced by either the cast or the marble is one of awe."[117] Journalist Lilian Whiting described Ezekiel's atelier in 1906 as "one of the fascinating interiors of the Eternal City" and mentioned a single sculpture, *Christ in the Tomb*, among "the best examples of his art."[118]

Like *The Martyr* and *Ecce Homo*, Ezekiel conceived Jesus in *Christ in the Tomb* with Semitic features; he most coheres to *Ecce Homo* with thick curls and a beard, but he closes his eyes in quiet but still humanized death. His head covering is a tallit, precise in detail down to the exact number of eyeholes for the fringes and an accurately stitched corner patch. Unexpectedly, though, he presents the supine Jesus displaying the ancient priestly blessing (fig. 31), which Ezekiel had adopted in a modified form for *Religious Liberty* and used more obviously in his Zionist-inflected bas-relief *Israel*, discussed in-depth in the subsequent chapter. A reporter noted the "Jewishness" of this quiet Jesus in the tomb, but the priestly blessing, displayed by both hands scarred with stigmata, went without mention: "The sculptor was free to choose from the idealization of centuries, but he created his own ideal, selecting the highest characteristics of the Hebrew race; and with the pitifulness, the suffering, and the horrors of death eliminated, it is one of majesty and calmest triumph."[119]

Determined to express Jesus's Jewishness beyond his Semitic countenance and his less easily discerned priestly blessing, the clay version left nothing to chance. On the side of the slab on which Jesus lies was the inscription "INRI." The letters were stacked, and the two *I*'s formed a cross to denote the Latin abbreviation referencing "Jesus the Nazarene, King of the Jews," as found in all four Gospels. The final marble omitted any inscription, indicating that Ezekiel did not like the design, perhaps because of its explicit Catholic reference. Marc Chagall, living in Paris, successfully navigated this dilemma by including the same words in Hebrew above a Jewish Jesus on the cross as he did for the Catholic signification in his painting *White Crucifixion*.

Despite de Bosis's misgivings, *Christ in the Tomb* did find a home. Soon after Ezekiel finished it, a woman he referred to as Mrs. James Jackson came to the Baths in 1897 to have a portrait relief made before she traveled to France. Characteristically, Ezekiel was taking his time to finish the relief, forcing Jackson to delay her journey. Because of that delay, she avoided a crowded annual charity bazaar in Paris, which was devastated by a fire that claimed the lives of 130 people, with hundreds more injured.[120] In remembrance of those who perished in the blaze, survivors built the Chapelle Notre Dame de Consolation. Mrs. Jackson expressed gratitude for her life to both a greater power and Ezekiel by purchasing *Christ in the Tomb* and donating the effigy to the chapel.[121]

A nonconformist and even at times a maverick, Ezekiel sculpted his biblical subjects with inventions stemming from his Jewish knowledge and background. Rabbi David Philipson, Ezekiel's principal biographer and friend, so noted in an address delivered at Rockdale Avenue Temple in Cincinnati: "He cut new channels. This unconventionality never appeared more strikingly perhaps than in his conception of the founder of Christianity. . . . Possibly none but a Jew would have thought of changing so radically the features and expression of Christianity's founder from the cast of countenance usually portrayed by Christian artists in all the Christian centuries and lands."[122] As such, Ezekiel subverted public expectations and, in doing so, his biblical works did not find eager patrons.

Ezekiel did execute a few commissioned works with biblical themes, among them one other known piece based on the Christian Bible: a marble relief of the Madonna and Child (1890s; sometimes called *Virgin and Martyr*) for his close friend Cardinal Prince Gustav von Hohenlohe-Schillingsfürst. The lunette sat over the door of a church in Tivoli, opposite the main entrance to the Villa d'Este, until it was destroyed during World War II. (Ezekiel's only other public sculpture in Italy, a life-size *Neptune* [1884] for a fountain in Nettuno, was also destroyed during World War II; a clay model is documented in a studio photograph.)[123] All that remains is a broad sketch of Mary in a flowing robe. Much of his other sponsored biblical works were for American patrons, namely Reform Jews, of whose thinking Ezekiel disapproved. The following chapter examines those works with biblical allusions, all but one commissioned, that convey Ezekiel's dogmatic proto-Zionist stance. They were spurred by his unwavering belief in the importance of a future Jewish homeland and disdain for the liberalization of American Judaism, lightning rod issues for late nineteenth-century Jews. Broader, complex religiocultural and historical factors shaped those diverse projects while at times still anchoring them in the sculptor's deep-seated religious convictions, which again initiated surprising artistic innovations.

EZEKIEL, ZIONISM, AND THE BIBLE

Chapter 3

The time would come when there would be a central government in Jerusalem again and that Palestine would flourish.
—Ezekiel, in conversation with Rabbi Isaac Mayer Wise, 1899

In the late 1890s, Ezekiel received a commission to make what is likely the first sculpture of a living rabbi modeled by a Jewish artist (fig. 32; a version was to be displayed in the censored Princeton exhibition).[1] After receiving a letter in Rome requesting his services, he responded quickly, expressing his gratitude for being chosen to execute the sculpture and outlining his immediate plans to visit the United States to undertake the work. Ezekiel stayed with family when visiting Cincinnati to complete the sculpture, a portrait bust of Isaac Mayer Wise, ordered by his congregation in celebration of the rabbi's eightieth birthday.[2]

One of Ezekiel's most influential American sitters, the Bohemian-born Wise, who immigrated to the United States in 1846, was the chief early exponent of American Reform Judaism. Initially a rabbi in Albany, New York, Wise relocated to Cincinnati in 1854 to assume the pulpit at B'nai Yeshurun synagogue, where he helped provide coherence to the German-based Reform movement and aimed to unify American Jewry. That year, he founded an English-language weekly, the *Israelite*, renamed the *American Israelite* two decades later—which remains in print to this day. The newspaper allowed Wise to espouse the ideology of Reform Judaism to a national audience, and B'nai Yeshurun stood as a flagship institution for liberal Jewish observance, with Wise the charismatic spokesman at its helm. B'nai Yeshurun adopted mixed-gender seating, introduced organ music during worship, and instituted shorter services while providing English translations to a wider audience. In 1875, Wise founded and became president of the inaugural Reform seminary in America, Hebrew Union College, also based in Cincinnati, which trained rabbis to lead Reform congregations throughout

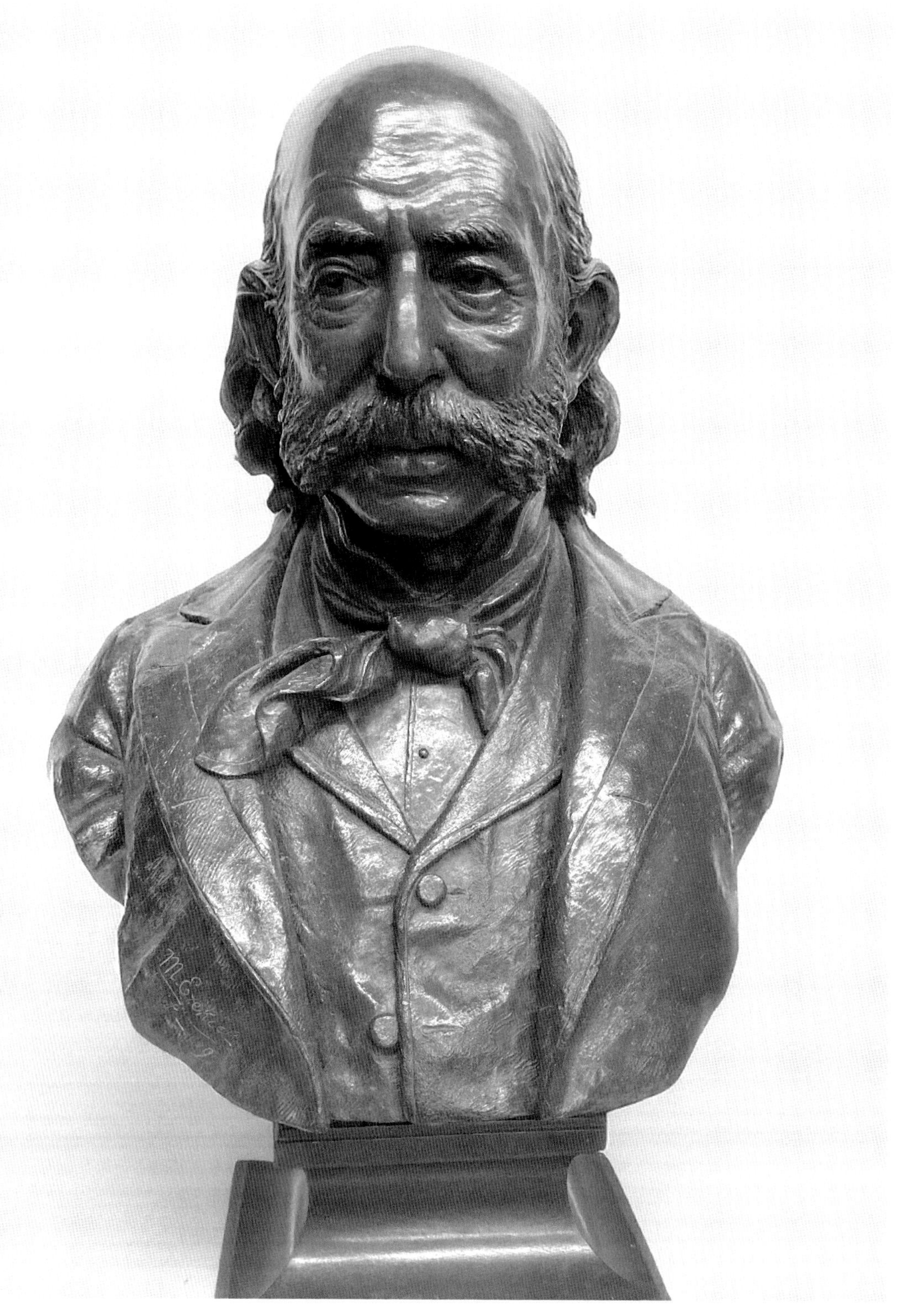

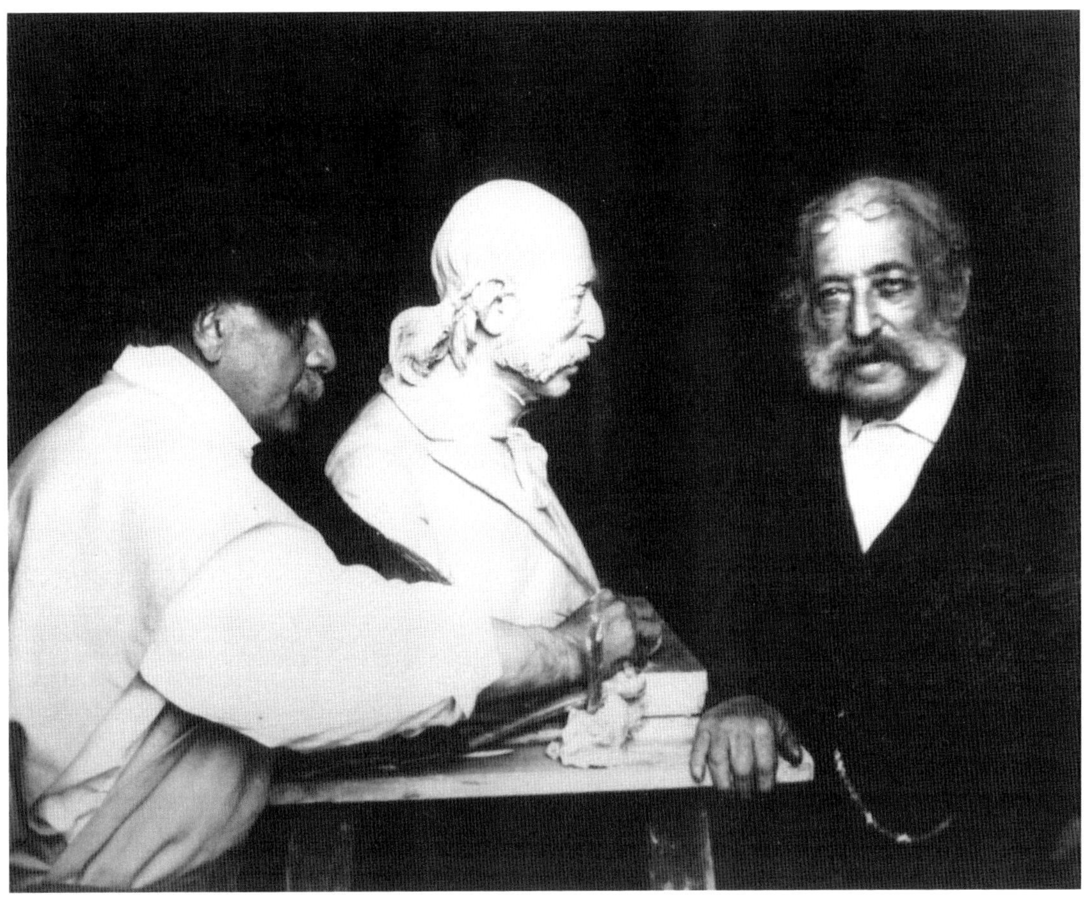

FIG. 32 (OPPOSITE) Moses Jacob Ezekiel, *Isaac Mayer Wise*, 1899. Bronze, 25 1/4 × 18 × 11 in. Collection of Skirball Museum, Skirball Cultural Center, Los Angeles, California. SCC 2012.3432. Photography by KeAnne Langford.

FIG. 33 Moses Jacob Ezekiel modeling *Isaac Mayer Wise*, 1899. Photograph. Courtesy of The Jacob Rader Marcus Center of the American Jewish Archives, Cincinnati, Ohio, at americanjewisharchives.org.

the country and now the world.[3] Branch campuses were eventually established in New York and Los Angeles in the 1950s, and in Jerusalem in 1963.

Ezekiel modeled Wise from life at the rabbi's farm, miles outside the city, waking early each morning because it took about an hour to reach his destination. Besieged by sweltering summer heat, Ezekiel complained of the conditions and marveled that he was able to do the necessary work.[4] A photograph of one of the final modeling sessions, taken through a window because Ezekiel did not want the clay moved, shows the sculptor in a heavy smock, staring intently at Wise, who wears a formal suit jacket and button-down shirt (fig. 33). The final conception accentuates Wise's high-buttoned vest, with one button undone, underneath a wide, V-notched lapel outercoat accentuating his shoulders. Wise has a jaunty ascot tied around his neck, the right corner partially tucked into his vest and the left crossing over onto his coat. His hair, long in the back, hangs a little past the bottom of his neck. A bushy mustache spreads over his cheeks to his thick sideburns, keeping his chin cleanly shaven.

Soon after moving to Berlin, Ezekiel wrote home to his mother, describing the appearance of Polish Jews he saw on the streets: "They all have a little curl in front of the ear and hair cut close behind to save the trouble of a comb and brush. Their long coat answers all purposes, for shirt, vest, and pants are not needed, and consequently not worn often."[5] Ezekiel and many American Jews, especially those in the South, were largely unfamiliar with this style of dress and certainly were not accustomed to seeing Jews of this ilk communing in large crowds. Rabbi Wise's appearance, like that of other Reform Jews, reveals how most assimilated Jews wanted to be perceived within the larger American population. Ezekiel's Sephardic family dressed in this fashion, as did the artist himself.

Following morning modeling sessions, the two men enjoyed lunches, which Wise's son Isidor recollected as "periods of delightful recreation for Dr. Wise."[6] They probably warmly remembered Ezekiel's father, Jacob, who had died a few weeks earlier. Jacob, who was a close acquaintance of Wise and had strong connections with Hebrew Union College, served as secretary of the board of governors for twenty years, which may have influenced his son receiving the commission. Wise had recently penned an editorial in the *American Israelite*, effusively eulogizing the elder Ezekiel. Among many accolades, Wise wrote, "His life was beautiful, and all who knew him are the better for that knowledge. Such a man does not die, as the world is forever brighter and better because of the life he lived in it."[7]

Ezekiel's memoir, again based on his journals so close in memory, relays that the sculptor and his sitter spoke about Zionism, the Hebrew Bible, Theosophy, and reincarnation, all subjects of great interest to Ezekiel. They disagreed on almost all points, with both backing their assertions by learnedly referring to biblical passages.[8] Despite these conversations, as the bust neared completion, Ezekiel wrestled with Wise's expression. Ezekiel felt that at their sittings he had aroused Wise's "moods and humors," but not the rabbi's zeal for his ideals, his "expression of absolute confidence, determination, enthusiasm and fire I know he exhibits when he is fighting for what he knows is the right," as Isidor Wise paraphrased the artist's sentiment. Isidor further remembered that someone suggested to Ezekiel that Wise's archetype was Moses, and questioning the rabbi about the great lawgiver's status might create the desired effect. With the sculpture complete, Ezekiel announced, according to Isidor Wise, "Moses turned the trick."[9] Ultimately, however, Wise does not look fiery. At eighty, he looks predictably weary, with tired eyes gazing slightly downward and circles underneath. Perhaps Ezekiel meant to suggest quiet determination, gleaned from the rabbi's knitted eyebrows, demonstrating his thoughtfulness and concentration. Ezekiel later rendered an ink drawing of Wise in profile at three-quarter length. Wise appeared with the same tired gaze, sitting in a chair and holding a rolled-up paper, assuredly a copy of the *American Israelite*.[10]

Wise died before the bust was cast but he did see the clay model which, according to his son, the rabbi had approved.[11] Shipped back to Europe, the model was bronzed. By then, Ezekiel had attained international fame, with his travels regularly followed in the news. The *New York Times* reported that he would personally courier the finished sculpture to the United States, after setting sail from Liverpool on May 19 of the new century.[12] Further demonstration of Ezekiel's celebrity at the time, the *Cincinnati Enquirer* covered his voyage across the ocean as well, adding that following his visit to the Queen City he would travel to Louisville apropos matters related to his Thomas Jefferson monument.[13] Two months passed, and the magazine *Monumental News* announced the arrival of the sculpture and its pedestal, adding, "It was pronounced a beautiful work of art."[14]

Ezekiel's bust of Rabbi Wise is one of a handful of works sponsored by American Jewish institutions after B'nai B'rith's commission of *Religious Liberty* for the Centennial. He became the artist of choice for Jewish Americans, especially Reform Jews, as they began to incorporate imagery into their institutions and organizations. The subsequent works, in three different media and referencing the Bible in different ways, uniquely impart the uneasy relationship in Ezekiel's day between those Jews who supported Zionism and those who saw America as the new Jerusalem. So, too, the reception of some pieces further demonstrates engrained conflicts with the Second Commandment. Paying close attention to the subjects and reception of these highly divergent works, this chapter discusses Ezekiel's avid concerns for the future of Judaism, a struggle that connects with the modernization of late nineteenth-century American Jewry championed by Rabbi Wise.

Israel, a Complicated Allegory

To understand Ezekiel's position on Zionism, as well as to further explore his artistic interest in the Bible, we must look backward to his first realized biblical work, which serves as a crucial foundation for his thinking and subsequent subject matter. That 1873 piece, an iconographically complicated bas-relief, titled *Israel*, can be partially fleshed out by parsing Ezekiel's conversation with Wise during their turn-of-the-century modeling sessions, together with his personal correspondence and other surviving documents. *Israel* was Ezekiel's initial use of Christological imagery, but as described in the previous chapter, not his last.

When enrolled as a student at the Royal Academy in Berlin, Ezekiel submitted two works for the Michael Beer Prize, a stipend earmarked for Jewish artists to live for a year in Rome: *Israel* (1873) and *Adam and Eve Finding the Body of Abel* (ca. 1873). A Jewish German poet from a wealthy, philanthropic family, Michael Beer died at age thirty-three. His will provided for a foundation to enable young artists "of the Mosaic faith" to travel to Italy.[15] *Adam and Eve Finding the Body of Abel*, depicting the aftermath of Cain's murder of his brother Abel, is lost. However, its title alone indicates a subject little depicted in the fine arts; portrayals of the actual murder were far more common, offering a dramatic, recognizable narrative. Ezekiel's bronze *Israel*, with a centrally engraved title to help orient the viewer of this opaque piece, earned him the prize as the first non-German to do so. *Israel* is also lost, but a 1904 version survives that replicates much of the original, with some elements omitted (fig. 34). An ambitious project for a young sculptor, and a rare bronze relief in Ezekiel's large body of work, *Israel* aligns with the popularity of relief sculpture at the time, particularly by Bertel Thorvaldsen. Another Roman expatriate, one who trained Crawford as a neoclassicist and was viewed as the heir to Antonio

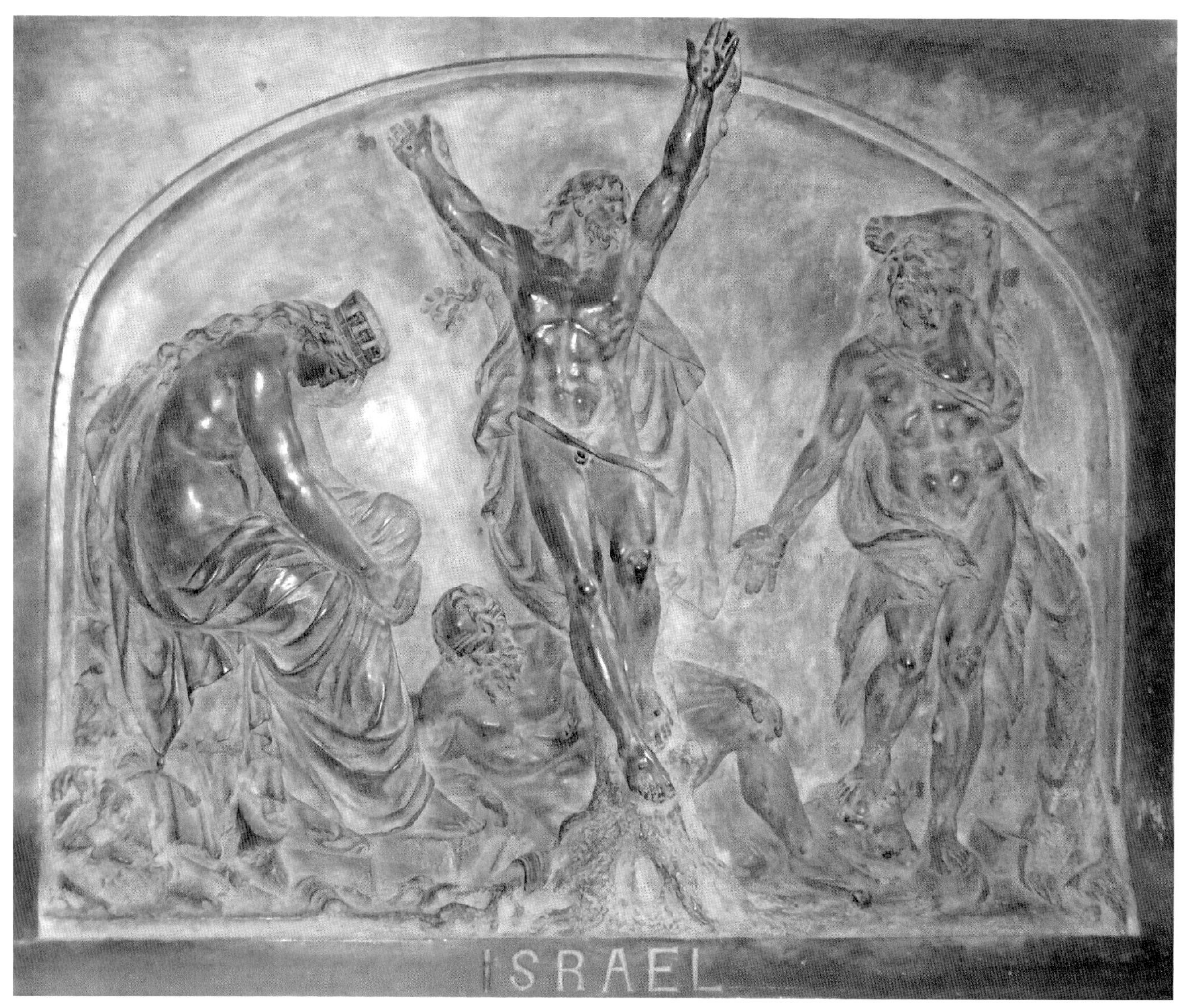

FIG. 34 Moses Jacob Ezekiel, *Israel*, 1904 copy after 1873 lost original. Bronze, 44 × 56 in. Skirball Museum of Hebrew Union College–Jewish Institute of Religion, Cincinnati, Ohio. Photo: Samantha Baskind.

Canova, the Danish Thorvaldsen had a substantial influence on American artists and beyond.[16] Ezekiel hoped to match his success.

Measuring 3 ½ feet high by 4 ½ feet wide, significantly smaller than the original at eight feet wide and six feet high, the surviving rendition of *Israel* was ordered by B'nai B'rith in March 1903. A representative sent Ezekiel a letter in Rome asking if he would contribute a piece of art for the Order's new building on the Lower East Side of Manhattan, which he deemed "the heart of the Jewish quarter."[17] In laying out his case, the letter writer explained that the building would serve recent émigrés from Europe, and the committee in charge had resolved to decorate the building with work by Jewish artists. He pointed to *Religious Liberty* as an example of Ezekiel's "genius and the patriotism of the B'nai B'rith," hoping the sculptor would make something similar. The letter further states that such a work would be appropriate for the building, since it offered a refuge for victims of religious persecution who had recently immigrated under duress to the Land of Liberty.[18] Attuned to the suffering of his coreligionists and always pleased to receive paid assignments, Ezekiel responded favorably; it is unknown whether other artists approached to contribute, including Henry Mosler, responded to the same request. Distressed about the future of European Jews during this era of intensified pogroms in the Pale of Settlement when contemplating the request, Ezekiel deviated from a sculpture hailing hopeful religious liberty and submitted a Zionist statement.

Initially intended only to comprise one figure, the narrative relief represents Israel allegorically four times. At center, Israel appears as a nearly nude Jesus crucified on a tree in the shape of a cross, with arms upraised and feet nailed to the tree stump. According to Ezekiel's notes, this Jesus/Israel figure stood on the right in the earlier version, and this move indicates its importance to the conception.[19] To emphasize Jesus's Jewishness, Ezekiel depicts him offering the ancient priestly blessing in line with the biblical text, with four fingers separated into two groups—shown later in Ezekiel's *Christ in the Tomb*—rather than with the modifications made for *Religious Liberty*. The blessing receives special attention for its extension above the arc framing the work. Near the feet of Jesus/Israel crucified, a despairing Israel bows his head in defeat, overcome by millennia of discrimination and humiliation. In both reliefs, a virile, almost-Herculean Israel with one arm cradled over his head gazes to the heavens. Accounts during Ezekiel's lifetime indicate that this "unconquered" man is meant to indicate Israel's hope; that figure stands at center in the lost rendition and to the right of Jesus in the surviving version. Fashioned as a resurgent Israel, he receives Jesus's/Israel's attention.[20] A female figure on the left side denotes Jerusalem. The main difference between the 1873 and 1904 reliefs is that Ezekiel's earlier rendering included a figure of David as psalmist with his harp, an Egyptian sphinx, and Moses with the Tablets of the Law above the arc depicting the main narrative.[21] One can only speculate about why Ezekiel abandoned this iconography, but perhaps he felt these extra figures distracted from his core message—the return of his people to the Land of Israel.

Unmistakably imbued with allusions to classical sculpture, the relief demonstrates Ezekiel's attraction to the antique and his attempts to harness the classical for ideologically modern ends. We do not know the musculature or precise poses of the figures in the first *Israel*, but the second version

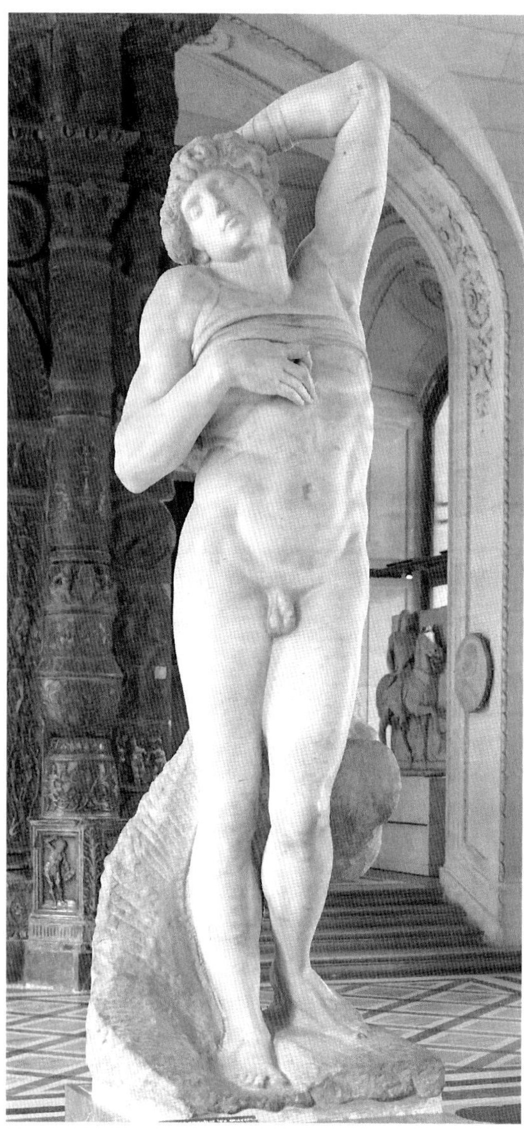

FIG. 35 Michelangelo, *Dying Slave*, circa 1513–16. Marble, 82 in. Musée du Louvre, Paris. Photo: Wikimedia Commons / Jörg Bittner Unna. CC BY-SA 3.0.

FIG. 36 (OPPOSITE) *Dying Gaul*, Roman marble copy, first or second century BCE. Marble, 37 × 73 7/16 × 35 1/16 in. Musei Capitolini, Rome. Photo: Steven Zucker, PhD.

summons familiar influences to which Ezekiel was exposed in Italy. *Israel* on the far right, with his pronounced contrapposto, strong musculature, thrown-back head, and arm reaching over his head, echoes Michelangelo's *Dying Slave* (fig. 35), originally made for Pope Julius II's tomb. The support behind *Dying Slave* was unnecessary for Ezekiel's *Israel* in relief, but he still preserved the structure. *Israel* on the ground partially parallels *Dying Gaul* (Greek bronze original, ca. 220 BCE; Roman copy, first or second century CE; fig. 36), an ancient marble widely recognized and reproduced in engravings, plaster, and bronze copies, and housed at the Capitoline Museum in Rome, Ezekiel's frequent haunt. Both works feature reclining bodies and necks torqued to the left, eyes downcast. Ezekiel's interest in *Dying Gaul* would only have been heightened by Michelangelo's restoration of the figure's right arm.

The Wandering Jew

A letter written to his father while executing the 1873 *Israel* provides some clarity about the difficult sculpture: "I cut the name *Israel* in the lower edge of the frame, although Ahasver would have been just as appropriate. . . . Ahasver is the traditional name of the Wandering Jew who is the type of Israel and the Wandering Jew gives the key to any understanding of my relief."[22] Indeed, in an influential early seventeenth-century telling of the Wandering Jew he was called Ahasver, and the name soon became synonymous with the mythical figure.[23] Based on a medieval Christian tale of a Jew who mocked Jesus on his way to Calvary, Ahasver—the Wandering Jew—was condemned as a result to roam the earth for eternity, or

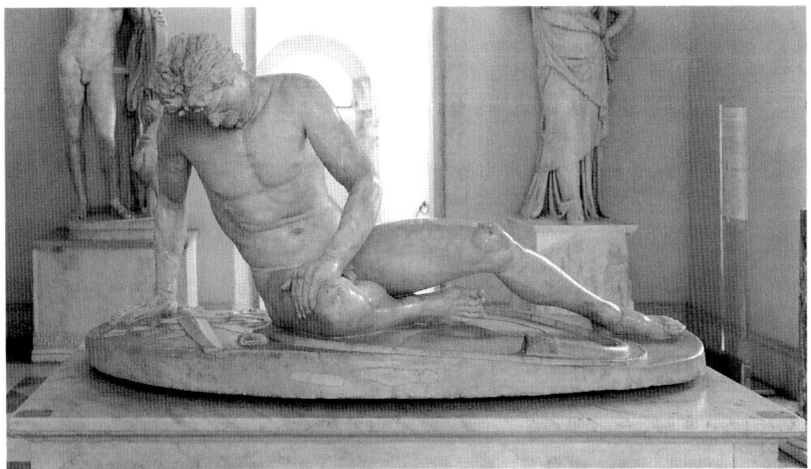

sometimes described as until the Second Coming.[24] The legend reaches back to the thirteenth century and was even in use in the twentieth century by Nazis for antisemitic purposes. It has been perpetuated in poetry, drama, opera, and other media, with special relevance here to the figure's plight in the visual arts. Malicious images of an antisemitic nature presented the Wandering Jew with certain attributes: a barefoot pilgrim with a staff; long beard and bent body to indicate old age and his extended years of wanderings; and often a money bag—thereby pointing to Jewish greed, expressly evoking the coins paid to Judas in return for his betrayal of Jesus. The most recognized visual representations of the Wandering Jew, by Gustave Doré, are a series of twelve dramatic, blatantly noxious large drawings. They were published several times as engravings in the mid- to late nineteenth century, first accompanying a poem by Pierre-Jean de Béranger.[25] The bearded, stooped Jew in the second image from Doré's series suffers for his taunting of Jesus and is thus doomed to roam (fig. 37). This pitiful figure also promulgates stereotypes of the weak and inferior Jewish body.

The anguish of the so-called Wandering Jew—both the legendary figure and the historically displaced Jew without a homeland, who is persecuted by the nations where he resides—was clear to Ezekiel. Being well-versed in Jewish history, he understood the travails faced by his people. His adopted city of Rome was the seat of the Christian triumph over the Jews: a five-month Roman siege in 70 CE destroyed Jerusalem and the Second Temple, and many survivors of the war were enslaved by the Romans. The Roman army's victory is publicly commemorated by the *Arch of Titus* (after 81 CE), located in the heart of Rome and past which Ezekiel walked innumerable times. Its relief panel overtly depicts the spoils looted from the Temple in Jerusalem.

Capitalizing on his experience writing as a correspondent for the *New York Herald* covering the Franco-Prussian War soon after he arrived in Germany, Ezekiel amalgamated his love of history, the Jewish people, and the written word within months of settling in the Eternal City. Then, he published a series of nearly twenty articles about the ghetto in Rome for the *Jewish Record*

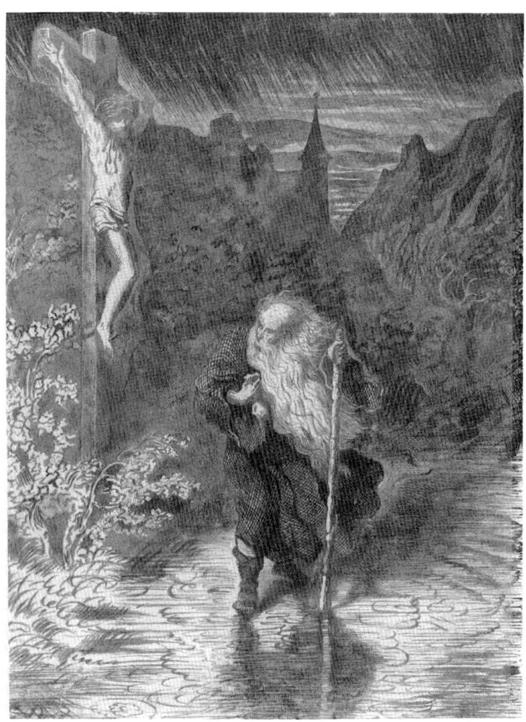

FIG. 37 Gustave Doré, *The Legend of the Wandering Jew, 7: Too late he feels . . .*, circa 1856. Drawing in pen and ink, 5 3/4 × 12 in. Photo © Victoria and Albert Museum, London. Given by H. H. Harrod, Esq.

of Philadelphia (October 22, 1875–September 8, 1876). Open about his extensive quoting of sources, especially the history of Roman Jews by Ferdinand Gregorovius (including his factual errors), Ezekiel penned dozens of pages about Roman Jewish history.[26] Nearing the end of the series, Ezekiel inserted his own voice. He expressed his admiration for Italian Jews' endurance in the face of oppression, of "bearing His name aloft amid the gorgeous ruins of pagan Rome and the cruelties of Christianity. . . . For, never in the world's history have any people cried so much and so bitterly as these Jews in Rome have done."[27] More than once, his memoir describes prior Jewish victimization in Rome; he points particularly to the traditional inaugural ceremony held in conjunction with the coronation of a new pope. Roman Jews, Ezekiel felt compelled to explain to his readers, were required to participate in the papal procession from medieval times, where for generations they gifted a Torah to the pontiff, who would in turn ceremonially offer a benediction rejecting a Jewish interpretation of the Bible.[28]

When Russian Jews were persecuted during pogroms in the early 1890s, Ezekiel spearheaded a relief committee to provide material aid for coreligionists expelled from their homes. In Italy, he marshaled a diverse group of non-Jews to assist him, quite remarkably including Cardinal Prince Gustav von Hohenlohe-Schillingsfürst and the mayor of Rome, who served as the vice president of the committee.[29] Ezekiel aimed to provide clothing and shelter for Russian Jews fleeing oppression, and then to use raised funds to create industrial and agricultural colonies in Palestine, as well as schools and hospitals.[30] Opposed to attempts by German philanthropist Baron Maurice de Hirsch to settle oppressed Jews in Argentina, Ezekiel instead advocated, he wrote in a letter to his father in 1891, "to repopulate Syria and Palestine with these refugees from barbarism. . . . There are 5 million Jews in Russia and they will all have to leave there sooner or later."[31] As a Jewish expatriate in Europe with close ties to Germany, Ezekiel was surely aware of the impending creation of the Jewish Colonization Association, funded by Hirsch and established two months after this correspondence. That same letter, dated squarely between the two versions of *Israel*, plainly outlines Ezekiel's hope: "There is no good reason why Palestine should not flower again like a garden and give corn, wine and oil to her inhabitants."[32]

Israel disrupts conventions by reclaiming the Wandering Jew as a figure that signifies the restless diasporic condition, instead of perpetuating the negative stereotype of the punished and pitiful migrant. The original bas-relief also serves as one of the earliest statements on modern Zionism in sculptural form. Heretofore, one of the most celebrated has been identified as an 1899 sculpture, *The Wandering Jew*, by Alfred Nossig, a Zionist from Galicia. That bronze has since disappeared but survives in photographs (fig. 38). Loosely derived from Michelangelo's muscular *Moses* (ca. 1513–15; San Pietro in Vincoli, Rome), Nossig's bearded Wandering Jew bears a Torah scroll adorned with the Star of David, a long-standing Jewish symbol self-consciously chosen by Zionists during the late nineteenth century to define the Jews as a distinct nation.[33] The Wandering Jew firmly leans on his massive staff, not to bear his burden but as a reference to the great rod used by Moses in parting the Red Sea during the Exodus. Confident and defiant, the aged but determined figure epitomizes assured leadership for a self-identified nation, whose Torah remains its enduring support, like the staff of Moses.

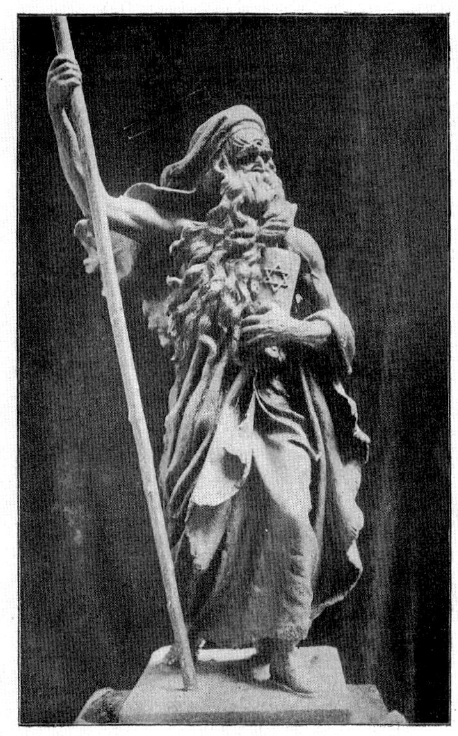

Der ewige Jude.
Skulptur von Alfred Nossig.

FIG. 38 Alfred Nossig, *The Wandering Jew*, 1899. Sculpture, lost. From *Ost und West* 1 (January 1901).

Nossig and Ezekiel's resilient and proud Wandering Jews have conscious intention, in contrast with those by Doré and other visual representations that picture a Jewish existence without purpose. (Ezekiel may very well have known Doré's engravings for their antisemitic impulse and widespread publication.) Instead of depicting weakness and stigma, Nossig's *Wandering Jew* proudly personifies the Jewish nation as he strides forward boldly, and Ezekiel's Wandering Jew demonstrates strength through a sturdy body. Ezekiel described his composition as one that intended to direct viewers' eyes to the "powerful figure of Israel, the unconquered one, the persistent, the Israel of the will to live." Crucified Israel, he continued, "extended his gesture of blessing toward the hopeful Israel, the Israel of the new age."[34] The early twentieth-century cultural monthly *Ost und West*, a widely circulated, Berlin-based, Jewish magazine hailing European Jewish culture and at times promoting Zionism, printed a reproduction of Ezekiel's relief within a larger 1903 profile about the artist.[35] Nossig's arresting, easily readable sculpture was understandably held up as a more lucid and effective Zionist statement at the front of the inaugural issue of *Ost und West* in 1901, adjacent to the magazine's mission statement.[36]

American Judaism and Zionism

For Ezekiel, steeped in traditional Judaism, the goal of his religion would be for Jews to wander no more and return to the Land of Israel, as Scripture dictates. Yet, with Judaism rapidly changing in late nineteenth-century America, most liberal Jews were not yearning for a renewed homeland. To a degree, the ever-wandering diasporic Jew was finally finding social acceptance in the United States and increased security under constitutionally protected religious freedom. The hopeful words uttered for ages at the end of the Passover seder, "Next year in Jerusalem," were no longer applicable for American Reformers, which dismayed Ezekiel because he strongly supported Jerusalem's rebirth. Despite his convictions, Ezekiel was ever ready to take commissions from Reform Jews—because he was starved for money, because he took pride in working for his people, and because he felt he could still transmit some of his Zionist ideals through his art.

When modeling the portrait bust of Rabbi Wise, Ezekiel—well aware of his sitter's thinking—argued with him about this point, and he chronicled the exchange in his memoir. Ezekiel, who criticized Reform Judaism, recalled Wise's opinion that "America was the Jerusalem for the Jews, and he did not believe at all in the restoration of the Jewish nation."[37] The pair's thoughts on American Judaism and Zionism could not have been more opposite, and Ezekiel described conversation about the subject as "hot." By then an ardent proto-Zionist, and three years away from his second version of *Israel*, Ezekiel firmly maintained, as he told the rabbi, "The time would come when there would be a central government in Jerusalem again and that Palestine would flourish." Wise admonished Ezekiel for such "an old-fashioned notion," as Ezekiel paraphrased it, and the rabbi's articles in the *American Israelite* bear out this point of view.[38] Wise opined in his paper in 1882, "The idea of the Jews returning to Palestine is no part of our creed."[39] The rabbi's perspective on Zionism, like that of many Reformers, was deeply rooted in a polarized moment in American Jewry.[40]

For millennia, Jews saw themselves as a nation in exile, striving to return to the Land of Israel. Since Reformers understood Judaism as a religion, not a people, their core values needed to be recontextualized. Reformers removed all prayers from their liturgy that asked God to restore them to the Holy Land; this was particularly noticeable in the Reform prayer book, *Minhag America* (1857), which was in great part created by Wise. In an 1885 "Declaration of Principles," commonly known as "The Pittsburgh Platform," Reform thinkers codified their dismissal of a Jewish state dictated by the messianic vision: "We recognize in the modern era of universal culture of heart and intellect the approaching of the realization of Israel's great Messianic hope for the establishment of the kingdom of truth, justice and peace among all men. We consider ourselves no longer a nation, but a religious community, and, therefore, expect neither a return to Palestine, nor a sacrificial worship under the sons of Aaron, nor the restoration of any of the laws concerning the Jewish state."[41]

Modern Zionism traces its roots to the mid-nineteenth century, instigated by a desire to reestablish a Jewish nation in Palestine.[42] In this initial period, European proto-Zionists advocating for active settlement include German philosopher Moses Hess. His Zionist treatise *Rome and Jerusalem* (1862) was first published in Germany; Ezekiel may have read the book, since he lived in

Berlin when studying at the Academy and was deeply interested in the subject. Like Ezekiel, Hess felt animosity for the Reform movement, concerned that its liberal ideas threatened the existence of Judaism. Hess took aim at the Reformers' "mission" to spread the values of Judaism and humanitarianism in the diaspora, which he considered contradictory: "What I don't understand is, how it is possible to believe simultaneously in 'enlightenment' and in a Jewish Mission in exile; in other words, in the ultimate dissolution and in the continued existence of Judaism at the same time."[43] Akin to many other proto-Zionists, Hess held that Jews could only find security on their own soil, because they would never truly be accepted by larger society. Like Ezekiel, he did not deem it necessary for all Jews to settle in Palestine. Rather, Hess saw the land as a haven for his people, spurred by an upsurge in Judeophobia. For the time being, Ezekiel was quite satisfied in Rome, and he equally saw an independent Jewish homeland as a refuge for beleaguered Jews in eastern Europe. He advocated their settlement through agrarianism, as did Hess.[44]

Regardless of whether he knew of *Rome and Jerusalem*—and the similarities between the two men's thoughts indicate that he did—the point is that Ezekiel lived in Europe, closer to Zionist thinkers and movements as well as the growing mistreatment of Jews, than Wise and the American Reformers. Ezekiel's expatriate status undoubtedly shaped his perspective. Further, after the Civil War, when Ezekiel expatriated to Europe, he might have felt even more rootless outside his original country, so that a revived Holy Land possibly held attraction as a fantasy. Or perhaps Ezekiel was more generally excited by the romance of a restored Israel; his idealism is exemplified by the beautiful home and cult of personality he nurtured in the decaying ruins of the thermae of Diocletian.

The true catalyst for the restoration of a Jewish state and the rise of modern Zionism was Theodor Herzl, an assimilationist from Hungary who studied law in Vienna. His position slowly evolved toward political Zionism as a result of the severe rise of antisemitism in Europe. Although he asserted that his beliefs were crystallized when working as a news correspondent in France covering Alfred Dreyfus's trial for Vienna's *Die Neue Freie Presse* (his successor at the paper, Max Nordau, was also pivotal to the founding of the modern Zionist movement), this perspective has since been questioned as revisionism on Herzl's part.[45] Still, the egregious antisemitism of the Dreyfus affair is broadly cited as a stimulus for Zionism, and to some degree shaped Herzl's core ideal that Jews could only achieve full emancipation by returning to the Land of Israel and forming a Jewish state.

Herzl's 1896 *Der Judenstaat* (*The Jewish State*), which led to the convening of the First Zionist Congress in Basel, Switzerland, the next year, outlined his goals for political action and urged that Jews reawaken to the importance of a national home as a solution to the "Jewish Question."[46] Soon, the Zionist movement took hold in Europe, with Herzl its undisputed leader, heralded for his spellbinding persona and inspired leadership. At the First Zionist Congress, one delegate exalted Herzl as "a royal scion of the House of David, risen from among the dead, clothed in legend and fantasy and beauty. Everyone sat breathless, as if in the presence of a miracle. . . . The dream of two thousand years was on the point of realization; it was as if the Messiah, son of David, confronted us; and I was seized by an overpowering desire, in the midst of this storm of joy, to cry out, loudly, for all to hear: 'Yehi hamelech!' Hail to the King!"[47] In America, however, Herzl's beliefs and spearheading efforts were controversial and even mocked by some, notably Rabbi Wise. Although Rabbi Gustav Gottheil of New York City's prominent Reform congregation Temple Emanu-El had early Zionist sympathies, the religious and political hopes of Zionism were largely discounted by American Reform Jews. Enjoying freedoms and opportunities unheard of in eastern Europe, they regarded their adopted homeland as a "new Zion."

The Book of Isaiah and Jerusalem as Woman

During conversations with Rabbi Wise while modeling the bust, Ezekiel cited the book of Isaiah to bolster his argument about an ancestral Jewish homeland. The book prophesies the deliverance of the exiles to Jerusalem and a Messianic Age when all nations of the world—Jews and non-Jews alike—will be welcome in Israel and will worship God there. Ezekiel remembered telling Wise, "According to chapter two of the prophecy of Isaiah, while all other nations would continue to exist and no Jew who lived in any other country could be required to go back to Jerusalem . . . peace and good will would reign upon the earth, and the simple faith for which the Jews had suffered so much would be recognized as being the true one."[48] These comments indicate that while Ezekiel felt the colonization of Palestine was essential to the survival of eastern European Jewry, he likewise believed in a religious claim to the Holy Land.

The book of Isaiah harks back to the Wandering Jew, Ezekiel's professed pivot of his *Israel* composition. That mythical figure's wandering could be curtailed with the end of Jewish exile from the Holy Land, signified by the woman on the left side of the bas-relief. Isaiah's writings, which emphatically employ a metaphor to describe Jerusalem as female, begin to clarify Ezekiel's complicated Zionist allegory. Ezekiel knew the book well, and he used either its words or made images inspired by the prophet's words in three works spanning his career (after the first version of *Israel*, in a seal for the Jewish Publication Society and later carved on his Arlington National Cemetery Confederate monument).

Ezekiel's female allegorical figure strikes the same pose in both *Israel* reliefs. In a letter dated 1873, Ezekiel describes the seminude, classically draped woman in *Israel* as representing Jerusalem, "bowed in grief, abandoned and with a demolished wall crown on her head."[49] Portraying her as such confirms Ezekiel's keen awareness of the Hebrew Bible, in which Jerusalem, as lamenting mother, is personified on several occasions. In the book of Isaiah, she says to God, "Can a woman forget her sucking child, that she should not have compassion on the son of her womb? Yea, these may forget, yet will not I forget thee."[50] So, too, accounts of Jerusalem's crown appear numerous times throughout the Bible, especially in the later prophets (e.g., Ezek. 16:12, Jer. 13:18). The Wandering Jew—the Jew in the diaspora—could be redeemed, as per Ezekiel's bas-relief, once a Jewish nation was restored. Then, Jerusalem would not be bowed and abandoned, and Jewish suffering would end.

By personifying Jerusalem as a woman, Ezekiel also followed biblical tradition. The Hebrew Bible refers to all cities in the feminine. Jerusalem, or Zion, has been allegorized as a woman in various texts and incarnations. In Isaiah, she is viewed as virgin (37:22) and bride (62:3), and elsewhere as daughter (2 Kings 19:21), menstruant (Lam. 1; throughout, Lamentations markedly ascribes Israel a female identity), and harlot (Jer. 2:20), among other metaphors. Even if some of Jerusalem's manifestations are undesirable, she is more frequently described positively, as beloved and beautiful. Most relevant here, the Bible repeatedly refers to Jerusalem as mother (e.g., Isa. 66:8), a figure customarily interpreted as a protector—in this case of the Jews—much like Ezekiel's *Religious Liberty*, who protects the American people from religious bigotry.

The woman/mother in *Israel* can be read as bowed and abandoned because the Jewish people had yet to return to their homeland; they still lived in diasporic exile, and most American Reform Jews were content there. Ezekiel's female personification of Israel wears a crown like her later American counterpart in the Centennial monument. However, while *Religious Liberty* gestures grandly and looks determinedly outward to the future, with a delicate thirteen-star crown on her head, Jerusalem gazes downward, her body curled forward defensively. Her crown—a "demolished wall," which may be a reference to the Temple destroyed by the Romans during the siege and subsequent Jewish exile from Jerusalem—weighs heavily on her head. Jerusalem as mother grieves for the loss of her children, whereas *Religious Liberty* resolutely safeguards them.

In Isaiah, the narrator commands Jerusalem, portrayed as a barren woman, to rejoice and prepare for children (the Jews' return) by extending her tents: "'Sing, O barren, thou that didst not bear, break forth into singing, and cry aloud, thou that didst not travail; for more are the children of the desolate than the children of the married wife,' saith the LORD. Enlarge the place of thy tent, and let them stretch forth the curtains of thy habitations, spare not; lengthen thy cords, and strengthen thy stakes."[51] Earlier, chapter 40 opens with an exhortation of reconciliation for the female Jerusalem: "Comfort ye, comfort ye My people, saith your God. Bid Jerusalem take heart, and proclaim unto her, that her time of service is accomplished, that her guilt is paid off."[52] If indeed Jerusalem's time of service is accomplished, if she is no longer abandoned, then the results of the Temple's destruction have been nullified, because Jews are no longer exiled—they are not wandering like Ahasver.
By adopting the image of Israel-as-woman as in the book of Isaiah, Ezekiel connects her to the ever-rootless Ahasver. To that end, Jerusalem can finally rejoice when her people return.

When *Israel* arrived in New York in 1904, the *Cincinnati Enquirer* reported on its artist, "the world-renowned sculptor" Ezekiel, and the sculpture, "justifying the high reputation the artist has so long sustained."[53] The sculpture, the paper further commented, "resting as it does in the very center of that little city within a great city, the Ghetto, will naturally make it the Mecca of many artists."[54] But it would not be so. While younger members of B'nai B'rith commended the relief, some older and more Orthodox members were unhappy because of its use of Christian imagery and a continuing misinterpretation of the biblical injunction against graven images.[55] The voices of those opposing the sculpture won out, so the complicated allegory, likely not understood as Zionist in theme, was never installed in the building. Stung by that rebuke, Ezekiel stayed silent on the commission's details. After the fact, for the permanent record—at least in his eyes—he wrote in his memoir about an encounter with an American visitor to his studio during which he displayed *Israel*. Ezekiel noted that the relief had won the Michael Beer Prize and relayed the visitor's reaction: "If you had never done anything but that one piece of work, it would have been enough for any one man to do."[56]

Isaac Mayer Wise as a Sculpted Rejoinder to Theodor Herzl

In contrast to *Israel*, Ezekiel's bust of Isaac Mayer Wise, as weary as he may seem, became a source of pride in the Jewish community and was replicated for other venues. Three months after Rabbi Wise's death, his wife, Selma Bondi Wise, donated the bronze to Hebrew Union College for rabbinical students to see daily as a likeness of the man who had long served as their leader.[57] (It is now held by the Skirball Cultural Center, Los Angeles.) At the request of Wise's son-in-law Adolph Ochs, publisher of the *New York Times*, four years later Ezekiel translated the portrait into marble for his patron's home, eventually donated to Cincinnati's Hebrew Union College by the rabbi's heirs. Another bronze bust of Wise, also dated 1903, is in the foyer of Mizpah Congregation in Chattanooga, Tennessee, almost certainly donated by Ochs, who owned and served as publisher of the *Chattanooga Times* and provided funds for the synagogue's new building in 1928.[58] In 1906, Ochs asked Ezekiel for a fourth copy of the bust, intended for display at the National Jewish Hospital for Consumptives in Denver (now known as National Jewish Health), an organization that Wise had supported. Since 1956, that marble resides in the lobby at the Hebrew Union College branch in New York City.

Considering Wise's well-known belief that Judaism is aniconic, it seems incongruous that he would submit to the sitting.[59] Four decades earlier, Rabbi Wise contested a portrait monument to philanthropist Judah Touro, who died in 1854 in New Orleans and gave generously to that city's institutions, both Jewish and non-Jewish. New Orleans Jews and non-Jews alike initiated a movement to memorialize Touro with a monument, which some American rabbis publicly and loudly condemned, based on the Second Commandment. Wise argued that scripture prohibited monuments, statues, and pillars, and wrote in the *Israelite* that supporters of the Touro monument (never erected) had "no right to break up a sacred law so conscientiously observed by our ancestors and contemporaries; a law which is essential and characteristic of Judaism with its purely spiritual monotheism."[60] Wise's later acceptance of a bust made in his honor demonstrates that his thinking about the Second Commandment had evolved, as had his congregants. Still, Wise's change in perspective has never been identified and merits brief supposition.

An article in the *American Israelite*, prompted by the bust on its display in Cincinnati, addressed "the interesting question of the relation of Jews to art."[61] The article begins by describing rigid interpretations of the commandment but quickly turns to examples of "artistic spirit" as described in the Torah: the decoration of the ark, tabernacle, and Solomon's Temple. Yet, painting and sculpture, the author asserts, were mostly rejected because these artistic modes "were employed for the most part in the service of religion and the abhorrence of the Jews for image worship and idolatry . . . naturally prevented the development of the plastic arts among them." The unidentified author notes the lack of Jewish art over the years and lauds "the Jew's proudest achievement that he taught the world 'the beauty of holiness.'" Nevertheless, the author argues for modern Jewish artistic production: "There is no reason in these latter days why, as a man, he shall not also aim at gaining a place among those who proclaim 'the holiness of beauty,' for both holiness and beauty are given of God to make life better, fuller and nobler."[62]

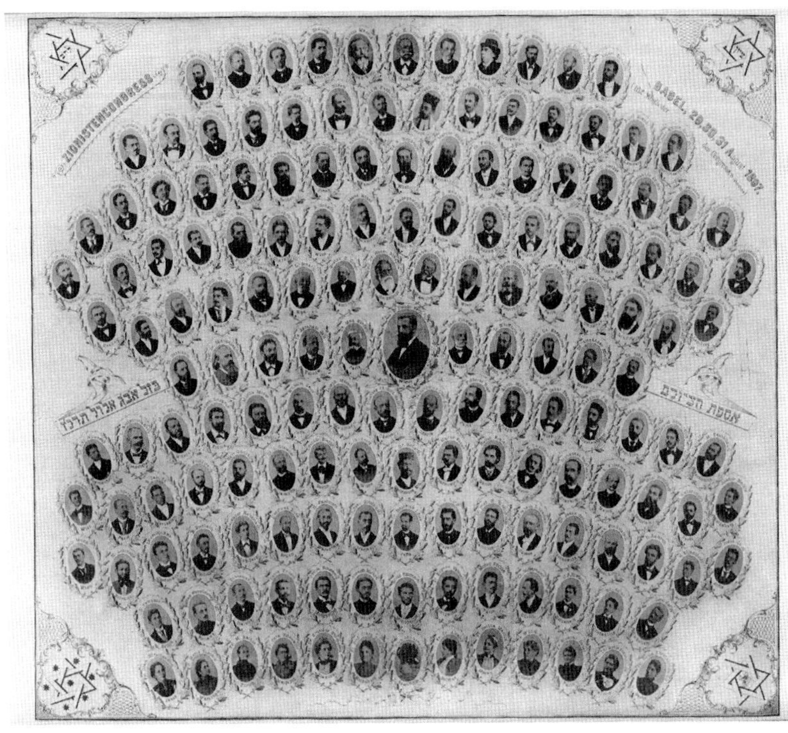

FIG. 39 "The Delegates to the First Zionist Congress, Basle, August 1897." In *Theodor Herzl: A Memorial*, edited by Meyer Weisgal (New York: New Palestine, 1929), following page 160. Photo: Wikimedia Commons.

Wise's dramatic about-face could be grounded in a broader, changing modern perspective about the Jewish arts, as described in his own newspaper. Moreover, he may have seen Christian clergy immortalized in sculpture and wanted to be acclaimed in the same manner. Wise's contemporary Henry Ward Beecher, a Christian preacher, was honored soon after his death with a full-length 1891 outdoor statue in New York by John Quincy Adams Ward. But considering the decisive historical moment, the congregation's commission may have been more than an opportunity to both contribute to the plastic arts and honor their esteemed rabbi. Perhaps the rise of modern Zionism instigated B'nai Yeshuran's desire to immortalize their rabbi in bronze—maybe even at Wise's suggestion. It cannot go unsaid that the bust's commission coincided with the strategic use of imagery depicting Theodor Herzl as part of the Zionist agenda. From the start, Herzl's face was deployed as *the* Zionist symbol in art, even more than a menorah, another key signifier.[63] The First Zionist Congress officially launched the modern Zionist movement and commemorated the event with a much-reproduced 1897 composite portrait showcasing Herzl as the figurehead at center, with his cameo being twice the size of the others (fig. 39). An 1898 Rosh Hashanah card highlighted Herzl's visage, which disrupted expectations of what Jewish men looked like—for instance, those Polish Jews that Ezekiel wrote judgmentally about to his mother. Herzl's distinctive appearance, handsome features, and physical appeal grew exponentially in importance for decades after Ezekiel's bust of Wise, especially through Zionist artist Ephraim Moses Lilien's iconic photograph of him, often used as a source in other media.[64]

While we will never know definitively why Wise acquiesced to having his portrait modeled, with Herzl's meteoric rise at the end of the nineteenth century, American Reformers were struggling with an extraordinary personality of arguably even greater pull than their own chief rabbi. Wise let his vitriolic opposition be known at the 1897 Central Conference of American Rabbis, where he called out Herzl specifically and Zionism broadly: "That new Messianic movement over the ocean does not concern us at all. . . . [Zionism is] a momentary inebriation of morbid minds, and a prostitution of Israel's holy cause to a madman's dance of unsound politicians."[65] Wise vehemently preached to his congregants and through the *American Israelite* that the nationalistic goals of Zionism jeopardized the Jewish position in their adopted country, allowing for questions about their patriotism and casting them as distinct from their fellow citizens. That a commission would be secured for a sculpted rejoinder to the growth of Zionism through Herzl's leadership and his elevation (even idealization) by means of visual culture—and by the preeminent Jewish American artist of his day—is worthy of at least conjecture and within the realm of possibility.

The First Seal for the Jewish Publication Society of America and Isaiah's Prophecy

After establishing himself as a successful artist working in the service of his religion for B'nai B'rith in the making of *Religious Liberty*, Ezekiel was asked to design the first seal for the Jewish Publication Society (JPS). The foremost nonprofit, nondenominational American press to focus on Jewish books, JPS was founded in 1888 and continues to produce books today. In making the seal, Ezekiel also turned to the book of Isaiah, further demonstrating his knowledge of the biblical text, penchant for originality, concern for the future of Judaism, and Zionist perspective.

Ezekiel's JPS seal, in use from 1890 to 1906 (fig. 40), was inspired by a messianic verse from Isaiah, proclaiming a time when there will be peace on earth: "And the wolf shall dwell with the lamb, and the leopard shall lie down with the kid; and the calf and the young lion and the fatling together; and a little child shall lead them."[66] Ezekiel described the seal in a letter dated July 13, 1889, addressed to Rabbi Joseph Krauskopf, secretary of JPS, a member of the first rabbinical ordination at Hebrew Union College, and a leader of American Reform Judaism: "I have placed over the Holy City the double triangular star, and in the centre of it and under the Child, the Lion and the Lamb, and the sprig of olive leaves—the words: 'Israel's mission is peace.'"[67] Two yods, the tenth letter of the Hebrew alphabet and a traditional connotation of God's name, sit inside the center of a radiant Star of David. Dominating the composition is a child playing with a serpent, which is not mentioned in the biblical passage. A recurring symbol of evil for Ezekiel—earlier found in *Religious Liberty* and *Eve Hearing the Voice*—the dangerous and duplicitous snake wraps around the boy's arm, tamed by the cherubic child who rests on a compliant lion. A lamb stands quietly nearby, and all species cohabit peacefully near olive leaves, a traditional symbol of peace. Ezekiel's correspondence with Krauskopf does not mention a path leading to the city of Jerusalem, rising resplendently in a Mediterranean landscape behind the central grouping.

Late nineteenth-century readers, both Jews and non-Jews, would see Ezekiel's seal on JPS

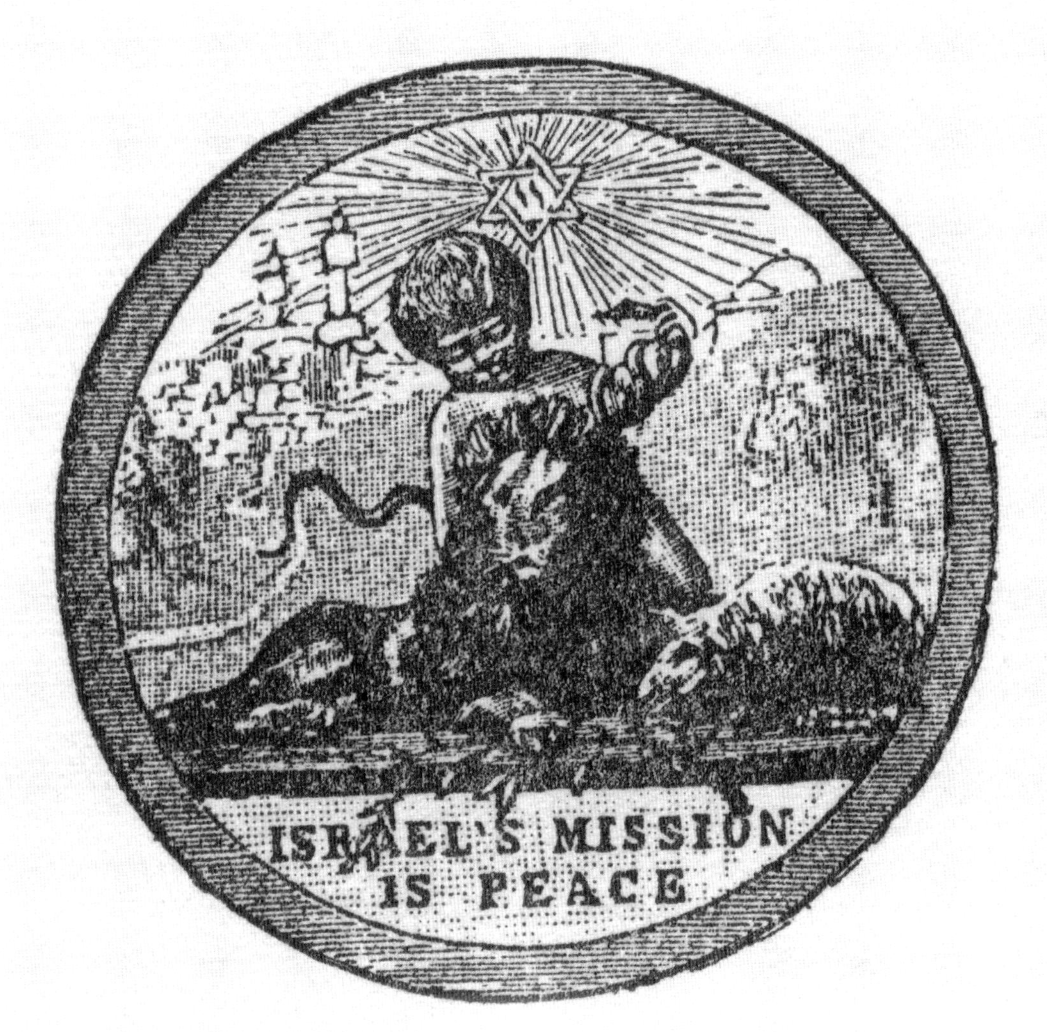

FIG. 40 Moses Jacob Ezekiel, Jewish Publication Society seal, 1889. Photo: Samantha Baskind.

books and come to it with little prior knowledge about the publishing house's goals. What might the insignia communicate about JPS? A good marketing team purposefully adopts an aesthetic to offer a so-called brand identity, as did two of the three earlier American Jewish publishing houses, but Ezekiel's seal does not offer that. The first Jewish press in the United States, the short-lived American Jewish Publication Society, was founded in 1845 by Isaac Leeser, a Philadelphia rabbi and indefatigable writer. That press aimed to distribute Jewish literature but did not use a seal. When a fire destroyed the society's building and most of its

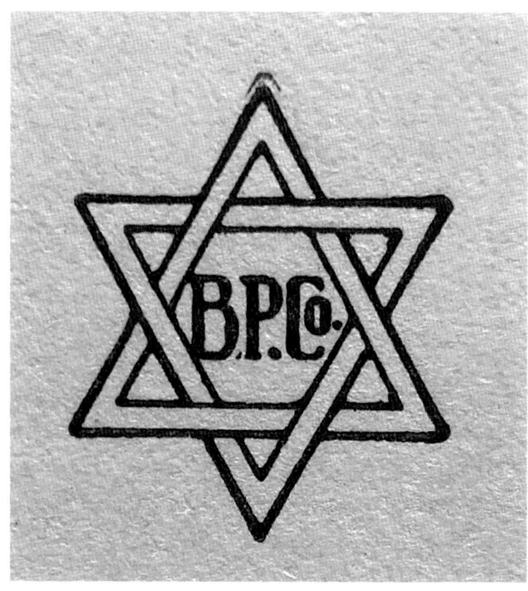

FIG. 41 Bloch Publishing Company seal, 1854. Photo: Samantha Baskind.

books in 1851, the press folded. The family-owned Bloch Publishing Company, which was founded in Cincinnati in 1854 by Isaac Mayer Wise's brother-in-law and published books as well as the *American Israelite*, used a simple legible seal—a Star of David with the press's initials inside (fig. 41).[68] That six-pointed star, now a common identifying symbol for Jews, was brought to America by German immigrants and saw its first conspicuous appearance in an 1845 stained glass program at the Baltimore Hebrew Congregation.

Nearly twenty years after the Bloch Publishing Company was established, in 1871, the Jewish community founded the New York based American Jewish Publication Society, which folded after five years for financial reasons. Most likely influenced by the visual precedent set out by the Bloch Publishing Company, the American Jewish Publication Society likewise utilized a Star of David with identifying initials, "AJPS," inside the star. On either side of the star are apt words that read, "For Torah and for testimony"—based on Isaiah 8:20. Despite Ezekiel's design significantly departing from these precedents and lacking coherence in communicating the purpose of the press, JPS nonetheless accepted the seal. In 1890, the initial book published, *Outlines of Jewish History*, was bound in red cloth with Ezekiel's seal embossed in gold on the cover. General readers, mostly Jews but also non-Jews, as well as Jewish schools, used the volume as a teaching tool for decades.

A year after JPS's founding, *The Menorah*, a B'nai B'rith journal billed as a monthly magazine for the Jewish home, reported that the first book was in the works, discussed the press's financial situation, and found it important enough to reprint Ezekiel's recent letter about the seal. Along with the original letter, Ezekiel sent a woodcut and two metal copies of his design, expressing his hope that the board would accept the work and that JPS "has for its main object[ive] the perpetuation of the interests and objects of pure Judaism."[69] Ezekiel was greatly troubled by the loss of "pure Judaism" as shown in his 1873 bas-relief for the Michael Beer Prize, which reflects his attachment to the return to Israel. He wrote disparagingly about Reform practice in an 1892 letter to Philip Cowen, editor of *American Hebrew*, a widely distributed weekly New York–based newspaper: "The operatic-hat-off ape-ism service is very distasteful to me. The difference between Judaism and *all other* Religions is simply this: Moses created *a people for a religion*—all others created a *Religion* for *the people*—and this latter is what the so called Reformers are attempting."[70] To reiterate, Ezekiel viewed Reform Judaism, for which he had a front row seat when living as a young man in Cincinnati, as a diluted form of the

Judaism he grew up with and preferred. "All the intelligent Christians I have met," he continued, "have *more* respect for a real Jew than one who apes him in a service dedicated to the one God."[71]

Ezekiel moderated his tone in the letter delivering the seal to the Reform rabbi Krauskopf. There, he wrote that even as he believed his first duty was to his country, he looked forward to "the dawn of that immense day when in reality Israel will rule the world, and God's name be acknowledged by the other nations as One."[72] Ezekiel's description contradicts the seal's origins in the book of Isaiah and its iconography, which clearly shows the Land of Israel. Ezekiel prudently measured his language to echo central Jewish prayers (the Shema and the Aleinu) to ensure that the seal would make it past the committee without offending his patrons due to his poor estimation of Reform Judaism. That is, by indicating his hope that the values of "Israel" (standing in as a name for Judaism, which it often did in nineteenth-century American parlance) be accepted by all, he hoped that the committee at JPS would accept his submission. JPS officials firmly agreed that by making the ideas and values of Judaism understandable through literature, this possibility would be furthered. It is curious that JPS approved a visual representation of Isaiah's prophecy for their seal, considering that part of his messianic vision is a rebuilt Jerusalem and some of the press's distinguished supporters and officers were Reform Jews and proud Americans of the same mind as Rabbi Wise. These laypeople included Ezekiel's father, author Simon Wolf of *The American Jew as Patriot, Soldier and Citizen*, and B'nai B'rith Centennial Commission Chair Adolph Sanger, who was instrumental in securing Ezekiel as the sculptor for *Religious Liberty*. After Ezekiel's seal was unveiled, his brother Henry Ezekiel served as a trustee (1892–96) and honorary vice president (1896–98).[73]

The Jewish Publication Society's original announcement in 1888 does not help sort out this puzzle. Unsurprisingly, it makes no mention of messianism. Instead, the notice focuses on the practical aspects of starting the press: what types of books would be published, the costs to join the Society, and its editors' desire to inspire young Jews, educate Christian neighbors, and aspire to good mechanical execution. On more than one occasion, the founding document stressed the nonpartisan, balanced nature of the publication house, one that "favors no special views and supports no particular party. . . . Holding these views the Society escapes the danger of sectionalism and narrowness."[74]

A sermon given by Rabbi Krauskopf to his Philadelphia congregation, "The Need of the Hour," delivered in December 1887, speaks to JPS's origins and may shed light on why Ezekiel designed the seal as he did. Krauskopf urged American Jews to cast aside their "awful lethargy" and remember their "proud *mission*," namely to disseminate the words of the Torah to the world. Krauskopf offered a short story about a "disgraceful predicament," which countered that mission: A rabbi preparing to dedicate a new synagogue could not find a Bible and was forced to borrow a copy of the holy book from a Christian. To that end, Krauskopf exhorted his congregation, quoting the book of Isaiah, "Think of these facts and then of the *mission* of Israel which we repeat so often and with so much gusto, and then of those words of Isaiah: 'And strangers shall stand and feed your flocks'" (61:5).[75]

The book of Isaiah refers to the Jewish people as "a light of the nations," a phrase central to Jewish liturgy and thinking: "I the LORD have called thee in righteousness, and have taken hold of thy hand,

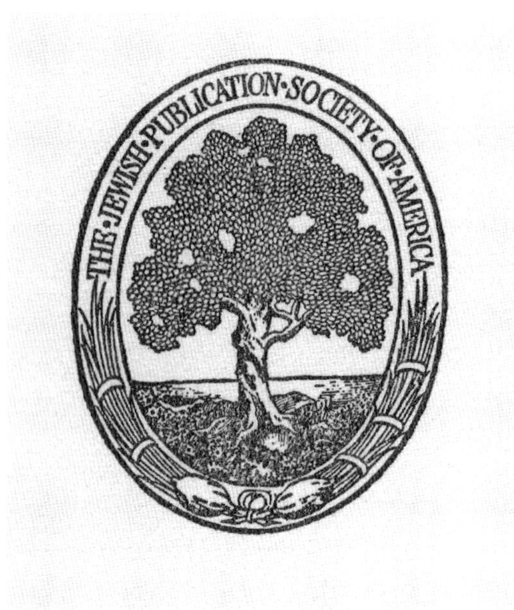

FIG. 42 Jewish Publication Society of America seal, 1906. Photo: Samantha Baskind.

and kept thee, and set thee for a covenant of the people, for a light of the nations."[76] Isaiah continues by invoking imagery of an ideal where strangers feed the Jews' flocks and aliens serve the Jews as plowmen and vine-trimmers. In the end, all will recognize the truth Jews hold, put them on a pedestal, and even serve them. The contemporary situation Krauskopf describes is the exact inverse. It pains him that Jews must seek a non-Jew to find a Bible instead of spreading the values of the Torah themselves. By quoting Isaiah, Krauskopf emphasized this inversion: the current reality in America versus how, as he and the Reform movement believed, Judaism should function and thrive as a unifier of humankind. The rabbi concluded that his coreligionists must support a Jewish publication house in America, because in doing so, Jews would be engaging "in the noble effort of fulfilling Israel's *mission*, of proving ourselves a blessing to all mankind."[77]

Krauskopf's sermons were published weekly and mailed all over the world, making it likely that Ezekiel had read "The Need of the Hour." Further, as the key sermon devoted to the importance of establishing a publishing house in America, for which Ezekiel was designing the seal, the artist would have sought out the spearheading sermon, or it would have been provided to him by Krauskopf or another member of the JPS board. In total, Krauskopf utters "mission" nineteen times in the sermon, which may have informed the textual element of Ezekiel's seal, considering the rabbi's preference for the word. Krauskopf's conception of mission, along with the larger Jewish notion of "mission"—from the B'nai B'rith brothers' creed to the Reformers' goals and beyond—was in step with a larger American concern with mission. The term was in parlance by the young country, still asserting its purpose; most challenging is its rationale of Manifest Destiny, which justified the displacement of Indigenous peoples from their land. American Zionists had their own idea of "mission," rooted in the same use of the idea but to different ends.[78] Then there is Krauskopf's reference to Isaiah; albeit different from Ezekiel's inspiration, it may have set the artist on a path to adopt some element of the book of Isaiah. As best can be surmised, either or both factors provided the artist with a prompt, even if the result was misguided.

Perhaps we should understand the seal as a failed attempt because Ezekiel tried to impart two ideas at once. Or it may be that JPS's first seal remains a conundrum since it was a didactic representation of one man's beliefs, which the press accepted because of Ezekiel's status as a Jewish artist of international importance. Possibly the most liberal JPS board members wanted to understand the seal as conveying the idea that the founding of a publishing house in the promised land of America, where Jewish books could be freely printed and disseminated, signaled something of a metaphorical messianic era. Whatever the case, Ezekiel's seal did not last long because it did not reflect the values and true goals of the press. In 1906, JPS debuted a new seal featuring the Tree of Life (fig. 42). That seal denotes the biblical ideal that learning and wisdom offer "ways of pleasantness, and all her paths are peace. She is a tree of life to them that lay hold upon her, and happy is every one that holdest her fast."[79] These words derive from a prayer that Jews say, or sing, when returning the Torah to the ark, acknowledging the gift of Torah and its study.

Different incarnations of the Tree of Life, some flowery and others stylized, still decorate the press's books as a symbol of knowledge as well as life. The various iterations of the JPS Tree of Life logo disclose more about design history than the Jewish Publication Society or American Jewish history but, most importantly, the seal offers a clear statement for readers. Namely, the updated seal provides an effective brand identity. In its earliest presentation, the logo looks like a formal seal one might find pressed into hot wax—appearing kingly, classic, and important—unlike Ezekiel's seal, which is visually noisy and difficult to read. A brand needs a quick read, and Ezekiel's seal offered anything but that. It was not until the introduction of the Tree of Life logo that the decoration of JPS books legitimized the content within the covers. The new insignia ensured that the publication house's seals and books would finally enjoy a reciprocal relationship.

JPS published a book in honor of the press's twenty-fifth anniversary in 1913, of course decorated on the title page with the newest Tree of Life seal. The book describes JPS history, prints letters of congratulations, and reproduces toasts made at the anniversary banquet, held at Dropsie College, the world's first state-accredited institution to offer a PhD in Jewish studies, founded in Philadelphia in 1907. The last toast extolled the press's silver anniversary and concluded by offering a "fervent wish of a 'sunny' future for The Jewish Publication Society of America." The reprint in the celebratory volume, after the closing encomium, features Ezekiel's discarded seal—the Star of David radiating beams of light like a sun—reproduced under this silly play on words.[80]

Culminating His Zionist Agenda (and Subordination)

Ezekiel's final religious-themed work was a 1909 stained glass window, commissioned in memory of Rabbi Wise for Philadelphia's Temple Keneseth Israel, the sixth-oldest Reform temple in the United States (founded in 1847). That window ideologically and visually culminated the artist's Zionist ideas. Tragically, Keneseth Israel's building burned in a fire in 1972, nineteen years after the synagogue had been acquired by Temple University for use as their law library. The stained glass artistic program can only be discerned through Ezekiel's one surviving sketch and descriptions of the design in various archival documents. Ezekiel's memorial window was dedicated on January 21, 1909, during the Twenty-First Council of the Union of American Hebrew Congregations, which met in Philadelphia that year. The *New York Times* provided advance coverage of the convention and a daily itinerary, making special notice of the dedication. The paper projected that the window, for which no details

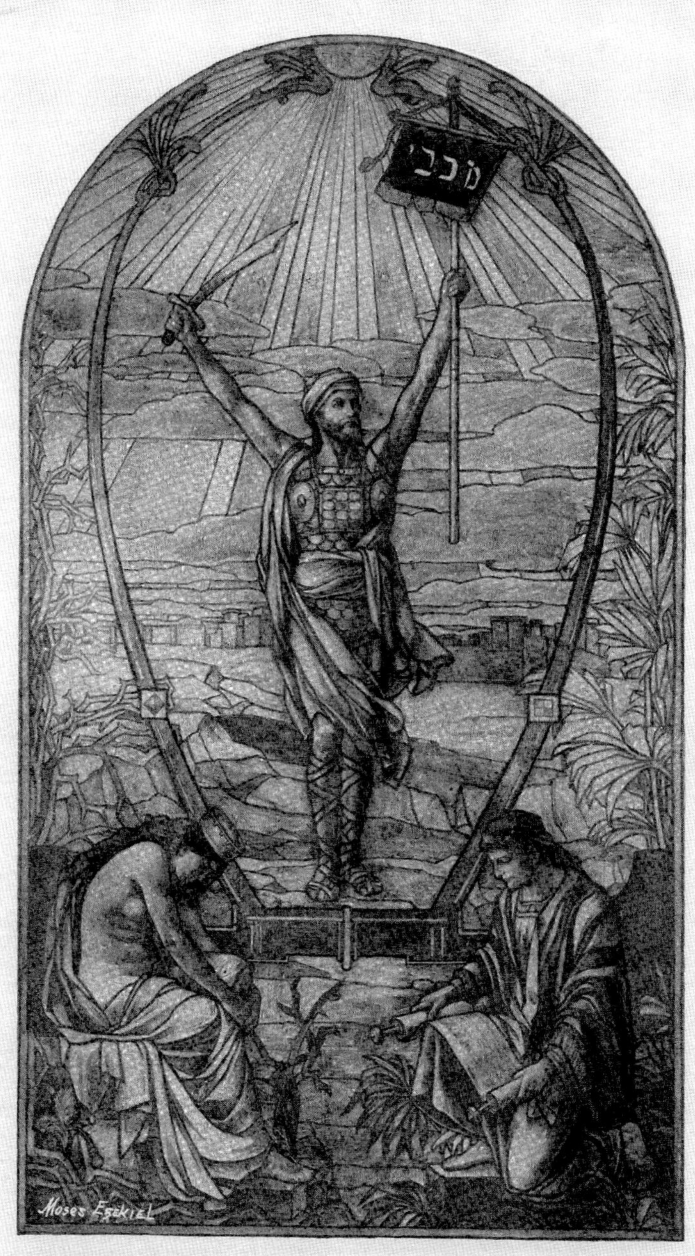
Moses Ezekiel

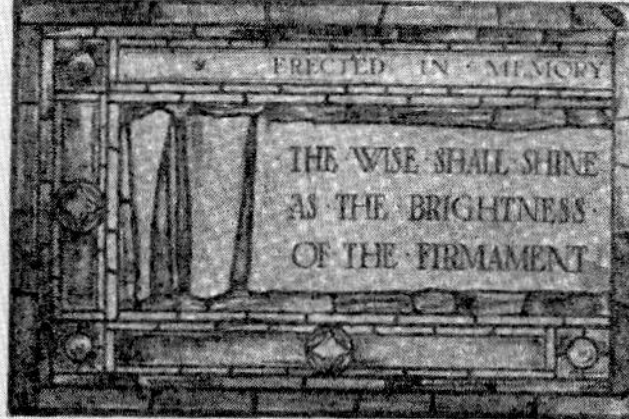
ERECTED IN MEMORY
THE WISE SHALL SHINE
AS THE BRIGHTNESS
OF THE FIRMAMENT

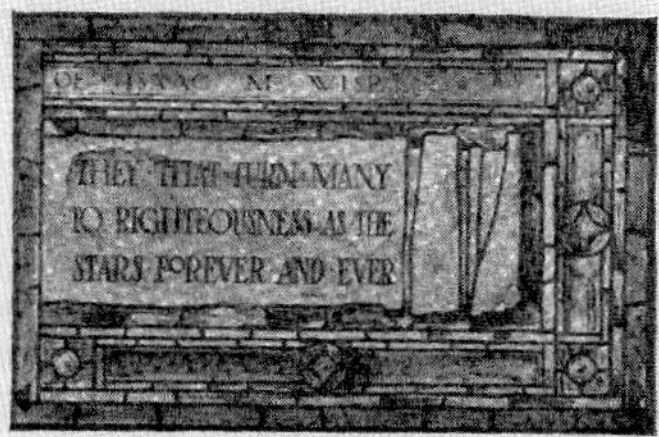
THEY THAT TURN MANY
TO RIGHTEOUSNESS AS THE
STARS FOREVER AND EVER

were yet available, would be so popular that reproductions in both black and white and color were to be made for Jewish homes.[81]

A short program for the ceremony contains Ezekiel's sketch of the window and portraits of both Ezekiel and Wise: Alfred Stieglitz's 1894 photograph of Ezekiel and a print of Wise. On the verso of a spread that shows Wise's portrait is a letter from the president-elect, William Taft, addressed to Krauskopf, rabbi of the congregation. In that letter, Taft—a Cincinnatian by birth who had visited Ezekiel's Roman atelier in 1902—politely declined Krauskopf's invitation to attend the dedication, because he was resting down south before he assumed the presidency. Taft offered fulsome praise for the deceased rabbi: "I knew Doctor Wise in his lifetime, and knew the universal character of his genius and of his interest, and have great veneration for his memory. . . . I am very glad to know that you are preparing such a suitable memorial for a man who certainly deserved well of his country and people."[82] The window was lauded in news coverage of the convention: "The conception and execution of this figure are of rare power and beauty."[83]

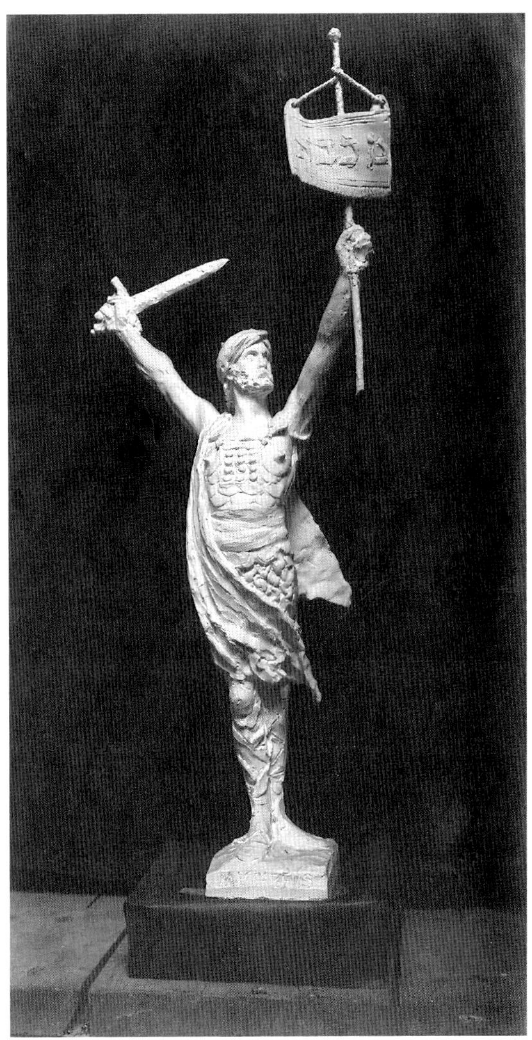

FIG. 43 (OPPOSITE) Moses Jacob Ezekiel, sketch for *Isaac Mayer Wise Memorial Window*, circa 1909. Beth Ahabah Museum and Archives, Richmond, Virginia.

FIG. 44 Moses Jacob Ezekiel, *Judah Maccabee*, circa 1909. Clay model (lost). Photo: Virginia Military Institute Archives, Lexington.

Placed in the southern wall of the synagogue and fabricated by Goodham Company of New York, based on Ezekiel's design (fig. 43), the window symbolized "the ideals and aspirations of the master of Reform Judaism in America," according to Keneseth Israel's board minutes.[84] In line with a clay rendition of Judah Maccabee by Ezekiel (fig. 44), the centrally placed warrior holds a sword aloft in one hand and in the other brandishes a banner emblazoned "Maccabee" in Hebrew. Judah Maccabee stood proudly at the window's center, "typifying the militant spirit of Wise," as a leading Reform rabbi wrote at the time.[85] The consecration speech delivered by the temple's leader, Rabbi Krauskopf, similarly describes Judah Maccabee as the perfect choice to personify Wise: "No truer likeness of the life and needs of Isaac M. Wise could have been conceived than that of the brave and loyal Judas Maccabee." He lifts his sword, "emblematic of the heroic and victorious battles he waged for Israel and Reform, against a foe mightly [*sic*] in number, and as unrelenting as the Syrian enemy of old." In this way, the warrior Wise is hyperbolically connected to a continuum of Jewish "heroes," extending from the biblical text to the modern day. Wise's great accomplishment, Krauskopf continues, was the antithesis of Ezekiel's beliefs: "He purified and rededicated the Temple of Israel. With the one hand he cleansed it of the mildew and decay which long and dark ages had imposed upon it, with the other he gave to American Israel that trend and vigor, that light and life which have made possible its mourning to turn into rejoicing, its despair into hope."[86] For Reformers, Wise was a hero. For Ezekiel and more traditional Jews, he espoused a watered-down version of Judaism that abandoned core values.

A son of Mattathias, Judah Maccabee in the Wise stained glass memorial is startlingly Zionist in origin. The Maccabees, a symbol for burgeoning Zionist sentiment, invoked ancient fighting Jews of yore for their heroics during the Maccabean revolt against the Syrians. Leo Pinsker's landmark Zionist nationalist pamphlet *Auto-Emancipation*, sparked by the 1882 pogroms, called out the woeful exilic condition of the Jews of his time. He argued for the resettlement of Jewish farmers in Palestine to relieve that condition (as did Ezekiel on this latter point)—by unfavorably comparing them to the valiant Maccabees: "What a miserable role for a nation which descends from the Maccabees!" Pinsker also compared the current Jewish condition to that of Ahasver to spur his coreligionists to provide humanitarian aid for resettlement in Palestine: "We must not admit that we are doomed to play on in the future the hopeless role of the 'Wandering Jew.'"[87] American Zionists, increasing in numbers at the turn of the century but by no means the majority, also saw the Maccabees as an exemplar for their cause. The Federation of American Zionists (later renamed the Zionist Organization of America) published a monthly periodical, titled *The Maccabaean*, from 1901 to 1920. Judah Maccabee as a subject piqued Ezekiel's Zionist interests for these very reasons, and his work unmistakably finds a precedent in an admired 1894 sculpture by Lithuanian-born Boris Schatz, *Mattathias, Father of the Maccabees* (fig. 45). Schatz's plaster model was exhibited to a wide, general audience at the 1900 Paris Exposition.[88]

By then mentored by Mark Antokolsky and living in Paris, Schatz crafted *Mattathias* the same year as the Dreyfus trial. Cast in zinc, it shows the determined aged patriarch in three-quarter view dramatically trampling a Greek soldier, passionately calling for action with his upraised arms and a knife, much like the figure in Ezekiel's stained glass window. Ezekiel's Maccabean figure, however, takes the form of Mattathias's son. Portraying Judah Maccabee allowed him to sculpt a younger, muscular body encased in armor and wind-whipped drapery, in sympathy with his decidedly classical predisposition, rather than a wizened, heroic elder with a flowing beard and long cloak. After influencing Ezekiel's own Maccabee, Schatz's sculpture reached a larger Jewish audience with a photograph published in 1903 in *Ost und West*, which had previously featured Nossig's *Wandering Jew* and later that year Ezekiel's *Israel*.[89] Schatz realized his Zionist ambitions when immigrating to Palestine, where in 1906 he established the art school Bezalel and has since been known as the "father of Israeli art."

To the left of the triumphant Maccabee, a seminude woman bends over in despair, which is a quote from Ezekiel's own bas-relief, *Israel*, symbolizing Jerusalem as a lamenting mother mourning the destruction of the Temple. Certainly, this reference would have been unacceptable if its nuance were understood by the Reformers commissioning the window. Board minutes instead describe the despairing Israel as Judea "mourning over her lost glory," countered on the right with "Judea regenerated, by means of a pupil studying and interpreting the Torah."[90] Ezekiel interpreted the second figure similarly but with a twist, as a "modern young rabbi studying the Torah under the palm leaves of peace (Israel's mission on Earth)."[91] This modified case of "Israel's mission is peace," the complicated formulation that doomed his Jewish Publication Society logo, here directly connects to the importance of Torah and reading—in line with JPS's mission—but merely as an aside in Ezekiel's musings on a stained glass window that had nothing to do with a Jewish press. Thorns nearby these figures denote Israel's suffering, a Christological reference that recalls the thorn imagery in Ezekiel's bronze sculpture *Ecce Homo* (see fig. 26) and accords with Max Rosenthal's painting for a Protestant church in Baltimore that was deemed unfit for display (see fig. 25).

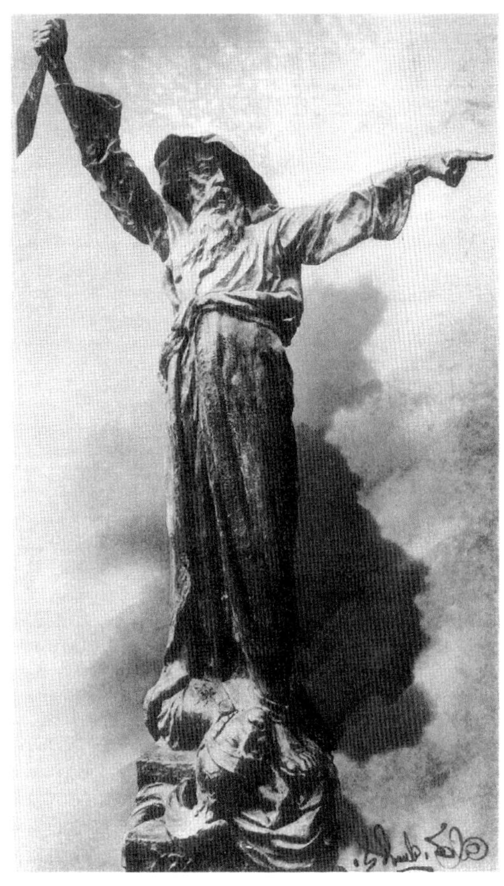

FIG. 45 Boris Schatz, *Mattathias, Father of the Maccabees*, 1894. Zinc (lost), 3 ft.

The overall message of the colorful window's iconographic program was meant to be the regeneration of the Jewish people, a revitalization that many Reformers attributed to Rabbi Wise: "The results of his achievements will partake of the immortality of Israel," Krauskopf declared.[92] Two textual elements incorporated into the window underscore Wise's accomplishments. Across the blazing sun at the top of the completed stained glass, the phrase "Let there be light" appeared in Hebrew, a design not yet present in Ezekiel's surviving sketch. "Let there be light" served as Wise's maxim, prominent on the masthead for *American Israelite*. At the base of the window, an abbreviated inscription from the book of Daniel, visible in Ezekiel's sketch, plays on his surname: "The wise shall shine as the brightness of the firmament. They that turn many to righteousness as the stars forever and ever" (12:3).[93] While this message contradicted Ezekiel's values, the artist adhered to the sponsoring body's request to acclaim Wise. And as might be expected, Ezekiel did manage to insert even more of his own dogma, beyond his allegorical grieving female figure. Ezekiel explained in a letter to his brother that the sun symbolized Jerusalem, contradicting Wise's belief that America, not a faraway country in the Middle East, was the Jerusalem for the Jews.[94]

Although he was hired to create art for American Reform Jews who saw themselves as a religion, not a nation, Ezekiel acted as a contrarian, even something of a sneaky iconoclast. In this final work, he again followed his own ideals rather than faithfully heeding his sponsors' needs. In doing so, he once more muddied the message by trying to express two ideas—inserting his Zionist philosophy while seeking to appease his clients. Ezekiel wanted to create art for the Zionist cause, but his ill-advised designs hindered the success of his conceptions.

Today, his artistic paeans to Zionism are all but gone. The seal has not been used for over a century; the original bas-relief of *Israel* is lost; the reconstituted bas-relief sits in an alcove of a seldom-visited museum lobby on Hebrew Union College's Cincinnati campus; and the stained glass window was devastated by fire. Another tragedy for Ezekiel's art in the current moment is close at hand: HUC Cincinnati will cease ordaining rabbis by 2026.[95] Krauskopf avowed in his consecration speech, "Here, in holy convocation, we pledge anew our fealty to our departed leader. Here we resolve anew to keep inviolate and intact the College, the Union, the Conference of his founding. Here we pledge ourselves to strive in his name, and in his way, so long and so well till our labor shall convert his cry 'Let There Be Light,' into 'There is Light.'"[96] With the college's flagship campus soon no longer inviolate and intact, Ezekiel's marble bust of Rabbi Wise and his cumbersome *Israel* bas-relief will need to find a new home. That may very well be storage in the basement of the New York City or Los Angeles branches of Hebrew Union College, far from Reform Judaism's founding city and even farther from the public eye.

Twelve days after Ezekiel died in 1917, the Balfour Declaration—pledging support for "a national home for the Jewish people" in Palestine—was issued by the British government. Like Moses and Theodor Herzl, both of whom died before they could reach the promised land, Ezekiel passed on before he could know about this significant step toward the eventual establishment of the State of Israel. Nor would he ever visit Palestine; Ezekiel's planned trip was thwarted by World War I.

As committed to Judaism as he was, Ezekiel still marched to his own drumbeat on some matters of spirituality, just as he formulated his own iconographic inventions, no matter the cost. He was a follower of Theosophy and joined the Theosophical Society, frequently visited the Masonic Lodge in Rome, and believed that dreams disclosed important messages, several of which are described in his autobiography.[97] Around the turn of the century, Ezekiel regularly hosted séances and believed he had a guardian spirit named "Donato."[98] Notwithstanding Ezekiel's mystical bent, his interest in the Bible figured prominently in his life and art. Discussed here and in the previous chapter, Ezekiel's biblical works constitute an intriguing portion of his oeuvre. They tell us how a nineteenth-century Jewish artist inflected otherness in his work, how American Jews incorporated the visual in their fledgling institutions, and how perceptions of Zionism diverged during a crucial moment in modern Jewry.

EZEKIEL, THE ARTS, AND THE ANTIQUE *Chapter 4*

I have a perfect enthusiasm for art, an enthusiasm that fires my whole soul and mind to such an extent that I am willing to relish poverty and every labour that would aid me in securing the object of my ambition.
—Ezekiel, letter to his brother Henry, 1866

The tympanum of the Renwick Gallery on Seventeenth Street and Pennsylvania Avenue in Washington, DC, features a relic of the building's past (fig. 46). A round medallion with a larger-than-life bronze relief profile portrait, distinctly drawing on Roman imperial portraiture, contains the visage of banker William Corcoran, who in 1858 chartered the building as the Corcoran Gallery of Art to house his renowned collection (fig. 47). Ornamental foliage decorates the tympanum, calling further attention to the visionary philanthropist honored inside the medallion. That portrait and the two bronze groups situated above the paired columns flanking the window were commissioned by Corcoran.[1] Desirous to select an American artist to ornament the building's facade, he handpicked Ezekiel for the job.[2]

Even more grand were Ezekiel's seven-foot-tall statues for the building's vacant second-floor external niches (fig. 48), depicting those whom he and Corcoran officials deemed the world's eleven greatest artists: Phidias, Michelangelo, Peter Paul Rubens, Rembrandt, Raphael, Titian, Albrecht Dürer, Leonardo, Bartolomé Murillo, Antonio Canova, and Thomas Crawford. Carved intermittently between 1877 and 1884, the sculptures, long gone from the edifice, have had a peripatetic afterlife. Ezekiel's sculptures of the artists he so ardently revered peppered the land around a swimming pool at a multimillionaire socialite's estate before they journeyed to an art dealer, and then private hands. For a time, one of the statues was on display at a major American art museum. Now reunited, since the 1970s all eleven statues brush against flora

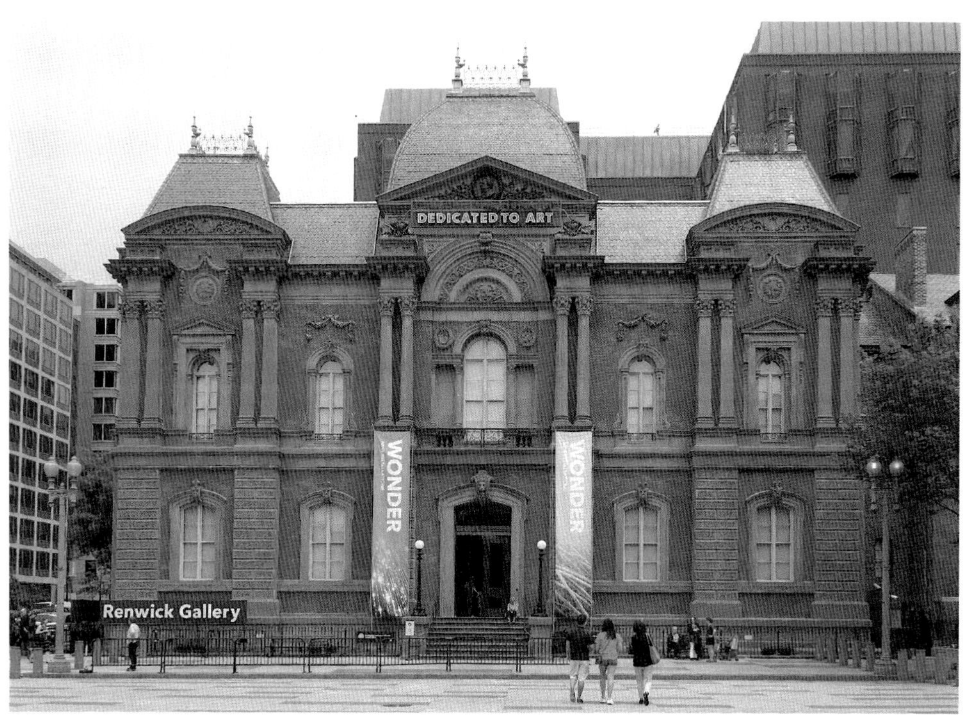
DEDICATED TO ART
WONDER
WONDER
Renwick Gallery

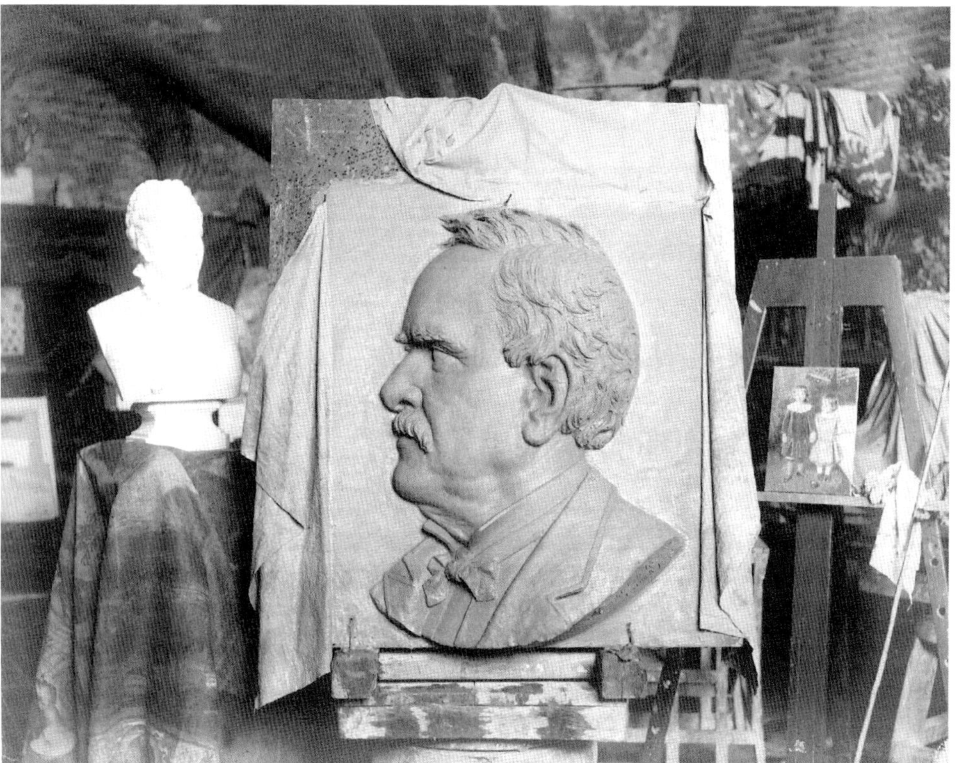

FIG. 46 (OPPOSITE TOP) James Renwick Jr., Renwick Gallery. Washington, DC, 1859–71. Photo: Wikimedia Commons / Tony Hisgett. CC BY 2.0.

FIG. 47 (OPPOSITE BOTTOM) Ezekiel's studio with clay model of Corcoran medallion, 1883. Courtesy of The Jacob Rader Marcus Center of the American Jewish Archives, Cincinnati, Ohio, at americanjewisharchives.org.

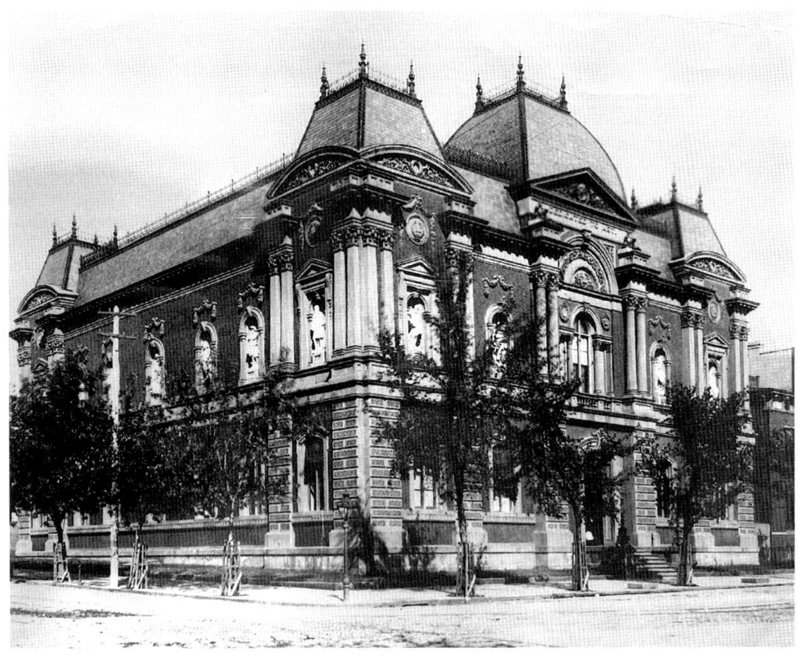

FIG. 48 Corcoran Gallery of Art with Moses Jacob Ezekiel's sculptures installed, circa 1884. Washington, DC. Photo: Virginia Military Institute Archives, Lexington.

and live among fauna at the Norfolk Botanical Garden in Virginia.

Erected at Corcoran's behest, the French Empire–style structure stands as the first building in the United States intended as a public museum for fine art. Placed advantageously in the nation's capital and within walking distance of the White House, the building later took on the name of its architect, James Renwick Jr. In 1861, it stood unfinished, a mere hollow structure. However, during the Civil War, Montgomery C. Meigs, quartermaster general of the Union army, took it over to use as a warehouse for records and uniforms. Eight years passed until Corcoran regained possession of his museum, swiftly restoring and completing it. The building's intended purpose as a repository of art was realized and finally opened to the public in 1874. The *New York Times* praised the new gallery as "a benefaction to the whole country . . . a Gallery of Fine Arts which will rival the most famous collections in the world."[3] By 1890, a second building opened adjacent to the gallery to serve as the Corcoran School of Art. Due to the success of the art school, known as "the Annex," the gallery's growing permanent collection, and the aspiration to mount temporary exhibitions, the Renwick building soon proved too small for its ambitions.

After seven years, the gallery and art school merged in the new Corcoran Gallery of Art, designed by architect Ernest Flagg in a Beaux Arts style with minimal exterior decoration, built just three blocks away. Less than two decades after their completion, Ezekiel's celebratory statues were removed from the original museum's exterior. The *Washington Post* morbidly reported that during their removal, the statues were "suspended by their necks from an improvised gallows," which "strongly resembled a lynching," before they were unceremoniously deposited in the back courtyard of the new building.[4] Ezekiel was as crushed by the short life of his sculptures as he was thrilled by receiving the prestigious contract. Summarily dismissed, his art was subject to the vagaries of taste, and not for the last time. The destruction and loss that plagued the Corcoran fiasco have extended to many other works in Ezekiel's oeuvre.

The odyssey of Ezekiel's Corcoran Gallery sculptures allows for a larger discussion about nineteenth-century art: its commissions, patronage, and architectural decoration; the establishment and goals of a museum in a young country only just assembling substantial collections; and the afterlife of works of art, considering how the Corcoran sculptures' intended function and meaning have been lost with their relocations. Yet, in their current home, they have garnered a different kind of attention that has unexpectedly extended the life of these sculptures, which had fallen into disfavor by the time they were removed from the Corcoran's facade. The Corcoran endeavor gave Ezekiel a taste for rendering men of the arts whom he esteemed, but the sculptor did so at great personal cost—physically, emotionally, and financially. Ezekiel surely had his heroes and, as the following pages will show, the immortals of his imagination—artists, musicians, and poets—surpassed the Confederates for which he is better known, if known at all.

The Corcoran Commission

Three years after the gallery opened, the board of trustees, a group of nine men to whom Corcoran deeded the building along with a $900,000 endowment (he deeded his art collection in 1873), finally set their sights on its decoration.[5] Corcoran's fateful encounter with Ezekiel led to a solution for his eponymous gallery's bland exterior. The art collector gave Ezekiel a tour of the collection when the sculptor visited the nation's capital after the unveiling of *Religious Liberty*. Recollecting that pleasant interlude, Corcoran wrote to Ezekiel in Rome about his thoughts on adornments for the front niches. Ezekiel suggested that statues of great artists, specifically Michelangelo and Raphael, would look handsome standing in the two front niches closest to the central window. Surprisingly, considering he was hoping for the assignment, Ezekiel also recommended two sculptures of idealized female nudes to serve as allegories of painting and sculpture. Ever ambitious, he advocated for the artist statues to flank the allegories in the outermost niches.[6] By 1877, the board approved the making of heroic sculptures for the facade's four front niches, choosing Phidias (fig. 49), Raphael (fig. 50), Michelangelo, and Dürer (fig. 51) at a cost of $600 per statue.[7]

Several years of transatlantic correspondence ensued, which included sketches, photographs, and negotiations over payment. Ezekiel initially asked for $1,000 per sculpture but was rebuffed. At other times, while toiling in Rome, he inquired about extra remuneration or complained about the agreed-on price.[8] Ezekiel rejected the suggestion that the sculptures be sandstone, which he felt was not durable enough, and recommended bronze-galvanized zinc, a cost-sensitive proposal on his part.[9] In later correspondence, which included photos of a marble *Faith* and plaster *Eve* for consideration, he pointed to second-class Carrara marble as the best possibility but noted that this would be more costly.[10] The Corcoran board did not authorize an increase in payment for marble but, nevertheless, Ezekiel agreed to proceed:

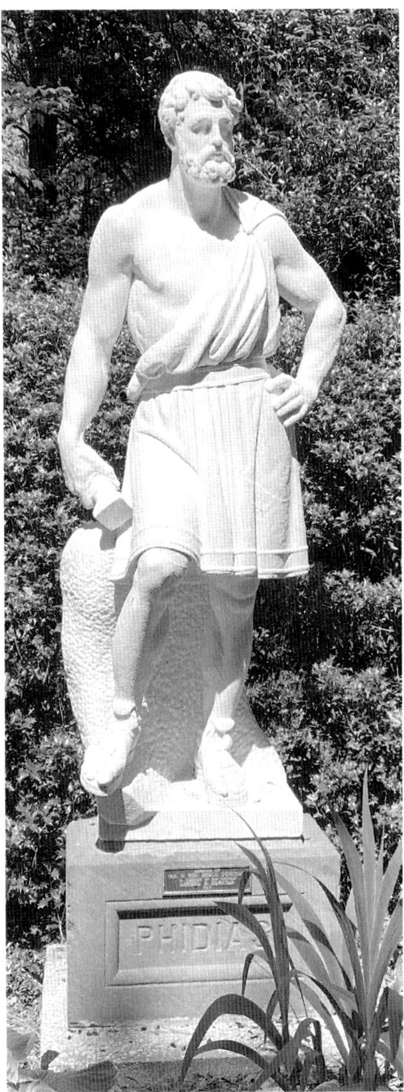
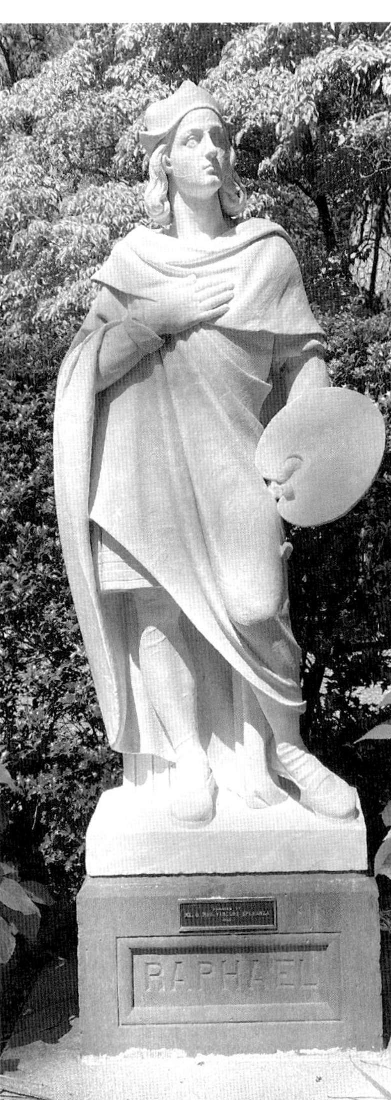

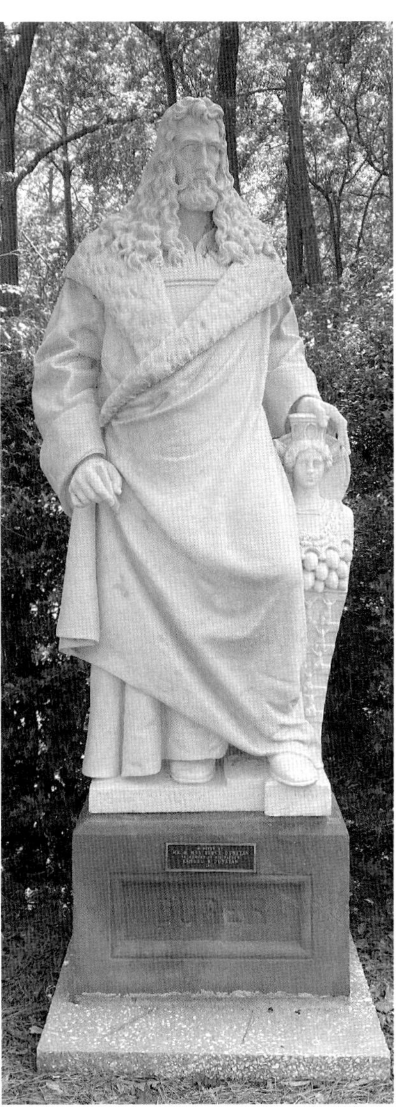

(LEFT TO RIGHT) FIG. 49 Moses Jacob Ezekiel, *Phidias*, 1879. Marble, 7 ft. Norfolk Botanical Garden, Virginia. Photo: Samantha Baskind.

FIG. 50 Moses Jacob Ezekiel, *Raphael*, 1879. Marble, 7 ft. Norfolk Botanical Garden, Virginia. Photo: Samantha Baskind.

FIG. 51 Moses Jacob Ezekiel, *Albrecht Dürer*, 1880 Marble, 7 ft. Norfolk Botanical Garden, Virginia. Photo: Samantha Baskind.

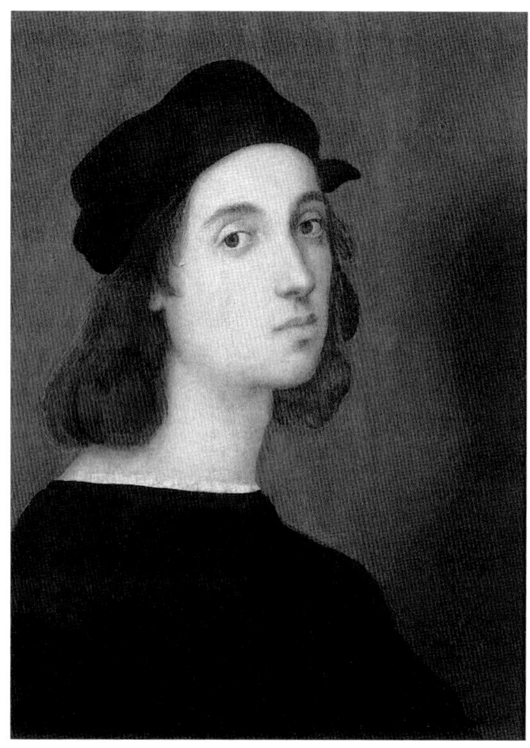

FIG. 52 Raphael, *Self-Portrait*, 1506. Oil on panel, 18.7 × 13 in. Uffizi Gallery, Florence. Photo: Wikimedia Commons.

FIG. 53 (OPPOSITE) Moses Jacob Ezekiel, *Titian*, 1881–83. Marble, 7 ft. Norfolk Botanical Garden, Virginia. Photo: Samantha Baskind.

"I have concluded to do them . . . of course it will not be a profitable work. . . . It is work at least wherein I can show in Washington what I am capable of doing."[11] Moreover, Ezekiel agreed to chisel the statues in marble at whatever price the board named: "It would be my especial pride to produce artistically good work without reference to the price, such as would most fitly add to the character of the 'Corcoran Gallery of Art.'"[12]

As Ezekiel labored, he wrote from Rome to Corcoran and the gallery's curator, William MacLeod, about his progress, and provided sketches and photographs at various times. Assessments of the sculptures' quality from those photographs gave MacLeod pause. In his journal, MacLeod remarked that *Raphael's* pose was "as bad as anything I ever saw in sculpture"; *Michelangelo* looked "deformed"; and *Dürer's* treatment was hampered because there was no overt sign of his status as an engraver, since he only held a pencil in his hand.[13] *Raphael* and *Phidias* arrived first, traveling by steamer and train to Washington, DC, in November 1879, when again MacLeod voiced uncertainty. He was hesitant about the color of the marble and judged Phidias's face as "not as strong and Grecian as it might be," but he was more satisfied with Raphael.[14] Phidias's face does have Roman features, but his clothes, a toga and sandals, are appropriately Greek in appearance.

Throughout the cycle, Ezekiel gave close attention to each figure's attire and took great care with the artist's faces. In this case, allegory was rejected in favor of literalism with some flourishes. Raphael resembles his quarter-length *Self-Portrait* in the Uffizi Gallery (fig. 52). Ezekiel adopted Raphael's three-quarter view of his face and askew cap, with the Renaissance painter's flowing cloak derived from his imagination. Dürer's stern physiognomy is based on one of the artist's self-portraits, familiar to Ezekiel from his time in Germany. In 1500, Dürer depicted himself with the long hair of the Nazarene (Alte Pinakothek, Munich), styling himself in the character of a type of Jesus, the Salvator Mundi, which Ezekiel adeptly captures. Responding to a letter from MacLeod, Ezekiel defended his choice of Dürer's attire, stating that he was sure the German painter's clothing "is historically correct" and based on a work by the artist.[15] From his studies in Germany with Albert Wolff, who in turn was trained by Christian Daniel Rauch, Ezekiel must have known of the latter's full-length bronze homage to Dürer (1849) in a Nuremberg plaza.

That figure wears a similar heavy cloak, adopts the same posture, and is shown as a Nazarene. For extra flavor, Ezekiel's *Dürer* rests his hand on a tall replica of the multibreasted Diana of Ephesus, an ancient statue imitated during the Italian Renaissance (e.g., by Raphael in the Vatican), including its adoption as a source for a fountain at the Villa d'Este at Tivoli, where Ezekiel summered at various times. *Titian* (fig. 53), to name another instance, closely coincides with his *Self-Portrait* in Berlin's Gemäldegalerie (ca. 1550), which Ezekiel saw when studying at the Academy. In accordance with the self-portrait, Ezekiel's sculpture shows Titian with his head cocked toward his right shoulder, his lapel tucked underneath his coat, two chains hanging around his neck, and his long thin beard and skullcap.

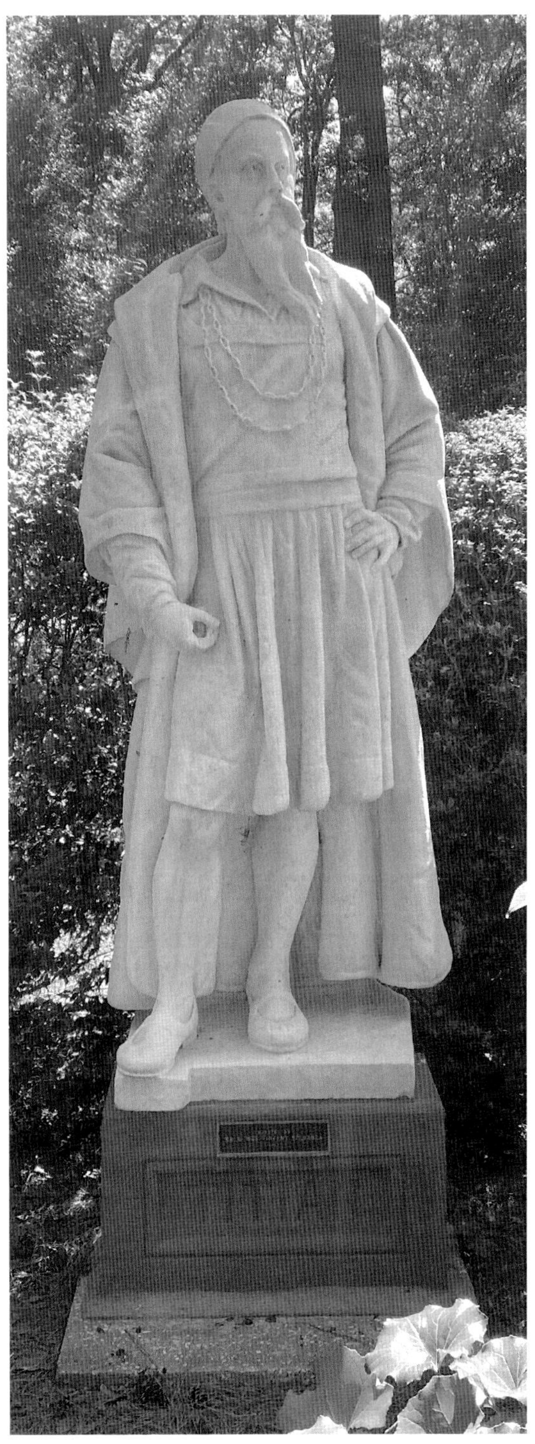

Even though Ezekiel sent measurements, the pedestals already installed in the second-floor exterior niches proved too high and were promptly redesigned.[16] Three months after arriving, in late January 1880, *Phidias* took his place to the left of the facade's center Palladian window, and *Raphael* to the right. *Dürer* and *Michelangelo* were raised into their niches on the Pennsylvania Avenue side soon after reaching American soil eight months later. Despite their reservations, in fall 1880, MacLeod and Corcoran concurred to order seven more statues, again at a cost of $600 apiece plus freight and pedestals, to fill the remaining niches on the building's Seventeenth Street side.[17] With a partiality to Italian art, Ezekiel suggested Giotto, Donatello, Leonardo, Benvenuto Cellini, Titian, Rubens, Rembrandt, and Canova as the final statues.[18] Ezekiel was following his own preferences but also a certain roster of artists who were canonized in late nineteenth-century art books. These popular books consistently repeated the same core group

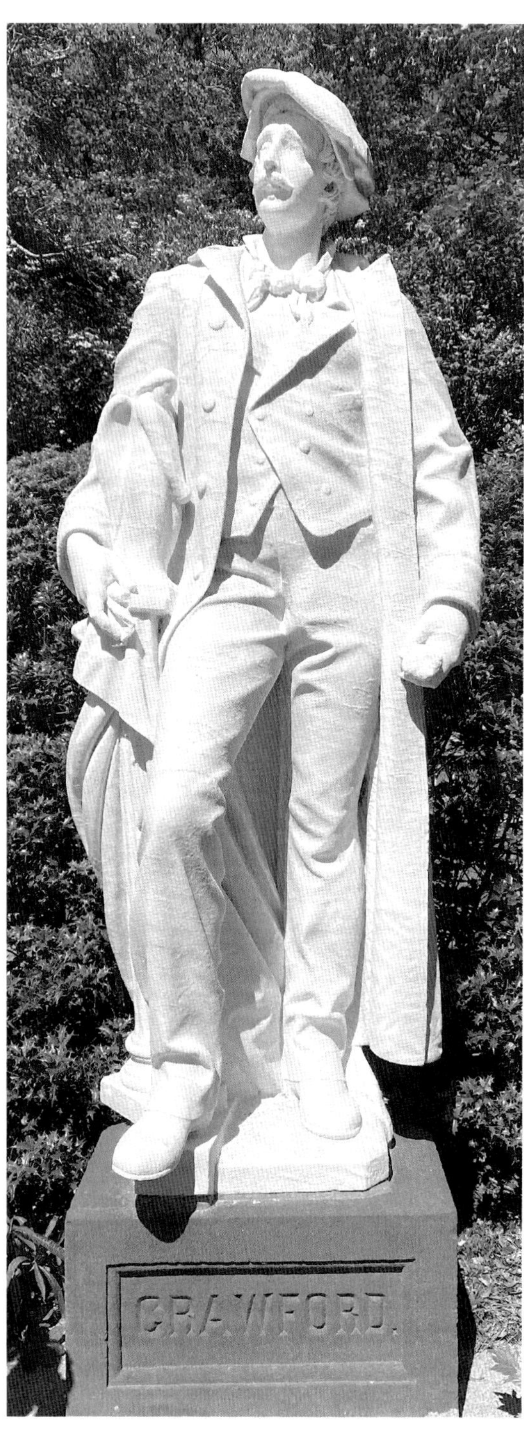

FIG. 54 Moses Jacob Ezekiel, *Thomas Crawford*, 1884. Marble, 7 ft. Norfolk Botanical Garden, Virginia. Photo: Samantha Baskind.

of white, male, European artists that ultimately appeared in the Corcoran niches.[19] Ezekiel pleaded for $650 each, explaining that $600 only covered material expenses, and he asked for an advance, which was approved.[20] Regarding Ezekiel's choice of artists, Corcoran noted that no American was slated to decorate the facade, and eventually the board's final choices differed slightly from those proposed by Ezekiel; he mentioned Anthony van Dyck and Paolo Veronese at different times as well.[21] *Leonardo, Titian, Rembrandt, Rubens, Murillo, Canova*, and the lone American and somewhat contemporary artist, *Thomas Crawford* (fig. 54), were all installed by June 1884.

The sculptor Crawford most especially aligned with Corcoran's goal of championing American art. The gallery's charter stated that the museum would be "used solely for the purpose of encouraging American genius, in the production and preservation of works pertaining to the 'Fine Arts' and kindred objects,"[22] although that mission was not always upheld. The most feted work in the collection though, American or not, was the first replica of Hiram Powers's *Greek Slave*, purchased in 1851. It held pride of place in the center of the Octagon Room on the gallery's second floor. Corcoran paid the highest price to date for a work by a living American when, in 1876, he acquired Frederic Edwin Church's painting *Niagara* for $12,500.[23] *Niagara* was just one of many American landscapes purchased by the patron, who desired American art to showcase the national character and to validate his patriotism, which Corcoran felt the need to defend after his self-imposed exile in Europe during the Civil War due to his Southern sympathies.[24] It cannot go without mentioning that Corcoran may have also been drawn to Ezekiel as the sculptor for his building's decoration because of the pair's common Southern loyalty and friendships with Robert E. Lee. The philanthropist donated funds for a monument to the general after his death, and later for his mausoleum. Corcoran presided over the general's memorial service in Washington, DC, and even served as the vice president of the Southern Historical Society of Richmond, Ezekiel's hometown.[25]

Crawford, too, aligned with Ezekiel's sensibilities. A generation earlier, when neoclassical sculpture thrived and Ezekiel would have found greater satisfaction, Crawford expatriated permanently to Rome—the first American to do so—and achieved great success. More than once, Ezekiel looked to Crawford's art as a model; most visibly, his *Statue of Freedom* atop the Capitol building stimulated *Religious Liberty*. It is possible that Crawford's full-length *Raphael* (1855; High Museum of Art, Atlanta) influenced Ezekiel's Corcoran conception, although it is uncertain whether he ever saw the marble. Smartly dressed in a vest, heavy coat, and askew cap, Ezekiel's *Crawford* jauntily stands with one leg forward in exaggerated contrapposto and holds a sculptor's tool in his left hand. No doubt, the superstitious Ezekiel, who never believed in coincidences, saw some plan of a mystic kind when Corcoran later purchased Crawford's winged marble *Peri at the Gates of Paradise* (1859; National Gallery of Art, Washington, DC), which Ezekiel's statue cradles in replicated miniature.

Nodding to artistic tradition, Ezekiel distinctly signed all but two of the statues with the Latin "Opus," a common practice in both antiquity and quattrocento Italian art. To name two examples, the monumental *Dioscuri* in Rome is signed thus, and Donatello, whom Ezekiel greatly favored, signed his *Judith and Holofernes* "OPVS/DONATELLO/FLO." After shipping *Phidias* and *Raphael*, Ezekiel decided to use this convention, with a numbering system that begins with Michelangelo, signed "ME OPUS XLVIII ROMA 1880," and continues roughly chronologically. Ezekiel signed other sculptures "Opus" around this time—for example, an 1879 bronze bust of munitions maker Benjamin Hotchkiss as "Opus XLV" (University of Cincinnati). But there is a lack of consistency as to which subjects were designated "Opus," making it unclear why some sculptures received this designation while others did not. Nevertheless, by associating his art with the great masters he admired and with the classical past, Ezekiel aimed to demonstrate quality and authenticity, thereby creating an aura around the sculptures. Such a mark, more conspicuous than Ezekiel's formulaic signature, creates a performative flourish that calls special attention to the artist and his art. These signatures were meant to assert his authority and artistic identity, creating a tie between himself, his esteemed predecessors, and the heritage of classicism.

In their original environment, the Corcoran facade's statues provided a glimpse through the precursors to what visitors would discover inside the gallery. They even served as a pleasurable yet didactic introduction to exemplars worthy of emulation and rivalry for nineteenth-century artists, some of whom Corcoran collected and knew personally. Michelangelo, Leonardo, and the other Greek and European artists embellishing the building were great masters, to be sure, so the American artists within the walls of the Corcoran, whom visitors would soon see, kept good company and ably extended the traditions of their honored forerunners.[26] But the architect of the new Corcoran building, a monolith devoid of ornament, did not design the structure to accommodate or feature

Ezekiel's sculptures, nor did the curators intend for them to be displayed inside the gallery. They were not even considered for the vast sculpture hall, filled with originals as well as dozens of plaster casts of major sculptures, among them the *Elgin Marbles*, *Discobolus*, and *Venus de Milo*.

Just a few years after Ezekiel's sculptures were set on their pedestals, in 1899, the Fifth Avenue facade of the Metropolitan Museum of Art in New York City was decorated with Karl Bitter's modest medallions representing six artists—Donato Bramante, Albrecht Dürer, Michelangelo, Raphael, Diego Velásquez, and Rembrandt—figures more appropriate for a survey museum than one dedicated to "American genius." (Phidias and Beethoven were among the suggested options that were not selected for the Met's facade.) Bitter also designed four caryatids representing the arts: painting, sculpture, architecture, and music.[27] But with the Corcoran Gallery's shifting identity and the increased focus on American art inside its walls, the European masters of a bygone era, whether crafted in marble by an American or not, made Ezekiel's monuments seem defunct. The European masters' position as role models was no longer the chief message the Corcoran Gallery wanted to convey. Thus, Ezekiel's sculptures were erased, became invisible, deemed a relic of the all-too recent past, in meaning, style, and subject. Instead, on the front of the new Corcoran building, eleven names were inscribed across the lintel in a simple manner. They include some that are in line with Ezekiel's statues but cover a wider geographical area and a longer time period. Curiously, still only one American artist, Washington Allston—a friend of Corcoran—joined the storied group, which no longer included Crawford. Winding around the top of the rounded structure in birth order are the names of traditional greats: Phidias, Giotto, Dürer, Michelangelo, Raphael, Velásquez, Rembrandt, Rubens, Joshua Reynolds, Washington Allston, and Jean-Auguste-Dominique Ingres.

The Afterlives of the Corcoran Sculptures

It goes without saying that the Corcoran sculptures' meaning changed after their various transits and physical displacements, quite remarkable considering the immobility of marble; each sculpture weighs approximately 1,500 pounds. Such a fate compares to works produced in the service of religion that are removed from the altar of a church and placed in museums. Another correlative is the afterlife of Works Progress Administration murals when their sites are repurposed, the murals relocated, or, in some instances, aesthetic or iconographic attitudes change, rendering their imagery controversial if understood ahistorically. Not only did Ezekiel's sculptures lose their site specificity when ripped from their context, but once removed from the facade of a building devoted to art, the statues were brought to the ground, which was not how they were meant to be viewed. Ezekiel designed the statues to be positioned within the measurements of the niches and permanently seen from below, and thus MacLeod's concerns when the sculptures arrived in Washington were mostly allayed once they had been hoisted to the second floor. Mindful of the sculptures' high vantage, Ezekiel cleverly signed *Phidias* on the sole of his right sandal. Just as relevant, in the years that the sculptures were separated, they were adrift without their companion pieces, which were vital for the larger program. The sculptures' placement was integral to their meaning, and their eventual displacement detrimental to the intended effect.

The statues' peregrinations merit further consideration for the ways they have subsequently been appropriated—initially debased and then surprisingly coveted and valued, much more than in their own day. After the sculptures were dismissed by the Corcoran, Washingtonian Evalyn Walsh McLean, who owned the forty-five-carat Hope Diamond, bought them to decorate the land around her swimming pool. She saw the statues as pretty trifles that served her purpose as a free-spending collector of beautiful things and a high-flying socialite. Thus, they were acquired as ostentatious conversation starters but certainly not the types of conversations Ezekiel imagined as he labored. When McLean's possessions were auctioned in 1948 to pay inheritance taxes, an article in *Life* magazine covered the event. One photograph shows potential buyers walking past the pool with two Corcoran statues visible in the background.[28] All eleven statues were bought by Elam L. Tanner Jr. for his Richmond estate. When Tanner moved four years later, an antique dealer took possession until the statues were purchased by two other Richmonders. Seven were sold to artist Bruce Dunstan and four to Vincent Speranza, all for less than $200 apiece. Dunston bequeathed *Crawford* to the Virginia Museum of Fine Arts in 1952, where it stood on a second-story terrace.[29] The terrace was closed to the public in 1954, and *Crawford* again disappeared. In 1960, the sculpture came out of isolation and was placed conspicuously outside the museum.[30]

Over twelve years, the Norfolk Botanical Garden slowly acquired all the statues.[31] In 1962, Marine Colonel J. Addison Hagan—a Virginia Military Institute graduate and Norfolk resident—discovered the sculptures' existence and learned that they were in private hands. He made their recovery and placement in a public venue his mission, motivated in great part by his memory of meeting Ezekiel at VMI during a fiftieth anniversary reenactment of the Battle of New Market, in which Hagan had taken part as a young cadet in 1914 (the sculptor was in the United States for the dedication of his Arlington Confederate monument). At first, Hagan tried to acquire the statues for his and Ezekiel's alma mater, but VMI did not have the funds to support that dream. Hagan did convince Dunstan to donate his six statues to the city of Norfolk, and Speranza to donate two in 1962. The last two sculptures in Speranza's possession came to the garden in 1974. Around this time, Hagan was also instrumental in persuading the Virginia Museum of Fine Arts to permanently lend *Thomas Crawford* to the garden.[32]

Founded in 1938 with a Works Progress Administration grant, the 175-acre Norfolk Botanical Garden is a more public, inclusive garden than those found on eighteenth- and nineteenth-century estates. Classical statuary has decorated aristocratic gardens for centuries, and the sculptures for those spaces are usually planned in tandem with the garden's original design. Ezekiel's sculptures mingle within the Norfolk Botanical Garden's carefully planned Statuary Vista (fig. 55). That long, grassy, and dramatic expanse forms part of a larger project, initiated in the 1960s and 1970s, to create an "International Outdoor Museum of Fine Arts." It includes signage about the donors of the Corcoran statues, information about Ezekiel's life, and, if concerns about the condition of the sculptures were not urgent, a beautiful effect.

The statues have severely deteriorated in their natural setting. Now scarred and disfigured, the

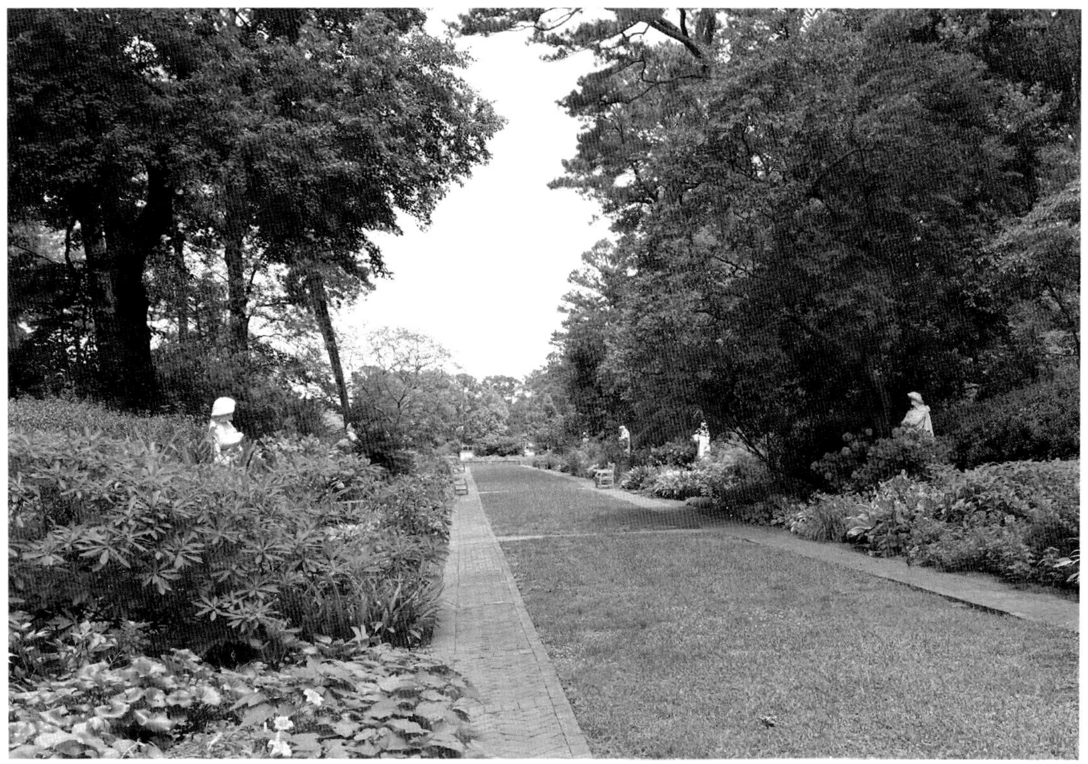

FIG. 55 Norfolk Botanical Garden, Statuary Vista, Virginia, 2021. Photo: Samantha Baskind.

marble has cracked and delicate pieces have broken off. Titian, Rubens, Rembrandt, and Raphael lost their noses, and the hands and fingers, so precious to artists, have broken on multiple statues. Raphael's palette broke long ago, and until a recent restoration Murillo's paintbrush had long disappeared. Lichen and moss growth can be found on all works. The life of Ezekiel's homage to the great artists has been prolonged in a deteriorated state. This in no way implies that the Norfolk Botanical Garden has been negligent. Well aware of damage done by the bitter elements, the institution launched a well-publicized capital campaign in 2013 to raise $500,000 to support the maintenance and restoration of the statues. By 2016, the sculptures were somewhat restored and the surrounding flora replanted to best highlight these artists of time past.

The legacy of Ezekiel's nomadic sculptures ends on a note of irony—and vindication. In 1899, the US Court of Claims moved into Corcoran's gallery and turned the exterior niches into windows. After the Smithsonian took possession of the landmark structure in 1964 and opened the edifice as the Renwick Gallery in 1972, officials finally recognized the worth of ornamenting the building during its renovation and, accordingly, the value of Ezekiel's statues. They approached the Norfolk Botanical Garden about returning the statues and were swiftly rebuffed. The garden instead permitted Italian sculptor Renato Lucchetti to create replicas of Rubens and Murillo. Lucchetti fabricated plaster molds and cast them with a durable marble mix, to which he added a patina to create an aged effect. "Ezekiel's masters," now in reproduction, rise high on red sandstone bases on the Seventeenth Street side, tucked into the only niches that were not converted into windows.

Still another institution desired the sculptures that Corcoran officials so easily discarded. In 1985, the Chrysler Museum of Art in Norfolk requested five of Ezekiel's statues for their building's niches, but again the Botanical Garden declined, arguing that separating the works would be unfavorable and depleting one cultural institution for another in the same city was nonsensical.[33] The Chrysler rejected a suggestion from the gardens to make copies for the niches, and the gardens rejected the Chrysler's offer to pay for reproductions in the gardens.[34]

In its day, the original Corcoran Gallery building was eulogized as the "American Louvre" and an "edifice destined to be sung by all the muses of history as the first Gallery built and endowed and dedicated to a community by an American."[35] The distinguished building, partly modeled on the famed Parisian museum, was indeed proudly "Dedicated to Art," as chiseled in bold capital letters underneath the tympanum featuring Corcoran's portrait. Critics of Ezekiel's statues, however, were not always so laudatory. Ezekiel's work fared poorly in a book about art treasures in Washington; twenty years after the erection of the new Corcoran Gallery, one author looked back at the original building's decoration and wrote, "His [Corcoran's] choice fell naturally upon Ezekiel, who had so notable a record of accomplishment, though the selection was more creditable to his zealous intentions than to his artistic judgment, as results amply proved." She concluded, "The whole idea of the statues was unfortunate, and, with the removal of the Gallery to its present site, no provision was made for them."[36]

Ezekiel had little to say about the Corcoran commission in his memoir, aside from grumbling about the price of his contract: "I knew that I could neither live well nor starve in making statues at such a price. But as artists in all the ages who have ever accomplished anything have always worked for their art and not for the money."[37] The loquacious artist wrote sparsely about his progress or ideas, subjects on which he typically spared few words, especially for major projects. Ezekiel's silence can only be interpreted as a consequence of the devastation he felt at how quickly the statues were cast away as irrelevant detritus. Spoiling away in the foliage and subject to the elements at the Norfolk Botanical Garden, but at least not left unseen in museum storage, detritus is what Ezekiel's homage to history's great artists will quite literally become in a few generations anon.

Franz Liszt, the Master

Ezekiel's Corcoran commission was one of the grandest of his career and unquestionably his most spectacular failure. Concurrently, he received an opportunity to sculpt a different artist that proved more successful, took much less of his time, and brought him immense satisfaction, even if his remuneration did not approach that provided by Corcoran. In 1880, the Royal National Hungarian Academy of Music requested Ezekiel to chisel a marble, half-length sculpture of the virtuoso pianist and composer Franz Liszt (fig. 56; a version of the bust was to be displayed in the censored

Princeton exhibition).[38] *Liszt* is a glorified representation—smartly not by idealization, a fashion that better served the previous generation, but through its striking realism. Liszt's face is framed by richly textured hair brushed off his forehead, which draws attention to his sunken eyes, the deep crevices on his cheeks and brow, as well as the protuberant moles on his left cheek, bridge of his nose, and forehead. He wears a coat buttoned down the front and holds one hand behind his back and the other hand below his breast, with his thumb tucked inside an opening. The maestro's long, thin fingers that proved so adept on the piano receive special consideration. Liszt consented to Ezekiel making a cast of his hands so that the artist could give them their due.[39] Viewers are left to imagine the composer's thoughts as they contemplate his internal stillness. Akin to some Corcoran sculptures, Ezekiel signed his *Liszt* with "Opus," numbered fifty-four. In doing so, he connected the master to a language appropriate for a musician as well as to his own sculptures of artists, broadly understood. Impressed with the bust and enjoying their growing friendship, Liszt wrote in a letter after the bust's completion, "I predict Ezéchiel's final success, particularly in America."[40]

When the marble was finished, Ezekiel crafted a bronze *Liszt*, displayed in the artist's atelier and later at the 1882 French Salon and the 1886 Roman Salon at the Palace of Fine Arts.[41] An art critic for the Italian newspaper *Il popolo romano* effused on the latter showing: "Of the many portrait busts exhibited there is one which has attracted marked attention. . . . The American sculptor has transfused into this work all of his greatest capabilities plastically, for a portrait of Liszt more expressive and lifelike than this one has never been seen."[42] The Grand Duke of Saxe-Meiningen so admired Liszt's portrait that he requested a copy, and Ezekiel, always eager to make money, complied. Subsequently, he created replicas in bronze in different sizes (extant are several eight-inch- and fourteen-inch-tall versions) and no fewer than two marble bust-length statues that did not include the master's arms or hands.[43] Only one marble half-length sculpture remains. In an 1882 letter to Marie zu Sayn-Wittgenstein, daughter of Liszt's longtime lover Princess Carolyne Wittgenstein, the composer writes of a version installed at Schillingsfürst Park, near Marienhof, and one on exhibition at the prestigious Galerie Goupil in Paris.[44] Yet another, a thirty-inch bronze version of the half-length *Liszt*, was sent to America for exhibition at the 1893 Chicago World's Columbian Exposition, a commemoration of four centuries since Columbus's discovery of America. Unfortunately, it arrived after the fair closed, just as Ezekiel's *Religious Liberty* and *Washington* missed their day in the sun at Philadelphia's 1876 Centennial International Exhibition. Eventually located in a storage warehouse, *Liszt* was returned to Ezekiel's brother Henry Ezekiel in Cincinnati. After Ezekiel died, Henry auctioned *Liszt* along with many other works from his brother's estate.[45]

Liszt was his generation's superstar, playing in majestic concert halls, followed by reporters, and venerated by legions.[46] The Hungarian spent considerable time in Rome, often enjoying hospitality at the Villa d'Este in Tivoli, Cardinal Prince Gustav von Hohenlohe-Schillingsfürst's palatial residence. He lived there annually, September to December, from 1870 until 1884. After Ezekiel made the German-born cardinal's acquaintance, the sculptor would stay at an apartment at the Villa for extended periods as well.[47] A patron of the arts in the spirit of his Este predecessors,

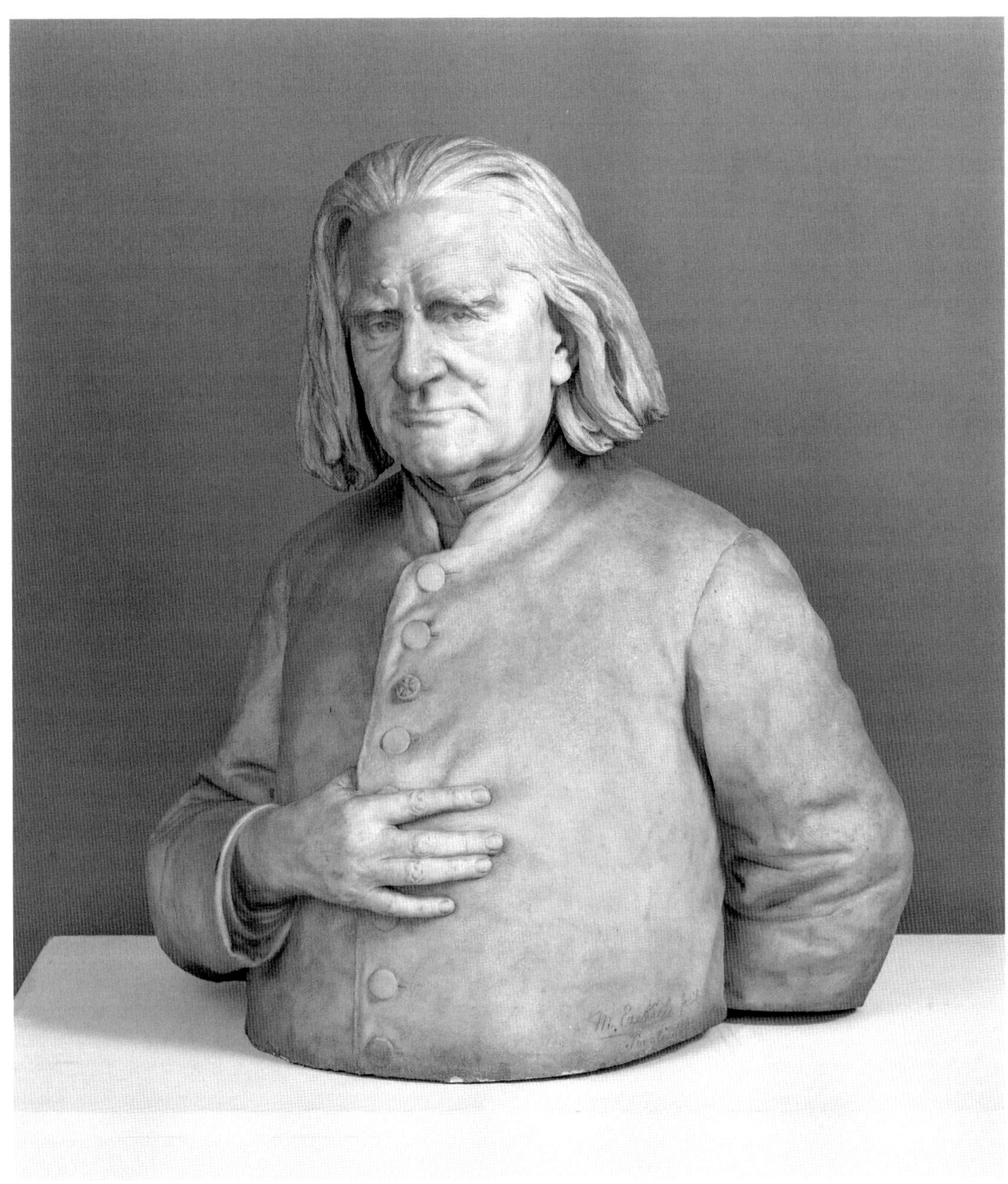

FIG. 56 Moses Jacob Ezekiel, *Franz Liszt*, 1881. Marble, 28 ½ in. Wadsworth Atheneum Museum of Art, Hartford, Connecticut. Presented by the heirs of Dr. Normand Smith, 1903.8. Photo: Allen Phillips / Wadsworth Atheneum.

Hohenlohe-Schillingsfürst restored and maintained the Villa and vast gardens and invited artists beyond Liszt and Ezekiel to enjoy the apartments. His precursor, the cardinal of Ferrara, had the grounds and extravagant fountains decorated with mythological creatures, whereas Hohenlohe-Schillingsfürst was motivated to decorate with religious statuary. One author states that Hohenlohe-Schillingsfürst commissioned Ezekiel to create a statue of *St. Sebastian* around 1890, which was placed in the Fountain of the Unicorn.[48] There is no evidence in Ezekiel's letters or in the posthumous list of works compiled by his family to suggest that he executed such a sculpture, and if he had done so, he would have certainly boasted about it. Hohenlohe-Schillingsfürst did ask Ezekiel to sculpt a marble relief of the *Madonna and Child* (1890s; chapter 2).

In an 1881 letter to Olga von Meyendorff, a longtime friend with whom Liszt kept a sixteen year-correspondence, he remarked on "a young sculptor named after a great prophet, Ezekiel," who "is spending this week at the Villa D'Este . . . working solely on a bust of poor me, larger than life."[49] Ezekiel carved the musician directly from marble during their sittings, the only portrait he ever chiseled from life and the only bust for which Liszt personally sat.[50] That gave the talented men an opportunity to talk, beginning their deep friendship. Ezekiel, who would whistle and hum when sculpting, was queried by Liszt, "What is that you are singing?" To which Ezekiel quipped, "It's a storm-march that was written by a man named Liszt; I don't wonder you don't recognize it!"[51] At another sitting, the two music lovers sang parts of Beethoven's symphonies.[52] Ezekiel's unedited memoir, brimming with details throughout the years about operas, orchestras, and other musical performances he attended, as well as those he hosted, particularly focuses on his time with Liszt.

Just four years into Ezekiel's life in Rome, Liszt received exceeding attention in the sculptor's memoir for the pair's social outings and for concerts that "The Master"—as Ezekiel referred to the composer—played on the upright piano, small organ, and Steinway at his home in the Baths of Diocletian. Ezekiel treasured his conversations with Liszt, discussing Wagner, the composer's son-in-law, and other eminent musicians and composers he knew. Ezekiel was one among many who were drawn to the singularly talented and charismatic Liszt. For Ezekiel, a man who cultivated his own celebrity and loved music, to be close friends with such a dazzling figure and one with alike artistic sensibilities was tremendously appealing.[53] That friendship would last until Liszt died, which Ezekiel mourned as "a sudden and a terrible blow to me."[54] It was Ezekiel who arranged Liszt's memorial at the Villa d'Este, where he placed his bronze bust of the composer on the altar.[55]

During these years, Ezekiel also formed a strong bond with Cardinal Hohenlohe-Schillingsfürst, of whom he produced an animated, waist-length sculpture of the man in his clerical robe, which conveys what Ezekiel experienced as his friend's generosity and convivial personality (1886; fig. 57). That marble bust, which he exhibited at the Via Nationale along with *Liszt*, is long lost, as are several copies.[56] Ezekiel was awarded the honorific title of "Cavalier's Cross of Merit" in 1887 from the Grand Duke of Saxe-Meiningen based on his busts of Liszt and Cardinal Hohenlohe-Schillingsfürst, the latter of which was praised by the European press.[57] Among its accolades, a critic from the Roman daily *Capitan francasa* effused, "It is a marvel of life-like reality," and the German

FIG. 57 Moses Jacob Ezekiel, *Cardinal Prince Gustav von Hohenlohe-Schillingsfürst*, 1886. Clay model (lost). Photo: Virginia Military Institute Archives, Lexington.

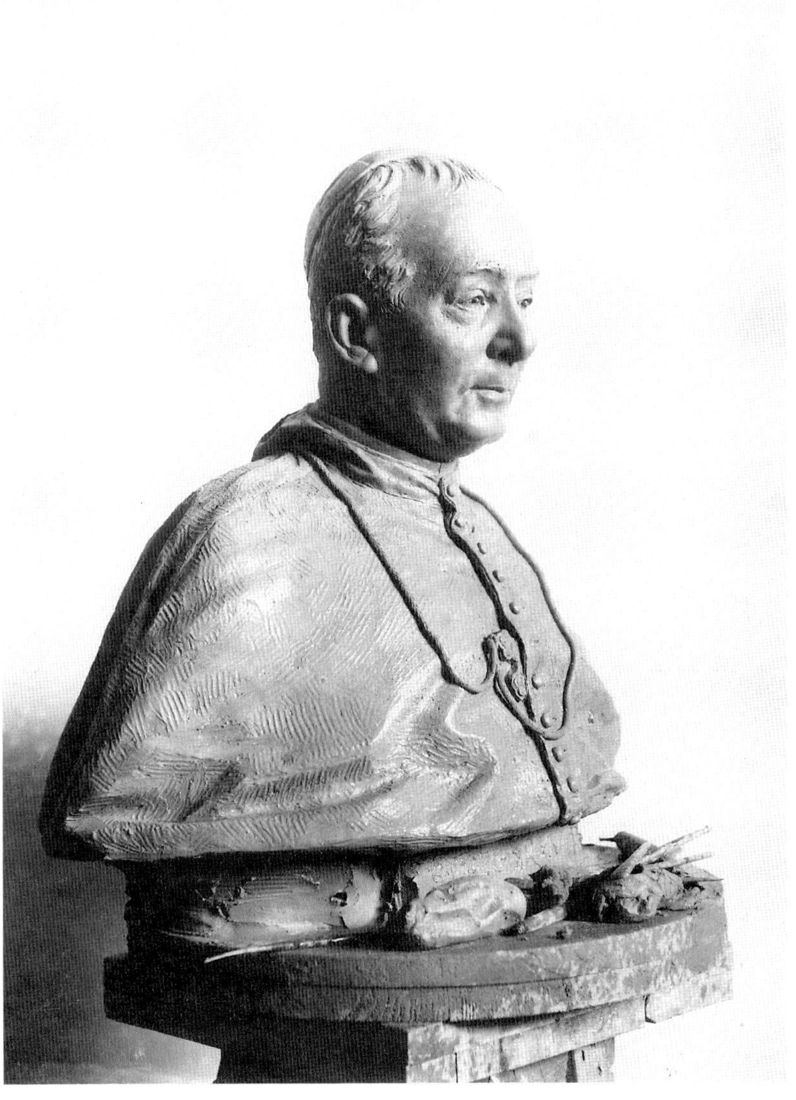

Frankfurter Zeitung described the bust as "one of the most perfect from the hand of this artist."[58] The open-minded Cardinal never disparaged Ezekiel for his Judaism and solidly advocated religious liberty. When Ezekiel formulated a pie-in-the-sky plan "to repopulate Syria and Palestine with refugees [Russian Jews] from barbarism," the cardinal offered his financial support.[59] One speaker at Ezekiel's memorial service in Washington, DC, addressed the relationship between Ezekiel, Liszt, and Cardinal Hohenlohe-Schillingsfürst: "An intimate friendship grew up between these three which lasted throughout their lives. They formed in themselves a lovely trinity of Art, Music, and Religion."[60] The Marine Band even played Liszt's "Liebestraum No. 3" (Love's dream) at the service.[61] While Ezekiel destroyed plaster models for lack of room, he kept either a bronzed version or the plaster model of *Liszt* in his living space until at least as late as 1909, along with his busts of the *Cardinal* and *Longfellow*.

Notably, Ezekiel only preserved two models for his Corcoran sculptures, *Leonardo* and *Titian*, seen for years by visitors to his studio.[62] This was despite the fact that Ezekiel wrote to Corcoran personnel that he would destroy all the models for the gallery's niche statues. Ezekiel claimed that he was asked to make copies of two of the Corcoran Gallery statues for a venue in Rome, unidentified in correspondence, but declined. Instead, he agreed to supply four of the heads for circular niches outside the building, though there is no evidence that the project came to fruition. But Ezekiel depicted one other great artist when he fabricated a now-lost bust of himself, undated, but based on his features from around the turn of the century.[63]

Ezekiel not only admired Liszt and was an amateur enthusiast of music, but he also dedicated his energies to excelling in the arts and championing music. He wrote about his "intense . . . fancy for music" and teaching himself to play piano, violin, and guitar as a child in Richmond, where his grandmother would take him to enjoy live music.[64] Once he lived in the Baths, Ezekiel hosted musical performances every Friday afternoon, and whenever possible he attended the opera and other musical events. The *New York Times* covered one performance: "Mr. Ezekiel now gives those musicales so much prized by foreigners as well as the Romans themselves."[65] In another instance, the *Times* pointed again to Ezekiel's musical events, which were "so popular . . . that no hostess dares to have Friday as a reception day."[66]

Ezekiel sculpted a bust of *Beethoven* (ca. 1893; lost), another musician he revered. Banking on the esteem for figures such as Beethoven, the sculptor fabricated the bust on speculation. No documentation has been found about the sculpture beyond Ezekiel's own admission: "I had never been able to dispose of it."[67] During a visit in 1893, Queen Margherita of Italy admired Ezekiel's *Beethoven* and asked the sculptor about his fondness for music. He replied that the string quartet that played for her each week had honed their skills in his salon for years before they regularly entertained the royal.[68] At that same visit, the Queen Mother spied a marble portrait relief of herself, again one that Ezekiel modeled simply because he wished to do so. He claimed that the queen deemed it very good, but she did not purchase the work.[69] *Beethoven* was hardly the first sculpture that Ezekiel executed without a sponsor, a practice employed by other nineteenth-century expatriate artists, among them Edmonia Lewis. Nearly all his biblical works were made on speculation, and many sat in Ezekiel's studio for years while he tried to sell them to countless visitors he knew, as well as tourists who stopped by. Ezekiel lamented that too many were either never cast or did not find a home. Moreover, his letters are filled with words touting how much those visitors enjoyed his works, in a further effort to sell them through that avenue.

His own best advocate, Ezekiel would take the initiative by enclosing photographs of his work with his ample correspondence and carry photographs of clay models when he traveled to the United States, in the hope of securing sales. In letters to Corcoran, for instance, Ezekiel mentioned available sculptures, among them *Eve Hearing the Voice*.[70] Ezekiel sent photos of a plaster *Eve*, described *Eve*'s inclusion in Vosmaer's book, and bragged that all who see *Eve* admire the sculpture. But he mentions that he cannot afford to bronze it without a commission. He remarks that his completed marble *Judith* would look good as pride of place in the Octagon Room, and he considers it "*my best work*": "I know of no place where I would rather have this work placed than in the Corcoran Gallery as it is eminently fitted *for a gallery*, and can be placed (I think, as all do who have seen it) in very good company." Always reaching for the stars, Ezekiel's aside about "very good company" implied Powers's *The Greek Slave*. Ezekiel also offered to discount one of his sculptures for inside the gallery and, acting as his best press agent, even sent letters suggesting further ornamentation on the building's facade, for which he was willing to send a sketch.[71] None of these propositions interested the collector. Ezekiel's ardent desire to make works in what he considered their handsomest form and thus to spend more than the agreed payment to achieve his aesthetic goals (and to donate time to make sculptures gratis), coupled with his steadfast devotion to classical subjects and styles, left him scrambling for money most of his years in Rome.

Literary Giants in Bronze and Marble

Having caught a whiff of excitement for working on a large scale with *Religious Liberty*, and motivated by his love of the classics, the ambitious Ezekiel created another group sculpture: *Blind Homer and Young Guide*, sometimes referred to as the *Homeric Group* and *Blind Homer with His Student Guide* (ca. 1881; fig. 58). *Homer* shows the aged, bearded author of the *Iliad* and the *Odyssey* on the seacoast, gazing blindly into the distance while reciting his poetry; an idealized nude boy playing a lyre at his feet adds to the tone of the bard's words. Homer's features, Ezekiel wrote, were based on a bust of the poet that he saw in Naples.[72] Leaning forward, transfixed by his companion's music, the sightless man gets a sense of his bearings by gently resting a hand on his guide's head. On one occasion, Ezekiel hosted a reading of Homer's poetry at his atelier, and at its end, a curtain was dramatically drawn back to reveal the sculpture.[73]

The *Homeric Group* languished in Ezekiel's studio. He wrote of watering the clay to keep the statue from drying out until it could be modeled in plaster. In an 1880 letter informing Corcoran that *Michelangelo* was completed and ready for shipment, he took the liberty of mentioning his work on *Homer*. Ezekiel vaunted, "So far as I know, this is the first group or figure of Homer that has ever been made and on that account has attracted some attention."[74] Patently, Ezekiel was hoping to entice Corcoran to purchase the sculpture. A different potential buyer, founder of the *Baltimore Sun* Arunah Abell, spoke to Ezekiel about a possible monument to Francis Scott Key, author of the "The Star-Spangled Banner," for his hometown of Baltimore, and the purchase of *Homer* for his summer residence. For the former, Ezekiel planned a monument that would stand twenty feet tall, topped by a draped female allegory of Maryland standing twelve feet tall, with her hand resting on fasces. One of the fasces would be topped with a flagstaff, and Ezekiel hoped that a real flag would be hoisted on it. A portrait relief of Key was to decorate one side of the square base, and a tablet inscribed with the words of the song on another side. But Abell died soon after the pair met in 1888, when he invited Ezekiel to Baltimore, and neither sale was realized.[75]

Attorney John Woodruff Simpson of New York saw a photograph of *Blind Homer and Young Guide* during Ezekiel's visit to the city in 1902 and

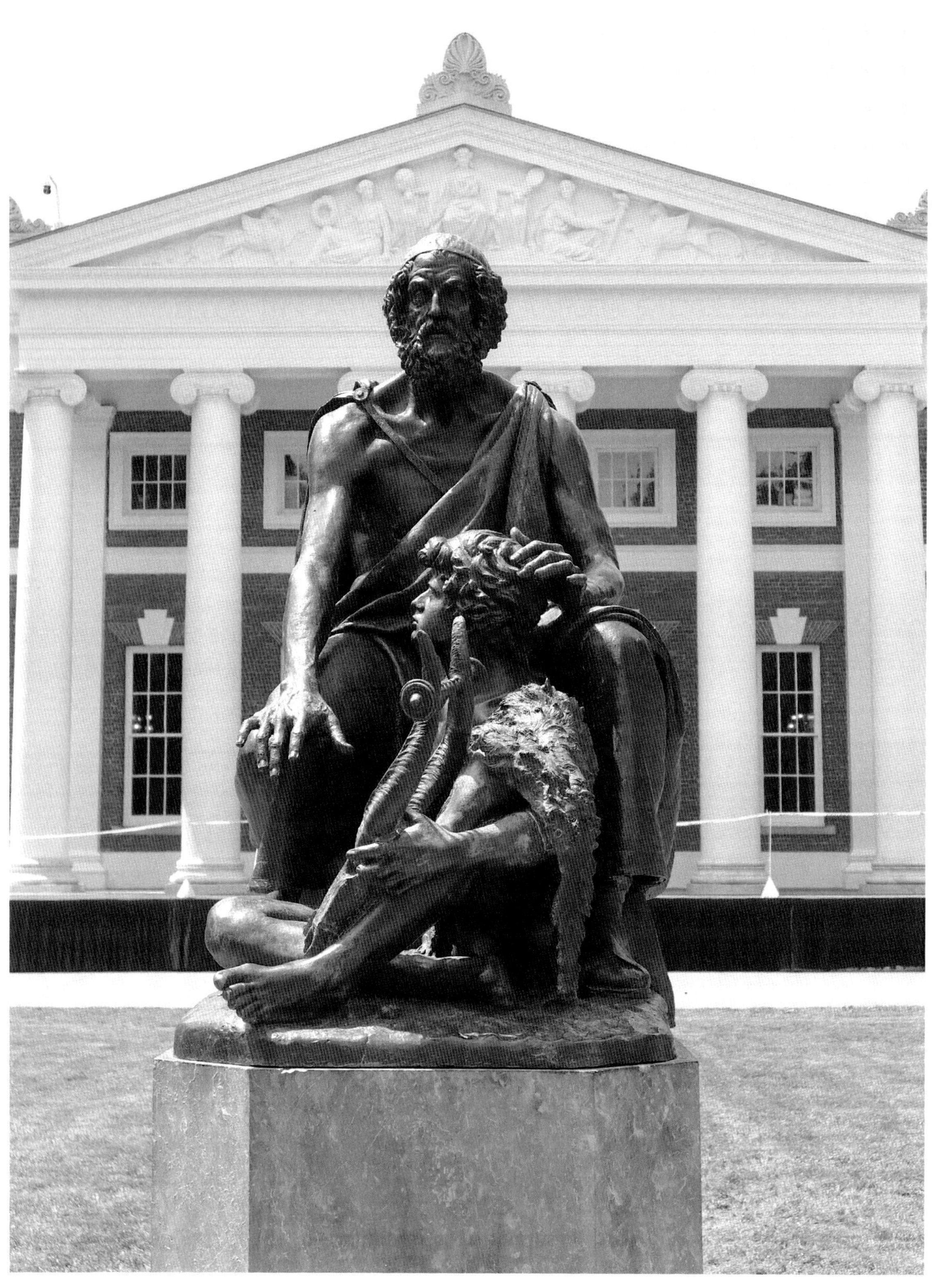

purchased the work for his alma mater, Amherst College. When plans fell through for erecting *Homer* at Amherst, Simpson generously authorized Ezekiel to choose an academic institution that he saw fit for the sculpture. Unsurprisingly, the Richmond-born artist picked the University of Virginia, where *Homer* still sits on the south end of the Lawn. To honor the donor, Ezekiel inscribed in Greek on the bard's strap, "Ezekiel from Richmond made me/it; Simpson dedicated it/me." Ezekiel gifted the sculpture's monolithic, black marble base to the university as a gesture of goodwill in hope of securing a commission for a monument to Thomas Jefferson on campus, which ultimately bore fruit (chapter 5).[76]

At *Homer*'s unveiling during commencement ceremonies in 1907, with the cord pulled by Ezekiel's sister Adeline Brauer, Robert Harrison of New York spoke on behalf of Simpson, who was too ill to attend. Harrison's speech reflected Ezekiel's thinking about the classics as well: "The donor of this group hopes that it will serve as inspiration to the young men who are now thronging your halls, teaching them there is something to be learned from the 'story of Troy divine' to elevate and kindle the soul."[77] Unable to attend the dedication, Ezekiel sent word by telegram, suitably written in the classical language of Latin: "Dum simulacrum Homeri lux circumfundit salutem dicit Ezekiel" (While the light surrounds Homer's likeness, Ezekiel sends greetings).[78] University of Virginia President Edwin Alderman cabled Ezekiel after the affair, "Statue unveiled. University deeply grateful," and Ezekiel responded by quoting the *Iliad* in Greek, here translated: "See, my son, how good it is / To give th' immortal Gods their tribute due."[79]

FIG. 58 Moses Jacob Ezekiel, *Blind Homer with His Student Guide*, circa 1881. Bronze, 67 in., pedestal 46 in. University of Virginia, Charlottesville. Photo: Samantha Baskind.

Earlier in the program, forced inside because of rain, US ambassador to Italy and author Thomas Nelson Page, President Alderman, and several others spoke. Most interesting are Page's remarks, for he was tasked to speak about Ezekiel, with whom he had developed a close friendship, and about the circumstances leading to the university's acquisition of *Blind Homer and Young Guide*. Extolling the distinguished sculptor as "Virginia's gifted son" and describing the expatriate's lingering "love and devotion to his Mother Virginia," Page underscored Ezekiel's devout commitment to "those lofty ideals of art. . . . His genius has ever been applied toward the accomplishment of the ideal."[80] Indeed, as quoted in this chapter's epigraph, Ezekiel penned more than once, "I have a perfect enthusiasm for art, an enthusiasm that fires my whole soul and mind to such an extent that I am willing to relish poverty and every labour that would aid me in securing the object of my ambition."[81]

During his auspicious visit to New York that led to the long-awaited purchase of *Homer*, Ezekiel stayed with William Milo Barnum, who had commissioned the sculptor to make a portrait relief of John Simpson, his law partner. Impressed with the portrait, Simpson and his wife, Katherine Seney Simpson, subsequently requested a torso of their five-year-old daughter Jean (1902; fig. 59) as well as seventeen small busts of writers and philosophers for his library.[82] The lost sculpture of Jean is astonishing for its excess of decoration. Jean's bounty of curls frames her fleshy face and merge with her torso, a cornucopia of flowers punctuated by a large rose near her right shoulder, thereby associating her with nature and innocence.[83] Even

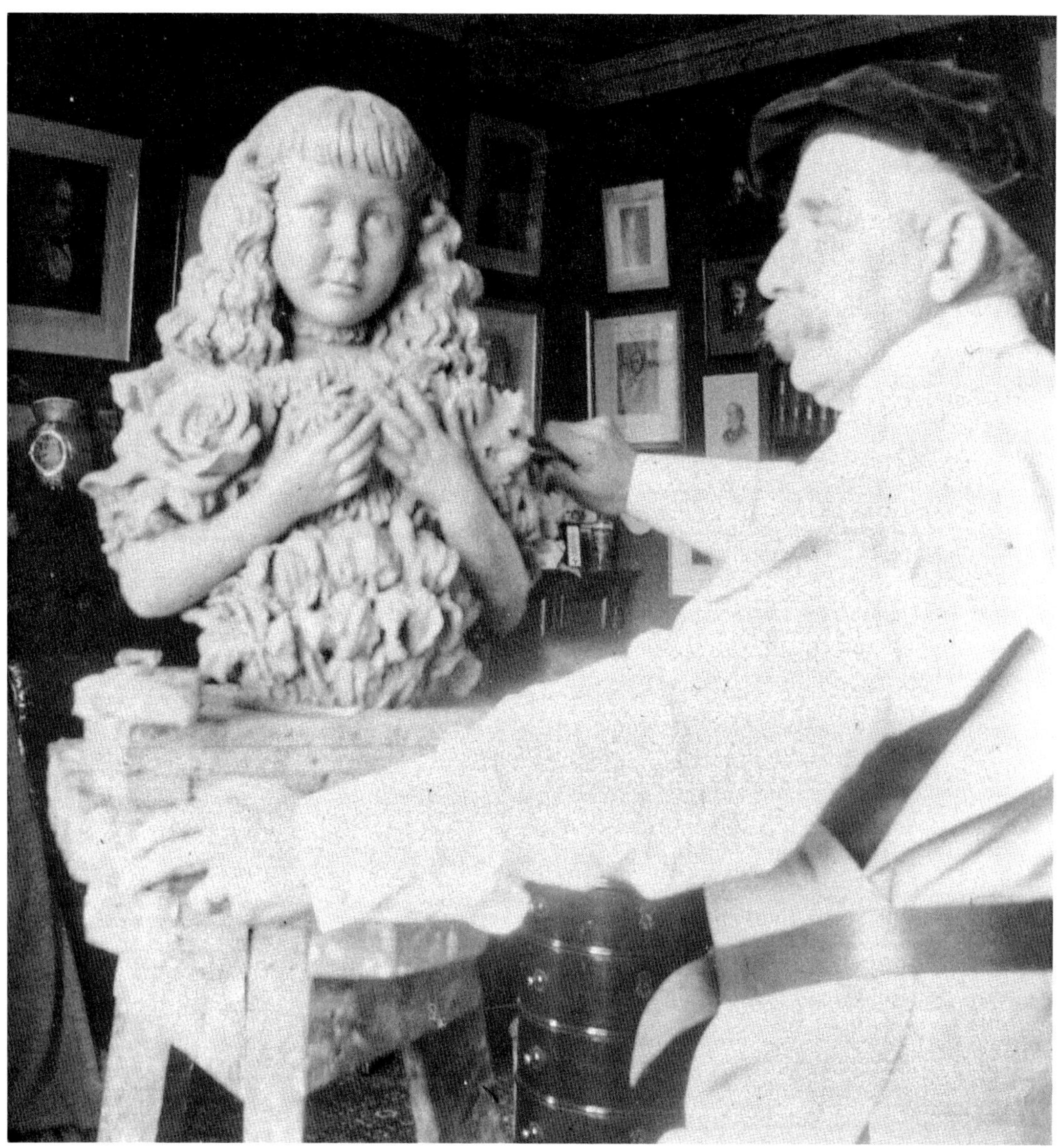

after the turn of the century, Ezekiel adhered to an idealizing allegorical neoclassicism with ornamentation of froth and frill that in this instance exceeds imagination.[84]

Jean Simpson, the most extravagantly decorated bust Ezekiel ever chiseled, is even more remarkable for a family that was among the great American champions of Auguste Rodin. Katherine Simpson donated over thirty works by Rodin to the National Gallery of Art and many to other American museums.[85] The same year that Jean sat for Ezekiel, the Simpsons later commissioned Rodin to make a bust of Katherine, Jean's mother and the sculptor's first American sitter (fig. 60). Rodin's conception

FIG. 59 (OPPOSITE) Moses Jacob Ezekiel, *Jean Simpson*, 1902. Marble. Lost. Simpson family collection, photo albums, 1902–3, New York. Photo courtesy of John Woodruff Simpson Memorial Library, East Craftsbury, Vermont.

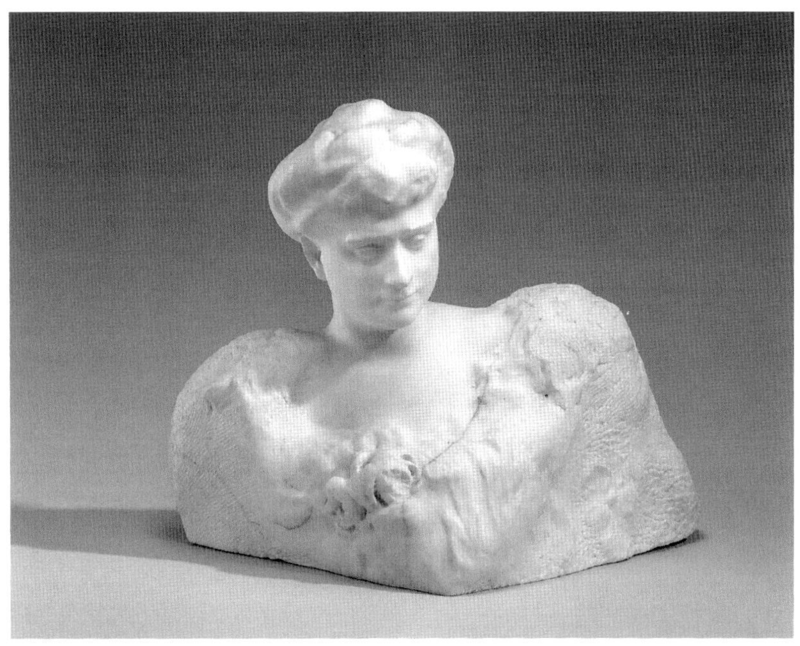

FIG. 60 Auguste Rodin, *Katherine Seney Simpson (Mrs. John Simpson)*, 1903. Marble, 21 13/16 × 27 3/16 × 16 5/16 in. Courtesy of National Gallery of Art, Washington, DC. Gift of Mrs. John W. Simpson, 1942.5.16.

of Katherine, made during sixty sittings and with the aid of a plaster mask to capture her likeness, is completely different from Ezekiel's young Jean and went against everything the American stood for as an artist.[86] Katherine is nearly subsumed by her amorphous, asymmetrical bust, rendered as a textured, bulky mass from which her head emerges. Rodin's suggestion of a rose near the center of Katherine's vague garment offers a subtle touch, unlike the flamboyant ornamentation of her daughter's portrait. By the early 1900s, it was an uphill climb for Ezekiel. The center of the art world was Paris, Augustus Saint-Gaudens and Rodin were in fashion, and Ezekiel's ideal was even farther in the past.

There are no studio photographs showing the Simpsons' commissioned busts of literati in progress, and Ezekiel only once comments on this large project—a wealth of authorial giants that would have been an apt counterpart to his full-length sculptures of the great artists at the Corcoran Gallery of Art. The lone sculpture that Ezekiel mentions regarding this commission is *Shakespeare* (ca. 1903; Robert Simon Fine Art, New York). Waning interest from the Simpsons, increasingly enthusiastic in their collection of modern art, could have doomed this exciting project. Or the bland, expressionless *Shakespeare* may have prompted the Simpsons to rescind the order. Ezekiel was disappointed again, not only because of this failed opportunity but also because he must have been thrilled to be making sculptures of the literary figures he keenly read. As a child, his favorite authors were Shakespeare, Shelley, and Keats, and of this trio he judged Shelley the best. Ezekiel's command of literature is all the more remarkable considering that he had to end his schooling at age twelve to work as a bookkeeper in his grandfather's store.[87]

Ezekiel found eager patrons for two vigorous marble busts of literary figures, both Romantic

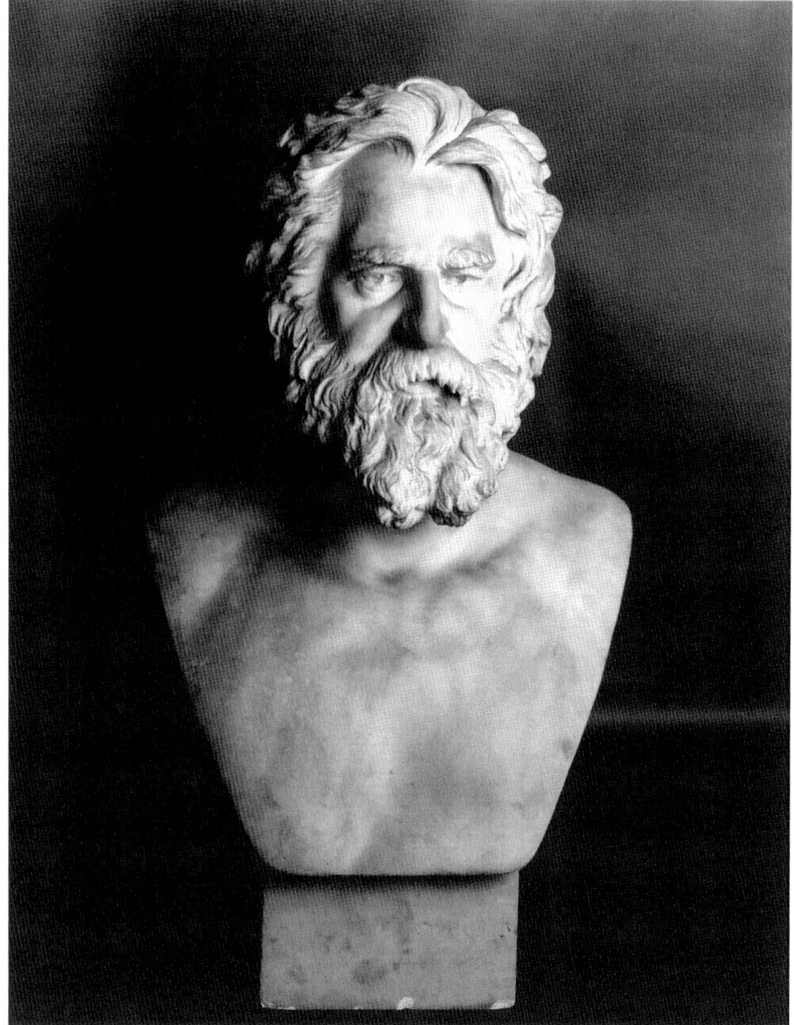

FIG. 61 Moses Jacob Ezekiel, *Henry Wadsworth Longfellow*, 1889. Marble, 31 13/16 × 22 1/2 × 17 3/4 in. Cincinnati Art Museum. Gift of Mrs. M. L. Schmidlapp, 1889.516. Photo: Cincinnati Art Museum.

poets who expatriated to Rome. Inspired in style by his love of the antique and neoclassical busts of literati by Americans from the previous generation, some of whom knew the writers, the first was a heroic bust of *Henry Wadsworth Longfellow* (fig. 61). A Cincinnatian named Mrs. M. Y. Schmidlapp met Ezekiel in the Queen City in March 1888 and spoke with him about a possible work for her to donate to the newly established Cincinnati Art Museum. She contacted museum officials to gain their approval of Longfellow as a subject, which they readily gave.[88] Chiseling Longfellow interested Ezekiel not only for his chance to join a legacy of artists who crafted portraits of writers and for the remuneration it offered but also for Longfellow's lyric poetry and his translations of Dante's *Divine Comedy* and Michelangelo's poetry from Italian.

A little over a year after the commission, Ezekiel sent the bust directly from Rome to the museum, where it was placed in the rotunda at the entrance on New Year's Day, 1890.[89] The *Cincinnati Times* applauded the thirty-two-inch sculpture as "a magnificent head, recalling the antique heads of the Roman Jupiter or the Greek Zeus."[90] Longfellow's heavy beard, worn because of scars on his face from trying to save his wife from a deadly fire, splits in the middle in line with past renditions of the poet. To name but two precedents, Edmonia Lewis's bust of Longfellow was based on observation from life (1871; Harvard Art Museums, Cambridge, MA), and Powers's bust of the poet was replicated at least three times (1869; Harvard Art Museums, Cambridge, MA).[91] Ezekiel's *Longfellow* shows the poet with wavy hair sweeping dramatically off his forehead, a stark contrast to his bare, tapered torso. Unlike other busts by Ezekiel, *Longfellow* was appreciated in the manner he intended—as a balm for the soul that could enliven museums, homes, and minds. As the *Cincinnati Times* critic exulted, under the article's subtitle "A Heroic Reminder of the Famous in Antique," "One seems lifted into a purer atmosphere in the contemplation of this exquisite chiseling of the beloved poet's features in fair marble, and unconsciously some familiar lines of the bard will come to one to be lovingly repeated while standing beneath the blessing of its art presence."[92]

The second bust presents Percy Shelley in stillness, staring wistfully into the distance (fig. 62). A shock of hair frames the poet's smoothly polished, oval, clean-shaven face like a halo. On the rounded base of the bust, terminating high at Shelley's shoulders, Ezekiel elegiacally incised in Latin, "Cor Cordium" (Heart of hearts), as inscribed on the poet's gravestone. Ezekiel surely agreed with Shelley, who wrote on subjects that ignited the sculptor. At various times throughout Shelley's essay "A Defence of Poetry," he connected poetry to pleasure, morality, imagination, inspiration, and the divine. Shelley hailed poetry's "wisdom which is mingled with its delight," early naming Homer as the first epic poet: "Homer embodied the ideal perfection of his age in human character; nor can we doubt that those who read his verses were awakened to an ambition of becoming like to Achilles, Hector, and Ulysses: the truth and beauty of friendship, patriotism, and persevering devotion to an object, were unveiled to their depth in these immortal creations."[93] It was that "ideal perfection" signaled out by Shelley that motivated Ezekiel's life and work, and was in turn lauded by Page concerning Ezekiel at the unveiling of his *Homer*: "His genius has ever been applied toward the accomplishment of the ideal."[94]

Indeed, Ezekiel's special affection for Shelley stemmed from his lyric poetry as well as the poet's understanding of the sensuality of sculpture. "The true poetry of Rome lived in its institutions; for whatever of beautiful, true, and majestic, they contained, could have sprung only from the faculty which creates the order in which they consist," Shelley wrote. "Poetry is the record of the best and happiest moments of the happiest and best minds."[95] In an 1818 letter Shelley observed, "Sculpture retains its freshness for twenty centuries—the Apollo and the Venus are as they were," and his 1820 "Ode to Liberty" exalted the remembrance of man "in marble immortality."[96] Nor was Shelley the only nineteenth-century writer to recognize the vivacity of sculpture. The narrator in Nathaniel Hawthorne's *The Marble Faun* (1860) described "marble immortality" and the emergence of a statue shining forth "with pure white radiance, in the precious marble of Carrara."[97] This glorification of marble and ancient sculpture in Hawthorne's

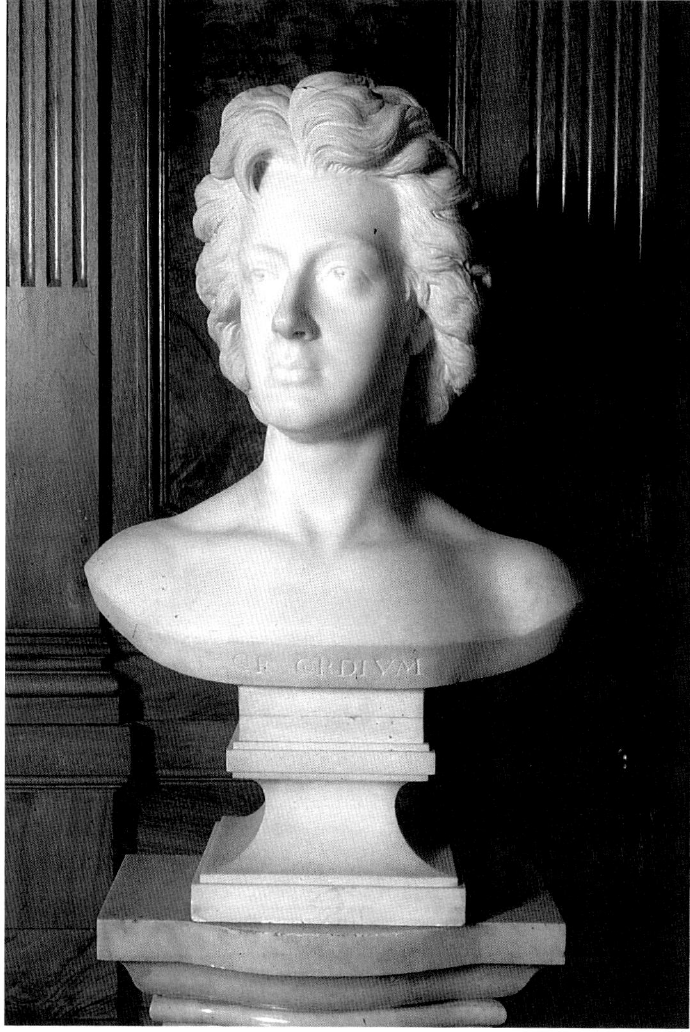

FIG. 62 Moses Jacob Ezekiel, *Percy Bysshe Shelley*, circa 1892. Marble, 24.4 in. Keats-Shelley House, Rome. Photo: Property of the Keats-Shelley Memorial Association.

popular romance sparked after he saw the *Faun of Praxiteles* in the Capitoline Museum, which Ezekiel visited often. Hawthorne's small cast of characters were partly shaped by his acquaintances with American expatriate artists in Rome: Harriet Hosmer, Louisa Lander, Paul Akers, and William Story, particularly the latter's *Cleopatra* and his convivial studio.[98] It goes without saying that when Carel Vosmaer and Mary Tincker used Ezekiel's work and studio as prototypes for their novels, the sculptor heartily drew a comparison to *The Marble Faun*. The latter had reached such popularity that it served as a guidebook for American tourists in Rome.[99] Travelers with a literary bent sought out the sculptures discussed by Hawthorne's characters, bringing attention to the ancient *Faun*, among other works, including the *Dying Gaul*, Ezekiel's model for *Israel*.

In 1892, *Shelley* was purchased by a wealthy New York man whom Ezekiel only refers to as

Mr. Leavitt, and whose brother's portrait relief he had crafted earlier (lost). Mr. Leavitt and his wife were visiting Ezekiel's atelier, where the couple saw the model of *Shelley*, yet another work made on speculation. To Ezekiel's delight, they asked him to chisel it for them.[100] Another marble of *Percy Shelley* found a place in a newly constructed memorial to Shelley and John Keats. In 1906, the house in Rome where Keats lived before his premature death was purchased by a committee of Americans and Englishmen. Soon converted into a Keats-Shelley memorial to honor the expatriates, the house features books and ephemera related to the poets. The king of Italy, the American and British ambassadors, and Shelley's grandson, along with other dignitaries, attended the inauguration—all in front of Ezekiel's *Shelley*, which he donated. At the proceedings, the sculptor was thanked for his contribution, which also included a donation of the first edition of Shelley's *Revolt of Islam* and Ezekiel's promise to make a bust of Keats soon; for reasons unknown (probably because he was not offered remuneration), he never did. Ezekiel's dear friend in Rome Adolfo de Bosis was commended for his translation of Shelley's writings to Italian, the first of its kind. Ezekiel himself covered the event with a substantial article published in the *New York Times*.[101]

When chiseling busts of Shelley and Beethoven without sponsors, Ezekiel believed that he was honoring his antecedents in the arts across disciplines, so he felt sorely disheartened when buyers did not recognize the works' artistic and intellectual value. At the same time, Ezekiel aimed to tap into a like-minded community of aesthetes and upper-middle-class intellectuals who wanted to celebrate the beauty, ideals, and achievements of creators, himself included, who made contributions to what in his mind were the supreme triumphs of world culture. While Ezekiel sensitively and intimately portrayed the psychological dimensions of his close friends Liszt and Cardinal Hohenlohe-Schillingsfürst, some of his idealized portraits honoring the wondrous accomplishments of his predecessors were not always as readily desired or viewed as the life-restoring gifts he meant them to be.

Fantasies of Ancient Romans and Greeks

Although not portrayals of artists, four like-minded works speak to Ezekiel's infatuation with antiquity and his desire to memorialize it in bust form. In 1903, Ezekiel set his sights on early Roman and Greek history with two busts of ancient Romans: the emperor *Marcus Aurelius* (fig. 63) and the statesman *Brutus*. With his heavy beard and swirling leonine curls, Aurelius's draped likeness would have been easily recognized by Romans of the time, not the least from the bronze equestrian statue of the man on Capitoline Hill. Likewise, the characters in *The Marble Faun* admired that ancient portrait, the "most majestic representation of the kingly character that ever the world has seen."[102] Still, Ezekiel carved the emperor's name at the bottom of the plinth for emphasis and aesthetic effect. No doubt Ezekiel admired Aurelius for his prowess as a military leader, and he may even have been thinking of his VMI teacher and personal military hero Stonewall Jackson, whom he would eventually depict for the West Virginia State Capitol and the Virginia Military Institute (chapter 6). Ezekiel would also have been intrigued by Aurelius's writings on philosophy. Considering Aurelius's eminence in Roman history, Ezekiel

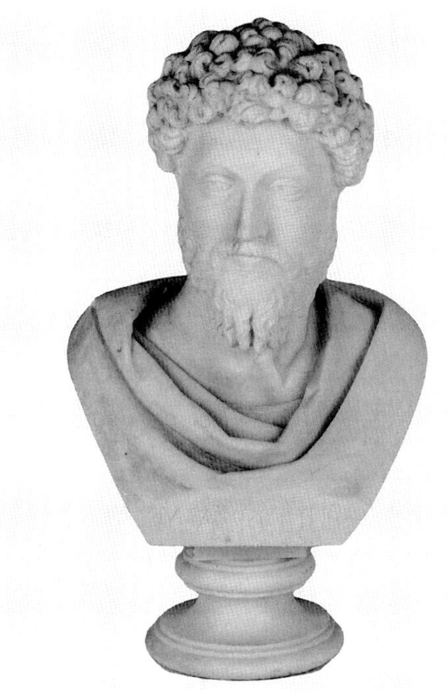

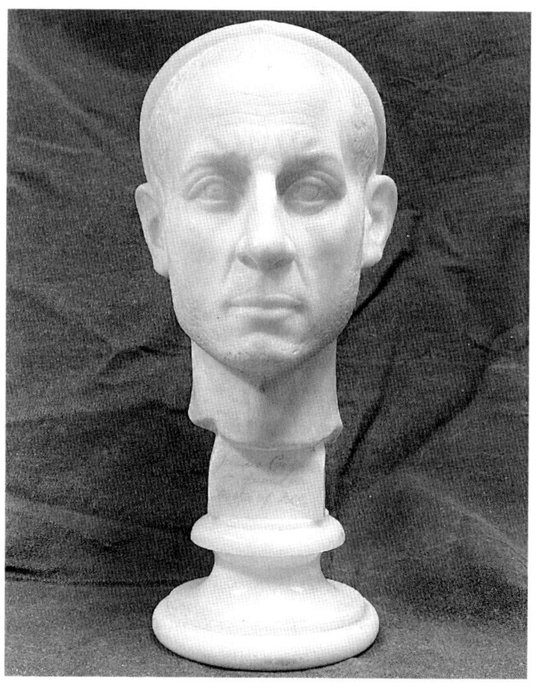

smartly chose this subject, as opposed to *Blind Homer and Young Guide*, which is hampered by its large size and an esoteric theme that contemporaries would less appreciate or have the means or space to procure. Regardless, in the new century, Ezekiel overestimated the audience for sculptures in imitation of the antique. Or perhaps his personal desire to give life in marble to those timeless figures who gripped his imagination was a risky proposition that he felt compelled to take. There is no evidence that *Aurelius* was purchased in Ezekiel's lifetime.

Conceived at the same moment was a bust of the Roman politician and orator Brutus, and again no provenance exists. (Both were sold at auction in 2022.)[103] Again, Ezekiel incised his subject's name in capital letters at the bottom of the marble bust, but otherwise the undraped portrait is much more austere. Ezekiel, who favored carving frothy curls and lush beards, followed tradition and showed a youthful, clean-shaven Brutus with strictly rendered hair, as per one of several renditions in Rome as a prototype. Aside from Brutus's fateful connection to Roman history for killing Julius Caesar, he purportedly uttered the Latin phrase "Sic semper tyrannis" (Thus always to tyrants) at the dictator's assassination. That phrase also serves as the motto of the Commonwealth of Virginia and decorates the state's official seal. Briefly, Ezekiel engaged in an unprecedented conversation with the antique when crafting a unique marble head of Caesar (fig. 64). Dated 1907, four years after his sculpture of Caesar's assassin, Ezekiel placed the ascetic head on a block of marble that he inscribed in cursive "Julius Caesar Found in Delta of Nile," as if recreating an object from antiquity.

A year after he sculpted *Aurelius* and *Brutus*, Ezekiel traveled to Greece, a stimulus for two

FIG. 63 (OPPOSITE LEFT) Moses Jacob Ezekiel, *Marcus Aurelius*, 1903. Marble, 19 × 12 in. Private collection. Photo courtesy of Clars Auction Gallery, Oakland, California.

FIG. 64 (OPPOSITE RIGHT) Moses Jacob Ezekiel, *Caesar*, 1907. Marble, 15 1/8 in. Virginia Military Institute Museum, Lexington. Photo: Virginia Military Institute Museum, Lexington.

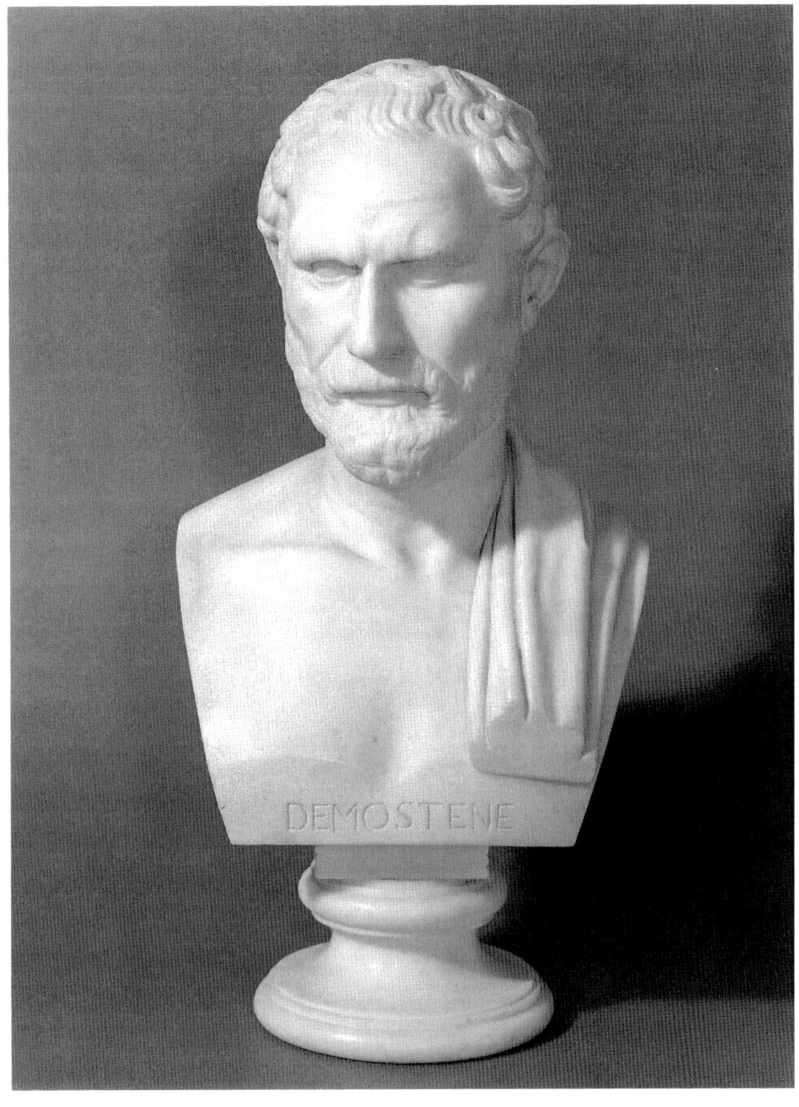

FIG. 65 Moses Jacob Ezekiel, *Demostene*, 1904. Marble, 18 7/8 × 9 5/8 × 7 1/2 in. Virginia Museum of Fine Arts, Richmond. Gift of Mr. and Mrs. Morton G. Thalhimer Sr., 67.44.1. © Virginia Museum of Fine Arts.

more noncommissioned marble portrait busts of famed Greeks: a modestly draped *Sophocles* the tragedian (1904; Virginia Museum of Fine Arts, Richmond), and the statesman and orator *Demostene* (fig. 65; Demosthenes, misspelled on the marble), figures that Ezekiel mentions when recounting his trip to the Hellenic Republic.[104] In 1901, Ezekiel went out of his way to write about attending an enjoyable performance of Sophocles's *Oedipus the King* and seeing a full-length marble *Sophocles* (30 BCE, after Greek bronze original 340–330 BCE) at the Lateran Museum in Rome.[105] Again, Ezekiel engraved these ageless figures' names on the front of their busts. Like the American sculptors Crawford and Saint-Gaudens, Ezekiel was drawn to copying an early Hellenistic statue of Demosthenes in the Vatican Museums.[106] In this faithful copy, *Demosthenes*'s brow furrows, his face is lined, and he gazes expressively toward his right. But still, these types of historical works were out of vogue. Crawford's bust dates to 1837 and Saint-Gaudens's to 1873. Crawford sometimes carved more than one copy, as he, too, was in the business of sculpture and found eager buyers on both sides of the ocean.[107] At some point, both of Ezekiel's busts made it to America, where they were acquired in the 1960s from a dealer on Cape Cod, Massachusetts, before they entered the collection of the Virginia Museum of Fine Arts.[108]

By presenting the virtues of the eminent men he portrayed in a manner used by the ancients, desired through the Renaissance and fashionable up to the Romantic period, Ezekiel harked back to a bygone time of intellect and heroism that greatly appealed to him. *Franz Liszt* and the *Cardinal* were more successful because of reciprocal bonds between the artist and his subjects, which offered a believable individuality and intimate level of description, which is lacking in the formal stillness of the busts inspired by Ezekiel's fantasies of his cultural exemplars. Accompanying Ezekiel's classical portraits from his imagination and his intimate representations of friends are dozens of naturalistically rendered commissioned busts in marble and bronze, and an occasional portrait relief, of distinguished living sitters. Those diverse figures, among others described throughout this book, include Rookwood Pottery founder *Maria Longworth Nichols Storer* (1893; lost), New York Senator *Rufus King* (1894; Cincinnati Law Library), German painter *Hans Peter Feddersen* (ca. 1900; lost), and Italian physicist *Alfonso Sella*, commissioned by the University of Rome after his untimely death (1907; lost).[109]

Edgar Allan Poe: American, Virginian, and Ezekiel's Last Sculpture

Ezekiel's last major commission was a sculpture of another poet, Edgar Allan Poe, a fellow Richmonder (fig. 66). Requested in 1907 by the Baltimore-based Edgar Poe Society, with the intention that the work would be unveiled for the centennial of the poet's birth in 1909, the commission was criticized. *American Art News* testified that some Baltimoreans, and the news correspondent agreed, felt the work should have been apportioned to an American resident, even one from the city. Ezekiel was praised, however, for visiting Baltimore in reference to the work, but a site had yet to be chosen.[110]

Poe was subject to several misfortunes but survives. The plaster model was destroyed by fire in 1913, when waylaid at a custom house en route to Berlin, where it had been shipped for casting. Ezekiel was out $7,000 because the packer failed to insure the work, and the sculptor estimated no less than a year would pass before he could model the piece again.[111] This financial blow was particularly demoralizing, because Ezekiel had already halved his asking price of $20,000 in sympathy for a poet born in his hometown, a fellow military man, and of course because of the prestige and visibility of the assignment. A second attempt at *Poe*, completed in 1915, was ruined in Ezekiel's studio during an earthquake. Enthusiastic about *Poe*, Ezekiel soldiered on and took an even greater financial hit. World War I delayed the third and final statue's shipment to the United States. And when it was finally sent across the Atlantic to be placed in Baltimore's Wyman Park in 1921, Ezekiel had been dead for four years. At least he did not live to see *Poe*'s further troubles: For months after

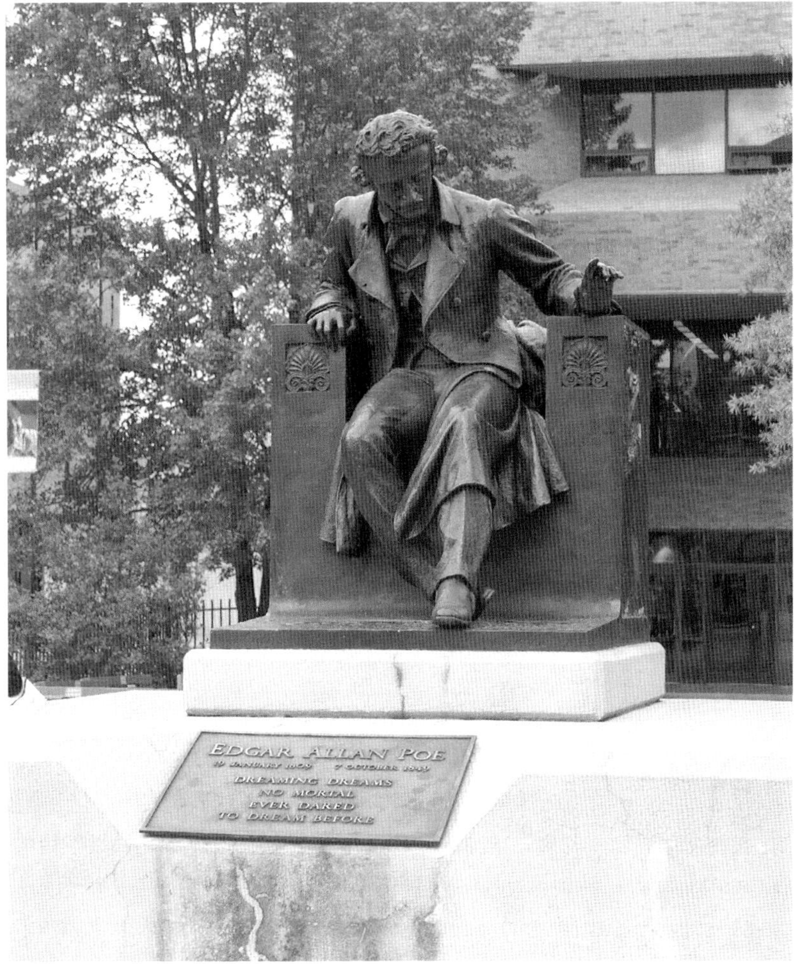

FIG. 66 Moses Jacob Ezekiel, *Edgar Allan Poe*, 1915. Bronze, 4 ½ ft. University of Baltimore School of Law, Baltimore, Maryland. Photo: Wikimedia Commons / Frederic C. Chalfant. CC BY-SA 3.0.

the statue's arrival, it sat in storage while the city laboriously approved its location.[112] Then, the Poe Committee noticed that inscriptions of the poems contained two errors.[113] In the ensuing years, *Poe* suffered from vandalism and harsh effects from the elements. The relief inscriptions on the sculpture's concrete pedestal, nearly unreadable from decay, necessitated its removal and replacement with a simple, unadorned base in 1983, when the sculpture was relocated to a more conspicuous location—a plaza at the University of Baltimore's Law School. There *Poe* has been adopted as a mascot, with students draping the sculpture with regalia during graduation and related accoutrements for other events. The sculpture's silhouette was once used as the university's logo.

Ezekiel crafted *Poe* in a new home, the Tower of Belisarius, after the Roman government evicted him from the Baths in 1910 to turn part of the land into a new branch of the National Roman Museum. When the city informed Ezekiel that he was to vacate with only ten days' notice, he was understandably upset and refused to move.[114] He mournfully and melodramatically reflected, "And thus ended my thirty years' reign on this spot which I had made a temple of art and which was known throughout the world as one of the most beautiful places in Rome."[115] Before leaving Rome in 1910 for a seven-month visit to the United States, the city awarded the esteemed sculptor with a different, historic residence: the Belisarius Tower, within the Aurelian Wall, built in 560 CE.[116]

More modern in conception than his previous representations of poets, the life-size third version of *Poe* portrays him seated in a chair and animatedly leaning forward into the viewer's space yet absorbed in his own reverie. His left hand rises in motion, and his right hand rests on the arm of the chair. Both chair arms are embellished in relief with winged muses of art and poetry. Ezekiel described his unusual interpretation: "As Edgar Poe was the one poet we have whose poetry does not seem to be based on anything that existed before his own, I conceived the idea of presenting him as seated listening in rapt attention to a divine melody and a new rhythm in his art."[117] Extraordinarily interested in textual inclusions (e.g., the heavily inscribed Louisville *Jefferson* [chapter 5]), sometimes to the detriment of his work, Ezekiel gladly decorated the now-ruined base with carefully chosen excerpts by the Poe Committee from the poet's works "The Raven," "Israfel," and "The Haunted Palace": "Dreaming dreams no mortal ever dared to dream before"; "To thee, the laurels belong, best bard"; and "Whose sweet duty was but to sing."

Sculpting his subjects in a chair was a fashion Ezekiel favored, and one used by artists he admired. Houdon's seated *Voltaire* (1779–81; Comédie-Française, Paris) possesses a similar vitality and sense of internal activity. Antokolsky's *Spinoza* (1882; Kyiv National Art Gallery, Ukraine) —which Ezekiel may very well have seen in plaster when visiting the artist in Paris and perhaps confirmed by his own attempt at the same seated portrait subject later in his life—is quietly pensive in his old age as he melts into his chair. Two other seated portraits by Ezekiel that reached fruition are an imposing eighteen-foot bronze monument of *Anthony Drexel* (1904; figure over eight feet tall), the founder of Drexel University, unveiled in Fairmount Park and now on site at the campus in his name, and a monument to Senator *John Warwick Daniel* (1913; chapter 6), located in Lynchburg. An unrealized, uncommissioned portrait of Otto von Bismarck (ca. 1893) in clay employed the same convention. Bismarck, who unified Germany, sits regally in a chair wearing his full military regalia. The portrait was likely sketched around 1893, based on the year German Emperor Wilhelm II and Princess Augusta Victoria traveled to Rome for the silver wedding anniversary of King Umberto and Queen Margherita. Ezekiel received the German royalty on Cardinal Hohenlohe-Schillingfürst's behalf at the Villa d'Este. When the couple visited Ezekiel's room at the villa, they saw a photograph of his clay model of Bismarck. Ezekiel recalled that the kaiser laughed at the photograph because he had forced Bismarck to resign three years earlier.[118] Among Ezekiel's many wounds is an order from 1888 that fell through for a colossal bronze statue of Charles West, who had recently died. West was a cofounder of the Cincinnati Art Museum and thus a perfect portrait subject for a sculptor of the arts, and the statue was supposed to depict him seated in an ornamented Savonarola chair. After failing to be paid even one installment yet having fully modeled the statue in clay, Ezekiel wrote, "I had no recourse but to destroy the whole of my work."[119]

Bolstered by his Roman environs, under the thrall of his adopted city's mystique, and with his own impractical penchant to immortalize his artistic idols in marble, Ezekiel worked with spirited energy. Responding to the call of ancient Rome, he came to Italy for the allure of marble antique statuary, for the glamour of the Eternal City in his mind's eye, and for museums that boasted great precedents, such as the *Apollo Belvedere* and *Dying Gaul* and later sculptures by Donatello, Michelangelo, and Canova.[120] But unlike his closer American forerunners—William Rinehart, Powers, and Crawford—Ezekiel, who suffered personally and professionally for his unremitting commitment to outmoded subjects and a bygone style, arrived in Italy a generation too late.

Ezekiel's troubles can be well summed up by an 1882 entry in curator William MacLeod's journal, in which he records Corcoran nodding to Ezekiel's financial exigencies and the effect of the sculptor's assiduous adherence to the classical:

> Mr. Corcoran came and read a letter to Miss Tunstall from Mr. Ezekiel, in which he complains of the unremuneratial [*sic*] price for his statues, of the silence of Mr. Corcoran and myself about them &c &c. Mr. C. expressed great sympathy over him, and intimated that he would finally present with $1000 over the cost of the work. Mr. E. writes in rather a morbid way about the want of encouragement of his works by Americans, whereas I suspect it comes from his devotion to High Art,—his Judith, his Homer, &c, and not to what may be popular.[121]

As for Ezekiel, after Corcoran agreed to pay him that precious extra $1,000 when he finished the entire project, he wrote gratefully to his generous benefactor: "Your letters have been a great relief to me—mentally and financially."[122]

Corcoran died in 1888, but it cannot be argued that had he been alive, the collector would have saved Ezekiel's sculptures from near oblivion. Early on, Corcoran expressed dissatisfaction with Ezekiel, who seemed to have bullied his way into sculpting all eleven sculptures. MacLeod wrote in his journal that after receiving a letter from Ezekiel accepting the patron's offer to make the niche statues, Corcoran "expressly disavowed having given the order to E. for he preferred to give the statues to different parties."[123] Three years later, MacLeod penned that the art collector regretted giving the order to Ezekiel, and Corcoran lamented his "attempts to benefit art seem to be thwarted by so many."[124] Frustrated with Ezekiel's progress and pandering for money, Corcoran complained to MacLeod in late 1883, who remarked in his journal, "I fear Mr. C's kindness has turned his head."[125] And then, in 2014, Corcoran's kindness was in fact heartbreakingly turned on its head when the 145-year-old, financially unsound gallery bearing his name closed its doors for good. The creations of both artist and patron were all too fleeting, but only the ever-aggrieved Ezekiel lived to see the day.

EZEKIEL AND THE PRESIDENTS *Chapter 5*

The greatest desire I have ever had was to see a good work of mine placed on my native soil.
—Ezekiel, speaking at the unveiling of his Thomas Jefferson monument at the University of Virginia, 1910

Photographs of the violent and deadly Unite the Right rally in August 2017, spurred by the decision to remove a monument to Robert E. Lee from a public park in Charlottesville, show hundreds of white nationalists encircling counterprotesters at the base of the towering Thomas Jefferson monument that rises grandly in front of the University of Virginia's iconic Rotunda. News articles about the hate-filled rally and its tragic aftermath almost always noted slogans chanted by right-wing extremists, carrying tiki torches and flags bearing Nazi swastikas, including "Jews will not replace us!" and "Jews are Satan's children." Yet, no article mentioned that the Jefferson statue was designed by a Jew, Moses Ezekiel, an example of his modern-day invisibility.

The country's third president held great allure for Ezekiel—as both a fellow Virginian and especially as author of the Virginia Statute for Religious Freedom. Ezekiel would sculpt likenesses of Thomas Jefferson on four separate occasions. Little known, the monument to Jefferson at the University of Virginia (UVA) is a full-scale replica of a turn-of-the-century commission by two Jewish men, philanthropist brothers from Louisville, Kentucky (fig. 67). The unusual approach taken by Ezekiel in conceiving the nation's third president and the complex allegorical program decorating the Liberty Bell on which he stands demonstrate how Ezekiel's carefully staged effort to memorialize Jefferson in a highly visible public space coincides with the American Jewish community's continued preoccupation with religious freedom. Such concern was already evidenced by B'nai B'rith's US centennial commission of *Religious Liberty*,

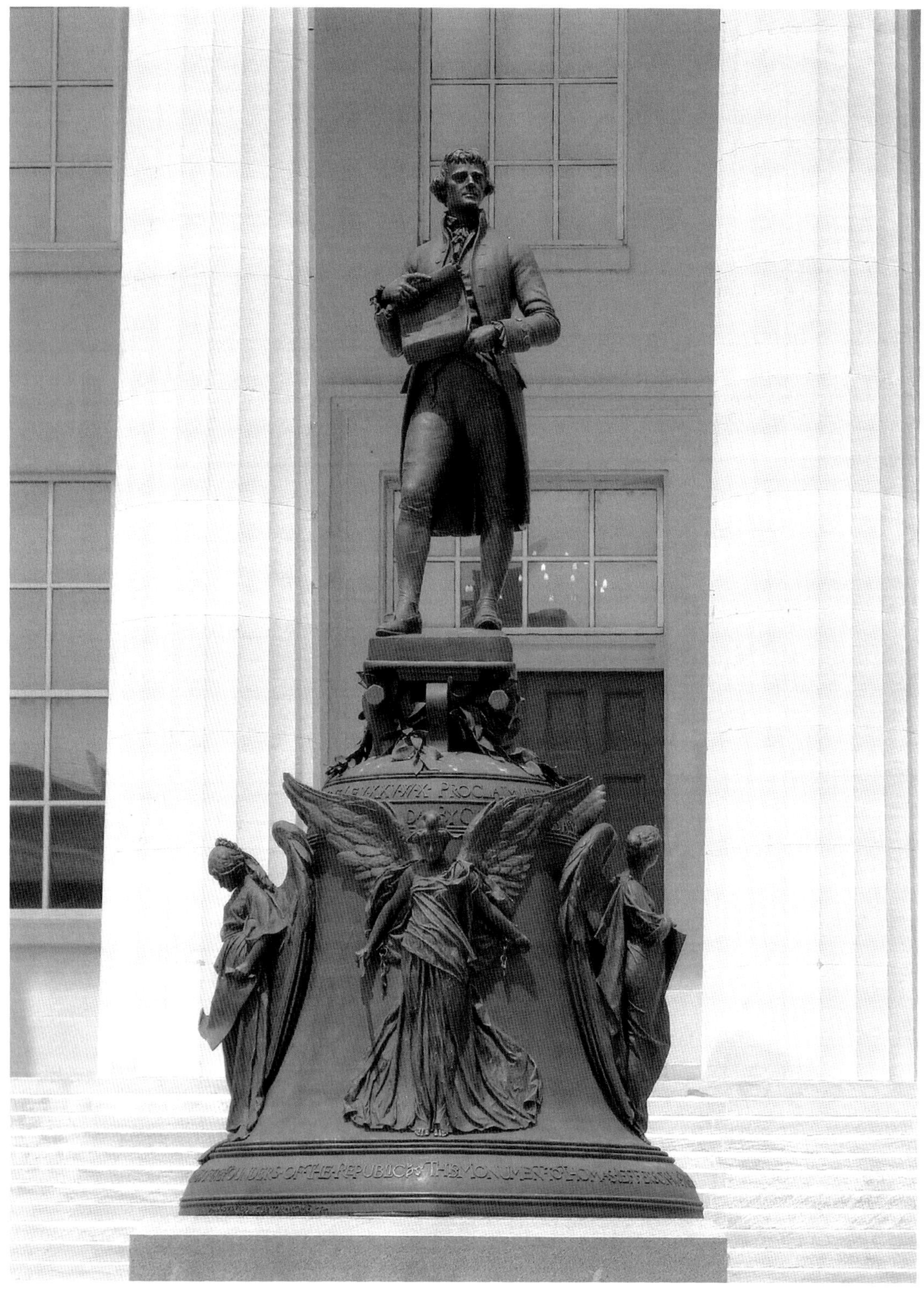
OF THE REPUBLIC

Ezekiel's earliest public monument, and then by this later public monument in front of the Louisville Metro Hall, formerly named the Jefferson County Courthouse. Examining Ezekiel's Louisville *Jefferson* provides insight into a fundamental Jewish interest that prompted this assignment at the dawn of the twentieth century. Further of consequence, particularly for the circumstances of their own commissions, are Ezekiel's Charlottesville replica and his portrait busts of presidents Jefferson and Abraham Lincoln, preceded by George Washington. Notably, the two Lincoln busts were also contracted by Jewish patrons.

George Washington, the Nation's and Ezekiel's First President

On his own volition, Ezekiel's first rendering of a president is a colossal plaster head of George Washington for the Centennial Exhibition (fig. 68; lost). Measuring approximately two feet tall and executed during his student days in Germany in 1872, the herm-type bust was exhibited at the Art Club in Berlin before it was shipped to America.[1] Ezekiel does not idealize the president; his presentation captures a serious Washington with tight lips, a strong, upraised chin, and hair coiffed high off his forehead. Washington wears no military attire, keeping the viewer focused on his resolute gaze (in contrast to Ezekiel's portrait of Rabbi Isaac Mayer Wise), slightly to his left, and the sinews of his neck. Sculpting Washington at the outset of his career and on such a grand scale was Ezekiel's ambitious attempt to place himself within a larger American artistic tradition, in varied media, that celebrated the Founding Fathers. In doing so, Ezekiel hoped to position himself for lucrative work as a sculptor of portraits and monuments during a moment in American history enamored with public art—one that Erika Doss aptly terms "statue mania."[2] Intended for display at the Centennial but unfortunately lost in transit, the plaster head would have been visible to millions. When the bust did finally arrive in the United States, Ezekiel placed it in storage, but that proved costly. In 1880, when laboring on the Corcoran statues, he wrote to curator William MacLeod asking if the gallery would be willing to store the plaster. Ezekiel's letter further indicates that he was hoping to get a government commission to chisel the head in marble for Washington's birthplace in Westmoreland County. Ezekiel even named a price of $3,000 and was clearly trying to garner help from Corcoran officials to secure such an assignment.[3] Based on later correspondence, the gallery agreed to house the head. Unfortunately, Ezekiel's brother Henry, who was facilitating the transfer from Philadelphia to the nation's capital, failed to send the bust in a timely fashion, and the piece remained adrift.[4] Eventually, Ezekiel donated the plaster to the Cincinnati Art Museum, but it has since been lost again, assuredly destroyed because of its fragile material; in 1965, curators unsuccessfully tried to locate the bust.[5]

From the late eighteenth to the mid-nineteenth century, art representing America's Founding Fathers proliferated among state and national governments. There was no lack of commissioned portraits, painted and sculpted, for public spaces presenting American heroes who successfully fought for the country's freedom during the

FIG. 67 Moses Jacob Ezekiel, *Thomas Jefferson*, 1900. Bronze, Jefferson 9 ft., bell pedestal 9 ½ ft., granite pedestal 5 ft. Front of Louisville Metro Hall, Louisville, Kentucky. Photo: Wikimedia Commons / Brent Moore. CC BY-NC 2.0.

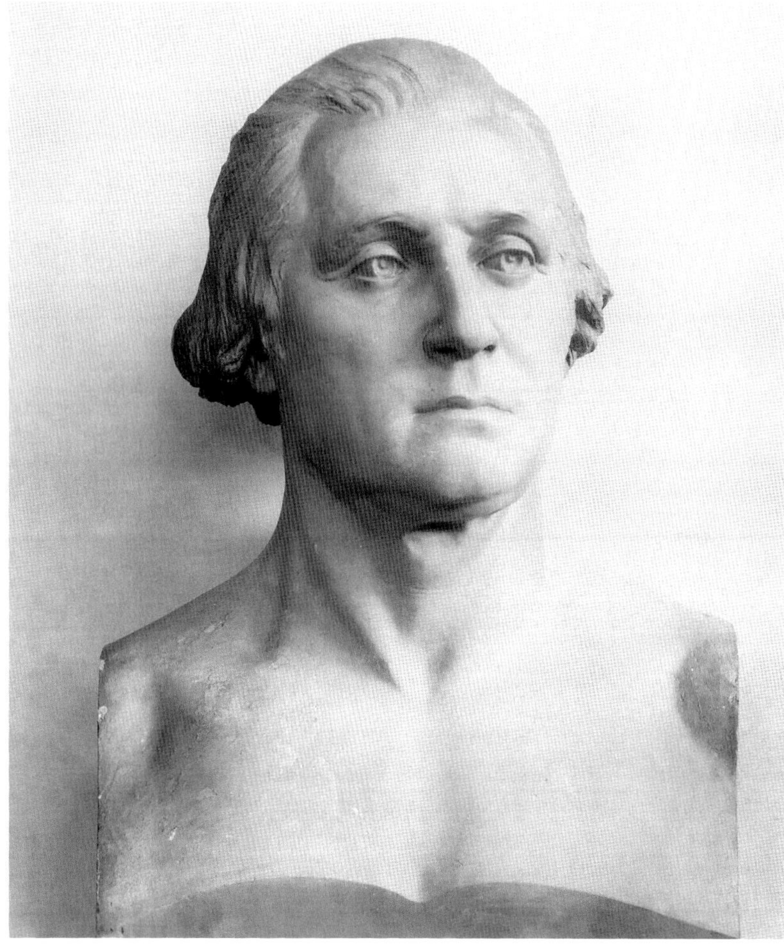

FIG. 68 Moses Jacob Ezekiel, *George Washington*, 1872–73. Plaster, approx. 2 ft. Cincinnati Art Museum. Missing. Gift of Moses J. Ezekiel, 1887.76. Photo: Cincinnati Art Museum.

FIG. 69 (OPPOSITE) Jean-Antoine Houdon, *George Washington*, 1788–92. Marble, 6 ft. 2 in. State Capitol, Richmond, Virginia. Photo: Steven Zucker, PhD.

Revolutionary War and then crafted laws for a nascent democracy. Meaningful for Ezekiel as a Virginian, and as the foremost portrait statuary in his hometown of Richmond, was Jean-Antoine Houdon's life-size, standing portrait of George Washington at the new Virginia State Capitol building (fig. 69). The first sculptural commission by the Virginia General Assembly and based on a careful study from life by the artist, Houdon's rendition shows the older statesman wearing his general's uniform. His cloak and sword rest on a bundle of fasces, both unnecessary with American independence firmly set and the elder statesman retired to his farm estate of Mount Vernon, so symbolized by the plow behind him.

Houdon's dignified statesman differs markedly from Horatio Greenough's controversial marble of a seated Washington wearing a Greek toga (1840), in part based on one of Houdon's studics of the president's head. The first federally funded monument to the nation's president and originally projected for the center of the Capitol Rotunda, it was soon deemed unseemly to present Washington bare to the waist and in the guise of a Greek god, with one hand pointed to the heavens. Merely three years after its completion, the sculpture was moved to the Capitol grounds and ultimately found a permanent home in the National Museum of American History.[6] Nonetheless, both Greenough and Houdon's works served as prototypes of major public monuments known to Ezekiel, offering valuable precedents for his own head of Washington and for the possibilities of advancement in his field. The model for Ezekiel's head of Washington derives from his memories of Houdon's life-size sculpture seen on visits to the Virginia State Capitol building as a child, and even more from a bronze copy at the Virginia Military Institute that faces toward the school's barracks. All other statues in front of the barracks face outward, but Washington was purposefully placed to observe the cadets during their daily routine, and for the cadets to observe the country's most revered citizen-soldier. Ezekiel's *Jefferson* at the University of Virginia was joined by a bronze copy of Houdon's *George Washington*, dedicated in 1913.

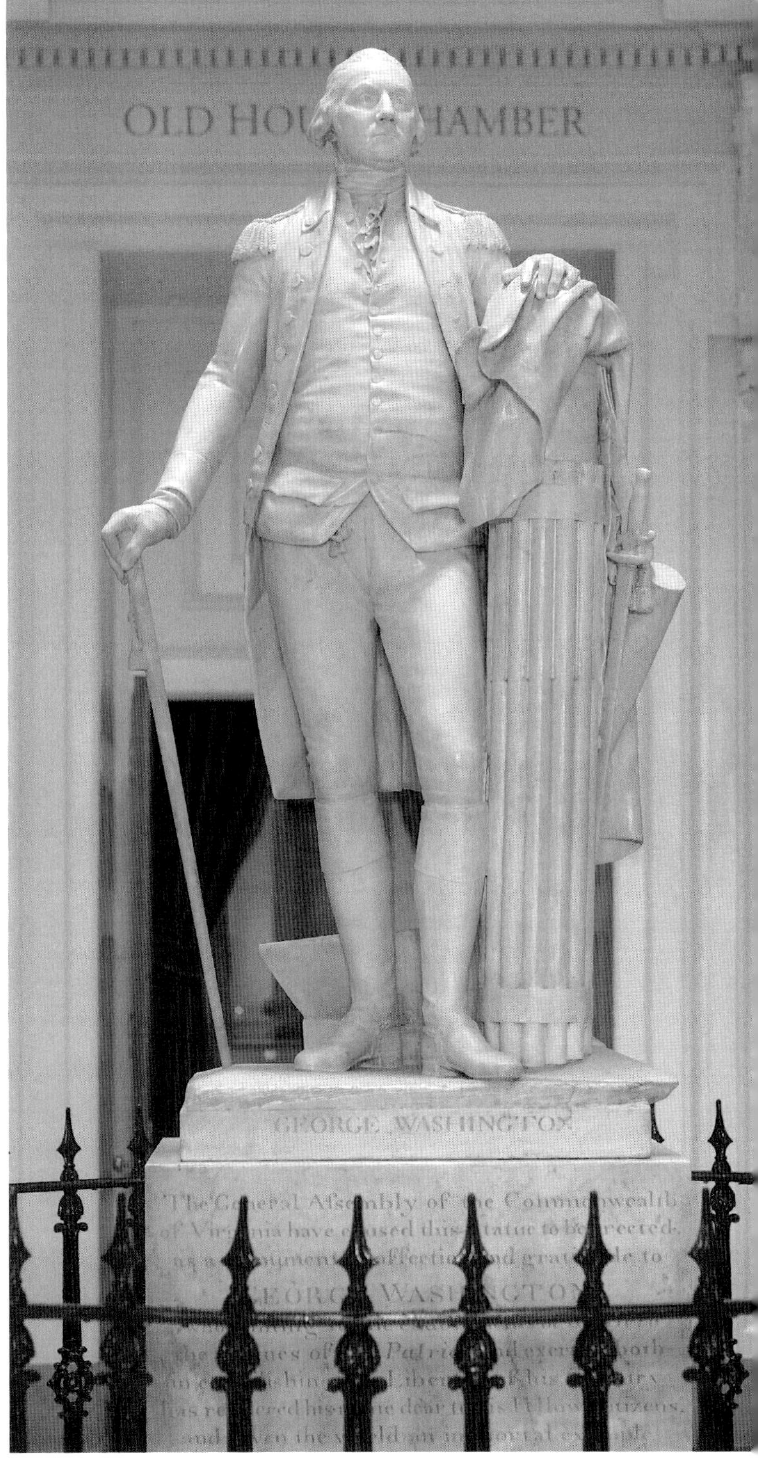

Aside from Houdon's *Washington*, one other major monument to the father of his country loomed large in Ezekiel's memory, also from his hometown. Thomas Crawford's bronze equestrian statue of Washington for the city of Richmond had arrived by ship from Italy in 1857, with Ezekiel among those citizens who helped pull it up from the dock and haul it to Capitol Square.[7] Exposure to these commemorative civic monuments in Richmond and their growing presence in major cities—to name but one more, the artist almost certainly knew of Cincinnatian Henry Kirke Brown's naturalistic equestrian statue of President Washington in New York City's Union Square (1856)—encouraged Ezekiel to pursue career opportunities he greatly desired.

George Washington had significant interactions with the Jewish community, who in small numbers arrived in the Americas as early as 1654 and were greeted with suspicion and subject to much the same bigotry they were hoping to leave behind. The open-minded president offered his support to the fledgling Jewish community, at the time between 1,500 to 2,500 people, engendering hope for the persecuted minority religion. Soon after his election to the presidency, the Hebrew Congregations of Savannah, Georgia, sent a letter of congratulations, which read in part, "Your unexampled liberality and extensive philanthropy have dispelled that cloud of bigotry and superstition which has long, as a veil, shaded religion [and] . . . enfranchised us with all the privileges and immunities of free citizens, and initiated us into the grand mass of legislative mechanism. . . . May the great Author of the worlds grant you all happiness." Washington responded, "May the same wonder-working Deity, who long since delivering the Hebrews from their Egyptian Oppressors planted them in the promised land—whose providential agency has lately been conspicuous in establishing these United States as an independent nation—still continue to water them with the dews of Heaven and make the inhabitants of every denomination participate in the temporal and spiritual blessings of that people whose God is Jehovah."[8]

When Washington visited Rhode Island during his first term in office, Moses Seixas, on behalf of Newport's Touro Synagogue, met with the president and read an address thanking him "for all the blessings of civil and religious liberty which we enjoy under an equal and benign administration." Washington replied in correspondence, quoting Hebrew scriptures, "May the children of the Stock of Abraham, who dwell in this land, continue to merit and enjoy the good will of the other inhabitants, while every one shall sit in safety under his own vine and fig-tree and there shall be none to make him afraid."[9] In celebration and remembrance of this essential letter about religious pluralism, which in its day was published in newspapers countrywide, Touro Synagogue hosts an annual public reading of Washington's missive, followed by an invited speaker. (Guests to the oldest synagogue in the United States have included Supreme Court justices Ruth Bader Ginsburg and Elena Kagan.) Washington's dealings with the Jewish community were unquestionably important to the artist, ever mindful of the opportunities accorded him and his coreligionists by the Constitution's separation of church and state, but even that was dwarfed in Ezekiel's mind by professional ambitions.

Ezekiel's *Jefferson* Holds Pride of Place in the Senate Chamber

Over a decade after making *Washington*, Ezekiel carved his first sculpture of Thomas Jefferson, a marble bust for the Senate's hallowed Vice Presidential Bust Collection, one of the earliest government commissions for that collection (1888; fig. 70). Documentation exposes Ezekiel's frame of mind as a young artist and provides a fuller picture of how the government solicited sculptors to decorate the Capitol in the nineteenth century. Extracts from the Joint Committee on the Library's minutes indicate an immediate desire to secure busts of the three living vice presidents—Hannibal Hamlin, William A. Wheeler, and Chester A. Arthur—at a cost not exceeding $800. These former vice presidents were asked to suggest a preferred artist to execute their busts. The next order of affairs was to acquire busts of the first two vice presidents: John Adams and Thomas Jefferson.[10]

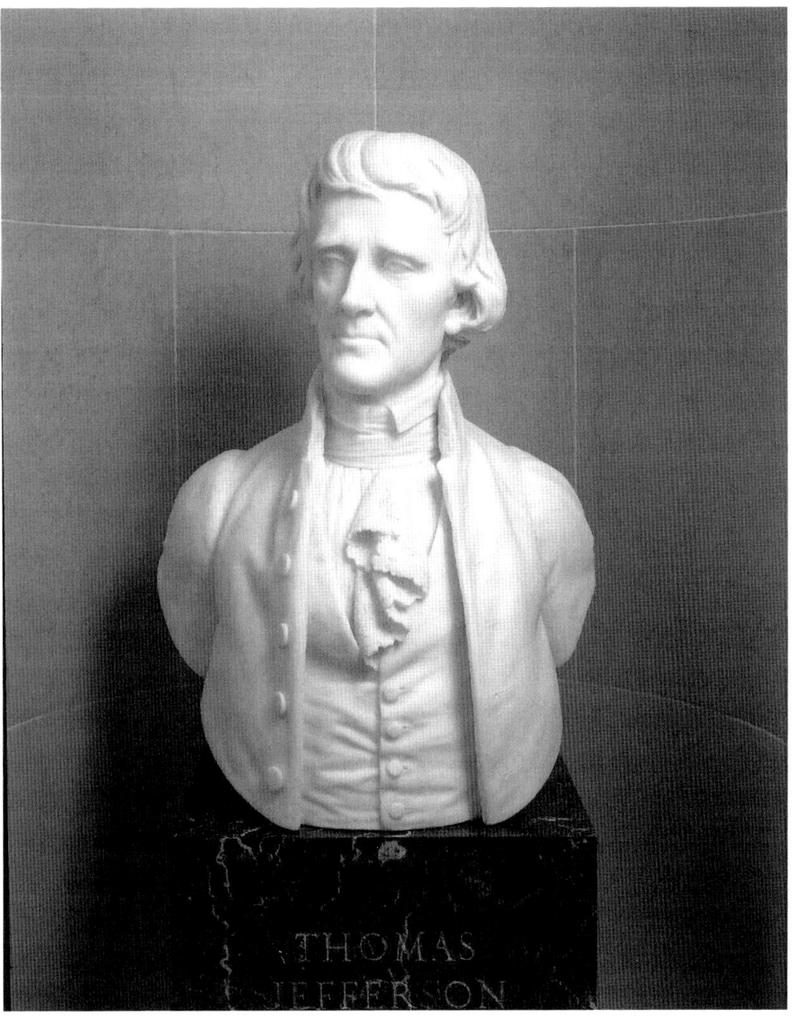

FIG. 70 Moses Jacob Ezekiel, *Thomas Jefferson*, 1888. Marble, 29 ½ x 20 x 16 ½ in. Accession no. 22.00002.000. Photo: US Senate Collection, Washington, DC.

In May 1886, Architect of the Capitol Edward Clark sent a letter to Ezekiel in Rome, requesting an overarching proposal for the Jefferson bust with all costs, including transportation. Chosen partly because he came from the same home state as his subject, Ezekiel initially misunderstood and thought that more than one bust had been ordered. Ezekiel wrote back, proposing a cost of $500 for each bust and mentioning that this is "a low estimate of price because I get $800 in Europe for every bust I make. But in consideration of a number of busts, and my desire to work for my Country—I am willing to undertake the work with pleasure."[11] Further correspondence from Clark in late June clarified the matter and provided preferred dimensions for the bust. A second letter from Ezekiel detailed a fee for a single bust at $1,000; but eager for the contract, he frankly wrote, "I will leave the matter of price with you and be satisfied . . . as I would like to have the commission, having at present no work on hand and needing it."[12] Over two years passed before Ezekiel notified

Clark of the bust's completion, along with his hope that it would "give you perfect satisfaction."[13] In his first letter to Clark, Ezekiel had informed him that custom duties for American artists are waived, and in this final stage Ezekiel filled out form number 155, declaring the work of art as the production of an American artist, which was notarized by the US consulate general in Rome before the bust shipped across the Atlantic.[14] Carved from Carrara marble and measuring 29 1/2 inches tall, the bust arrived at the Capitol in late March 1889 for the agreed-on price of $800.

Situated on a black marble pedestal, Jefferson, with slightly elevated nostrils and a protruding chin, tilts his head upward regally and toward his truncated right shoulder. Wavy hair falls to Jefferson's ears, and he furrows his eyebrows in thought. Ezekiel accentuates the president's thin build and elongated torso, with his cravat high on his long neck and embellished with lace at the bottom. A row of buttons on Jefferson's waistcoat pulls ever so slightly at the seams, allowing Ezekiel to make evident his skill at rendering material. Jefferson's shoulders slope awkwardly, perhaps to portray him with hands clasped behind his back. Whatever Ezekiel's intention, his source is unclear. Jean-Antoine Houdon's plaster Jefferson busts (1789), made from life when Jefferson served as minister to France, offer a more naturalistic, expressive appearance and clearly did not provide the younger artist with his paradigm.[15] In 1889, Ezekiel's bust was unveiled on the one hundredth anniversary of the establishment of the Senate, along with Daniel Chester French's bust of John Adams. The niches surrounding the Chamber have subsequently been filled, with newer busts now stationed throughout the Senate wing. Jefferson's bust holds pride of place, sitting conspicuously albeit somewhat stiffly in a niche on the gallery level, just to the right of the presiding officer's central desk, visible to all visitors to the Chamber and seen at televised proceedings.

Additional correspondence from Ezekiel says much about the plight of a nineteenth-century sculptor. Unlike paintings that can be created inexpensively and sold on the open market, chiseling a piece from marble or having plaster bronzed in a foundry requires significant costs for materials, housing, and labor. Sensing an opportunity to earn more money, the proactive and unabashed Ezekiel sent letters to several authorities, asking to execute more busts for the Senate collection. After receiving notification that the bust reached America safely, Ezekiel wrote again to Clark in hope for another order, enclosing papers that he had signed for remittance of his fee: "A commission to make the balance of the busts for the niches would be very acceptable indeed to me, and be of help to me in my life and work, as my other commissions are now exhausted, excepting a bust of Lord Sherbrooke which I am now doing for London. I get twice as much for it as for the Jefferson—but that is no matter. I need the work, and you would do me, and our Country I believe, a service if you would continue your favor in my behalf."[16] Whether Ezekiel received double the fee for his bust of Sherbrooke is unknown, and his mention of it may very well be a calculated move to establish his worth. Busy that same day writing letters, Ezekiel penned New York Senator William Evarts, chair of the Senate Committee on the Library, with an analogous message requesting further assignments and nodding to his bust of Lord Sherbrooke.[17] A letter with the same theme was sent to Anson McCook, secretary of the Senate.[18] These are hardly the only times when Ezekiel pounded the pavement; recall, to name one instance, his correspondence with

Corcoran officials about *Eve Hearing the Voice* and other sculptures.

The sculptor sometimes struggled for commissions, in part his own doing, because he loathed competitions. Early on, he was burned by a competition for an equestrian monument in Cincinnati to President William Henry Harrison.[19] Ezekiel had been invited to submit a model in 1887, along with over a dozen other sculptors. He was not chosen, he bemoaned, because the competition "was only a hoax" and a single judge had been given carte blanche.[20] This assertion cannot be substantiated. Prickly in defeat, Ezekiel was likely not chosen to sculpt the monument because the judges simply preferred Louis Rebisso's statue, unveiled at the World's Colombian Exposition in Chicago before it was transported to Cincinnati in 1896. As the years passed, Ezekiel often provided his services gratis or subsumed substantial fees, and so often complained about his finances.

Ezekiel's go-getter approach, the nearly indefatigable hustle that carried through his artistic career, patently counters words written to his father from art school in Berlin:

> What the Government or Societies do not choose to give upon the merits of a model in open competition, I am not the man to hanker after; and I would not lose a moment out of my studio to gain the good will or vote of the best congressman that exists. Neither do I hold it consistent with the dignity of an artist to be called upon to exhibit himself with his works and to advocate his claims to superiority as has just been done in Washington. I would never do it. . . . I do not intend to go into the sculpture business, sink or swim.[21]

In 1886, two years before he was offered the Senate's Jefferson bust, Ezekiel sent a letter to his grandmother, writing, "I feel very badly indeed when I think that my own country has repudiated me and that I have nothing to hope for at home—I shall never have any work to do for my own land if I have to mauevere [*sic*] and lobby for it. . . . I would never want a commission given to me, if I had to sacrifice my self respect and honour as an artist to get it. . . . My status cannot be established . . . by a commission of judges in Washington."[22] Having recently been spurned by competitions, as he was repeatedly during the ensuing decades, a young Ezekiel voiced insecurities that unfortunately were reinforced throughout the years. Ezekiel became his own worst enemy, losing out on opportunities because of his reluctance to put himself on the line or cutting off his nose to spite his face with his peevishness. Ultimately, Ezekiel was almost always bereft of money and gave away major works or reduced his price simply to have his sculptures erected, especially Confederate monuments. During this particularly barren period, the Corcoran sculptures behind him and compounded personally by the death of Franz Liszt, Ezekiel despondently wrote, "The few little commissions I have got in the last few years, were like drops of water in the ocean, and I find myself so embarrassed that I hardly know which way to turn."[23]

Ezekiel's *Jefferson* Rises High in Downtown Louisville

During a vacation in Rome in early 1896, Isaac Bernheim, who amassed a fortune as a whiskey distiller with his younger brother Bernard, visited Ezekiel to negotiate terms for a proposed gift to their adopted city of Louisville.[24] Because of his

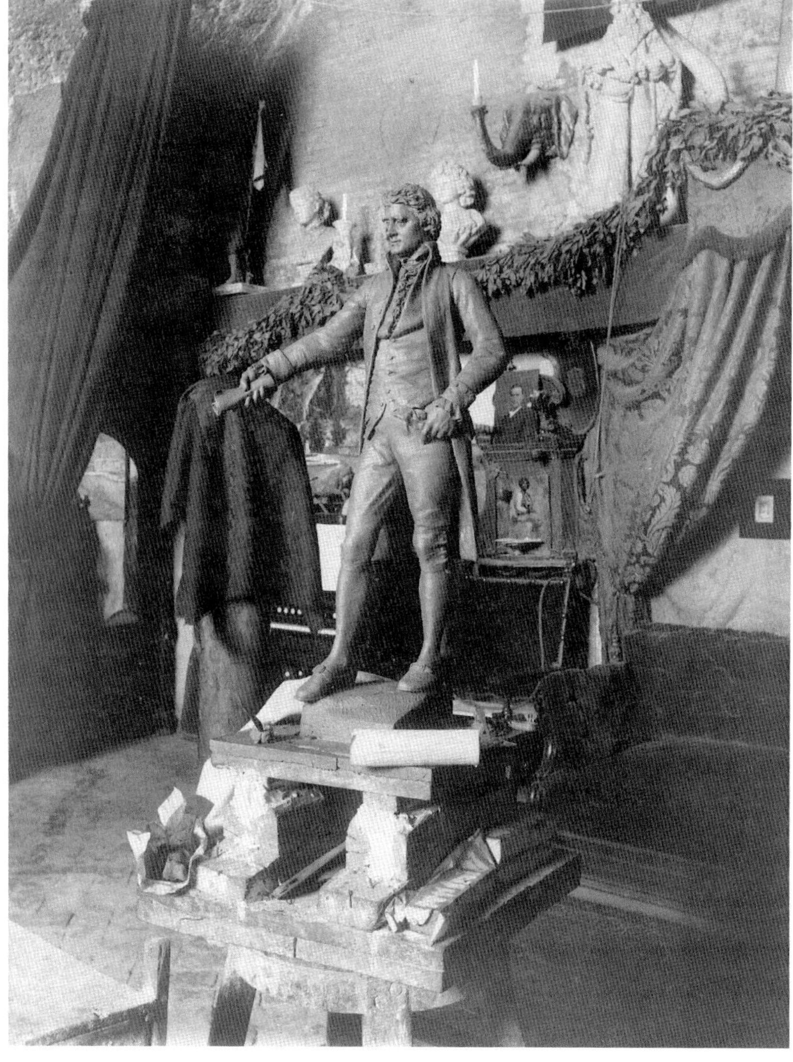

FIG. 71 Moses Jacob Ezekiel, *Thomas Jefferson*, circa 1899. Clay sketch. Courtesy of The Jacob Rader Marcus Center of the American Jewish Archives, Cincinnati, Ohio, at americanjewisharchives.org.

FIG. 72 (OPPOSITE) Hiram Powers, *Thomas Jefferson*, 1860–62. Marble, 8 ft., 4 in., pedestal 29 1/4 in. Collection of the US House of Representatives, Washington, DC. Photo: US House of Representatives.

negative experience with competitions, Ezekiel was adamantly against submitting plans in advance, so the brothers granted him full latitude to sculpt Thomas Jefferson. This subject resulted in a wholly original conception, an eighteen-and-a-half-foot-tall bronze monument to the third president for a payment of $20,000. The Bernheims ordered the bronze three years prior to securing approval from the city of Louisville, which they finally asked for in a letter dated September 18, 1899. They presented to the city a sculpture of "one of the world's greatest statesmen," in part as "education" for the city's inhabitants. Additionally, the brothers provided a permanent, invested fund of $10,000 for the monument's maintenance and a celebration at its base every Fourth of July, and an annual prize awarded to public school children who wrote the best essays commemorating a national event or person connected to the life and times of Jefferson. Only two days passed before the city's board of park commissioners responded, gratefully accepting the Bernheims's "magnificent offer."[25]

At nine feet tall, Jefferson stands atop a replica of the Liberty Bell, 9 1/2 feet tall with the corbel and nearly ten feet in diameter, all atop a ten-foot base with steps.[26] He appears as drafter of the Declaration of Independence while holding the document outward. Ezekiel depicted Jefferson in his thirties, an inventive approach, indicating the future president's age at the time when he wrote the new nation's charter. For Ezekiel, rendering Jefferson in this manner was a matter of authenticity: "Jefferson was a young man, able to stand unsupported by chair, cane, or column; I have shown him as such. Many have made him middle-aged, with a large Declaration in his hand, though, as a matter of fact, the Declaration was written on a small sheet, which I have measured."[27] An earlier exploration of his subject in clay, rejected by the artist, has Jefferson extending a rolled-up Declaration of Independence, also of small size, toward his audience (fig. 71). Both deviate from recent portrayals of Jefferson, particularly from Hiram Powers's full-length sculpture, ordered by President James Buchanan and installed on the House side of the Capitol in 1863 (fig. 72). Powers received $10,000 for the work, and the same amount for a sculpture of Benjamin Franklin that was delivered the previous year.[28] Ezekiel had been to the nation's capital twice since the installation of Powers's sculpture, which presents Jefferson holding a scroll of the Declaration by his side, so he most likely saw it. He was in Washington, DC, to speak with B'nai B'rith's lawyer about *Religious Liberty* in 1874, and in late 1876, when he met with William Corcoran to tour his gallery. Always interested in demonstrating his originality and offering a twist on the formula (e.g., *Eve Hearing the Voice*), sometimes to

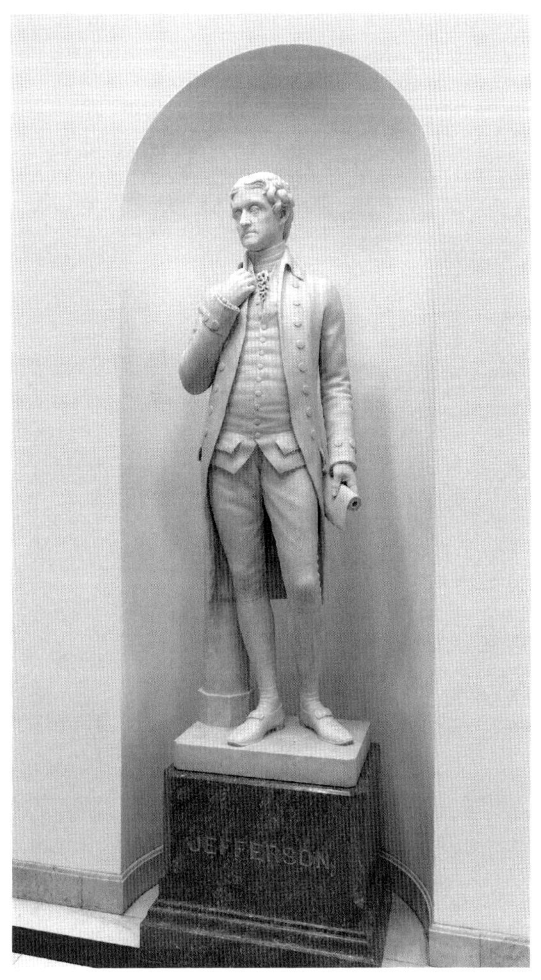

an extreme, Ezekiel opted for Jefferson to display the document facing outward and to implement an extensive allegorical program.

Four winged females, each 5 1/2 feet tall and at regular intervals, surround the bronze bell, the most recognizable symbol of American freedom. Those angelic figures embody Jeffersonian ideals: Liberty, Equality, Justice, and the Brotherhood of Man. A term Ezekiel coined for religious freedom, "Brotherhood of Man" likely derived from the use of the word "brotherhood" to denote members of the fraternal Order of B'nai B'rith. The Order promoted inclusivity for all levels of Jewish observance, much as Ezekiel hoped for unity among the world's religions. Written on the monument are two inscriptions. An inscription in relief from the book of Leviticus (25:10) encircles the top of the bell, copied exactly from the actual Liberty Bell in Philadelphia: "Proclaim liberty throughout all the land unto all inhabitants thereof (LEV. XXIV)." The relief inscription in uppercase letters around the bottom of the bell indicates the donors' names and their motive for bequeathing the sculpture: "This monument to Thomas Jefferson was presented to the people of Kentucky, July 4, 1900, by Isaac W. and Bernard Bernheim to perpetuate the teachings and examples of the founders of the republic."

On the highly polished, five-foot tall Quincy granite pedestal are four gold-gilded inscriptions: two are drawn from the Declaration of Independence and one from the Virginia Statute for Religious Freedom, the documents most synonymous with Jefferson's name. The tolerant Jefferson understood religion as a personal matter, both for himself and others. He wrote in a letter, "I never told my own religion, nor scrutinised that of another. I never attempted to make a convert, nor wished to change another's creed. I have ever judged of the religion of others by their lives."[29] On the sculpture's pedestal, the lines of interest from the Declaration of Independence begin, unforgettably, "We hold these truths to be self-evident: that all men are created equal." Markedly relevant is Ezekiel's quoting of the Virginia Statute for Religious Freedom, drafted in 1777 but not enacted into law for nearly a decade, when future President James Madison shepherded its passage through the state legislature; the Statute serves as the prototype for the First Amendment of the Bill of Rights, ratified in 1791.

Ezekiel had inscribed pivotal points from the Statute on the front of the sculpture's pedestal, most visible for viewers. He used the essential words at the start of this decisive document and then cherry-picked key points from the remainder: "Almighty God hath created the mind free. All attempts to influence it by temporal punishments or burthens—are a departure from the plan of the holy author of our religion—No man shall be compelled to frequent or support any religious worship or ministry or shall otherwise suffer on account of his religious opinions or belief, but all men shall be free to profess and by argument to maintain their opinions in matters of religion. I know but one code of morality for men whether acting singly or collectively." Another indispensable statement on religion, from Jefferson's first inaugural address (March 4, 1801), is carved on the rear: "Equal and exact justice to all men, of whatever state of persuasion, religious or practical." Gilded text on the west side of the pedestal in Louisville reads, "I have sworn upon the altar of God eternal hostility against every form of tyranny over the mind of man," which is drawn from a September 23, 1800, letter from Jefferson to Benjamin Rush.[30] In using this mode of inscriptions, sometimes to a fault, Ezekiel hammers home the message his patrons desired and the points he wanted to emphasize. Crucially, none of these quotes are on the base of the 1910 replica sculpture at the University of Virginia. They are specific to this monument of Jefferson, commissioned by two Louisville Jews at this particular moment, rather than the more universalized presentation on UVA's campus meant to simply stand for its founder.

During his monthslong trip home to the United States in 1896 to visit family and attend to business matters, Ezekiel sketched on paper

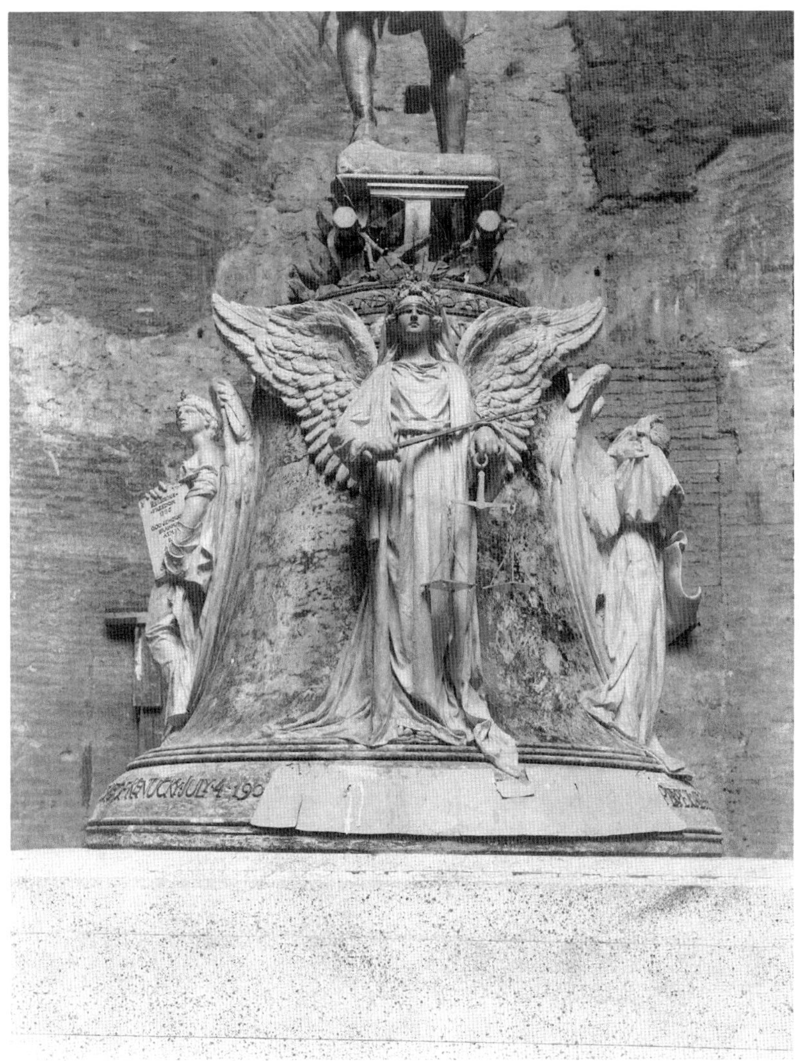

FIG. 73 Moses Jacob Ezekiel, *Justice*, 1899. Detail of the plaster model of *Thomas Jefferson* monument. Courtesy of The Jacob Rader Marcus Center of the American Jewish Archives, Cincinnati, Ohio, at americanjewisharchives.org.

some ideas for the *Jefferson* monument, which he quickly crafted as a small maquette. He stopped in Louisville, where he was Isaac Bernheim's guest at his country home. The artist surveyed the physical space mapped out for the monument and showed his maquette to the Bernheims, who expressed their enthusiasm. Upon returning to Rome, Ezekiel spent a year working on the sculpture. Because of its size, Ezekiel was forced to build a second, larger studio on the ground floor of the Baths of Diocletian. During its making, Ezekiel wrote of carting away mountains of dirt and spending thousands of lire to put in pavement, windows, and a roof.[31] Several remarkable photographs show the enormous plaster model of *Jefferson* nearly becoming one with the walls of the ancient space (fig. 73). It remained so until Ezekiel was evicted from the Baths in 1910, substantiated by King Victor Emmanuel III's visit to the studio the previous year, covered by the press, which reported the royal pronouncing *Jefferson* "the most original monument he had ever seen" and congratulating "America on having such a sculptor and Rome on being his home."[32] A strike at Quincy Quarries, fittingly on land once owned by John Adams, Jefferson's predecessor in the presidency, stymied the completion of the Louisville base.[33]

Despite the quarry strike that postponed the Louisville dedication, the monument's arrival was greatly anticipated. *Monumental News*, the *Courier-Journal*, and the *New York Times* announced that the monument was shipped on May 7 from Berlin, where it had been cast. Six weeks later, the *Times* touted the upcoming unveiling at the city's Fourth of July celebration.[34] Reaching New York in early June 1900, the sculpture stalled in its journey. Tunnels on direct railway lines from New York to Louisville were insufficient to accommodate the minimum of seventeen feet of clear space needed to transport Ezekiel's Liberty Bell; Jefferson could be laid down lengthwise, but the bell could only sit flat. The solution was to send the freight to its ultimate resting place via Buffalo.[35] Notwithstanding the delay in New York, *Jefferson* still arrived on time for the July Fourth dedication, but there was no base on which it could stand. Akin to *Religious Liberty*, another major work by Ezekiel that could not be unveiled on its intended date—a second Independence Day disappointment, twenty-four years later. *Jefferson* was not dedicated until November of the following year, which brought Ezekiel back to the United States after a mere fourteen months.

Three of the four allegorical figures adopt recognizable iconography. The winged figure occupying the front of the statue symbolizes *Liberty*, wearing a sleeveless, flowing garment that envelops her body. Resolute, she holds a dagger in one hand (recall that an abandoned version of *Religious Liberty* held a dagger) and powerfully breaks the chains from her arms, evident from her flexed muscles and the open shackles behind her. At the rear, a blindfolded *Justice* holds balanced scales in one hand and wields a drawn sword that crosses her body in the other. Initially, Ezekiel planned to dress her half in armor and half in clothing of peace, but he discarded this idea. The allegorical program would have been even more complex had Ezekiel pursued his idea of incorporating two angelic baby figures in relief, flying among clouds toward *Liberty*. One would bear a flaming torch with "Common Sense" and "The Rights of Man" inscribed on it, and the other angelic figure would have the bound staves of the Union on his shoulder.[36] Instead, wisely, *Justice* stands tall and stately with a pointed halo around her head to demonstrate her "divine" status. *Equality*, angry and intent, is situated on the left side of the bell, tearing up a large document, dated October 14, 1776, and inscribed "Laws of Primogeniture." She stamps on a document at her feet to symbolize the destruction of such obsolete laws.

On the right side of the bell, the *Brotherhood of Man* tenders the most novel, unfamiliar conception (fig. 74). An article in *Monumental News* did not even attempt to describe the personification, whereas attention was paid to the other three.[37] The *Brotherhood of Man* looks up over her left shoulder to the heavens at God. Remarkably and progressively, she holds a tablet bearing the inscription "The Statute of Religious Freedom," along with the names of several deities: "Jehova" (Hebrew God), "Brahma" (creator god in Hinduism), "Atma" (individual's essence in Hinduism), "Ra" (ancient Egyptian sun god), and "Alla" (Muslim name for God).[38] In the upper left corner, Ezekiel placed the Om of Hinduism in Sanskrit, and in the right corner, he singled out his own God, written in Hebrew, "Adonai Echad," meaning one God. Ezekiel described the *Brotherhood of Man* in a letter to his brother: "On the right-hand side the figure *Vox Populi, Vox Dei* holds jealously to her heart the tablet upon which the names of all the gods that have ever been worshipped on earth are inscribed," and decisively adds, "all of them equal under the laws of our country."[39] Years later, Ezekiel penned his father, in respect to his understanding of this female personage's embrace of all religions, "The God of the Bible is an individual personal God."[40] Ezekiel carefully planned his artistic program and purposely placed the figure denoting religious freedom between Liberty and Justice in order to signify that under US law, regardless of religion, all have equal rights and protection. Of the four angels surrounding the bell, only the wings of the *Brotherhood of Man* cradle her body. *Liberty*'s wings expand aggressively, as do those of the blindfolded *Justice*. Defiant *Equality*, turned on an angle, does not enjoy the comfort of winged protection. But the *Brotherhood of Man* possesses calm tranquility, as she is safely embraced by her elegant wings. Simultaneously majestic and delicate, the *Brotherhood of Man*'s form conveys the same rights for which she stands. For Ezekiel, religious liberty was both the most majestic and fragile of rights.

Initially, the Bernheims considered having Ezekiel make a monumental sculpture of Abraham Lincoln rather than Jefferson but soon thought otherwise, confident that the sixteenth president's home state would honor him. Isaac Bernheim wrote retrospectively that this change of heart also related to the opportunities afforded him in America as an immigrant who lived in freedom because of Jefferson's good works: "After deliberation, it occurred to me, that as my brother and I were foreign born, had been naturalized in and protected by this government, and under its benign rule had enjoyed so many blessings, that it would be a fitting thing to present the statue of him who had done more than any other man to make this country free, and who had made our success and happiness possible by inspiring Americans with the truth and justice of that immortal declaration, All men are created equal."[41]

Such freedoms were nearly taken away during the Bernheim brothers' and Ezekiel's lifetime, when Ulysses S. Grant issued General Orders No. 11 in December 1862, expelling all Jews "as a class" within twenty-four hours from districts occupied by the Union army in Kentucky, Mississippi, and Tennessee. Grant erroneously branded Jews as traitors to the Union, accusing them of smuggling cotton. Ezekiel dubbed the Order "infamous" and "anti-Jewish," mentioning it twice in his memoir.[42] So appalled by the Order, when Grant ran for president, Ezekiel penned what he termed "a very scathing letter" against his candidacy, published in several newspapers: "The Jew who does not with all his heart, soul and means, oppose the election of this second Pharoah, deserves to be publicly branded as a renegade to his faith."[43] That letter further urged his coreligionists "to oppose by every means in their power the efforts that are being made to place a man in power who, by a mere scratch of the pen, can deprive us of all the rights and benefits of a free country."[44] In correspondence nearly four decades after the fact, Ezekiel describes the incident in some depth and declares, "I denounced General Grant, comparing him to the worst czars of Russia for his famous or rather infamous Order No. 11."[45] Soon, Ezekiel received a retaliatory letter from the Richmond Union League

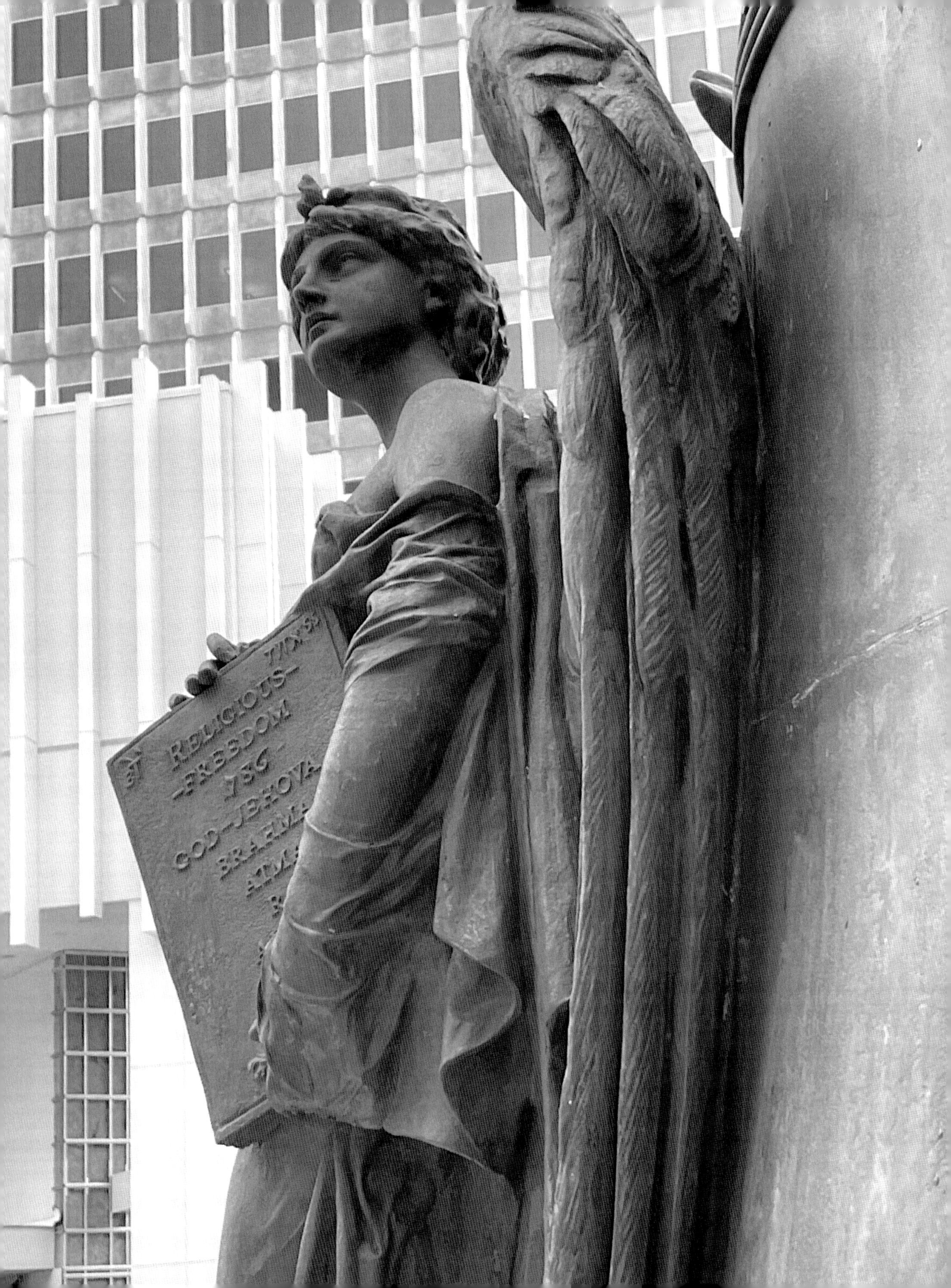
RELIGIOUS
FREEDOM

Association, informing him that his life was in danger if he did not leave the city.[46] One evening, when walking home from medical school, a shower of rocks fell from an archway, breaking windows but not hitting him. Ezekiel melodramatically described this incident as the only assassination attempt on his life. When Grant ran for a second presidential term, he toured Europe, and in Italy, he asked for an audience with Ezekiel. The artist agreed, citing Grant's recent public denouncement of the Order. (In repentance, during his presidency Grant appointed more Jews to office than any previous president.) The visit went smoothly—the hospitable artist offered him mint juleps, whiskey, and cigars—and afterward, Ezekiel attended a reception in Grant's honor. Ezekiel heard from the US consul that Grant deemed his visit to the Baths of Diocletian as his "pleasantest hour in Rome."[47]

As a testament to Ezekiel's renown, Grant was not the only president he met. President Theodore Roosevelt invited him to visit the White House in January 1902 and summoned Ezekiel back for an evening reception. While Roosevelt was busy with his guests, Ezekiel tried to sneak out, but he was waylaid by the president, who requested he stay to talk when the event ended. Ezekiel recounted that later in the evening, he and Roosevelt strolled and spoke about Rome and "matters in general there."[48] William Taft called on Ezekiel at his Roman studio, and as president, he invited the artist to be his guest at the White House. There, Ezekiel spoke with Taft about Italy's "political and financial conditions" and, as he put it, "gave him as good a report as the most patriotic Italian could have done."[49]

FIG. 74 Moses Jacob Ezekiel, *Brotherhood of Man*, 1900. Detail of *Thomas Jefferson*, Louisville, Kentucky. Photo: Samantha Baskind.

Jefferson's Louisville Unveiling and the Rewards of Religious Freedom

Four thousand people attended the unveiling of the Louisville statue, with former Kentucky Governor William O'Connell Bradley delivering an address underscoring Jefferson's teaching in favor of religious freedom, one of the underlying principles of America's government (fig. 75). "The Star-Spangled Banner" was intoned by the large crowd before Bernard Bernheim's six-year-old daughter ceremoniously pulled the cord, gracefully releasing the white canvas from the enormous bronze. Back in the United States little more than a year since his last visit when the monument's original dedication was delayed, Ezekiel, the *Courier-Journal* wrote on the front page, "sat like one transfixed when the cloth slipped from its fastenings and fell in a heap to the ground. There was a sudden burst of applause. The sculptor's black eyes brightened and he chuckled with true delight. It was his work. He had made the figure with his own hands. From material without shape or form, he had wrought a likeness, almost perfect in detail, of Thomas Jefferson, and the applause meant that hundreds of people around him approved his work."[50]

The crowd cried out for Ezekiel, who mounted the platform. Someone in the large gathering shouted for Ezekiel to make a speech, but he demurred and hid behind two dignitaries, according to a newspaper account.[51] Rabbi Hyman G. Enelow delivered a prayer at the ceremony's end, and all stood again and sang "America the Beautiful." The brothers could have quietly donated the monument to the city as immigrant citizens of the United States without any religious components at the unveiling. Instead, the Bernheims very publicly announced their Jewishness to their hometown,

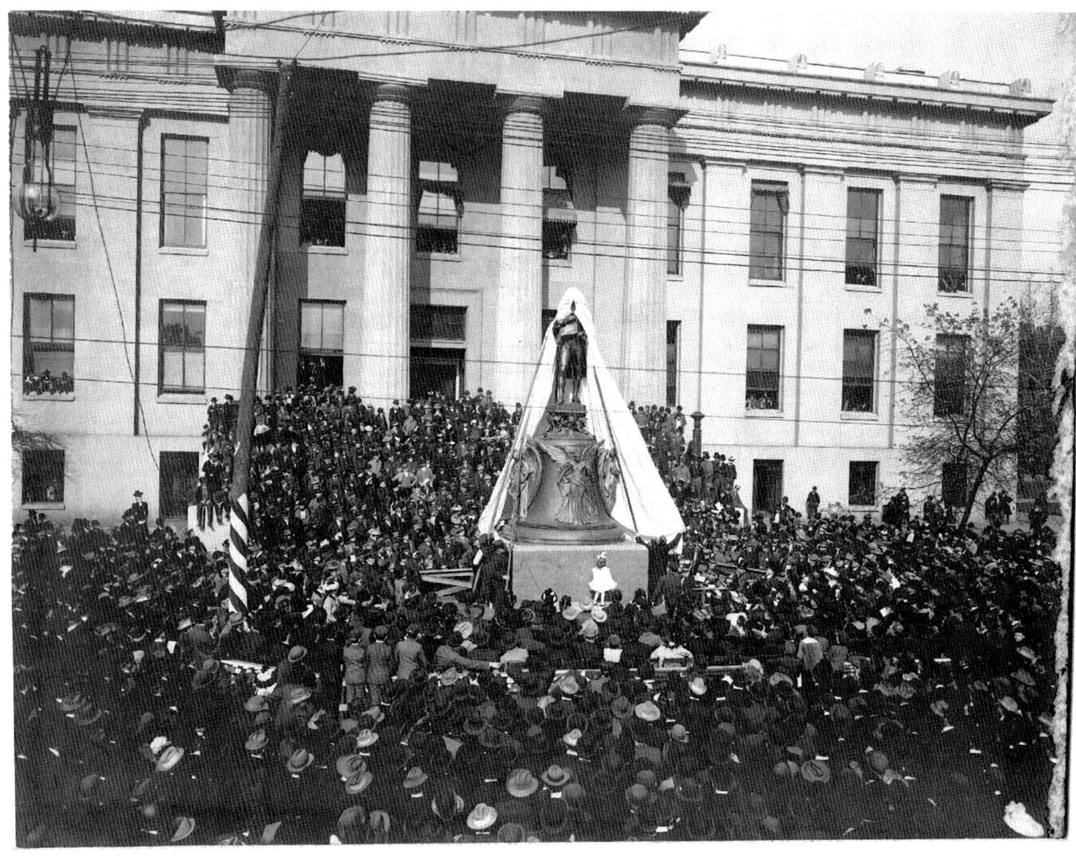

FIG. 75 Dedication of Thomas Jefferson statue, November 9, 1901. Photo: The Filson Historical Society, Louisville, Kentucky.

unconcerned about flouting their religiocultural heritage and feeling safe enough as Jews in democratic America to ask Rabbi Enelow to offer the benediction.

The brothers' Jewish American experience could not have been more different from that of the eminent, American-born sculptor.[52] Originally from Germany, Isaac Bernheim immigrated to the United States at age eighteen with four dollars to his name. Following a stint in New York, he worked as a peddler, traveling with horse and wagon through Pennsylvania selling household items. When his horse died, Bernheim moved to Paducah, Kentucky, where he had family. He gained work experience there and began bookkeeping for a liquor company, Loeb, Bloom, and Co. After saving enough money, Isaac brought Bernard to the United States in January 1870. Within two years, they set up their own successful distilling business, which the brothers eventually moved to Louisville to expand their opportunities in a larger city. Philanthropic and active in Jewish communal life, Isaac was involved with the Union of American Hebrew Congregations (now the Union for Reform Judaism) and in 1890 funded the renewal of the Young Men's Hebrew Association in Louisville, which had been shuttered since the Civil War, for which he served as the first president; renamed the Jewish Community Center, it exists to this day.

An art enthusiast, Isaac Bernheim sponsored two statues to represent Kentucky in the Capitol from artist Charles H. Niehaus, who was born in Cincinnati, studied art in Germany, and lived in Rome for a time. Those bronzes—of Kentucky statesman *Henry Clay* (1929) and surgeon *Ephraim McDowell* (1929)—remain in National Statuary Hall and the Capitol Visitor's Center, respectively. Bernheim ultimately did sponsor a full-length statue of *Abraham Lincoln* (1922) by George Grey Barnard for outside the Louisville Free Public Library. Here again, a rabbi, Bernheim's nephew, delivered the invocation.

Unlike Ezekiel, Isaac Bernheim was sympathetic to Reform Jews, whom he termed "advanced Hebrews," and firmly believed that "it was impossible for the ancient habits of the orthodox Jew to compete with the customs of the country in which he lived."[53] A practicing Reform Jew and devotee of Rabbi Isaac Mayer Wise, Bernheim contributed to the rabbi's newspaper, *American Israelite*, and generously donated monies to Hebrew Union College, establishing the seminary's library. Also unlike Ezekiel, Bernheim held Rabbi Wise in high esteem for his liberal approach to Judaism. "He had the foresight to know that the old-fashioned Oriental form of Jewish worship was out of place in our progressive, Occidental civilization, and that to hold the interest and claim the loyalty of the rising generation in Israel it had to be adapted to the advanced and enlightened spirit of the age," Bernheim wrote.[54] No matter their different ideologies, this collaboration between Jewish patron and sculptor was based on a shared admiration for Jefferson and appreciation for the rewards of religious liberty.

Bernheim's status as a Jew who could find freedom and success in America was never far from his mind. Years after the erection of the Jefferson monument, he extolled the virtues of religious liberty on American soil, conspicuously co-opting the term Ezekiel introduced for his allegorical figure: "The most thrilling prospect before us to-day [*sic*] is the vision of the Brotherhood of Man, and it is by toleration alone that this vast and kindling harmony of races and creeds can be achieved. In this respect America and Australia lead, and they will be the pioneers for the rest of the world."[55]

An early scholarly volume on the subject similarly viewed protection of religion as America's great contribution to the world. Published soon after the *Jefferson* dedication, Sanford Cobb's study on religious liberty in America aims to demonstrate the sharp contrast between American and European governments. As stated in Cobb's preface, his book traces "those influences and events which guided the American republics to their unique solution of the world-old problem of Church and State—a solution so unique, so far-reaching, and so markedly diverse from European principles as to constitute the most striking contribution of America to the science of government."[56] Ezekiel concurred that religious liberty was especially unique to America. Mary Argyle Taylor's appreciation of Ezekiel paraphrased his thoughts on the subject: "Once he told me that he had tried to give the figure of religious liberty on the Jefferson monument a peculiarly American type of face because he considered religious liberty so peculiarly an American gift to civilization."[57] While the female personification of *Religious Liberty* in Philadelphia is mature, even motherly as she physically protects the young *Faith*, Ezekiel's vision for a personification of all the religions of the world is a lovely and innocent young woman who knows of no strife.

Ezekiel's *Jefferson* at the University of Virginia

The full-scale copy of the Louisville monument in Charlottesville was in great part a gift from the artist (fig. 76). Some years earlier, Andrew D. White, cofounder and first president of Cornell University, had encouraged Ezekiel to visit UVA's campus to look over the buildings and grounds to evaluate fitting locations for new works of art, which he did in 1900. This suggestion was made after White, for whom Ezekiel sculpted a bust of his wife, Clara Dickson White (1888; Cornell University, Ithaca, NY), saw *Jefferson* at the bronze foundry in Berlin prior to being shipped to Louisville, and he recognized the suitability of the monument for UVA's campus. White wrote to the Bernheims from Europe in 1900, "I know of no memorial statue or group superior to this . . . the grouping of the whole is masterly."[58]

The Charlottesville replica was executed at the suggestion of Thomas Nelson Page, who spoke so highly of Ezekiel at the *Homer Group* dedication. Page visited Ezekiel in Rome and admired his model of the Jefferson monument. There, the ambassador learned from Ezekiel that at one time a New York–based alumnus of UVA had attempted to raise funds for a replica, but that individual unexpectedly died, so the project stalled. Page renewed these efforts and facilitated the gift. Delighted to replicate the sculpture for his home state, Ezekiel donated his time to modify the wording on the bell support. In early discussions, Ezekiel offered the sculpture with the caveat that UVA defray the cost of casting, pedestal, and transportation. However, in the end, Ezekiel even paid for the nearly eight-foot red marble pedestal. Ezekiel remembered having the sculpture lifted with a chain and pulley to build up temporarily what would in due course be its red marble base.[59] Ezekiel's generosity vis-à-vis *Jefferson* surpassed his gift of the old bard's base.

Additional funding for *Jefferson* was provided by Page and many others, including alumnus George C. Thomas, who saw the model in Ezekiel's studio. An itemized list of donations in the university's alumni bulletin indicates that Page and Thomas gave $1,000 each.[60] Some donors were not UVA alumni but donated because of a broader belief in Jefferson's ideals. Perhaps most interesting is a contribution by Joseph Bryan: $500 in memory of a deceased "Jewish friend, a brilliant fellow-student" named Gratz Cohen, who perished on the battlefield at Bentonville when fighting on the Confederate side during the Civil War.[61] The author of an article in the UVA alumni bulletin speculated that Bryan contributed in honor of Cohen because he recognized the importance of Jefferson's stance on religious freedom for American Jews: "Many of his [Ezekiel's] race have found the University of Virginia what its great founder must have desired it to be: an institution where a man shall count as a man, and where neither race nor creed shall be allowed to weigh in the balance."[62] Other noteworthy donors include Jews without ties to the university: financier Jacob Schiff ($250); Jefferson and Isaac Seligman ($100 apiece), descendants of banker Joseph Seligman; Isidor Straus, co-owner with his brother of R. H. Macy and Co. ($200);

FIG. 76 Moses Jacob Ezekiel, *Thomas Jefferson*, 1910. Bronze, Jefferson 9 ft., bell pedestal 9 ft., marble base, 7 ft. 10 in. University of Virginia. Charlottesville. Photo: Samantha Baskind.

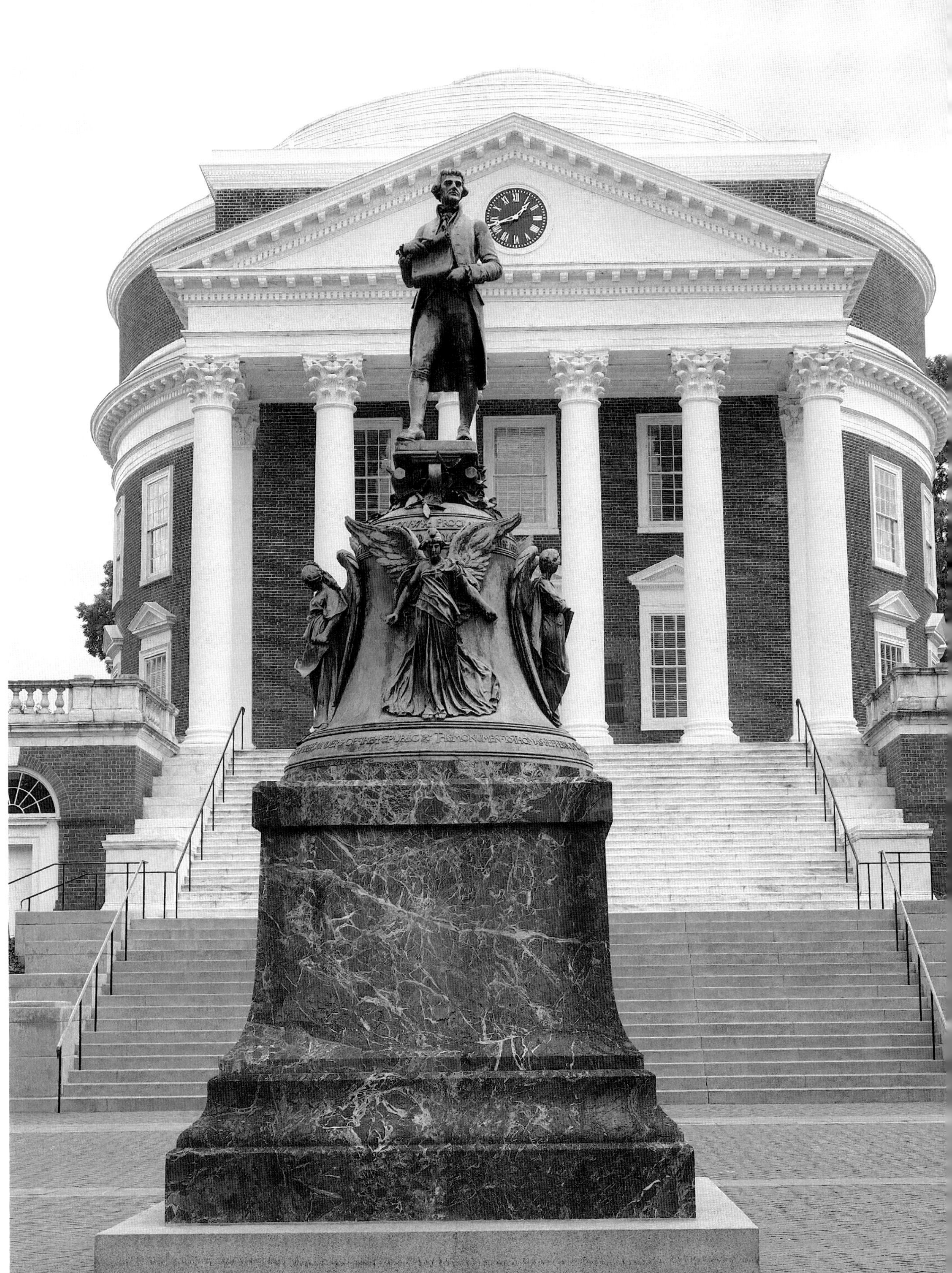
OF THE REPUBLIC
THIS MONUMENT TO THOMAS

and B'nai B'rith ($100). Rabbi Cohen of Richmond spearheaded a subscription in support of the city's eminent sculptor, raising $200 from nineteen additional donors, most if not all Jewish, based on their surnames. Total funds raised equaled $7,633.50.[63]

On the north end of the Lawn, the monument faces Madison Hall and sits in front of the university's Rotunda (1822–26), designed by Jefferson himself. Modeled after the Pantheon in Rome (though half its height and diameter), the Rotunda serves as the visual focus of Jefferson's "Academical Village." The sculpture's stately presence is enhanced by Corinthian columns situated behind it in Virginia and the Doric columns of the Greek Revival courthouse in Louisville. In contrast to Louisville's *Jefferson*, the UVA statue adopts only two inscriptions: the quote from Leviticus, plus an abridgment of the earlier quote around the lower edge of the bell for the Louisville *Jefferson*, omitting the names of donors: "To perpetuate the teachings and examples of the founders of the republic this monument to Thomas Jefferson was presented to the people." The size and placement of Ezekiel's monument in front of the Rotunda makes it the most prominent sculpture on campus; it holds additional significance as the centerpiece before the building that anchors the university. Chapels typically anchored institutions of higher learning, but Jefferson, intent on separating education from religion, envisioned the "holy temple" of his university as a library, housed inside the Rotunda until 1938.

Ezekiel's classicizing bent and allegorical conception contrast strongly with other statues of Jefferson on campus, among them the university's first, a nearly one-ton marble by Alexander Galt, a fellow expatriate Virginian and Confederate, who carved the marble sculpture in Italy in 1861 on commission from the Virginia state legislature.[64] Situated in the Rotunda, Galt faithfully renders the statesman in classical simplicity at full length, holding the Declaration of Independence at his breast. After settling in America by his early twenties, Karl Bitter, an Austrian-born sculptor, designed several sculptures of the third president at different ages, including a bronze portrait that depicts an elderly Jefferson sitting in a chair with a document in his lap.[65] Bitter's *Jefferson* is also devoid of allegory in preference for naturalism (1915; fig. 77). Less visible than Ezekiel's monument, Bitter's sculpture dwells in an obscure, leafy niche near the Lawn.

Ezekiel's penultimate trip to the United States, in 1910, was eventful. He crossed the ocean for four occasions: the unveilings of *Jefferson* in Charlottesville, *Stonewall Jackson* in Charleston, West Virginia, and a lone soldier monument on Johnson's Island at Lake Erie; and at VMI's commencement exercise, he conferred Jackson-Hope medals to the two cadets with the highest academic achievements. The *New York Times* covered his visit for the UVA dedication, more accurately referring to him as "Cavaliere Moses Ezekiel," not Sir Moses Ezekiel, but the paper erroneously states that the monument was on a smaller scale than the Louisville version. Interviewed for the article, Ezekiel explained that he had not been home for five years because of the pressure of his current workload, and that he was currently modeling in clay a statue of Napoleon at St. Helena (see fig. 97).[66]

Following UVA commencement exercises, Senator Thomas Martin, a classmate of Ezekiel's who had fought with him at the Battle of New Market, presented the monument, remarking on the four allegorical spirits as symbolizing Jefferson's "chief aspirations and purposes of his life," a phrase he employed twice.[67] President Alderman accepted

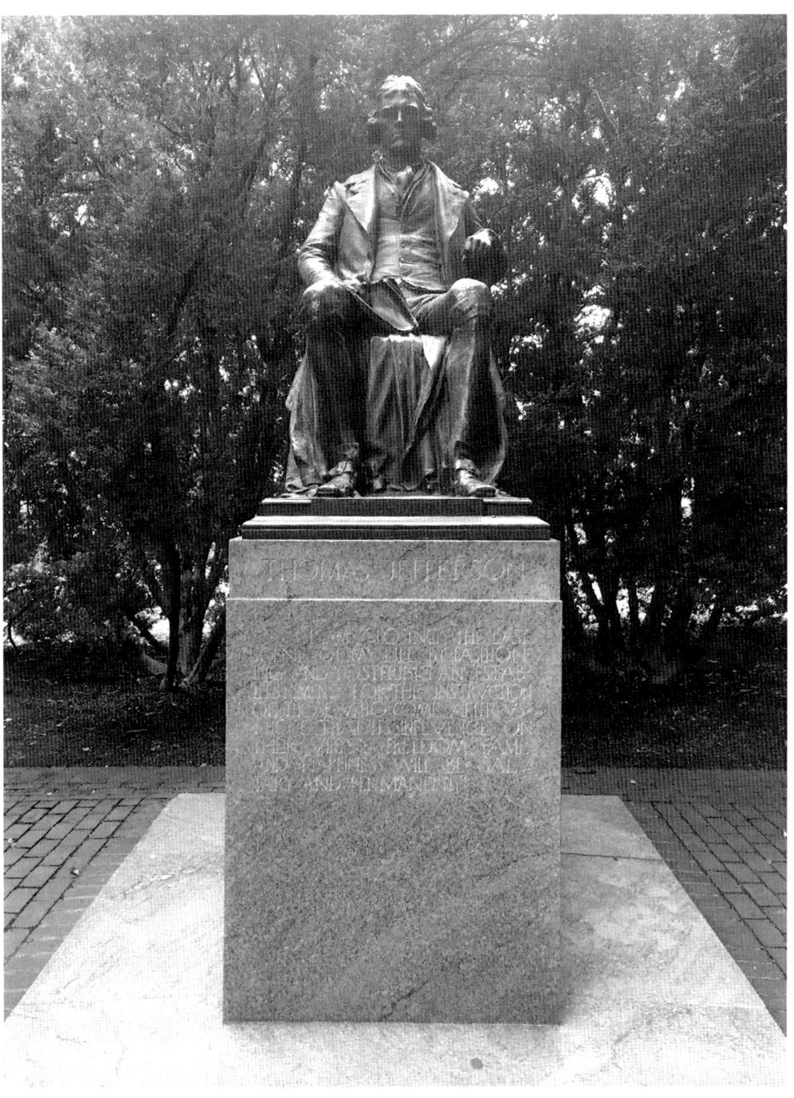

FIG. 77 Karl Bitter, *Thomas Jefferson*, 1915. Bronze, Jefferson, 5 ft., 5 in., pedestal 4 ft., 1 ¼ in. University of Virginia, Charlottesville. Photo: Samantha Baskind.

"the noble statue" and heralded Ezekiel's devotion to Virginia by voicing his gratitude "to the man of imagination whose genius created this work of art, whose patriotism desired that it should stand upon the soil of his native State."[68] The young son of William X. Randolph, a descendant of Jefferson, drew the veil. But the moment was marred by a prank. A student placed a chamber pot on Jefferson's head, which was discovered only when the sheet was removed. Ezekiel, who preferred not to speak in public, gave a brief address—still the longest of his career—effusively eulogizing his love of the Commonwealth:

> Nobody ever loved Virginia any more than I. Every stone, every piece of earth, everybody, everything in Virginia has remained in my heart just the same as when I was a boy down to the present moment, and the greatest

desire I have ever had was to see a good work of mine placed on my native soil. When you speak of gratitude, there is no gratitude due to me. I owe the gratitude to [you] to feel that I am worthy to have my work placed where the spirit of Thomas Jefferson hovers and where it will ever be.[69]

Neither passing years nor absence lessened Ezekiel's filial affection for his mother state.

Ezekiel's gratitude for Thomas Nelson Page's intercession apropos the Jefferson monument at UVA was so great that around 1910 he gifted his friend with a quarter-scale replica of the monument (49 × 25 in.).[70] Only two of this size are known; the other one, donated by the artist to VMI in 1914, is currently on display at the Virginia Museum of the Civil War in New Market Battlefield State Historical Park. Rosewell Page inherited the bronze after his brother's death and bequeathed the sculpture to the Commonwealth of Virginia in 1924, in memory of Thomas Page. It was exhibited in downtown Richmond's Thomas Hunter Blanton Office Building, renamed the Jefferson State Office Building, then moved to the Library of Virginia, which holds a copy of the Virginia Statute for Religious Freedom. In addition, Ezekiel fabricated a small, twenty-four-inch statuette of Jefferson holding the Declaration of Independence outward, standing only on a platform and without the Liberty Bell or its allegorical decorations (ca. 1900).

It is worth briefly revisiting the dedication of *Blind Homer and Young Guide* for the affair's unforeseen connection to Jews and religious freedom. Unable to attend the unveiling of *Homer* in June 1907, Ezekiel chose UVA alumnus Rabbi Edward N. Calisch of Richmond to speak on his behalf:

There is no class of people that appreciates and loves the University of Virginia more than the Jewish people. Thomas Jefferson was the champion of religious liberty and the founder of the University. His spirit hovers yet over this favorite child of his, and makes it to be the home of justice, of liberty and of equal opportunity. The Jews are handicapped in the schools of the Old World to-day, and in the years that have gone the benches upon which they were compelled to sit in the school of life were hard indeed. Therefore do they rejoice in this gift from one of their heaven-dowered children unto this University, symbolizing their devotion and their affectionate appreciation.[71]

Although *Blind Homer and Young Guide* has no religious undertones, Rabbi Calisch capitalized on an opportunity to remind a large audience about Judaism and religious liberty when speaking on the grounds of the university founded by the American statesman most affiliated with that freedom. Like Bernheim, Ezekiel and Rabbi Calisch realized an occasion to introduce a rabbi and the Jewish religion to the greater populace in conjunction with a widely publicized and well-attended event.

Uriah Phillips Levy, Thomas Jefferson, and Monticello

The first full-length portrait statue for the Capitol building, a seven-foot-tall bronze of Thomas Jefferson by French sculptor Pierre-Jean David d'Angers (1834; fig. 78), was also commissioned by a Jewish patron: Uriah Phillips Levy, the first Jewish commodore in the United States Navy. Levy's illustrious career included service in the War of 1812, when he and the rest of the crew were taken prisoner by the British and held in captivity for sixteen months, and he spearheaded the banning of flogging in the navy.[72] D'Angers's straightforward bronze of Jefferson shows the president holding in his right hand a quill pen and in his left a scroll, which runs along his body from the top of his thigh to his feet, with legible text from the Declaration of Independence in its entirety, including signatures. At his feet lie two books, possibly denoting the collection that Jefferson donated to the Library of Congress, and a laurel wreath of poetry. On the marble and granite pedestal, d'Angers austerely incised one word in capital letters, "Jefferson," whose simplicity speaks for itself. The bronze base indicates the donor's name and intent: "Presented by Uriah Phillips Levy of the United States Navy to his fellow citizens, 1833."[73]

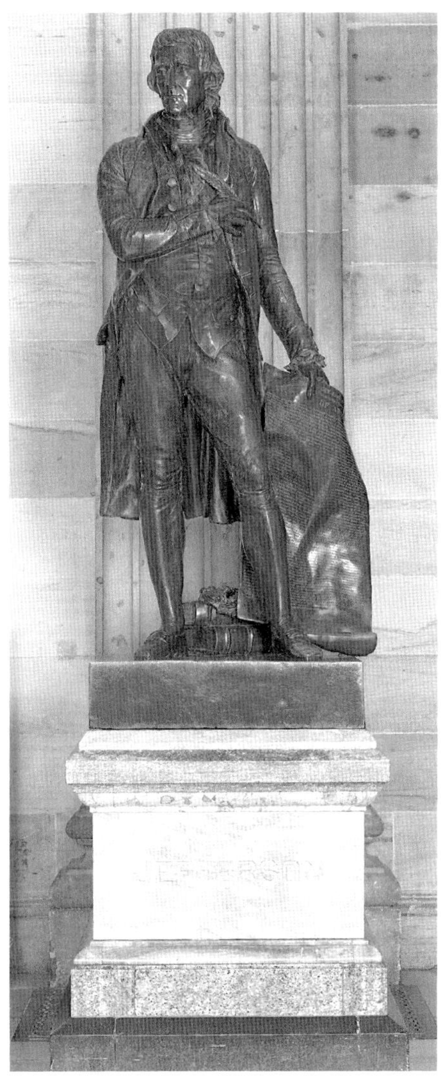

FIG. 78 Pierre-Jean David d'Angers, *Thomas Jefferson*, 1834. Bronze, 7 ft. Capitol Rotunda, Washington, DC. Courtesy of Architect of the Capitol.

Like his fellow Jews Ezekiel and Bernheim, Levy admired Jefferson's principles, especially religious freedom. He faced antisemitism throughout his naval career but remained openly Jewish. At a naval review in 1857, Levy proudly announced to the Court of Inquiry, "My parents were Israelites, and I was nurtured in the faith of my ancestors. In deciding to adhere to it, I have but exercised a right guaranteed to me by the Constitution of my native State and of the United States, a right given to all men by their Maker, a right more precious to each of us than life itself."[74] Levy's gift is the only privately sponsored work of art in the Capitol. At the same time, he gifted a bronzed plaster model for d'Angers's Jefferson to the city of New York, where it stood in the City Hall council chamber until its removal in 2021, over objections to the third president's slaveholding history; the sculpture now resides in the New-York Historical Society.[75] In a letter from 1832, Levy explained his motivations: "I consider Thomas Jefferson to be one of the greatest men in history. . . . He did much to mold our Republic in a form in which a man's *religion* does not make him ineligible for political or governmental life."[76] Echoing Isaac Bernheim, Levy continued, "As a small payment for his determined stand on the side of religious liberty, I am preparing to personally commission a statue of Jefferson."[77]

It is largely unknown that Jefferson's mountaintop home Monticello owes a significant debt to Jewish American generosity.[78] Levy, who gained great wealth investing in real estate, so appreciated Jefferson that he purchased a run-down Monticello in 1836 and was pivotal in restoring the mansion and its grounds. When Levy died, he left Monticello to the US government. His will specified that if the government declined his offer, then next in line for the estate was the Commonwealth of Virginia, followed by the Sephardic synagogues of Newport, New York, and Philadelphia. The philanthropic Levy generously donated to Jewish causes and acted as the first president of the Washington Hebrew Congregation. Seventeen years later, after the government failed to maintain the home, leaving Monticello in disrepair again—in part because the Confederacy had seized the estate during the Civil War—another Levy became a steward of the property. Uriah Levy's nephew, Jefferson Monroe Levy, a three-term congressman from New York who found similar success in real estate, carried on his uncle's legacy by once more preserving and restoring the property. For almost a century, the Levys tirelessly spent time and fortune to save Jefferson's home and grounds from ruin, until 1923, when the newly founded Thomas Jefferson Foundation acquired Monticello from Jefferson Levy.

During his trip to Charlottesville in 1900 to assess locations for his *Jefferson*, Ezekiel made it a point to visit Monticello, which he describes in some detail. He evaluated the quality of the art and the furniture in the home, expressing regret that very little had belonged to Jefferson. During this visit, Ezekiel met Jefferson Levy, who invited him to dine. Ezekiel enthused about the experience (he used one of the few exclamation points in his autobiography; another was employed when relaying his acceptance of an order to sculpt Lincoln): "I found myself at last, in the old dining room of Thomas Jefferson!"[79] A member of the Levy family suggested that when Ezekiel visited the university, he should see Galt's ideal statue of the president, which the artist did and found lacking. Paying his respects at Jefferson's grave, Ezekiel saw the epitaph that the onetime governor of Virginia scripted for his own tombstone, which underscored the bill for religious liberty:

> Here was buried
> Thomas Jefferson
> Author of the
> Declaration
> of
> American Independence
> of the
> Statute of Virginia for Religious Freedom
> and Father of the
> University of Virginia

As a man who epitomized democracy and wrote the Virginia Statute for Religious Freedom, Jefferson stood for the religious liberty so attractive to Jews like Levy and the Bernheims. Ezekiel's work celebrates that same freedom, as did his earlier centennial monument on the theme. He initially planned the Philadelphia group's pedestal to be a Liberty Bell; but instead, it is plainer and more angular, bearing an engraved inscription explicit in purpose: "Religious Liberty, Dedicated to the People of the United States by the Order B'nai B'rith and Israelites of America." The freedom afforded Jews in America, a country Ezekiel loved to his last day, was of great importance to him and his coreligionists who sponsored prominent sculptures of Jefferson.

A Southern Patriot's Unlikely Busts of Lincoln

Sometime in the late 1880s, Ezekiel attended a dinner party in Rome with guests, including Alessandro Fortis, an Italian politician who would in time serve as his country's first Jewish prime minister. Seeking to impress the young American, who subsequently became a good friend, Fortis offered a toast to the memory of Abraham Lincoln. Ezekiel responded by explaining that he had fought against Lincoln and General Grant but "did not object to drinking to Lincoln's health, although I had not yet quite recovered from the shock of Southern subjugation." He remarked that his dining companions "seemed to be horrified at the idea of my having fought for slavery and were very much surprised when I explained that we had never fought for slavery, but for states' rights and for free trade."[80] This was not the only instance when Ezekiel espoused Lost Cause ideology (chapter 6).

At a different time, Ezekiel more derisively and dismissively called Lincoln a "sectional president . . . who had not received a single vote in all of the fourteen Southern states." (Lincoln did receive Southern votes but did not carry any Southern states.)[81] Remembering seeing Lincoln walk up Richmond's Main Street in April 1865, Ezekiel negatively judged the president's appearance: He wore "an uncouth beaver hat on his tall ungainly figure."[82] Ezekiel's perspective on Lincoln counters that of Simon Wolf, the spearhead for *Religious Liberty* and a man fully against slavery, who recognized the sixteenth president as "the very incarnation of all that was just, true and manly, not only for the Christian but for the Jew, not only for the white man but for the negro, not only for the American but for all men, no matter from what part of the world they came."[83] Uriah Levy, also an abolitionist, purportedly offered Lincoln his fortune to support the Union.[84]

In 1896, the artist who asserted that he "had not yet quite recovered from the shock of Southern subjugation" chiseled a marble bust of Abraham Lincoln for Nathaniel Myers, a philanthropist in New York who donated liberally to Jewish causes.[85] When meeting Myers in New York City, the lawyer asked Ezekiel if he could overcome his "scruples" to carve the sixteenth president. Aware of the irony, Ezekiel put it, with emphasis, "I was to make the War President of America!"[86] Characteristically in need of funds, Ezekiel was indeed able to quash his political scruples and unyielding Southern patriotism. Ezekiel cited two sources that greatly aided him: an etching drawn from life provided by Myers and a copy of Lincoln's life mask.[87] The sole surviving photograph of the now-lost marble, published in the *New York Times* three decades after its completion, shows the bust sitting on a dark columnal pedestal. A caption notes that the work is interesting because it was produced by a Confederate soldier.[88]

Even if Ezekiel found Lincoln disagreeable because of his abolitionist stance, or at least for his so-called subversion of states' rights by eradicating slavery across the nation, the artist must have felt some gratitude for his quick action after Grant issued General Orders No. 11. When the Jews of Paducah, Kentucky, received papers notifying them of the Order, some rallied and sent a telegram to Lincoln indicating their outrage over "this inhuman order; the carrying out of which would be the grossest violation of the Constitution and our rights as good citizens under it."[89] Fearful and desperate to quash the Order, Prussian-born Cesar Kaskel, a Union man, successful merchant, and Jewish citizen of Paducah, quickly traveled to Washington, DC, to speak with the president. Such expedience proved warranted since Lincoln had not heard about the Order until Kaskel informed him. An oft-quoted, somewhat poetic (and unlikely) exchange between Kaskel and the president has Lincoln responding to news of the Order by saying, "And so the children of Israel were driven from the happy land of Canaan?" To which Kaskel replied, "Yes, and that is why we have come unto Father Abraham's bosom, asking protection." Lincoln declared, "And this protection they shall have at once," and then he speedily revoked the Order.[90] Lincoln's sympathy for Jews further manifests by his appointment of Jewish chaplains and officers to the Union army.[91]

Around the turn of the century, Ezekiel crafted a series of undated, 15 1/2-inch-tall bronze busts of Lincoln cast from the plaster (fig. 79; the bust was to be included in the censored Princeton exhibition).[92] Thus, we know that Ezekiel's sculpture for Myers shows the president's head cocked toward his right, capturing the Great Emancipator's elongated face and deep-set eyes but not overemphasizing the cragginess of his features or his typically gaunt, haggard countenance. A more successful bust than *Jefferson* in the Senate collection, *Lincoln* looks thoughtful, more convivial than serious, with a smile nearly playing on his lips. The folds of his jacket, vest, and shirt are naturalistic, and the lopsided, casual manner by which his tie hangs conveys affability.

It appears that the bronzes were not sponsored; rather, the entrepreneurial Ezekiel made them as reasonably priced parlor pieces for a receptive, middle-class audience eager to purchase a likeness of their beloved, martyred president. Sculptor John Rogers provided a prototype for this approach, although on a larger scale and at a much lower price point. Rogers churned out approximately eighty thousand factory-produced statuettes in his lifetime, some depicting the life of everyday Americans and Civil War subjects, at an average cost of fourteen dollars.[93] These hugely popular, editioned, plaster "Rogers Groups" included *The Council of War* (1868) in three slight variations. Storytelling in nature, *The Council of War* portrays a seated Lincoln holding a map of the Union's war campaign, accompanied by Secretary of War Edwin M. Stanton and General Ulysses S. Grant. It is unknown who purchased Ezekiel's Lincoln busts, except for one. The Bernheim brothers acquired a copy in 1900.

Plans to acquire the bust were reported by the *Courier-Journal*: "If there is proper response from the art loving, as well as patriotic people of the city, a magnificent bronze bust of Abraham Lincoln will soon grace some conspicuous site in Louisville."[94] While Ezekiel's monument to Jefferson had yet to be installed in front of the Louisville courthouse, news of the enormous statue and its famous sculptor had been the talk of the town and the bust was keenly anticipated. Isaac Bernheim organized a campaign to raise $1,500 by popular subscription to purchase the bust, aiming to create a sense of ownership and civic pride. He hoped for contributions from 1,500 people at one dollar each, enough to defray all expenses. Before a real effort to secure monies, over one hundred people had subscribed to the fund.[95] The *Lincoln* bust was housed but not exhibited until the arrival from Europe of the pedestal, measuring 4 1/2 feet tall and part of an antique column, which Ezekiel procured from a Roman temple and cut to the required size.

There was some breakdown in fundraising because the Bernheims alone gifted the bust to the state of Kentucky in May 1901. Governor Augustus

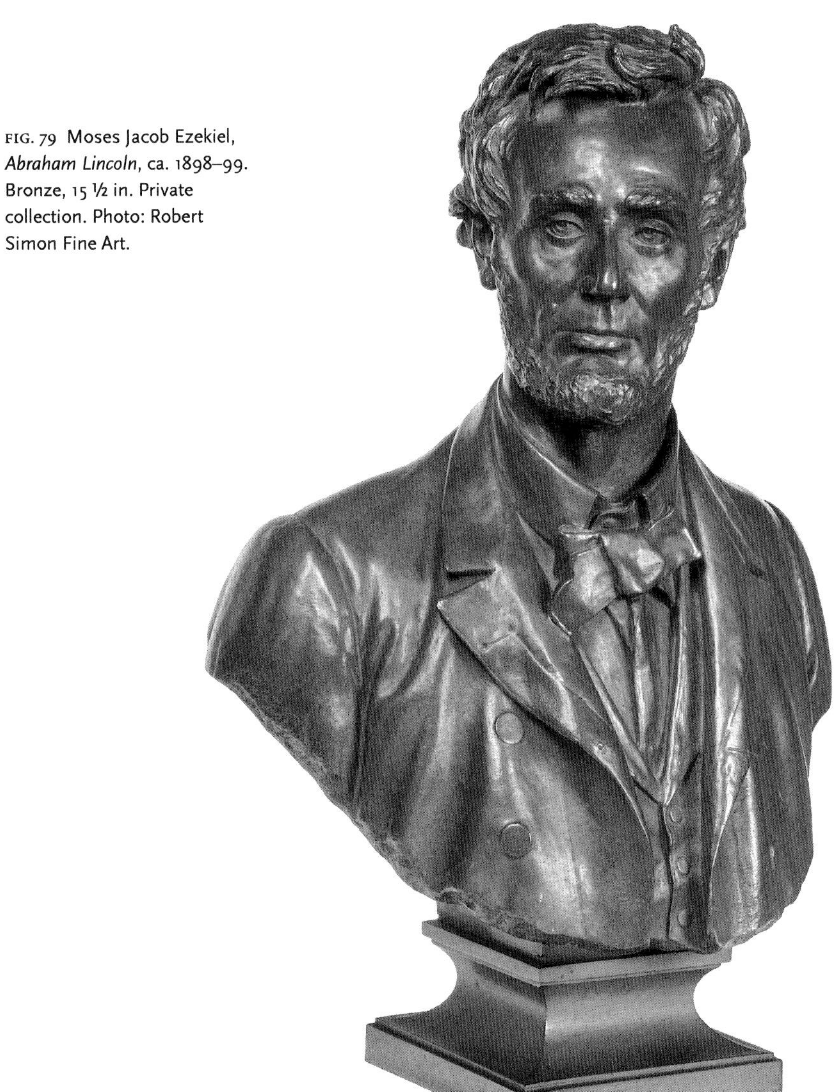

FIG. 79 Moses Jacob Ezekiel, *Abraham Lincoln*, ca. 1898–99. Bronze, 15 ½ in. Private collection. Photo: Robert Simon Fine Art.

Willson himself thanked them for their "generous and patriotic present," which the brothers proposed be placed in the center of the state's capitol rotunda. The governor, however, expressed reservations that the bust might be too diminutive for the large rotunda and ultimately deemed it better suited for one of the central corridors on the second floor. Willson indicated that until a larger sculpture could be fashioned for the rotunda, Ezekiel's bust would hold that place of honor.[96] The bust never found any home in the state's capitol building, and ownership was officially transferred to the Louisville Free Public Library. Small brass plaques on the back of the pedestal tell the sculpture's history. In flowery script, the plaque reads, "Presented to the State of Kentucky by Isaac W. Bernheim and

Bernard Bernheim, May 1901." Underneath, a second plaque indicates, "Transferred to the Louisville Free Public Library upon the request of Isaac W. Bernheim and Bernard Bernheim, Act of the Legislature, Feb. 24, 1914." Eventually, the bust was moved to its current, remote location at the Crescent Hill Branch of the Louisville Public Library system.

Past and present renditions of Thomas Jefferson strongly differ from Ezekiel's inventive monument, which in its use of allegory attempts to record not only the third president's likeness but also his cardinal beliefs. Ezekiel had an agenda and a real personal investment with many of his sculptures, among them *Jefferson*, *Religious Liberty*, and his Confederate monuments *Virginia Mourning Her Dead* and the thirty-two-foot-tall *New South* formerly at Arlington Cemetery (chapter 6). Ezekiel well knew the importance of his artistic decisions and how they contributed to his works' meaning. In particular, the elaborate Jefferson monument underscores Ezekiel's propensity for pedagogical storytelling. His deliberate choices for the sculpture in Kentucky, where he was given free rein, were an attempt to remind Americans of the great president's principles and perpetuate them. Those principles, so critical to the Jewish people's freedom and successes in America, were realized by other Jews drawn to Jefferson, with the Bernheims and Levys among the most public instances. Regrettably, they were not always abided by Americans outside the Jewish community. Foremost for Ezekiel was the crafting of public memory in visible venues, but in the process, the idealistic sculptor sometimes veered into excess, muddying a monument's effect with complicated allegory and extravagant inscriptions, which also obscured his technique.

Indeed, in the first survey of American sculpture, published two years after *Jefferson* was unveiled in Louisville, Lorado Taft assessed the monument as "somewhat whimsical . . . novel and interesting, though too fanciful to be impressive. There is much beauty of modelling in various parts of the work, particularly in the subordinate figures."[97] Nonetheless, Ezekiel's monumental sculpture fulfilled his own strong career ambitions and his belief that art could effect change. Ezekiel, too, strove to make vital connections with his country's not-so-far-away founders, as per his patrons' and his own ideals, and as an appeal to fellow Americans to remember the nation's core values—in this case, religious liberty.

EZEKIEL AND THE CONFEDERACY *Chapter 6*

I love my art above everything in the world except the land of my birth and my Confederate record.
—Moses Ezekiel, circa 1910

Ezekiel's Civil War statues are enmeshed with questions about how Americans reckon with a public landscape dotted with sculpted remembrances honoring racial oppression. As I write this book, Confederate sculptures are coming down or being relocated at a rapid pace in response to Black Lives Matter protests beginning in 2013 and intensified by the death of George Floyd in police custody seven years later. Three of Ezekiel's sculptures were up for public debate.

Most people rightly view Confederate monuments with incredulity. How, in the twenty-first century, could there be resistance to the removal of an equestrian statue that lionized General Robert E. Lee, a white supremacist who led the South's attempt to divide the nation, on Richmond's very public Monument Avenue? How could opposition to removing a Lee statue in Charlottesville, Virginia, have been so vehement that it led to death and injury at the 2017 Unite the Right rally, necessitating the declaration of a state of emergency? Opponents, including then-President Donald Trump, argued that tearing down such monuments erases the nation's history. In truth, most Confederate monuments were erected between the 1890s and the 1940s, decades after the Civil War, commissioned by sponsors to shape and rewrite the nation's history, and to perpetuate continued hatred and subjugation of Black Americans. Indeed, most Confederate statues, including all but one by Ezekiel, were created long after the Civil War to reinforce Jim Crow laws and impose a topography of terror. Equally relevant, the racism made concrete by these monuments still exists, deeply affecting the lives of Black Americans.

Ezekiel's unique position—distinct among all as a boy veteran and native of the capital of the Confederacy who permanently evacuated his home in ransacked, postwar Richmond—adds another layer of perspective to Confederate monuments and the complexity of his oeuvre. Ezekiel provided almost all his Confederate works at little cost. Many were gifts, not commissions, and gifts have an inalienable connection to the giver in a way that a commodity does not. Ezekiel saw his Confederate statues as part of his life story and personal narrative rather than mere commodities with exchange value. In the vast debates about what sculptures should be toppled and which should remain, notice of the artists who fashioned them is often negligible and certainly not central, with Ezekiel's name rarely mentioned.[1] On the occasion that Ezekiel's identity as the maker of a statue receives notice, his Confederate service as a boy is almost always elided, even though this biographical fact is central to many of his artistic choices.

This chapter recovers Ezekiel's perspective in conjunction with these monuments and, above all, examines the unexpected biographies of the objects themselves. Ezekiel's earliest Confederate monument, *Virginia Mourning Her Dead*, sui generis in the memorial landscape, especially merits discussion of the sculpture's origins and subsequent mutability. His final Confederate monument, for Arlington Cemetery, warrants deeper understanding of the contradictory historical forces that shaped its commission and reception in the immediate period after its dedication. Ezekiel's other Civil War monuments provide context for these two pivotal works, both studies in deeply disquieting contradictions, and offer a full perspective of his works in this genre.

Virginia and Ezekiel Mourning Their Dead

In May 1864, the Virginia Military Institute, America's first state-sponsored military college, sent 257 teenage cadets to fight for the Confederacy at the Battle of New Market—the only time in US history that a student body was called from their classrooms and deployed in pitched battle under their own command as a unit. That combat is remembered as the "field of lost shoes" because many boy soldiers lost their boots in thick mud during their four-day, eighty-some-mile march in heavy rain from VMI to the Shenandoah Valley.[2] As part of the Virginia Valley Campaigns, the cadets and approximately five thousand other soldiers defeated the much larger Union army of around eight thousand men, temporarily keeping the region from capture. An unexpected Confederate victory, the Battle of New Market left ten Confederate cadets dead and forty-seven wounded. Ezekiel was one of those surviving cadets (fig. 80).

Five years after the war, Ezekiel modeled his first sculpture as an art student in Berlin: an elegy to his slain friends, poetically titled *Virginia Mourning Her Dead* (fig. 81). Eager to find an audience for the statue, Ezekiel sent a photograph of the model to Richmond in 1872, where it was on view at a local store. The *Richmond Whig* found it of note: "The anatomy of the figure, as far as can be judged from the picture, and the details of the drapery and other accessories are designed in a most skillful manner and indicate a high degree of talent in the young artist."[3] One of his less intricate sculptures so as not to confuse its message, *Virginia Mourning Her Dead* straightforwardly presents a 6 1/2-foot-tall, bronzed allegorical female figure (7 3/4 feet including the lance), symbolizing a sorrowful Virginia. Wearing a helmet and draped in classical robes, with chain mail on her breast, she holds a reversed lance in her left hand, a reminder of service in war and, because it is inverted, a symbol of mourning. Her right foot rests on top

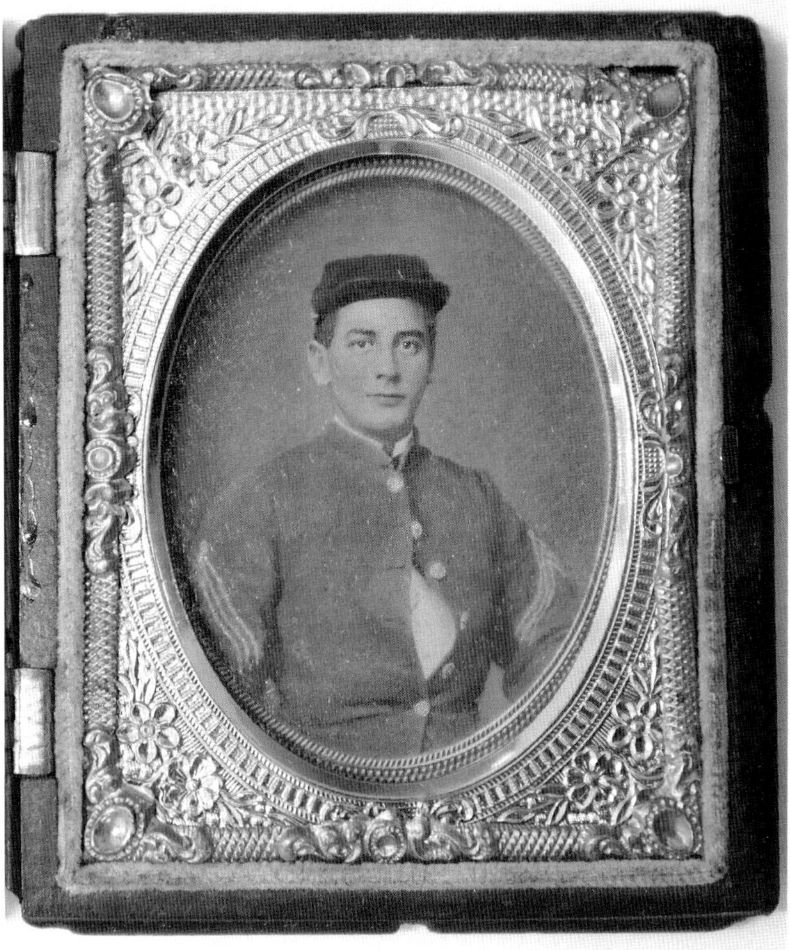

FIG. 80 Moses Jacob Ezekiel in his cadet uniform, 1864. Daguerreotype. Photo: Virginia Military Institute Archives, Lexington.

of an ivy-covered broken cannon barrel, symbolic of the destruction of war. She bows her head in grief for the young sons of the South who fought and died for her at war. (The female in *Israel* also mourned, in that case for the Jewish exile from Jerusalem; chapter 3.)

Ezekiel's "Virginia" purposefully shares commonalities with the Roman goddess Virtus, or Virtue, who anchors the official seal of the Commonwealth and the state's flag. That state flag—used as a model for flags carried by army regiments (fig. 82)—bears a strong resemblance to the seal, featuring Virtus with one foot triumphantly stepping on a personification of Britain. A toppled crown indicates the vanquishing of British rule, emphasized by the words "Sic semper tyrannis" (Thus always to tyrants), an impetus for Ezekiel's *Brutus*, conceived the same year that *Virginia* was bronzed. Ezekiel's monument to the cadets of New Market does not show Virginia as a conqueror or a broad-shouldered Amazon but as a feminine, classical goddess enveloped in the folds of her garment. Her more sympathetic appearance is underscored by her tilted head and slumped

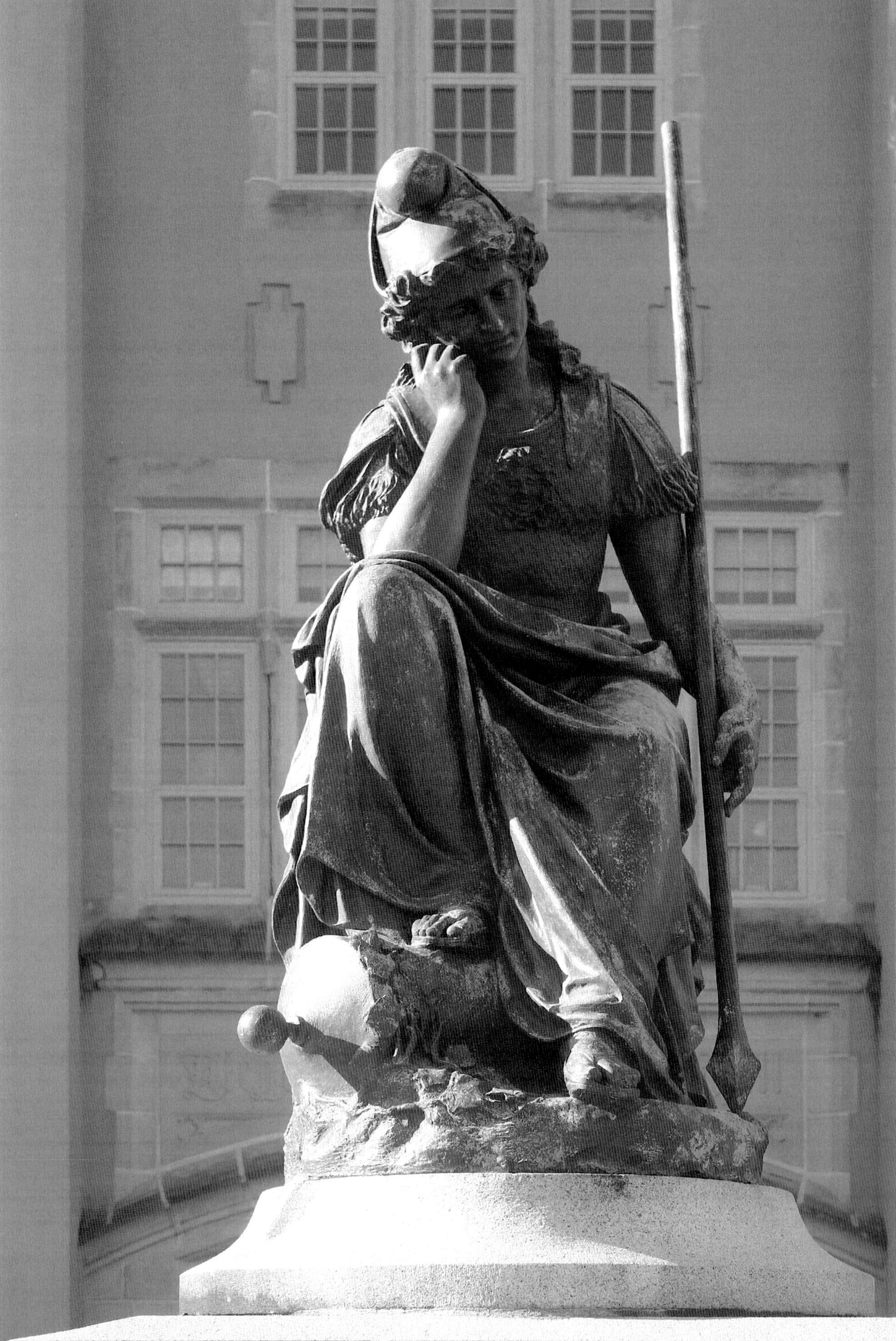

shoulders, as opposed to the defiant figure with erect posture on both the seal and the flag.

Still an amateur sculptor with no commissions to his name, Ezekiel embarked on *Virginia Mourning Her Dead* fully of his own volition. His memoirs and other correspondence demonstrate that it was a sculpture he urgently needed to make, born of the unimaginable trauma of watching his friends die, his memories of warfare, and the horrifying task he undertook after fighting ceased of combing the field in search of the scattered dead and injured. The tremendously personal nature of *Virginia Mourning Her Dead*, the creation of which Ezekiel dubbed "one of the most sacred duties in my life," is central to its understanding.[4]

Shattered by what he saw, Ezekiel dedicated eight pages of his memoir to the battle and its aftermath—both its unmitigated devastation and the pride he felt at its success.[5] He referenced New Market in multiple letters and once, when prompted, powerfully narrated his experience for Louisville's *Courier-Journal*.[6] In these accounts, Ezekiel underscored the discipline of the cadet battalion's advance to war in the cold and rain as "beautifully in line . . . in as perfect order as if on dress parade," and romanticized their charge through the mud to surprising triumph.[7] At the same time, he recalled gruesome details: a friend struck in the head by an exploding bombshell who sank to death next to him, bodies torn to pieces, and being grazed by bullets in his leg and chest. He was soon relieved when he slipped his hand into his jacket and found blood but no mortal injury.[8] New Market cadet John Clarke Howard wrote a detailed recollection for *Confederate Veteran*, in which he, too, celebrated the boy soldiers' "call to the test of fire" alongside the carnage of "that bloody day."[9] A different cadet, John S. Wise,

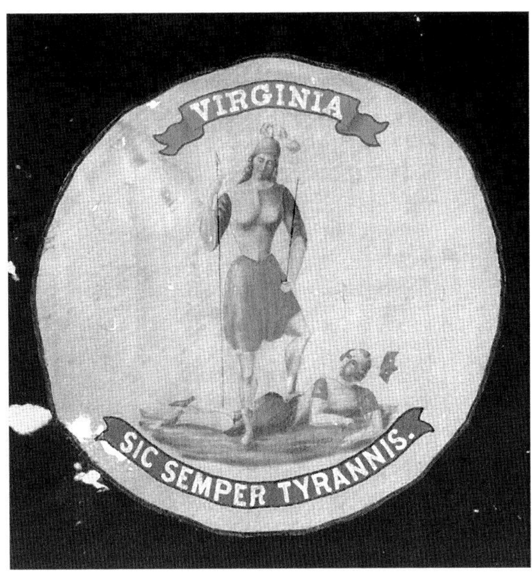

FIG. 81 (OPPOSITE) Moses Jacob Ezekiel, *Virginia Mourning Her Dead*, modeled 1870, cast 1900 (detail). Bronze, statue 7 3/4 ft., with lance, pedestal 11 ft. Virginia Military Institute, Lexington. Photo: Samantha Baskind.

FIG. 82 Civil War–era Virginia regimental flag, circa 1862. Virginia Military Institute Archives, Lexington. Photo: Virginia Military Institute Archives, Lexington.

who later served as a member of the US House of Representatives, remarked on his "gallant" friends who advanced shoeless, exhausted, and wet "with great grit and eagerness." But he could garner little enthusiasm for the Pyrrhic victory: "Our victory was almost forgotten in our distress for our friends and comrades dead and maimed."[10] He discovered William McDowell dead on the field, recollecting, "It was a sight to wring one's heart. That little boy was lying there asleep, more fit, indeed, for the cradle than the grave. . . . I had come too late."[11]

Among those Ezekiel found wounded was his roommate, Thomas Garland Jefferson, the great-great-nephew of President Thomas Jefferson.[12] Ezekiel managed to transport Jefferson, who had a severe chest injury, to a nearby home.

At Jefferson's request, Ezekiel read to him from the Christian Bible as means of comfort until he died in his Jewish friend's arms. Before Jefferson's burial, Ezekiel washed his bloody shirt, cleaned his body for burial, and cut a lock of his hair, which he gave to Jefferson's mother after returning to Richmond. *Virginia Mourning Her Dead* memorializes Jefferson and Ezekiel's other compatriots, boys who sacrificed their lives, and remembers those who survived and courageously answered the call to duty, even if for a treasonous cause. The sculpture, by far Ezekiel's most visually compelling, was fashioned by a grieving young man who modeled his anguish in clay, evident in the pathos of Virginia's quiet pose. Dewy morning rain on her face gives the impression of weeping, augmenting the intended effect.

The poignant simplicity of the final sculpture was nearly obscured by Ezekiel's compulsive penchant to overillustrate, as he did for his *Thomas Jefferson* statue and, as will be described below, even more with Arlington's Confederate monument, which has been rightly characterized as a "textbook in bronze" and "audacious" in its excess.[13] Years before VMI even considered a monument to the New Market cadets, Ezekiel wrote to officials about *Virginia Mourning Her Dead* and included his thoughts on a potential pedestal. He proposed a pedestal decorated on all four sides. As explained in a letter as early as 1886 to VMI's superintendent, Ezekiel planned to execute bas-reliefs on two sides: one of the officers and cadets preparing for conflict, and the other showing the immediate aftermath of battle. On the front of the pedestal, he suggested an inscription chosen by a committee at VMI and on the back the names of the ten boy soldiers who died.[14] The pedestal's bas-reliefs would have been an autobiographical statement: One was to portray excitement about combat, while the second would depict a defining moment of Ezekiel's life. To use his words, Ezekiel planned the second bas-relief to show "a cadet standing amidst ruins and desolation on the ground where some of his comrades lie dead."[15] These artistic choices would have diminished the potency of *Virginia Mourning Her Dead*, devoid of iconography beyond her own pose and expression. He eventually concluded that there should be no ornamentation on the tablets, which instead austerely list all the New Market boy's names, not just those who died (fig. 83).

VMI officials had yet to set their minds to memorializing the cadets, and so the plaster sat waiting in Ezekiel's various European studios for almost three decades since its initial conception, until his alma mater at long last planned to erect a monument to his slain brethren.[16] When hearing the news, Ezekiel promptly contacted the selection committee and presented *Virginia Mourning Her Dead* for a fraction of its actual cost and labor incurred. Cast "so that [my dead comrades'] memory may go on in imperishable bronze, sounding their heroism and Virginia's memory down through all the ages and forever," as Ezekiel movingly wrote, he shipped the 1,750-pound sculpture across the Atlantic.[17] He proudly signed the sculpture "Ex-Cadet M. Ezekiel, cast Rome, 1900 15, May." May 15 marked the thirty-sixth anniversary of the Battle of New Market and the annual date of a VMI ceremony remembering the fallen cadets. Stones in memory of each of the ten cadets claimed by the battle sit behind *Virginia Mourning Her Dead*, with six of the ten casualties—including Thomas Garland Jefferson and William

FIG. 83 Moses Jacob Ezekiel, *Virginia Mourning Her Dead*, modeled 1870, cast 1900. Photo: Samantha Baskind.

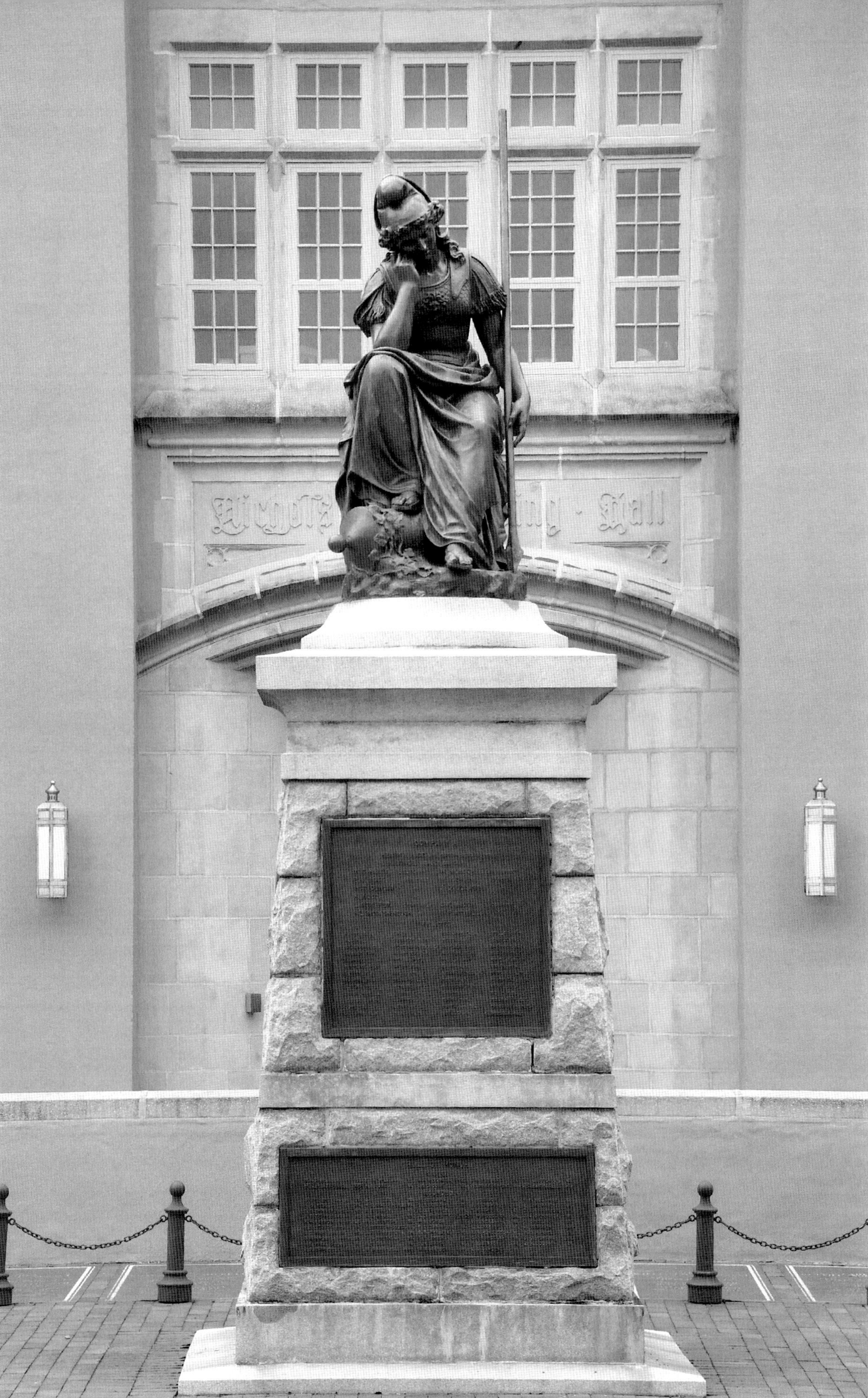

McDowell—later reinterred beneath their markers. The monument was dedicated on June 23, 1903, on the parade ground of VMI. Unable to attend despite entreaties to change the date to suit his travel schedule, Ezekiel cabled a telegram, penned in Latin: "I am there and remember and faithfully offer congratulations."[18]

Undeniably, Ezekiel's Confederate statues, political art fraught with contention, were closest to his heart. His memories of New Market, the exhilaration of unexpected victory but even more the horror of watching his friends die, were ever present in his mind, most likely mingled with his own survivor's guilt and post-traumatic stress.[19] One of the most compelling episodes establishing Ezekiel's frame of mind came soon after the artillery fire stopped. Barefoot throughout the fighting, at its end Ezekiel saw his friends taking shoes off the feet of the Union dead. In a 1901 interview, Ezekiel underscored this trauma: "I stooped down by the closest [dead Yankee] and I started to take off his shoe. But something made me look at his face. His eyes were wide open and his look went right through me. He was little more than a boy, and there was a red gash and smear, where a shot had torn away part of his face. I went back to his feet in a hurry and I got my shoes."[20] A teenager drafted with little notice, Ezekiel's carefree training as a cadet did not prepare him for such acute violence or the actions he was forced to take to ensure his own survival.

Consequently, Ezekiel became a casualty of war. The "riddle of death," as Drew Faust so rightly demonstrates in her seminal study on death and the Civil War, "exceeded language and understanding."[21] Undoubtedly, the bloodletting Ezekiel saw in combat irrevocably shaped the rest of his life. Painter and Confederate veteran Conrad Chapman, who as a young man enlisted for over three years and was injured in the Battle of Shiloh, explicitly acknowledged the lasting effect of his war service: "My character was formed in the armies of the south and for better or worse I must abide by it."[22] A Union soldier who saw active duty at Shiloh, writer Ambrose Bierce stands out for his rejection of glorifying war and his exceptionally gruesome and nihilistic prose. Bierce strikingly described being haunted by "phantoms of a blood-stained period" and "sentenced to life" by his war service.[23] Similarly, Ezekiel turned to the language of art to express his individual sorrow. Ezekiel would have agreed with poet Walt Whitman, who, when asked, "Do you go back to those days?" responded, "I have never left them."[24] The long shadow of Ezekiel's cadet experience and Civil War service are themes that run through decades of correspondence.

In many ways, Ezekiel also conflated his identity as a Virginian with his heady days of youth and friendship at VMI before New Market. Sentimentalizing that time, he sought to visit Lexington on every trip to the United States and was delighted to address the cadets at graduation in May 1909. Designed by Ezekiel with the seal of Virginia in relief at the center of the simple bronze medal, the New Market Cross of Honor was presented in 1904 to veterans of the New Market corps on the fortieth anniversary of the battle, an event the sculptor regretted he could not attend because of work responsibilities.[25] Of his alma mater, Ezekiel wrote affectionately, "Every stone and blade of grass is dear to me—and the name of Cadet of the VMI the proudest and most honored title I can ever possess."[26] More than Judaism, Ezekiel worshipped the past: the artistic past, military past, and Southern past. Throughout his life, Ezekiel recollected his VMI years so fondly and at times espoused a noxious Lost Cause narrative—an engrained belief system that attempts to whitewash the fact that slavery was the impetus for the Civil War by asserting the rebels were nobly fighting for states' self-determination—likely because that was the only way he could reconcile the carnage he wrought, the carnage he saw, and the unbearable loss unleashed by the reverberations of the Battle of New Market.[27]

Virginia Mourning Her Dead complicates calls for the unilateral removal of Confederate-related monuments. The sculpture speaks to the importance of considering the larger context, partially because of its function as a monument erected out of sorrow and respect, and more crucially because its symbolism has grown beyond Ezekiel's original, heartfelt intent. In this instance, the mutability of allegory allows for such an evolution. *Virginia Mourning Her Dead* now has a broader meaning for the fledgling citizen-soldiers at VMI, divorced from the Civil War. Today, Ezekiel's statue exists as a tribute and memorial to the more than six hundred VMI alumni who have died in military service since 1839.[28] In this way, the sculpture not only memorializes Ezekiel's loss but also acknowledges VMI's losses throughout history rather than celebrating the values of the Confederate States of America. To clarify how her message has been broadened and to annul the taint of the sculpture's birth from the Civil War, VMI has determined to remove the plaques listing the New Market cadet's names from her base.[29] Too, the New Market affair is now held up by the institute as an example of what a VMI education can cultivate in its cadets—discipline, bravery, and coolheadedness in combat—divorced from the stench of the Civil War. The *Richmond Times-Dispatch* so noted in 1903, "It would be hard, indeed, to remember a list of names more representative of the best blood of Virginia than that which will be inscribed on the Institute's battle monument. But it is well to remember that there are thousands of men who have gone out from the Institute would as willingly risk their lives for the old State that claimed the lives of those gallant boys in '64."[30] And finally, *Virginia Mourning Her Dead* can also be understood as a reminder of the cost of war—any war—and the solemn responsibility of leaders who have the power of committing young men and women to conflict.

His Own Worst Enemy

While *Virginia Mourning Her Dead* languished for decades, Ezekiel actively sought other opportunities to memorialize his beloved South. On three occasions, Ezekiel entered competitions to create a proposed Monument Avenue statue in the former capital of the Confederacy, slated to depict Robert E. Lee, the sculptor's friend and mentor, whom he called "our Hero."[31] As Ezekiel eagerly awaited word in 1877, news came that the project was canceled due to financial reasons and rivaling sponsors, and subsequent attempts to reopen the competition were hampered by sponsors' differing agendas and challenges with juries.[32] In 1886, a renewed opportunity to sculpt Lee heartened Ezekiel. When the models were initially planned for exhibition at the Corcoran Gallery, Ezekiel prevailed on curator William MacLeod to put in a good word for him; however, with around twenty submissions received, the location needed to be changed for lack of space.[33] Even as Ezekiel's entry received favorable mention and a $1,000 prize from distinguished jurors—the sculptors Augustus Saint-Gaudens and

John Quincy Adams Ward, along with Architect of the Capitol Edward Clark—it was not chosen.

Ezekiel submitted a wax equestrian model of Lee in CSA military garb commanding his energetic horse Traveller (fig. 84). The pair surmounted a massive base elaborately festooned with laurels and an inscription. That proposed statue represented Lee, as he put it, "reining in his horse to a perfect standstill, showing his unwillingness to go forward when all hope was lost," thereby extolling the general for his understanding of when to accept defeat.[34] The inscription on the base, "He that ruleth his spirit is greater than he who taketh a city," buttressed the idea that the greatest conquerors are those in command of self, and closely paraphrases the book of Proverbs: "He that is slow to anger is better than the mighty; and he that ruleth his spirit than he that taketh a city."[35] The same figure crafted for *Virginia Mourning Her Dead* sat in front of the central frieze of the base, reinforcing Ezekiel's remembrance of the Civil War as inexorably linked to his military service and its deadly aftermath for several of his fellow cadets. As much as some sponsors desired that a Southerner like Edward Valentine or Ezekiel sculpt Lee, that allegorical touch, equivalent in size to Lee himself, doomed the sculpture. So, too, jurors were unimpressed with the relationship between Lee and Traveller; the horse's crouching position and Lee's attempt to rein him in were assessed as only possible if the general were lassoing a wild animal.[36] Kirk Savage argues that the committee preferred a quiet, lucid depiction of Lee atop a submissive horse, thereby depicting the relationship between a benevolent master and his equine inferior, a coded message about white benevolence toward Black inferiors.[37] While the erection of such a monument was partly to support racist structures by elevating a secessionist and thus to provoke fear in people of color, Ezekiel's statue spoke more to dignity in defeat. Moreover, nodding to his own experience, he memorialized the loss of life—further making his submission undesirable.

The only Lee sculptures ever completed by Ezekiel were a modest 1870 silver bust profile relief encircled with a wreath of leaves and framed against velvet (lost), at the request of the general's widow, Mary Custis Lee, for a benefit at her church; and a failed effort in the 1880s to secure a contract for a statue of the general as a boy for his home in Westmoreland County, Virginia.[38] After completing a clay sketch and believing that he had already been commissioned, Ezekiel generously cast an eight-inch bronze bust of the general wearing his tasseled campaign hat at his own expense to help with fundraising.[39] Several editions of that bust survive, among them one in the collection of the Smithsonian American Art Museum, but the sculpture of Lee as a boy never reached fruition. In 1886, Ezekiel wrote to the Corcoran Gallery about the busts, asking the museum to house a box of them. The box contained seventy-four busts priced at ten dollars each, and Corcoran officials indicated that they desired to immediately secure copyright.[40] Given William Corcoran's Confederate sympathies, his interest in the reproductions was unsurprising, and the gallery successfully sold reproductions.

On sundry occasions, Ezekiel wrote letters to friends and officials expressing his frustration at being passed over for monuments to Lee and spurned by the South: "In my home I am

FIG. 84 Moses Jacob Ezekiel, *Robert E. Lee*, circa 1877. Wax model. Courtesy of The Jacob Rader Marcus Center of the American Jewish Archives, Cincinnati, Ohio, at americanjewisharchives.org.

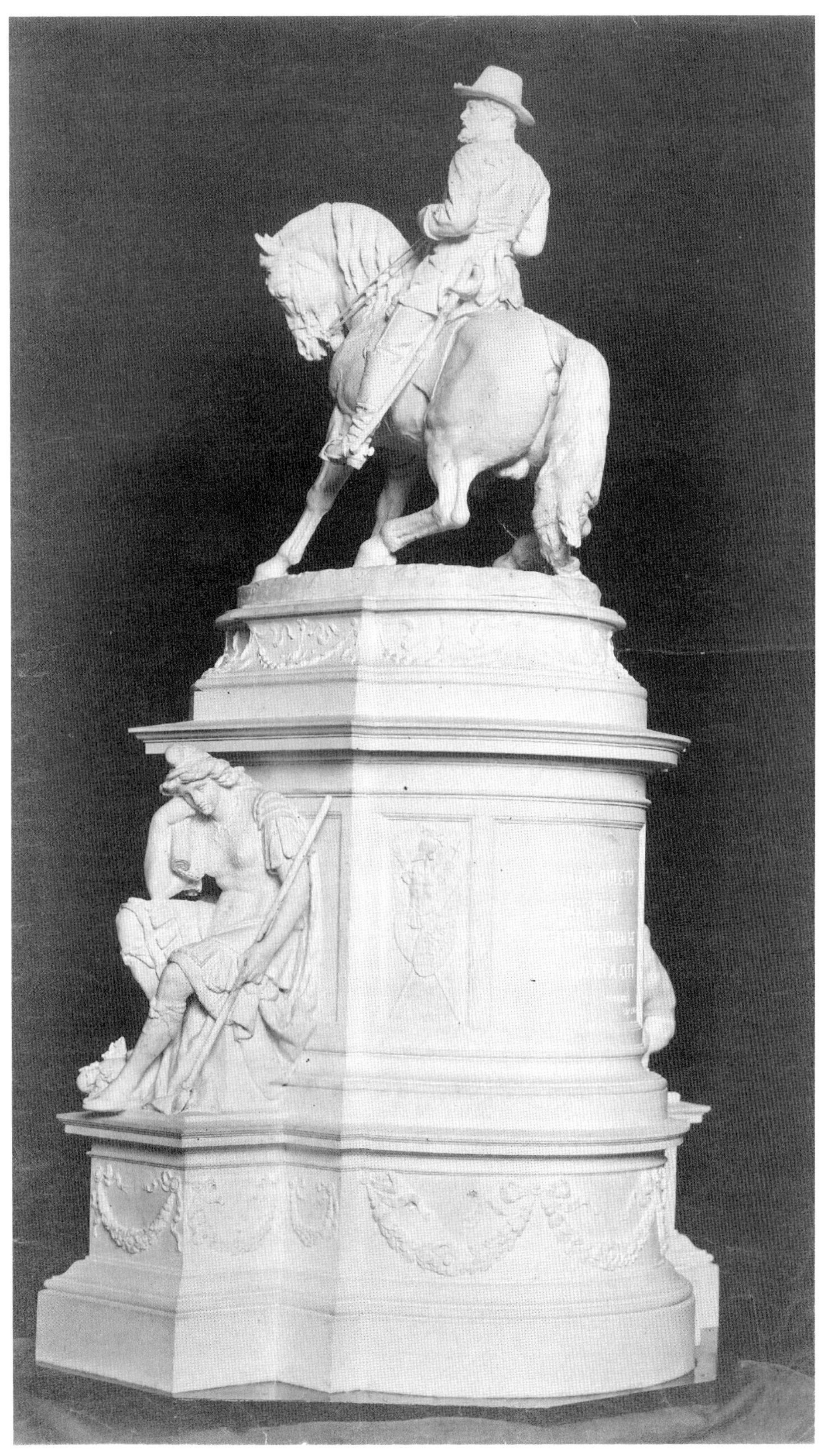

considered a weak artist not equal to the task of making a *Lee* monument. They expect to see a finished work in a small model, and they do not take into consideration what I have done in my art all these years without them."[41] To VMI Superintendent Scott Shipp, a commander of cadets at New Market, he wrote, "My whole heart and soul were infused [in the Lee monuments]. I had given up all hope as far as my native state is concerned."[42] Ezekiel lamented that he had risked his life for Virginia but to no avail: "The Lee monument competitions ruined me."[43] Awash in defeat and depression, Ezekiel further despaired, "My studio was filled with unbought works, and no one could be in reality more miserable than I was, but I managed to keep my face clear, to eat my own sorrow and disappointment. . . . I sacrificed everything for my art and so far had only bitter results. Yet I was so perfectly happy when at work. It was the ingratitude and the injustice that rankled, and nothing else."[44]

These experiences led to the peevishness that gave Ezekiel a reputation for being difficult and instigated his aversion to competitions. One glaring example is a different Confederate monument opportunity that he sabotaged for no other reason than his prickly insecurity. Around 1899, Ezekiel was personally sought out by the Confederate Soldiers and Sailors Monument Association to sculpt a monument for Richmond's Libby Hill Park. He submitted models for the statue, which the committee found lacking. Eager to have the venerated sculptor and veteran execute the piece, the group asked Ezekiel to provide revised models, name his price, and communicate a sense of when the statue would be completed. Upset that his work was deemed unsatisfactory, Ezekiel irritably responded that he could suggest no definite time for delivery. As summarized in the *Richmond Times-Dispatch* and reiterated variously among other national publications that covered the public tiff, Ezekiel stressed that his "services were very valuable, and his work would be worth all the money that could be raised for the purpose."[45] Not only did Ezekiel fail to submit a second set of models, he left unanswered a letter requesting them. Six months after the sponsors' follow-up letter was sent to Rome, the group lost patience with Ezekiel's petulance and contracted a different sculptor to make the statue. The eventual monument was an imposing, seventeen-foot-tall bronze soldier surmounting a seventy-three-foot-tall Corinthian column, comprising thirteen stone cylinders representative of the Confederate states. Erected in 1894, it stood in Libby Hill Park until its removal in 2020.

Ezekiel did not take the bad press lightly. In response to the *Richmond Times-Dispatch*'s story, he sent a letter to the editor criticizing the article as "very unjust" and tried to clarify the matter. Ezekiel explained that he inquired about the price to estimate his material costs and was willing to complete the work without payment for his labor, while indicating that the problem was "a question of doing honor to the Confederate soldiers and doing a work for my native city." He felt that being painted as a "mercenary individual in a matter in which the highest sentiments of my nature are involved" dishonored him as an ex-soldier who "did his duty" during the war. Ezekiel publicly bemoaned his troubles with competitions and the "injustice that has put the execution of memorials to our fallen heroes and southern statesman into the hands of men who have no more ability than some of the southern sculptors possess, and certainly no more sentiment for our past history." Unquestionably, Ezekiel's ego as an artist was hurt, but just as much, his pride as a Southern veteran.

His own worst enemy, Ezekiel expressed disinterest in taking part, even if a competition opened for the work, having already spent more time, labor, and money on the project "than I, as a poor man, can afford," he wrote.[46]

As a rejoinder to these perceived failures, the year before he died, a still aggrieved Ezekiel began sketching in clay an equestrian portrait of Stonewall Jackson: "I have no object in making this sketch as I never expect to have anything to make for my native city. But it will serve some day as a comparison with what ever kind of a monument that the [Richmond] committee have secured—just as my models for the Lee monument will serve in future ages to show the works I did (and there were three different ones) that cost me years of labour, and all in vain."[47] With no extant model and only Ezekiel's word, it seems that, akin to his *Thomas Jefferson* monument, the sides of the massive pedestal were to be decorated with allegories, in this case representing War, Peace, Sorrow, and Fame.[48]

A bronze bust of Pennsylvania Governor Andrew Gregg Curtin for Philadelphia's Smith Memorial Arch (1897–1912) also left a sour taste in Ezekiel's mouth, and perhaps not only because of challenges with his sponsors (fig. 85).[49] Funded by private citizen Richard Smith, the semicircular Smith Memorial Arch acts as a gateway to Fairmount Park, the site of the Centennial Exhibition and first home for *Religious Liberty*. Fourteen sculptures by thirteen artists populate the Civil War monument, which pays tribute to Pennsylvania's military heroes and, in the case of Curtin, a leading civilian during the war effort. A staunch supporter of the Union army who regularly convened with President Lincoln, Curtin would seem an unexpected subject for Ezekiel. Not only was he a Northerner, but Curtin worked with the War

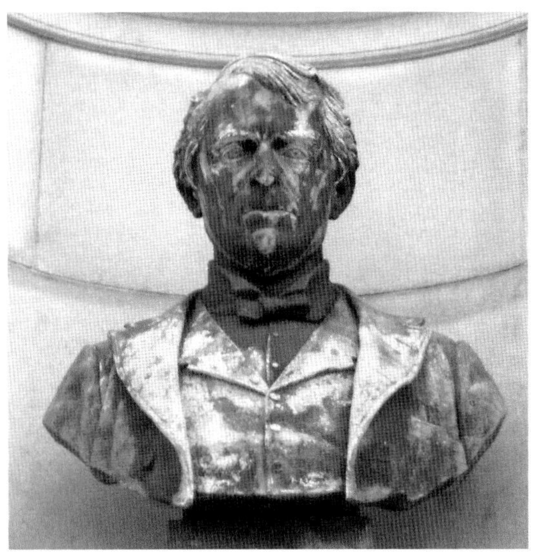

FIG. 85 Moses Jacob Ezekiel, *Governor Andrew Gregg Curtin*, 1903. Bronze. Smith Memorial, Philadelphia, Pennsylvania. Photo: Wikimedia Commons.

Department to squash General Lee's crossing of the Susquehanna River during the Battle of Gettysburg. Even closer to home, the Fifty-Fourth Pennsylvania Infantry Regiment faced off against the cadets at the Battle of New Market.

But Ezekiel did not turn down the opportunity to sculpt one of nine busts accompanying three full-length figures and two equestrian statues as part of the memorial; Daniel Chester French designed a monumental figure of Major General George Gordon Meade, and John Quincy Adams Ward executed an equestrian statue of Major General Winfield Scott Hancock. Flattered by the selection committee, which sent a circular to Rome in 1897 asking him to suggest a design, desirous to hold company with the esteemed French and Ward, and of course in need of the fee ($1,800), Ezekiel supplied a sketch based on a photograph and eventually a finished model in 1901. The sponsors found that model unfavorable and requested that Ezekiel rework it, which he delayed for a year. It was not until the end of 1903 that Ezekiel's contribution was bronzed and placed in the monument, the last of all busts installed.[50] Katherine Cohen, also a Jewish American, created a more successful work for the Memorial Arch. Lively in expression and infused with immediacy, her bust of *General James Beaver* contrasts with the tepid, psychologically wanting likeness of Curtin. Ezekiel's bland, unflattering contribution may have been a passive-aggressive act on the Confederate veteran's part—another instance where his war experience informed his monument making.

Years before, Ezekiel again willingly put sectional loyalties aside in pursuit of an interesting opportunity. In 1873, Ezekiel entered a competition for a monument to Union Admiral David Farragut in Washington, DC, that was ultimately awarded to Vinnie Ream, who earlier had also lost out on the Monument Avenue Lee competition despite enthusiasm for her conception.[51] Ezekiel railed, "It made me very sorry to think that I had tried to overcome my Southern reluctance to make any kind of monument to the Yankee Admiral Farragut."[52] Around the same time, Ezekiel submitted a model for a monument to General James B. McPherson, one of the highest-ranking Union officers killed in the Civil War, which was not chosen. He rankled about a commission lost in the early 1890s for a bronze equestrian monument to William Henry Harrison in Cincinnati.[53] Around 1907, Ezekiel was contacted by the United Daughters of the Confederacy (UDC) about making an equestrian monument to Confederate General John Hunt Morgan in Lexington, which he consented to do for a small price because he hoped to have "some kind of justice shown to me in my native South." For reasons unknown, he did not make the monument, which was eventually executed by Pompeo Coppini and erected in 1911.[54] More satisfactory to Ezekiel was his work on a Stonewall Jackson statue, which he rightly described at the time in both frustration and relief as, after forty years, "the only commission I ever received from the South."[55]

Ezekiel's Devotion to the South Realized

As a student at VMI, Ezekiel heard about the teaching legacy of Thomas "Stonewall" Jackson, later the highest-ranking Confederate officer killed during the war. After Jackson died by friendly fire and his remains were returned to the Institute, Ezekiel was appointed a member of the honor guard watching over his coffin in the general's old classroom before burial. On the third anniversary of Stonewall Jackson's death, in 1866, with his admirers still grieving, Ezekiel wrote to his cousin from VMI, where he had resumed studying postwar and graduated last in his class of ten: "Lexington has put on her mourning garb today, the school rooms are deserted, the stores are closed. . . . The Southern people need no flaring epitaphs inscribed on mammoth mausoleums to bid them remember and cherish the names and deeds of their fallen heroes."[56] Yet, Ezekiel's greatest dream was to do just that.

His devotion to the South, Ezekiel's truest muse, was finally realized with a 1909 bronze for the UDC, which tasked him with a Jackson statue for the grounds of the West Virginia Capitol building (fig. 86), in the general's hometown.[57] The eight-foot tall, half-ton bronze sculpture portrays Jackson standing erect, with chin upturned, gazing resolutely into the distance. He holds field glasses in his right hand and grips a sword in his left.

His conspicuous sword belt buckle, emblazoned with "C.S.A.," betrays the weapon as one used in defense of the Confederate States of America. The jacket of Jackson's Confederate uniform appears dramatically blown by the wind, as if he were still on the battlefield at Chancellorsville, where he was mortally wounded. Considering their patent resemblance, Ezekiel had in mind Augustus Saint-Gaudens's *Farragut Monument*, exhibited in plaster at the 1880 Paris Salon and erected in New York City in 1881 (fig. 87).[58] Saint-Gaudens portrayed the determined Civil War naval admiral similarly holding binoculars and with wind whipping open the bottom of his overcoat but with greater realism, immediacy, and lively texture, a hallmark of his Beaux Arts training in Paris. The monument, which marked a break from neoclassicist idealism, was highly visible and much lauded.[59] The bold shadows created by Saint-Gaudens's animated bronze surfaces were in direct contrast to Ezekiel's predilection for smooth, contoured marble. *Jackson*'s windblown, bronzed coattail alludes more closely to the wet drapery found in marble works from antiquity, perhaps offering the general as a votive monument in the vein of *Nike of Samothrace* (ca. 200–190 BCE; fig. 88), much as Edward Valentine imbued his recumbent, draped Robert E. Lee with glorifying, Christlike connotations (see fig. 29).

Ezekiel's lifelong concern for accuracy (e.g., his interest in sculpting *Jefferson* at the age he signed the Declaration of Independence rather than as an elder statesman; *Religious Liberty*'s chain mail), alongside his personal connection to Jackson, amplified the importance he placed on the task of properly memorializing the general. He wrote to Valentine, requesting a copy of the life mask used to sculpt his own *Stonewall Jackson* monument, marking the Jackson family burial plot in Lexington, less than a mile from VMI.[60] A rival for Confederate commissions and jealous of Ezekiel, Valentine did not send the mask. Ezekiel persisted, asking an administrator at the Confederate Museum in Richmond for the same mask as well as the loan of two Confederate buttons, a belt buckle, and a sword strap, for which he was again rebuffed.[61] Eventually, Ezekiel got his hands on some key objects to help him craft what he hoped would be an authentic, well-received statue worthy of its subject—and worthy, he also hoped, of the artist, a patently proud son of the South. Orchestrating the date for the Charleston dedication to coincide with the 1910 unveiling of his *Jefferson* statue at the University of Virginia and his standing soldier monument *Southern* on Lake Erie, Ezekiel joyously attended. He was joined by thousands on hand, including seventy-five VMI cadets detailed by the governor to join the festivities.[62] Ezekiel had specifically asked Superintendent Edward Nichols for the corps' presence at the ceremony.[63]

Even more joyous for Ezekiel, although not financially prudent, was a replica of Jackson that he donated to VMI, which varied from the Charleston prototype only by its pedestal and inscription. So eager was Ezekiel to have a sculpture of Jackson on his cherished alma mater's campus, he waived his fee and personally paid for some of the materials. The general stands on a 9 1/2-foot inscribed pedestal that reads, "Stonewall Jackson / The Virginia Military Institute will be heard from today / General Jackson at Chancellorsville / May 2, 1863." It is said that this was the general's final battle call, and its inclusion is a grander gesture than the modest inscription on the West Virginia pedestal that only mentions Jackson's name, the title "Confederate

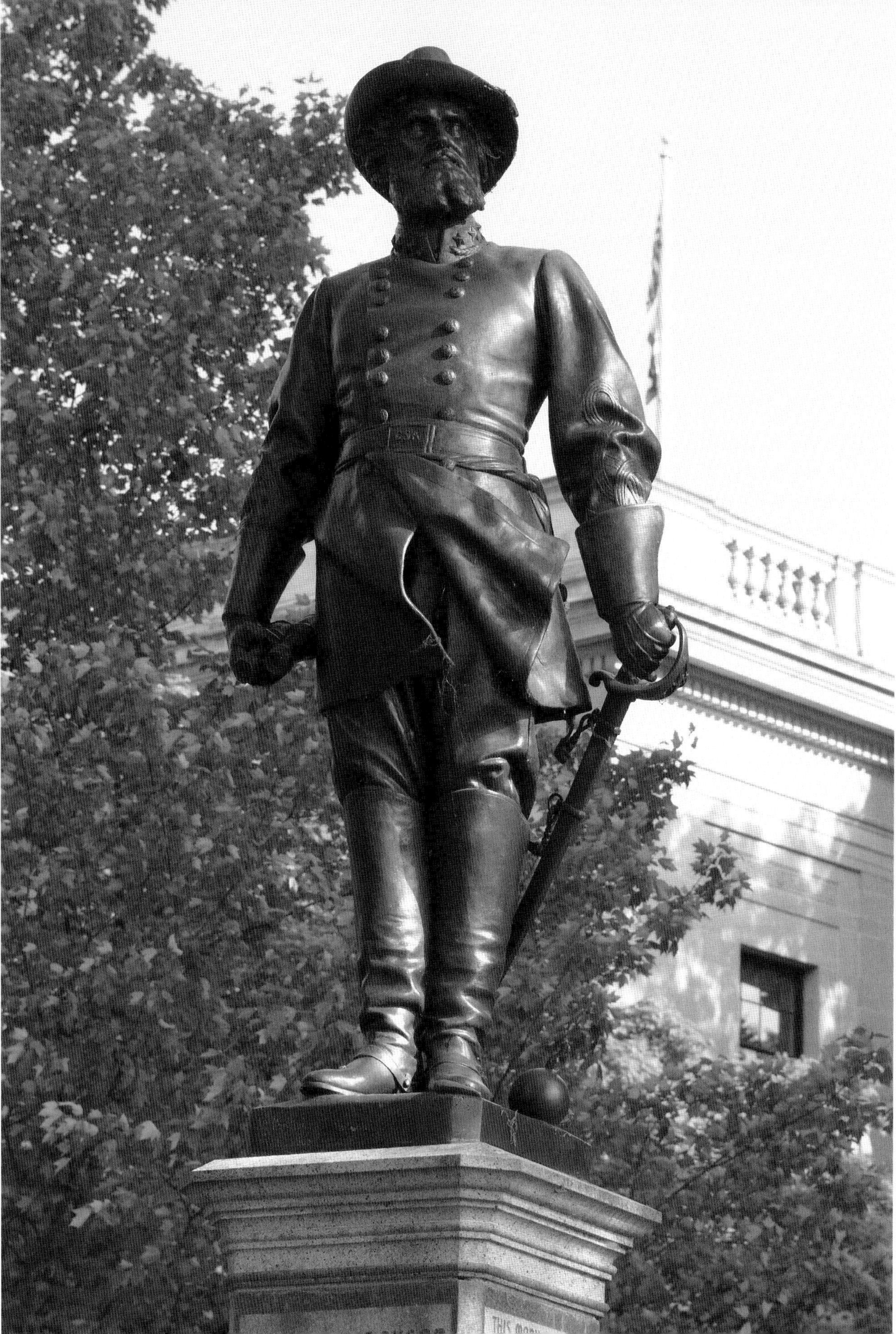

General," and his lifespan. Nearly two dozen insistent letters sent across the ocean chronicle Ezekiel's suggestions for Jackson's placement on campus; instructed dimensions for the foundation, pedestal, and plinth; shipping timetables and customs fees; the nature of the pedestal's inscription; and the statue's progress.[64] At times, he voiced concern about *Virginia Mourning Her Dead*, which was being moved to a new location to make room for *Jackson*.[65]

During commencement exercises in June 1912, *Jackson* was dedicated on the parade ground with fanfare. A large crowd gathered, including Civil War veterans, Southern patriots, and VMI alumni, some of whom had fought alongside Jackson. It was curated as an extraordinary celebration of the general's achievements—his strategical and tactical prowess, his service during the Mexican-American War and Civil War, and his teaching accomplishments as professor of physics and artillery tactics at the Institute. Jackson's widow and other family members stood symbolically and proudly by, with the general's twenty-two-month-old granddaughter ceremoniously pulling off the bunting as the sculpture was officially unveiled. Speeches lauded Jackson as the school's "greatest hero" and detailed his accomplishments, mostly as a Civil War general. The presiding reverend prayed "that the Corps of that day and for all time be influenced by the character and strength and truth of the man being honored."[66]

Not touted at the unveiling were qualities that inflamed formerly enslaved people and abolitionists, and now most twenty-first-century Americans: Jackson was also an enslaver of six people and a fundamental member of the rebel forces. Following a 2020 *Washington Post* exposé of widespread

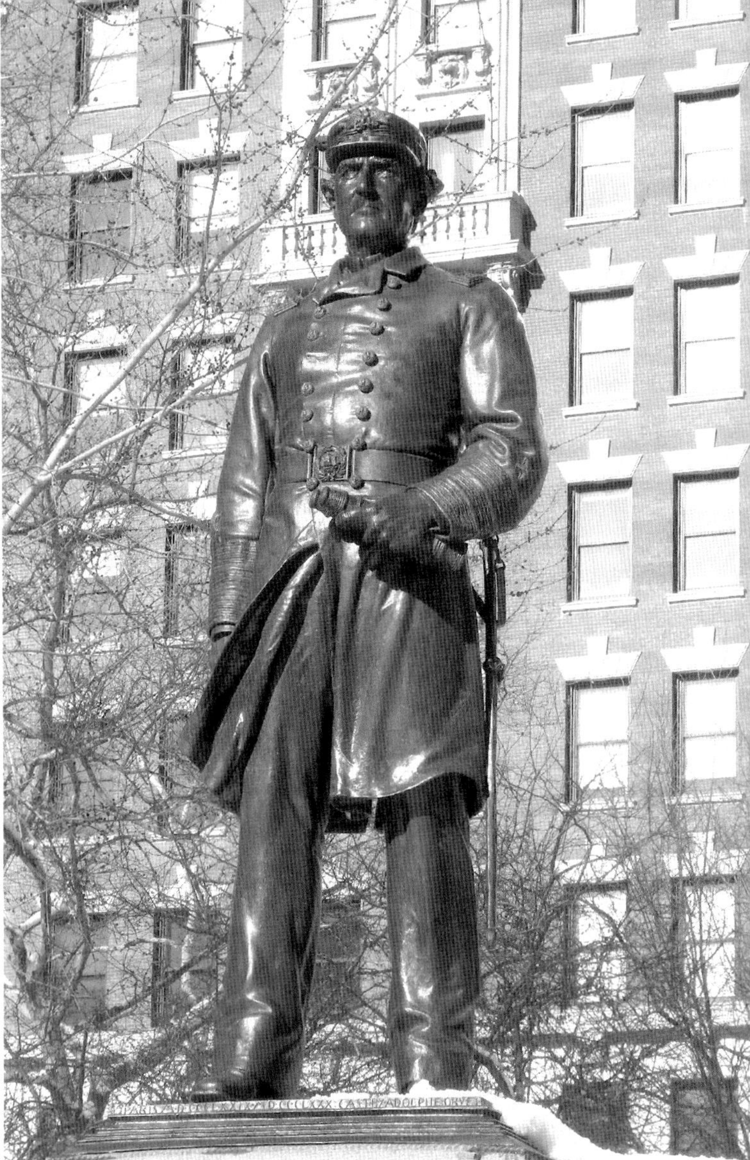

FIG. 86 (OPPOSITE) Moses Jacob Ezekiel, *Stonewall Jackson*, 1909. Bronze, figure 8 ft.; with pedestal 12 ½ ft. Charleston, West Virginia. Photo: Wikimedia Commons / Judson McCranie. CC BY-SA 3.0.

FIG. 87 Augustus Saint-Gaudens, *Farragut Monument*, 1877–80. Bronze, figure 8 ft. 3 in.; with pedestal 15 ft. 3 in. New York City. Photo: Wikimedia Commons / Jim Henderson.

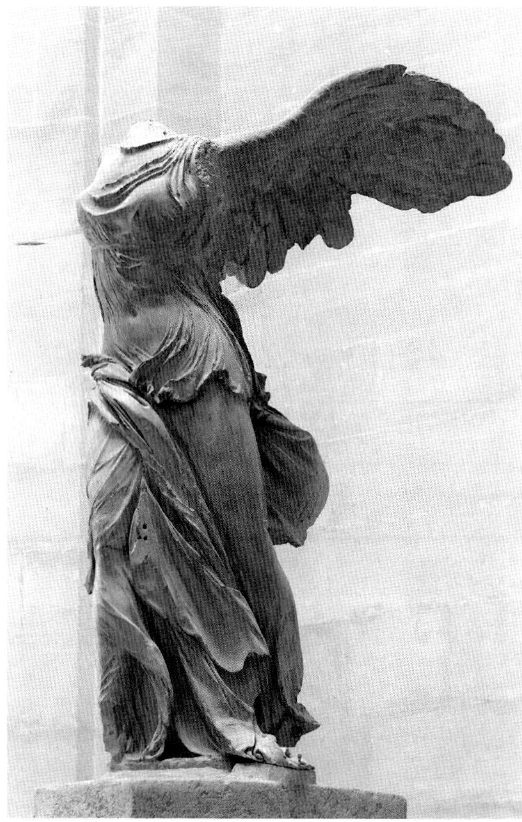

racism at VMI and the Virginia governor's subsequent order for an independent investigation of the allegations, these facts finally took precedence and the institute's "greatest hero" was decisively removed from the front of the barracks after more than a century.[67] VMI owns an identical quarter-size statuette of *Stonewall Jackson*, on exhibit in the Ezekiel gallery at the school's art museum, the first public museum in the Commonwealth.

Stonewall Jackson has been relocated to New Market Battlefield State Historical Park, isolated at the site where Ezekiel fought with his young comrades and close to the quarter-scale bronze of his *Thomas Jefferson* statue. Colonel Keith Gibson, director of the VMI Museum system, explained the institute's logic: "Placing the Jackson statue at the Virginia Museum of the Civil War, New Market Battlefield State Historical Park, puts Jackson in the geographic center of the theater which brought his international acclaim, his famed 1862 Valley Campaign. We aren't discarding Jackson's lessons and legacy. We are placing him in a new location to put him in a position to help viewers understand the legacy of his military standing."[68] In the rapidly changing landscape of Confederate sculptures, moving them—instead of removing them—to battle sites has provided one alternative to total dismissal. Now absent from VMI's heavily trafficked parade ground, the monument no longer acts as an everyday perpetuator and reminder of the country's history of systemic racism.

The same cannot be said for the Charleston version of *Stonewall Jackson*. After years of debate about dismantling the more public monument, erected solely to promote Jackson's commitment to the Lost Cause rather than his other military and teaching accomplishments (for some, a debatable rationale), the sculpture surprisingly remains on the Capitol grounds. Its placement at the seat of government power would have made its meaning all the more pernicious in the era of Jim Crow when racism surged, functioning as an intimidation tactic and reminder of a brutal, racist past. Despite recent widespread support to tear down the monument, multiple Capitol Building Commission meetings in 2020 and 2021 failed to reach a decision on the statue's fate.[69]

Less publicly debated because of the subject's dual loyalties, and depicting a man not readily recognizable as a figure affiliated with the Confederacy, is Ezekiel's statue of *John Warwick Daniel* (1913; fig. 89). Funded by subscription, the sculpture still stands in the Confederate major's hometown of Lynchburg, Virginia. Daniel, whom Ezekiel called "our Southern hero," later served the US government in Congress for over twenty years after the war. "The eminent Virginia sculptor, Sir Moses Ezekiel, himself an ex-Confederate soldier," the *Alexandria Gazette and Virginia Advertiser* reported, "has consented to make the figure, so no fears as to the excellence of the bronze presentment need be entertained."[70]

Ezekiel would not only have been pleased with the financial benefits of the Confederate commission but also would have perceived sculpting the major an honor because Daniel delivered a lengthy and well-received 1883 keynote speech at the dedication of Edward Valentine's *Recumbent Lee*. Wounded at the Battle of the Wilderness and dependent on crutches for the rest of his life, Daniel earned the alliterative moniker "Lame Lion of Lynchburg." Ezekiel worked out the dilemma of Daniel's disability by placing him in his senatorial chair, with crutches tastefully resting off to the side. As such, the sculpture focuses on Warwick as a statesman, not as a warrior. The documents Warwick holds in his right hand and in front of his body are more visually obvious than his crutches, a by-product of his war service, and he wears the clothes of a citizen, not a soldier.

Daniel is still on view, justified by authorities for his loyalty following the war, front and center in the statue's presentation—but in its day, the major's earlier fight for secession was just as significant to its purpose. As the pedestal partly reads, "Major in the army of Northern Virginia and for twenty-four years a senator of the United States from Virginia." At the dedication, Daniel—whose secessionist past was forgiven to such an extent that he delivered an address at the dedication of the Washington Monument—was jointly and paradoxically praised for

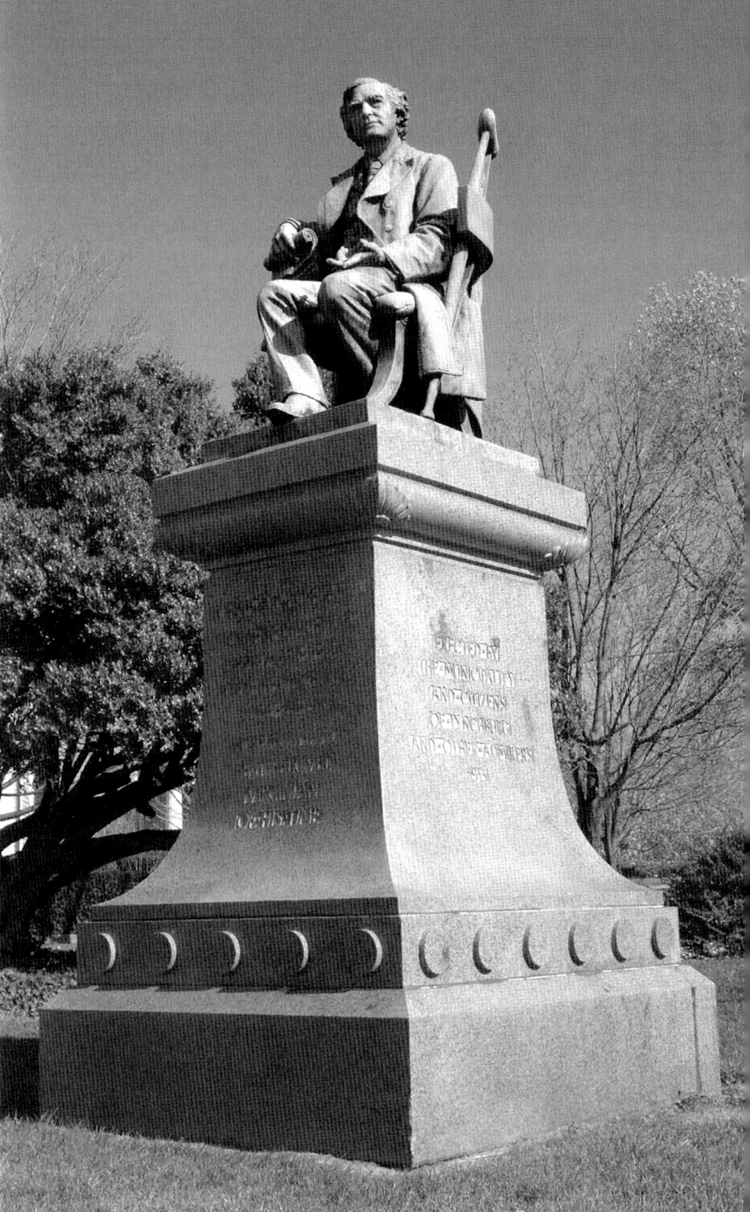

FIG. 88 (OPPOSITE) *Nike of Samothrace*, circa 200–190 BCE. Marble, 9 ft. Louvre, Paris. Photo: Wikimedia Commons / Marie-Lan Nguyen.

FIG. 89 Moses Jacob Ezekiel, *John Warwick Daniel*, 1913. Bronze, figure, 7 ft.; granite pedestal 10 ft. Lynchburg, Virginia. Photo: Keith Gibson.

his positions in the US government, his daring on several battlefields including the Battle of Bull Run, and his adherence to the Lost Cause. Virginia Governor Henry C. Stuart opined in his address, "His surpassing eloquence reached its sublimest heights as he expounded Southern principles, [and] defended Southern motives. . . . His tributes to Jefferson Davis and to Robert E. Lee . . . will endure longer than their monuments of bronze erected by grateful people."[71] While *Daniel's* pedestal is devoid of injurious, valorizing language, his introduction at the unveiling, squarely in the Jim Crow era, demonstrates that the statue's original agenda was to maintain an irredeemable way of thinking.

Self-Portrait of the Artist as a Soldier

Conversations about whether Confederate monuments should be toppled or stay put revolve around their subject, as well as the location where they were erected. Alongside relocation to battlegrounds, cemeteries provide another solution, and sculptures already in cemeteries, erected out of sorrow or respect in a commemorative context, are mostly immune to removal, including three by Ezekiel: an architectural gateway, a lone soldier monument, and the country's national monument to the Confederacy at Arlington Cemetery. (The latter was removed after this book was sent to copyediting.) The first, a UDC commission for the Hickman City Cemetery in Kentucky (1913), was named the *Tyler Confederate Memorial Gateway* in memory of a young private from the county who died during the war. Designed in an Egyptian Revival style, and conspicuously reminiscent of the facade of the building housing the Medical College of Virginia where Ezekiel studied after his war service, the gateway memorializes seventy-nine soldiers buried under the shadow of the austere twenty-nine-foot tall, twenty-five-foot-wide structure (fig. 90). A simple blocked font delineates the soldiers' names on the columns. On each side above a pedestrian entrance, a short poem reads, "Each soldier's name / Shall shine untarnished on the roll of fame / And stand the example of each distant age, / And add new luster to the historic page." A complete anomaly in Ezekiel's oeuvre, he agreed to undertake the project at a reduced cost.[72]

Ezekiel's over-life-size infantryman in Sandusky, Ohio, is more complex and typical of his work (fig. 91). An early monument to the South on Northern soil, *Southern* was placed on Johnson's Island in 1910 at the site of a former Confederate prison where more than twelve thousand soldiers were once confined, and now operates as a cemetery for those who perished. The irony that Ezekiel easily received an order from the North—or at least a ready audience, considering he donated it in full—to commemorate the Confederacy after decades of pleading for many from the South was undoubtedly not lost on him. The Cincinnati-based Robert Patton Chapter of the UDC purchased the neglected island to care for the 206 soldiers' graves and beautify the grounds, which in their minds necessitated a public monument. Ezekiel's sponsors requested the most common monument type of the Civil War: a lone citizen soldier.[73]

Donated by Ezekiel, who only requested payment for materials, the sculpture, alternately called *The Lookout* and *Southern* (the latter in relief capital letters on the base), may have been a repurposing of his rejected design for the Confederate Soldiers and Sailors Monument for Libby Hill Park. *Southern* presents a uniformed, rank-and-file soldier clutching a rifle affixed with a bayonet cocked

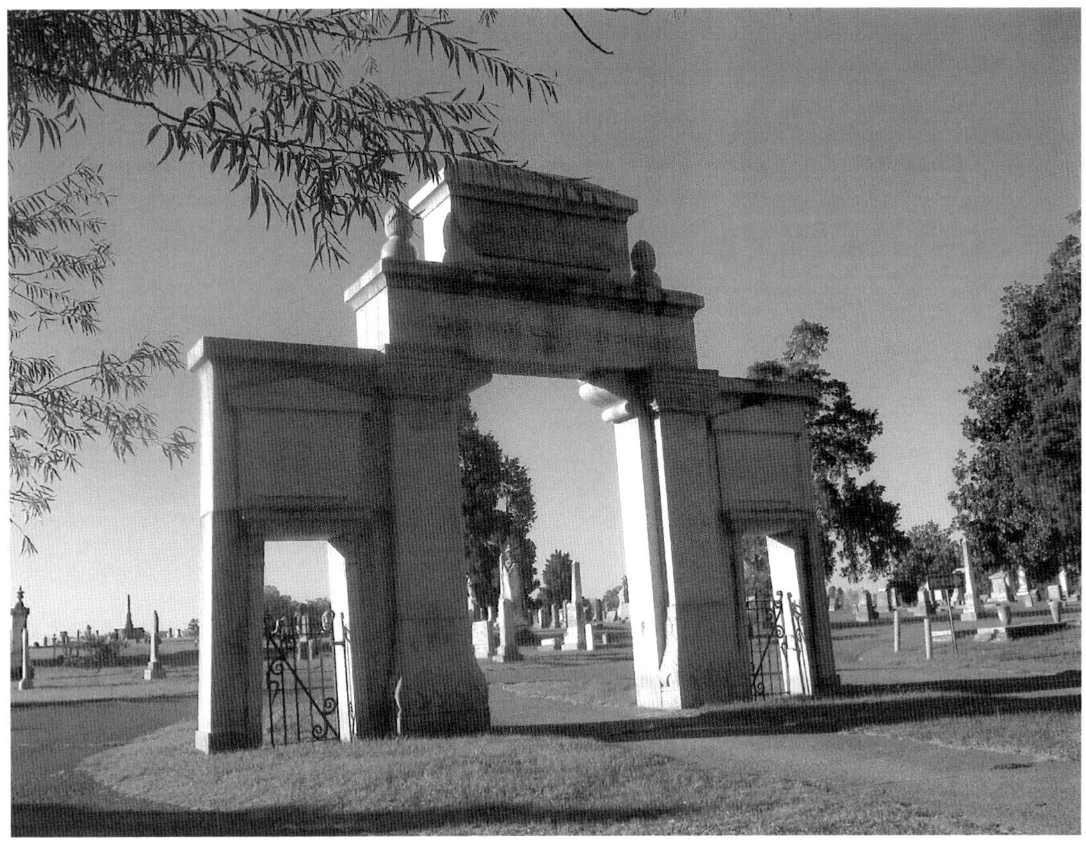

FIG. 90 Moses Jacob Ezekiel, *Tyler Confederate Memorial Gateway*, 1913. Granite, 29 × 25 ft. Hickman, Kentucky. Photo: Wikimedia Commons / C. Bedford Crenshaw.

to one side, with his hand held over his eyes. Characteristic of interchangeable mass-produced citizen soldier monuments in the North and South, *Southern* stands at parade rest, although the soldier's pose is not nearly as static or generalized as his prefabricated counterparts. Commissioned by the UDC, the Confederate monument in front of Alabama's Sumter County Courthouse was erected in 1908 (since removed), during the same period as *Southern*. This "typical" soldier monument, here one of a kind in marble, shows a formulaic staid soldier atop a vertical shaft, holding his rifle perfectly erect in line with his body (fig. 92). In contrast, *Southern*'s jaunty, contrapposto pose, with his left foot stepping off the plinth and hand at his forehead, shows the animated soldier as a man of action. As he was wont to do, Ezekiel defied the standardized formula of the genre in which he was working—in this case, cookie-cutter, Silent Sentinel monuments proliferated by both the Union and Confederacy—by introducing innovations.

Rank-and-file monuments were intended to honor and mourn anonymous, ordinary, white soldiers through generalization, but the face of *Southern* could not be more particularized: Ezekiel imbued the figure with his own features,

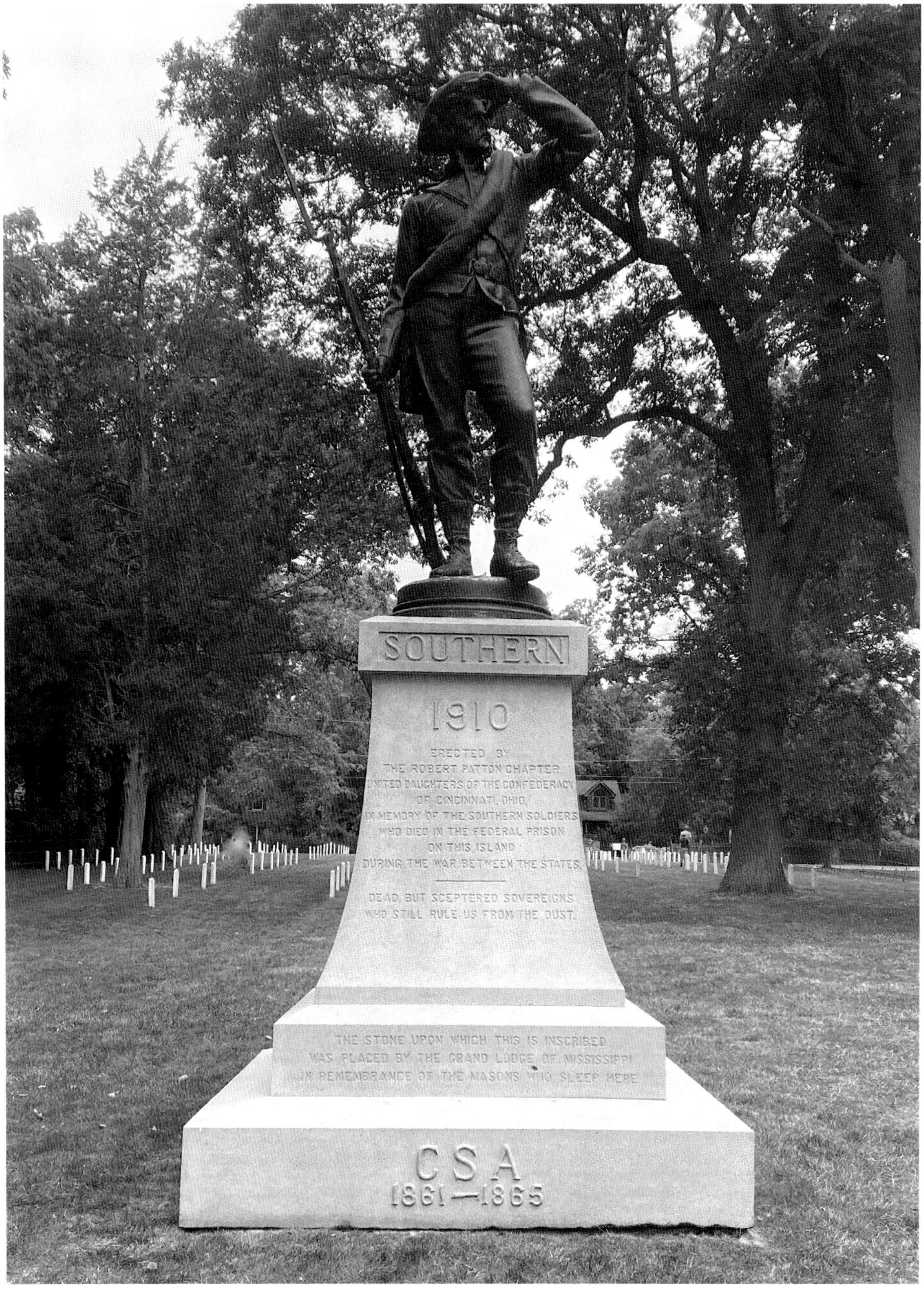

SOUTHERN
1910
ERECTED BY
THE ROBERT PATTON CHAPTER
UNITED DAUGHTERS OF THE CONFEDERACY
OF CINCINNATI, OHIO,
IN MEMORY OF THE SOUTHERN SOLDIERS
WHO DIED IN THE FEDERAL PRISON
ON THIS ISLAND
DURING THE WAR BETWEEN THE STATES.
DEAD, BUT SCEPTERED SOVEREIGNS
WHO STILL RULE US FROM THE DUST.
THE STONE UPON WHICH THIS IS INSCRIBED
WAS PLACED BY THE GRAND LODGE OF MISSISSIPPI
IN REMEMBRANCE OF THE MASONS WHO SLEEP HERE.
CSA
1861—1865

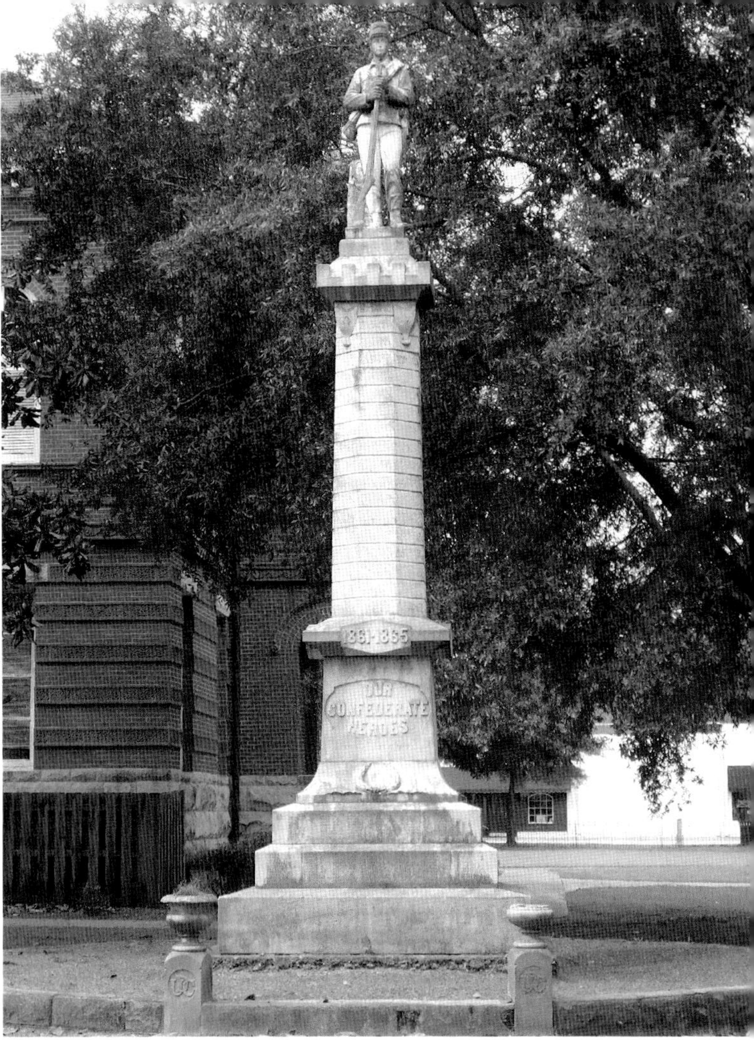

FIG. 91 (OPPOSITE) Moses Jacob Ezekiel, *Southern*, 1909. Bronze, 19 ft. Johnson's Island, Sandusky, Ohio. Photo: Samantha Baskind.

FIG. 92 *Sumter County Confederate Monument*, 1908. Marble. Livingston, Alabama. Photo: Jimmy Emerson. CC BY-NC-ND 2.0.

thereby fabricating a self-portrait as a soldier in bronze—again, a highly personal Confederate statue. Not only did *Southern* recognize the dead on Johnson's Island, but the statue was a paean to Ezekiel's own Confederate record, to the respect he believed he deserved for his lofty service and consequently the commissions he should receive as a noble veteran. The direction of *Southern*'s gaze is somewhat ambiguous. While *Southern*/Ezekiel may be looking into the distance, the tilt of his head indicates that he may also be subtly looking toward the heavens, in remembrance of the fallen soldiers of the Confederacy, some of whom were his New Market comrades. Or perhaps his expression, unlike the resolute frontal gaze of most lone soldier monuments, could be read as one of questioning, searching in the distance for some understanding about the physical and emotional costs of war, which Ezekiel knew well. The importance of this monument to Ezekiel, and its proximity to Cincinnati, drew his brothers Henry, Walter, and Louis to the dedication, where he delivered a brief address.[74] Ezekiel's modifications to the common soldier monument, tucked quietly away on a local island, are rarely seen. In contrast, the largest Confederate monument on a burial ground was readily seen for over a century on the busy acres at Arlington, the nation's largest military cemetery.

An Elaborate Symbol of Reunification and a Lost Cause Apologia

After the outrage and tragedy in Charlottesville at the Unite the Right rally, direct descendants of General Robert E. Lee issued a well-publicized statement in *Newsweek*. The Lees censured white supremacists' promulgation of hate spurred by the removal of the general's equestrian sculpture, and underscored that a postwar Lee "implored the nation to come together to heal our wounds and to move forward to become a more unified nation."[75] Asserting that his great-great-grandfather "never would have tolerated the hateful words and violent actions of white supremacists, the KKK, or Neo Nazis," Robert E. Lee V advocated moving all Confederate sculptures into museums, where they can be contextualized.[76]

Less well publicized is a similar statement published three days later by twenty-two of Ezekiel's descendants in the form of a letter to the *Washington Post*. They wrote to advocate for the removal of one of the country's most visible monuments to the Confederacy: their kin's thirty-two-foot high, classically styled, highly allegorical bronze sculpture, which then rested four hundred yards away from the Tomb of the Unknown Solider at Arlington National Cemetery, on the land where General Lee himself once lived (fig. 93). That 1,100-acre family estate, inherited by Lee's wife, Mary Custis Lee—a descendant of George Washington and a good friend of Ezekiel, who drew her portrait and regularly corresponded from Rome—was seized by the US government during the Civil War. The Ezekiel family declared their pride in Ezekiel's "artistic prowess," but urged that since the monument "intended to rewrite history to justify the Confederacy," it should be placed in a museum with proper contextualization.[77] That was not a realistic option, as it weighs several tons, measures taller than the floor of any building, and is over ten yards long on its side. Until Ezekiel's family released their statement, few groups had called for the toppling of Arlington's Confederate monument. That would change a few years later, not because of the Ezekiel family's encouragement, but because the country finally began to take notice of the abhorrent public commemoration of the Confederacy in "the land of the free." As the following pages will show, the statue served as a physical reminder of oppression and institutional racism in an authoritative venue, and indeed glorified the Confederacy.[78] For some, though, the monument's purpose as a memorial marking grave sites in a cemetery, and sanctioned by the US government, suggests nuance. Here, too, Ezekiel included personal references to his Civil War service.

In 1910, Ezekiel received the commission to sculpt Arlington's Confederate monument, which he felt truly vindicated his love for the South. The massive, five-tiered statue comprises over thirty life-size figures and is topped by a classically dressed woman typifying the South, much as a woman typified religious freedom in his sculpture for B'nai B'rith.[79] Towering over the cemetery's segregated Confederate graves, she wears a crown of olives symbolizing peace in a reunited America, and her left hand holds forth a laurel wreath toward the South, crowning and honoring the dead buried below. Ezekiel made iconographical use of a laurel wreath because it loomed large in his mind as a memento of his Confederate service, yet another autobiographical touch. He recalled the trek back to VMI with fellow cadets after the Battle of New Market, when hundreds of citizens greeted the soldiers appreciatively and one girl placed a laurel wreath on the boys' cadet flag.[80] Staying at his sister Hannah's house during the 1899 visit to Cincinnati to model the *Isaac Mayer Wise* bust, Ezekiel found the wreath tucked away with other sentimental belongings and donated it to VMI.[81] At present, the pristinely preserved wreath hangs on a wall in the Institute's art museum.

The monument's female figure holds a pruning hook in her right hand, and behind her sits a plow. Distinctly quoting the plow in Jean-Antoine Houdon's *George Washington* (see fig. 69), whose fasces provided inspiration for *Religious Liberty*, the plow in the Confederate monument nods

FIG. 93 Moses Jacob Ezekiel, *New South* (Confederate Memorial), 1914. Bronze, 33 ft. Formerly Arlington Cemetery. In storage as of January 2, 2024. Photo: Keith Gibson.

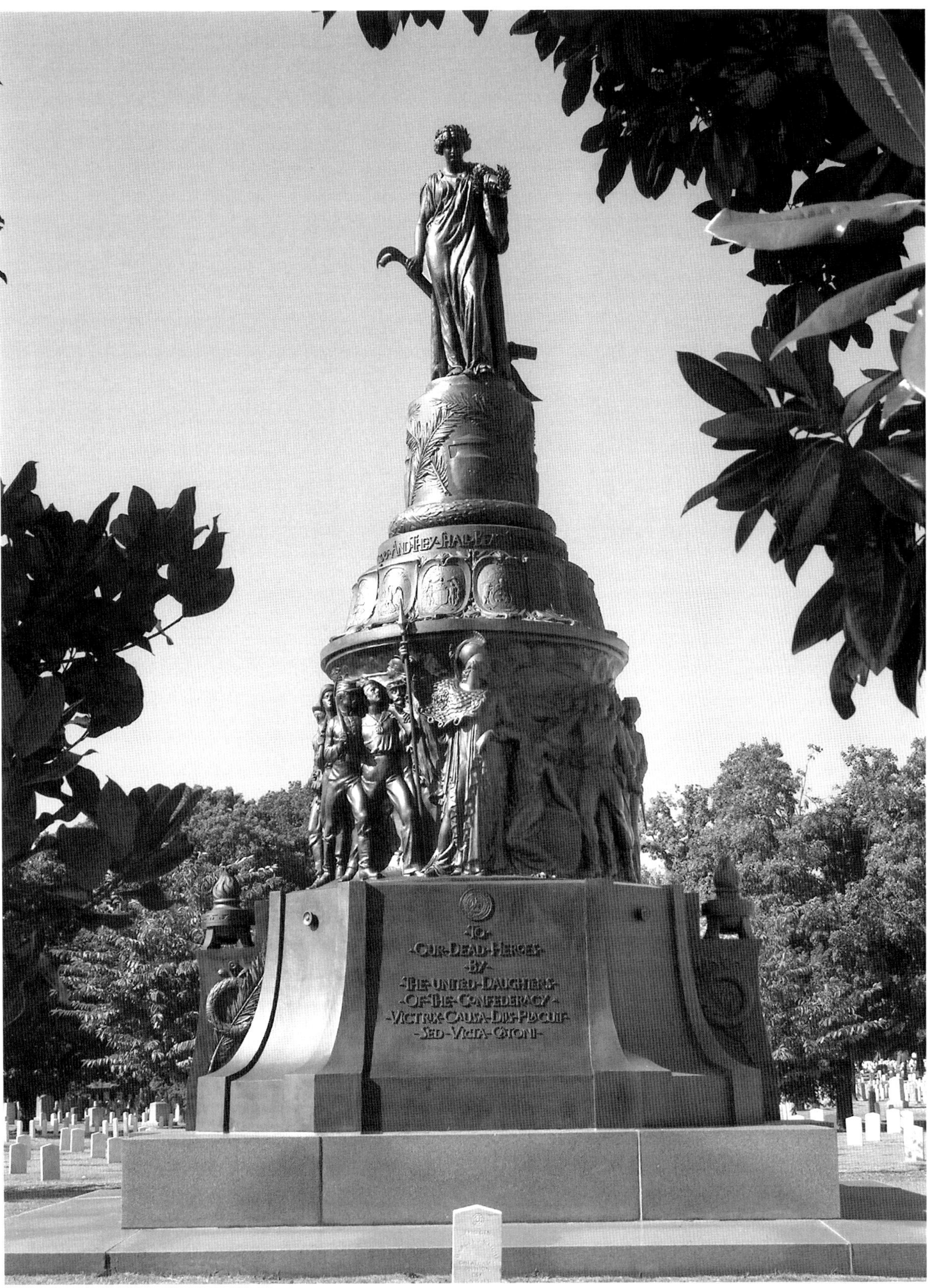
TO
OUR DEAD HEROES
BY
THE UNITED DAUGHTERS
OF THE CONFEDERACY
VICTRIX CAUSA DIIS PLACUIT
SED VICTA CATONI

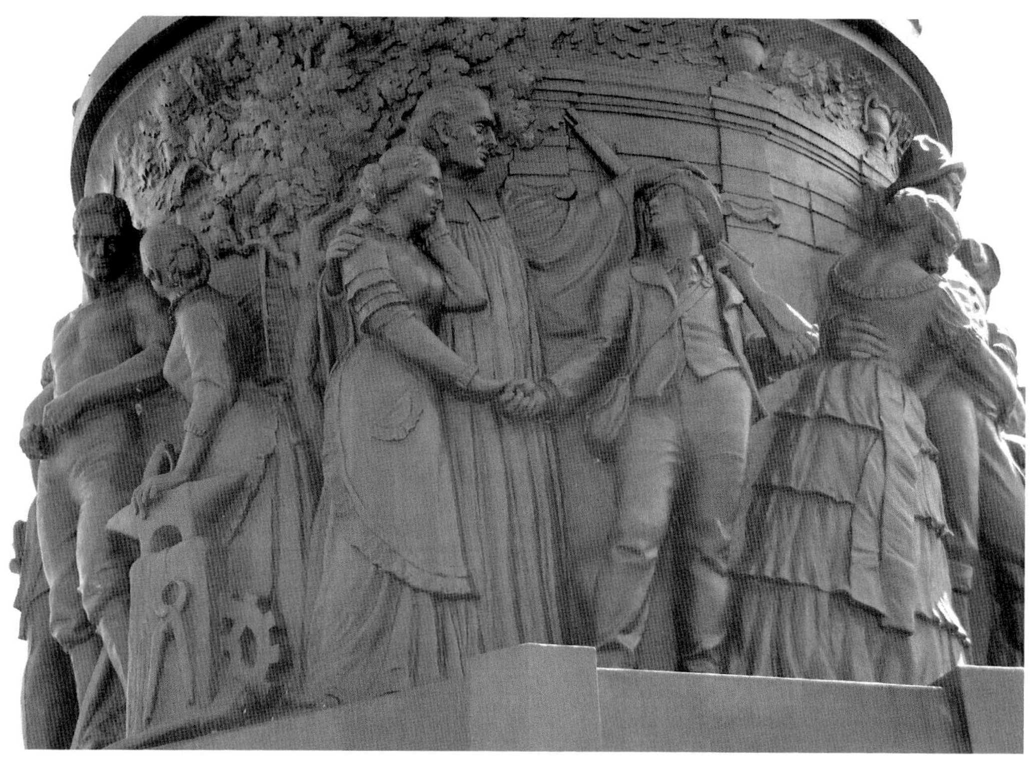

FIG. 94 Moses Jacob Ezekiel, *New South* (Confederate Memorial), 1914 (detail). Photo © Dell Upton.

toward peace and the exchange of a sword for a plow after government service. That message is further emphasized by a quote from the book of Isaiah that wraps around the center of Ezekiel's sculpture (remember that Isaiah was one of Ezekiel's favored biblical books, central to his conceptions of the bas-relief *Israel* and the JPS seal): "And they shall beat their swords into plowshares and their spears into pruning hooks."[82] The female allegory appears atop four bas-relief funerary urns inscribed with the dates of each year of the Civil War, and a plinth directly below the biblical passage bears fourteen shields. Each shield represents a single coat of arms from the thirteen Confederate states and the border state Maryland, which did not join the secession but provided material support.

The largest, most complex, and most controversial section of the massive monument features an eight-foot circular frieze of high-relief figures underneath the shields. At center, Minerva, the goddess of war, glances at the collapsed woman on her left, whom she tries to prop up. Another allegorical representation of the South, and one considerably less benign than *Virginia Mourning Her Dead*, this defeated figure barely grasps her shield, inscribed with the word "Constitution." Soldiers flank the pair, and hovering above are spirits of war, calling them to offer the South assistance. Carrying weapons, those soldiers heartily answer the call to service. Ezekiel preferred to sculpt his frieze in an archaic style, one that stemmed from

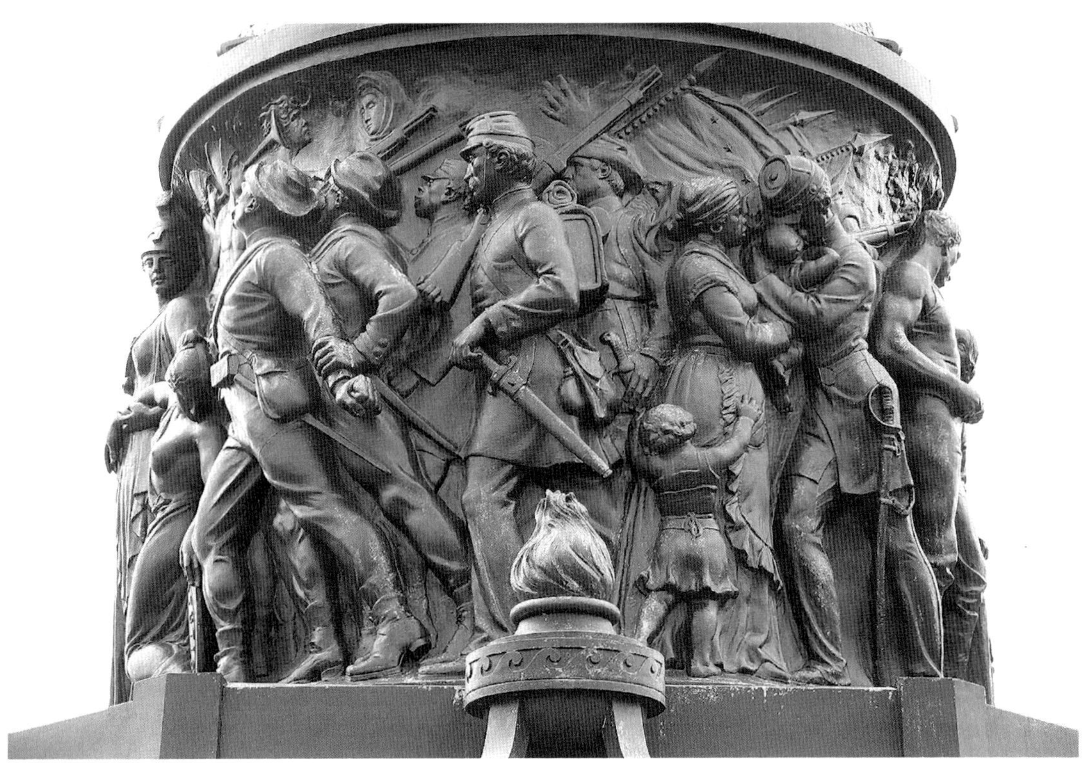

FIG. 95 Moses Jacob Ezekiel, *New South* (Confederate Memorial), 1914 (detail). Photo © Dell Upton.

his German training with Rudolf Siemering at the Royal Academy. Siemering's 1871 monument to *Germania*, in process during Ezekiel's subsequent stint in his studio, used the same, and similarities between the two conceptions are strongly apparent. This approach was common when depicting processionary scenes, as in the Parthenon frieze (ca. 443 BCE), another aspect of its appeal for Ezekiel.

Vignettes surrounding the central grouping were meant to demonstrate the sacrifices that families made as their men went off to fight for the very Constitution that the South, according to the Lost Cause, tried to protect: a strapping blacksmith who has forged his sword for war and takes leave of his wife; a young woman fastening her beau's sash around his waist as she bids him farewell; and a clergyman and wife blessing their uniformed son, a boy surely not ready for battle—much as a teenaged Ezekiel was far too young for war (fig. 94). Tremendously problematic are two depictions of Black figures: a faithful enslaved man wearing the uniform of the Confederate States of America, who follows his master to battle; and an officer kissing his baby goodbye in the arms of an enslaved caregiver, who also has a toddler tugging at her skirt (fig. 95).

In his book-length chronicle of the monument's history written soon after its unveiling, Hilary Herbert—an officer in the Confederate army, chair of the Executive Committee of the Arlington

Confederate Monument Association, and later secretary of the US Navy during President Grover Cleveland's administration—delves deep into the monument's meaning. He stressed a (contrived) message of benevolence between enslaved people and their masters: "And there is another story told here, illustrating the kindly relations that existed all over the south between the master and the slave—a story that cannot be too often repeated to generations in which 'Uncle Tom's Cabin' survives and is still manufacturing false ideas as to the South and slavery."[83] As both Ezekiel and Herbert make plain, in image and word respectively, key elements of the monument's design are undeniably shaped by Lost Cause propaganda, the ultimate in revisionist thinking and vindication.

The narrative Ezekiel conveys, one of devoted servitude, was born of his own experience, for which Black viewers in his time and most twenty-first-century audiences are justifiably critical and most appalled. After he expatriated, Ezekiel drew portraits of his "favorite mammy" Keziah that he intended to illustrate his memoir (the posthumously published edited version does not include any drawings), and he sent her loving letters from Rome. Addressed to "My dear Mammy," Ezekiel wrote a letter of "gratitude": "I often think of you dear Mammy and the older times when you made me as happy as a a King. . . . Although I have eaten and enjoyed myself in the presence of real kings and princes it has never tasted as good to me as when I was your child."[84] This private letter is not the posturing and revisionism of the faithful slave narrative espoused by Lost Cause ideologues, nor the sanitized mythology proposed by those who preferred a monument to content, loyal, caregiving enslaved women.[85] Rather, from *his* perspective, Ezekiel truly formed a relationship with his enslaved caregivers, whose point of view we cannot access and which is likely very different. As Sterling Brown smartly observed of Thomas Nelson Page's nostalgic Plantation tradition stories, "Thomas Nelson Page was not lying in his eulogy of the mammy. . . . Page's feeling is honest if child-like. I am sure that he loved his mammy to death."[86] Page, a friend and champion of Ezekiel's who helped him procure the *Thomas Jefferson* commission at the University of Virginia as well as the Arlington Confederate monument, had long made his name as a Southern apologist whose sentimental, racist fiction about the bygone antebellum South was heavily informed by Lost Cause falsehoods.

Ezekiel was partly raised by Keziah and other enslaved women, all of whom he affectionately called "aunt," while surrounded by more enslaved people in his grandparents' household. His grandfather owned Richmond's clothing store for enslaved people. To be readied for auction, they were brought to the store for appropriate attire. Recalling one particularly devastating episode when Keziah witnessed her son Robert auctioned to a new family, Ezekiel wrote, "Robert looked indifferent and sad. I felt very badly about it, but I had seen so many separations of parents and children, of wives and husbands, that I did not then appreciate the full depth of his misery." Later that day, as the sun set, Ezekiel watched Keziah slip into the kitchen and "heard a low sob and something like a wail, so painful and sad that my flesh crawls today to think of it."[87] He also writes warmly about a reunion in Richmond soon after the war with Keziah and recollected her motherly care but later complains in racist, shameful fashion of seeing "an ignorant negro [who] was sitting in the speaker's chair in the House of Representatives where Thomas Jefferson once had sat."[88] Ezekiel's monuments are a study in contradictions, just like the man himself.

"Israelites with Egyptian Principles"

Considering the Jewish people's own experience with persecution and slavery, it comes as a surprise to some that a fair number of Jews, like Ezekiel, supported the Confederacy, even though it should be self-evident that anyone can retain noxious political affiliations and advocate prejudicial thinking. On those grounds, the American and Foreign Anti-Slavery Society presented a paper at its 1853 annual meeting in which it strongly denounced the issue of Jews and slavery: "The objects of so much mean prejudice and unrighteous oppression as the Jews have been for ages, surely they, it would seem, more than any other denomination, ought to be the enemies of *caste* and the friends of *universal freedom*."[89] To be sure, Jews would seem unlikely supporters of white domination, but Ezekiel acts as a reminder that Jews—despite their sense of themselves as others—can ally with oppressors. Mirroring the general population, Jews were both abolitionists and slaveholders. In Ezekiel's family alone there were divisions: His father was a Union man and his maternal grandfather a slaveholder. Numbers differ, but it is estimated that approximately two thousand Jews fought for the Confederacy, out of a total Jewish population of between twenty thousand and twenty-five thousand in the Confederate states.[90]

Judah Benjamin, the first openly Jewish US senator and onetime nominee to the US Supreme Court, served as attorney general of the Confederacy before he became secretary of war and eventually secretary of state. During the Civil War, Ohio Senator Benjamin Wade underscored the bifurcation of Benjamin's allegiances when referring to him and other proslavery Jews as "Israelites with Egyptian principles."[91] While not as public as Benjamin, other Southern Jews sanctioned slavery, arguing that, as Solomon Cohen wrote in a letter, "God gave laws to his chosen people for the government of their slaves, and did not order them to abolish slavery."[92] Rabbi Morris Raphall of New York invoked (and twisted) Jewish tradition when admonishing abolitionists: "When you remember that Abraham, Isaac, Jacob, Job—the men with whom the Almighty conversed, with whose names he emphatically connects his own most holy name . . . —that all these men were slaveholders, does it not strike you that you are guilty of something very little short of blasphemy?"[93] In Richmond, a few Jewish auctioneers sold slaves, and one Jew, Abraham Smith, was a slave dealer. Even Richmond's rabbis defended slavery. Rabbi Max Michelbacher, spiritual leader at Beth Ahabah Synagogue where the Ezekiel family worshipped, created a prayer for Confederate soldiers.[94]

An influence close to home led Ezekiel to war when his mother urged him to fight: "I remember when the Civil War broke out that she said she would not own a son who would not fight for his home and country."[95] Ezekiel claimed, in words that echo the Lost Cause myth, "We were thoroughly imbued with the idea that we were not fighting for the perpetuation of slavery but for the principle of states' rights and free trade, and in defense of our homes, which were being ruthlessly invaded."[96] Oscar Straus's observation in his memoir may partly explain Ezekiel's experience: "As a boy brought up in the South I never questioned the rights or wrongs of slavery. Its existence I regarded as matter of course, as most other customs or institutions."[97] The first Jew in the cabinet of an American president when he held the position of secretary of commerce and labor under Theodore Roosevelt, Straus evolved his thinking over the years; he dedicated his memoir to his grandchildren "and their contemporaries of every race and creed."[98] Straus, whom Ezekiel met during one of his stays with the Stieglitz family and visited the artist in Rome, has been commemorated with his own memorial: a marble fountain by Adolph Weinman, decorated with allegorical figures and located in the Federal Triangle (1947).[99] Isaac Bernheim, who sponsored Ezekiel's *Thomas Jefferson* monument in Louisville, connected the enslavement of Blacks and Jews in a way that Ezekiel never did. Bernheim explained his solidarity with the Republican Party: "It stood for liberty in that it had freed the negro of his shackles. Being of a race that had long known the oppressor, this one principle alone appealed to me with great force."[100]

After the war, some Jewish women in Richmond founded the Hebrew Ladies' Memorial Association for the Confederate Dead, an organization of the same mind as the UDC. They cared for the graves of Jewish secessionists killed in action and raised funds to erect a monument in their memory (never realized). Members of the association rationalized that when antisemitism inevitably reared its ugly head, they could offer up their dead coreligionists as proof that Jews were loyal citizens of the nation, at least as they saw it play out in their Southern communities.[101] While this argument holds some weight, considering what was then a widespread canard that Jews shy from fighting for their country, it obviously does not absolve Jewish Confederates. Nonetheless, unfair disparagement of Jews and the military was a real concern, as evidenced by Simon Wolf's book, *The American Jew as Patriot, Soldier and Citizen* (chapter 1).[102]

The Arlington Commission

Part of the controversy around the Arlington Confederate monument stems from the dueling goals of the two groups involved with its making: the UDC and the US government. Postwar women's groups, most visibly the UDC, took on the tasks of burying their dead and maintaining private cemeteries because their kin were excluded from the newly formed national cemetery system.[103] After Congress passed a law in 1900 allowing the Confederate dead entrance into Arlington, in part initiated by a speech delivered two years earlier by President William McKinley in which he advocated for government care of Confederate graves, members of the UDC lobbied for a monument to the newly interred. With renewed hope for reconciliation, Secretary of War and future President William Howard Taft granted that request in 1906. Many of the dead already interred at Arlington, and others from neighboring cemeteries, were reburied in concentric rings in the newly designated Confederate section.[104] Members of the UDC promptly turned their attention to memorialization, and Ezekiel's name was at the top of their list.

During his 1910 trip to the United States for his *Thomas Jefferson* unveiling at the University of Virginia, Ezekiel received an invitation to meet with Colonel Hilary Herbert. The purpose of the invitation was vague, but an intrigued Ezekiel traveled to the nation's capital, where he stayed with Thomas Nelson Page. Together, the men called on Herbert, who was waiting with members of the UDC. The group offered Ezekiel the opportunity he ardently desired since the Civil War's end, on par with *Virginia Mourning Her Dead*. "I had been waiting forty years to have my love for the South recognized," Ezekiel wrote in his memoir. (He wrote nearly the same of his Stonewall Jackson monument.)[105] At this initial meeting, Herbert and members of the UDC preempted Ezekiel's biggest concern by letting the inflexible sculptor know that he had free rein with the design. When prompted, Ezekiel sketched an idea, which the enthusiastic committee immediately accepted. That conception closely resembles the final monument, much as *Religious Liberty* remained true to Ezekiel's original vision. Four years later, that bronze statue, one of the largest erected in Arlington, would be dedicated as the definitive monument to Confederate soldiers and remains one of the best-known statues of the war that nearly claimed Ezekiel's life.

Unquestionably riddled with egregious iconography and textual elements, in some other important ways Ezekiel's sculpture differs from Confederate statues peppering the South. *New South*, his preferred title for the monument, diverges, for example, from Charlottesville's 1924 sculpture of Lee, a private commission once in a public park that bore the general's name—and which sparked the Unite the Right rally. Akin to Ezekiel's *Tyler Confederate Memorial Gateway* and *Southern*, from the start *New South* was intended for a cemetery, not a public square. But in this instance, the work was created for a national cemetery rather than a regional one. Even more, *New South* was sanctioned by the federal government, including both Congress and three presidents (McKinley, Taft, Wilson), in part to remember Americans who died on American soil, however indefensible their views had been; and as a symbol of a reunited country. As President Taft declared in a speech to members of the UDC in 1912 at a reception after the laying of the monument's cornerstone:

> You are not here to mourn or support a cause. You are here to celebrate, and justly to celebrate, the heroism, the courage and the sacrifice to the uttermost of your fathers and your brothers and your mothers and your sisters, and of all your kin, in a cause which they believed in their hearts to be right [as Ezekiel alluded in the text on the back side of the monument], and for which they were willing to lay down their lives. That cause ceased to be, except in history, now more than half a century ago. . . . I rejoice in the steps that I have been able to take to heal the wounds of sectionalism and to convey to the Southern people, as far as I could, my earnest desire to make this country one.[106]

Taft voiced a similar sentiment when Ezekiel visited the president by invitation at the White House in 1910. There, the pair spoke about Ezekiel's recent agreement to sculpt the monument in Arlington. Ezekiel recounted Taft expressing his pleasure that the esteemed sculptor had received the assignment, as Taft had heard about Union and Confederate soldiers fraternizing at *Southern*'s dedication, in keeping with a spirit of reunion that was sweeping the country. Newspapers corroborate Ezekiel's account. As reported by the *Cincinnati Enquirer*, veterans of the Blue and Gray marched together carrying their respective colors, ultimately resting both flags against the statue draped in an American flag before its unveiling.[107] "Politically speaking," Ezekiel quoted Taft, "you have contributed a great deal towards the peaceful solution of our affairs."[108] At Ezekiel's funeral, President Harding's eulogy intoned the same about Arlington's Confederate monument: The statue "carries the plea for a truly united nation. . . . It speaks to us the ardent wish, the untiring purpose, to help make our people one people."[109]

At the Arlington unveiling, President Woodrow Wilson, the first Southern president since the Civil War, reiterated the passing of sectional antagonism as he accepted the statue on behalf of the government. Deeming *New South* an "emblem of a reunited people," Wilson declared, "This chapter in the history of the United States is now closed, and . . . we now face and admire one another."[110] In his waning years, Ezekiel voiced this perspective as well, quoting Robert E. Lee in his memoir and agreeing, "I have buried the past with my sword," which was, in part, the message of his Lee submission that was roundly rejected for placement on Monument Avenue.[111] Ezekiel expressed this standpoint more than once: "I remembered how General Lee had buried it all when he sheathed his sword at Appomattox and how he had asked me to do the same thing. . . . I do think that as Americans we ought to be united now that the war is over. . . . It can serve no purpose and only injure us to keep up any kind of animosity now that it is all over."[112] To be clear, Ezekiel agreed that the past should be the past, yet he still did not admit that what the Confederates had fought for was not a lost cause but a wrong cause.

Under a darkening sky and the threat of heavy rain, hundreds of Confederate veterans and some Union counterparts, along with over four thousand civilians, attended the unveiling of *New South*. Wilson processed with former soldiers carrying US flags of Stars and Stripes as well as the Confederate Stars and Bars. The long program featured several speeches, notably by President Wilson and Robert E. Lee's grandson, delivered in an attempt to repair the torn fabric of the nation. Confederate veteran Rev. Randolph McKim began the ceremony by invoking to God that the "monument may stand as a perpetual memorial of the reconciliation between the people of the States once arrayed against each other in deadly conflict," and quoted Isaiah as inscribed by Ezekiel on the monument.[113] Among other dignitaries on the platform were the commander of the United Confederate Veterans and the commander in chief of the Grand Army of the Republic, a fraternal organization of Union veterans. Both parties promoted the monument as a tribute to the Confederate dead and a symbol of the reunification of the fractured country after the Spanish-American War, where the direct descendants of Confederate and Union soldiers could be found "marching side by side in peace and amity."[114] Incontestably that is idealism at its apex, but the Spanish-American War did unite kin from both sides of the Civil War, who fought shoulder to shoulder against a foreign enemy. Still, the sculpture's hammering home of a false Lost Cause narrative provides a challenging and highly troubling contradiction. So does the UDC's choice to honorifically hold the unveiling on the anniversary of Jefferson Davis's birthday.

Those contradictions continue. Even in the twenty-first century, government officials acknowledged Confederate Americans at Arlington Cemetery. From President Theodore Roosevelt onward, most US presidents sent a wreath to the monument on Davis's birthday. George W. Bush chose instead to lay a wreath on Memorial Day. Amid calls to cease this tradition, America's first Black president, Barack Obama, sent a wreath to both the Confederate Monument as well as the African American Civil War Memorial on Memorial Day.[115] Much as Thomas Ball's *Emancipation*

Memorial (1876) serves as the country's monument to emancipation in the nation's capital despite its complicated and contested portrayal of a submissive, recently emancipated man at the feet of a paternalistic Abraham Lincoln, the tensions inherent in the country's national monument to the Confederate dead as well as the premier symbol of sectional reunion incited extreme positions about its future on either side of the divide.

Arlington's elaborate Confederate monument sits atop an octagonal base that bears additional nomenclature aimed to reinforce its visual vocabulary and didactic, exculpatory purpose. Underneath the Confederate seal at the front, Ezekiel inscribed in Latin, "Victrix Causa Diis Placuit Sed Victa Catoni." Translated as "The victorious cause was pleasing to the gods, but the lost cause to Cato," the bold phrase connects the "cause" to Roman antiquity, when the common man fought to prevent Julius Caesar from becoming dictator of Rome. In other words, the quote casts Lincoln as a dictator and the Confederates as righteous men who aimed to preserve the rights they saw enabled by the Constitution—which for most allowed slavery. On the back of the monument, Ezekiel sculpted a poem in high relief, credited to Reverend McKim (who delivered the invocation at the unveiling):

> Not for fame or reward
> Not for place or rank
> Not lured by ambition
> Or Goaded by Necessity
> But in Simple Obedience to Duty
> As they understood it
> These Men suffered All
> Sacrificed All
> Dared all—and died.

Without a doubt, the poem reads problematically, but at least it extends a brief conciliatory note by acknowledging Confederate ideology as one of duty "as they [secessionists] understood it." A year after the unveiling, *Monumental News* published a one-page article about the monument with a full-page reproduction. The anonymous author stayed politically and critically neutral, save for an observation that the monument "is one of the most elaborate sculptured memorials on any of our battlefields and exemplifies an unusual form of public memorial."[116]

Ezekiel's allegiance to the South never waned; it was ever present in his mind and, as often as possible, in his art. This was especially evident in the abundantly symbolic and self-indulgently decorative *New South*. While Ezekiel subtly encoded Judaism in *Religious Liberty*, there is little subtle about *New South*. His preferred title references the term "New South," coined in the 1880s by *Atlanta Constitution* editor Henry Grady. Grady's vision was for a South revitalized by modern industry, moving beyond its pre–Civil War agrarian economy; however, his plan did not include equal treatment for African Americans.[117] Like Grady's vision, the "new," only present in the monument's title, is overshadowed by the old in highly visible and troublesome ways. Nonetheless, the monument was meant to act as a binding agent, a remedy for the country's wounds, and in its day *New South* did just that. Its failure to live on in history, however, lies in the fact that while *New South* was intended to be designed as a "peace monument" (to use Ezekiel's words), its creator went rogue. A precedent for this subordination is the Jewish Publication seal, where he inserted iconographical inventions not specified by the sponsoring committee. To put it plainly, Ezekiel ruined the government's sincere goals for the monument with his overzealousness, which more than pleased the UDC and its sympathizers.

As a symbol of reconciliation for white Americans, the monument worked. Southerners were pacified and grateful to be afforded the same consideration as other American soldiers. The impetus for a Confederate monument—to fortify national solidarity as an "emblem of a reunited people"—at least, was a noble one, notwithstanding tainted aspects of its conception.[118] But in the end, the monument shows how white Southerners won the memory of the Civil War with an overriding narrative asserting that the rebels were fighting for states' self-determination rather than the right to own human beings—a perspective that links to the current-day persistence of white supremacy. An understanding of the historical forces that shaped the monument's commission and reception in the immediate period after its dedication in no way excuses its message. Rather, it deepens our understanding of how a eulogy to the Confederacy could rest for over a century just four hundred yards from the Tomb of the Unknown Solider.

Ezekiel wrote in an 1886 letter, "Monuments in enduring bronze and marble are the legacies we bequeath to future ages as the most reliable records of our culture as well as our deeds."[119] In reality, this is rarely the case, because as this chapter (and book) has demonstrated, monuments can be moved, mutilated, and mutate in their meanings. Even more, as framed in their own day, most Confederate monuments are the least reliable records of one's deeds. Their reliability comes to the fore when we see them not for what they were meant to be but for what they really are: an enduring legacy of reliable symbols denoting power and suppression that make insidious claims for inequality.

Yet, as has also been shown, some monuments have unknown histories beyond their surface appearances that warrant excavating and considering. *New South* stood as the country's failed monument to both sectional reconciliation and a Lost Cause, and *Virginia Mourning Her Dead* mourned the dead from the day Ezekiel conceived her, soon after the war's end, not decades after the fact. Not motivated or shaped by questions of white superiority, and devoid of Lost Cause imagery and twisted language, *Virginia Mourning Her Dead* served as a salve to wash away the trauma of Ezekiel's experiences on the battlefield rather than celebrating a single individual with racist principles. Certainly, one could look at *Virginia Mourning Her Dead* one-dimensionally and argue that it originally commemorated boys who fought in defense of the Confederacy, and thus slavery, and rip the sculpture down. One could note that VMI did not find it suitable to erect the statue until the Jim Crow era. One could point to Ezekiel's other Confederate monuments—such as his *Stonewall Jackson* on the grounds of the West Virginia Capitol building in Charleston or the iconography of his Arlington monument—to subvert any defense of *Virginia Mourning Her Dead*. One could further dismiss the sculpture because, throughout his life, Ezekiel remained a proud Confederate veteran and never showed remorse for his participation in the Civil War. The rebel flag hung until his death in his Roman home, and he saw himself, as he put it in his later years, as "the old soldier hermit in the Baths of Diocletian, who still has the Confederate flag and colours, and *his* coat of arms of the Old Dominion, as the chief ornament of his Den."[120] His autobiography was originally titled "Memories of a Southern Veteran," and at times he regurgitated the myth of the Lost Cause.

But that would ignore the nuances of Ezekiel's profoundly personal and visceral monument, and its distinctive place in the history of commemorative statuary—crafted by a veteran under the strain of his war memories to honor the death of conscripted boys. *Virginia Mourning Her Dead* serves as Ezekiel's Mourner's Kaddish to his slain brothers in arms. It bears repeating that he described the making of the statue as "one of the most sacred duties in my life."[121] Symbolic of their lasting influence on his life is one of the two dedications at the front of his memoir: "To the memory of my cadet comrades who fell in a victorious defeat."[122] Notwithstanding, the long shadow of one man's crushing experience does not absolve a sculpture that fails to acknowledge the unmistakable fact that what the boys were fighting for was wrong. This is especially significant given the sculpture's location at a twenty-first-century American campus that sent these individuals to fight for slavery. Yet still, for some, *Virginia*'s afterlife redeems her as she teaches us about the politics of the past and the present, and thus she remains in the public sphere. While *New South*'s intended conciliatory purpose in its own day is negated by its literal, contemporary, politically infused iconography, *Virginia Mourning Her Dead*'s broadened purpose in the current day is allowed by its timeless allegorical iconography. She raises questions about the sometimes-challenging ambiguities of America's legacy of monumental hatred as we right the wrongs of our country's ugly history of segregation, apathy, and hate. While this book recovers Ezekiel's work, recovery does not have to include acceptance.

CONCLUSION

Moses Jacob Ezekiel's Misfortunes in Art and History

All that I did and do wish was and is to be able to devote myself independently to my own art, which is everything to me. I have hungered and suffered for it . . . but have always kept up a cheerful face and let the world believe that I was having a great success such as I had a right to deserve.
—Moses Ezekiel, circa 1890

If Ezekiel were asked to name what he viewed as his most important sculptures after his monuments to the South, among them would be two yet unmentioned: a twelve-foot-tall memorial to Jewish philanthropist Jesse Seligman, sponsored by Jewish American patrons; and a noncommissioned life-size monument of Napoleon.[1] The genesis for the works, the artistic choices Ezekiel made, and the afterlives (i.e., deaths) of these sculptures epitomize Ezekiel's misfortunes in art and history.

While the Corcoran sculptures still exist, albeit not in their finest form nor in their intended venue, a commission about which Ezekiel wrote considerably more, an 1895 memorial to Jesse Seligman, is assuredly destroyed (fig. 96). A Bavarian-born Jewish philanthropist, Seligman arrived in America as a boy and later amassed a fortune in his family's banking business. He supported sundry causes, with the Hebrew Orphan Asylum in New York City, established in 1859, closest to his heart; Seligman founded the organization and then served as its president for nearly twenty years.[2] After Seligman died in 1894, orphanage directors ordered Ezekiel to make a sculpture commemorating their esteemed leader, funded by public subscription.[3] Years earlier, in 1882, Ezekiel himself showed support for the orphanage by arranging an auction in Cincinnati of donated artwork for its benefit. His donations included an autographed letter and a bronze statuette of the highly influential but excommunicated seventeenth-century Jewish philosopher *Baruch Spinoza* (ca. 1880; Skirball Museum, Cincinnati).[4]

The *Jesse Seligman Memorial* strongly stresses religious freedom and recycles some of the lexicon of iconography from *Religious Liberty*. Its base comprises the ruins of Assyria, Egypt, and ancient Rome in allegorical form as emblematic of these civilizations' xenophobia, from which modernity rises symbolically as a column of the Union. A serpent attacked by an American eagle, in the same configuration at the base of *Religious Liberty*, coils around the back of the column. The eagle of liberty, period documents explain, destroys the serpent of intolerance, which has poisoned the earlier ages denoted on the base.[5] Atop the column sits a lush wreath, and atop that rests a bronze bust of Seligman. After Asylum personnel decided that Ezekiel would execute a statue in their leader's honor, the sculptor aimed for authenticity by crafting a death mask of Seligman when his body arrived at Temple Emanu-El, the first Reform congregation in New York City.[6] Standing in front of the column as a separate entity, a bronze, life-size, barefoot orphan girl in tattered clothes holds an unfurled scroll, on which Ezekiel has inscribed, "His charity knew no race or creed."[7] The words "true liberty destroys intolerance" appear between the decorative base and the orphan's feet. Ezekiel's conception was considerably more than requested or expected.

It is unknown how the asylum's directors reacted to the final product, but from a current perspective, the sculpture—though beautiful in its separate parts—does not add up to a cohesive conception. Nor does the addition of the religious liberty iconography—an eagle, a serpent, a column of the Union, along with the fallen dynasties at the base—express a clear message about Seligman. Perhaps Ezekiel meant to suggest that because of America's religious freedoms, the Jewish Seligman could become a Gilded Age millionaire and thus offer material support for worthy causes, but that message would be too complicated for most viewers. Trying to shoehorn meaning into the monument, former New York City Mayor Abram S. Hewitt spoke at length during the unveiling "upon the prosperity of the Hebrew sect," and of Seligman as a man: "Simple as a child, wise as a serpent, and gentle as a dove."[8] Some might have been taken aback by Seligman's bust, which shows him undraped and without a shirt, nipples apparent. Ezekiel may have been ill-advisedly thinking of Horatio Greenough's marble of a seated, shirtless George Washington (chapter 5), thereby presenting Seligman similarly. For years, the monument decorated the entrance hall of the orphanage's building on Amsterdam Avenue and 138th Street, unveiled in April 1896 on the second anniversary of Seligman's death, with Ezekiel in attendance.

Ezekiel invested a massive amount of time and energy into the piece, delayed a trip to the United States to work on it, and wrote to his father that he made his "fourth plan a success."[9] Documents indicate that the orphan, eagle, laurel, and bust are different color bronzes, the column is red marble, and the base yet another color marble; a black-and-white photograph substantiates tonal gradations. The monument cost significantly more to make than the fee allotted by the Asylum, but that did not matter to Ezekiel: "This project will

FIG. 96 Moses Jacob Ezekiel, *Jesse Seligman Memorial*, 1895. Marble and bronze, 12 ft. Lost. Courtesy of The Jacob Rader Marcus Center of the American Jewish Archives, Cincinnati, Ohio, at americanjewisharchives.org.

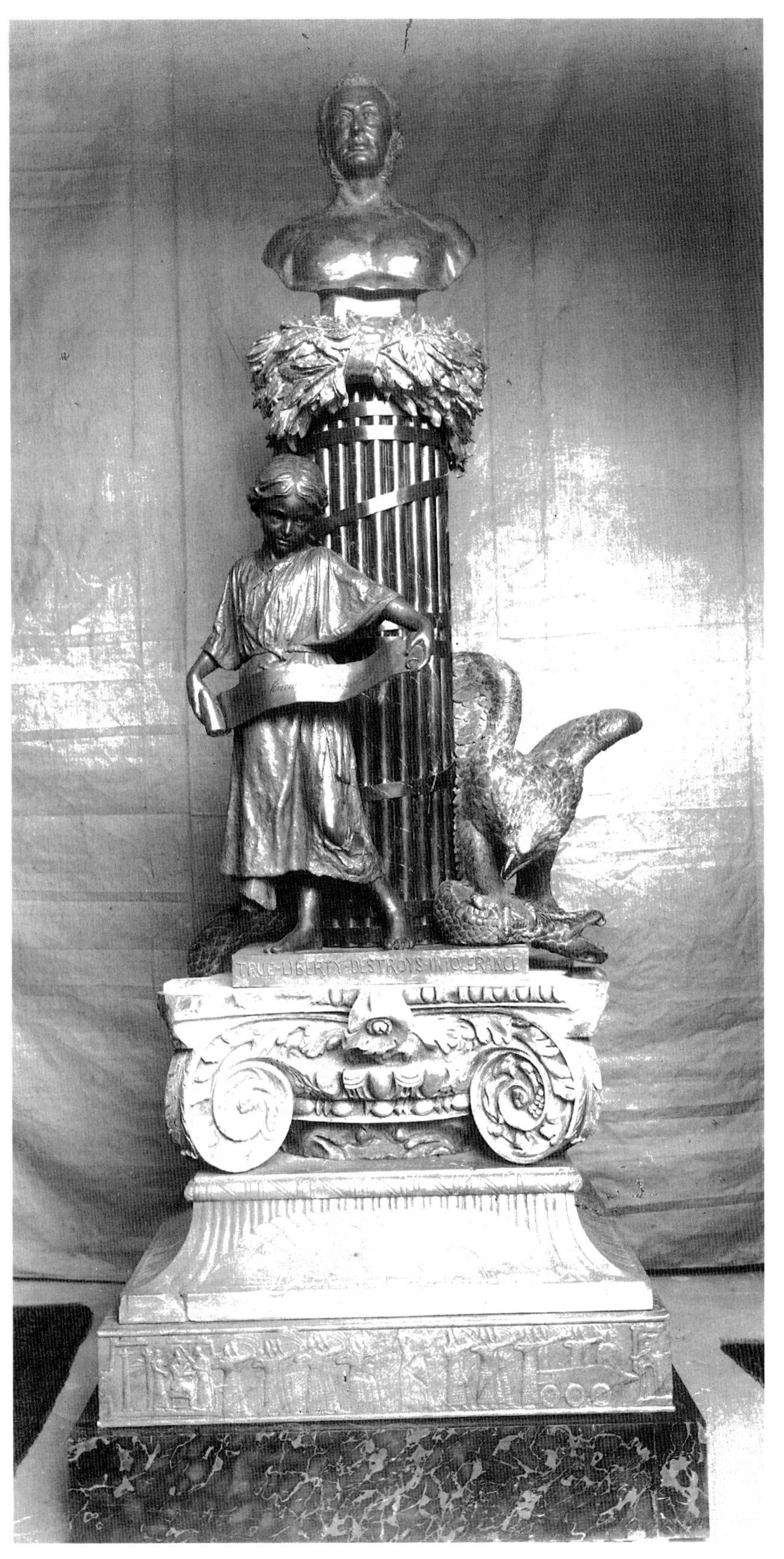
TRUE·LIBERTY·DESTROYS·INTOLERANCE

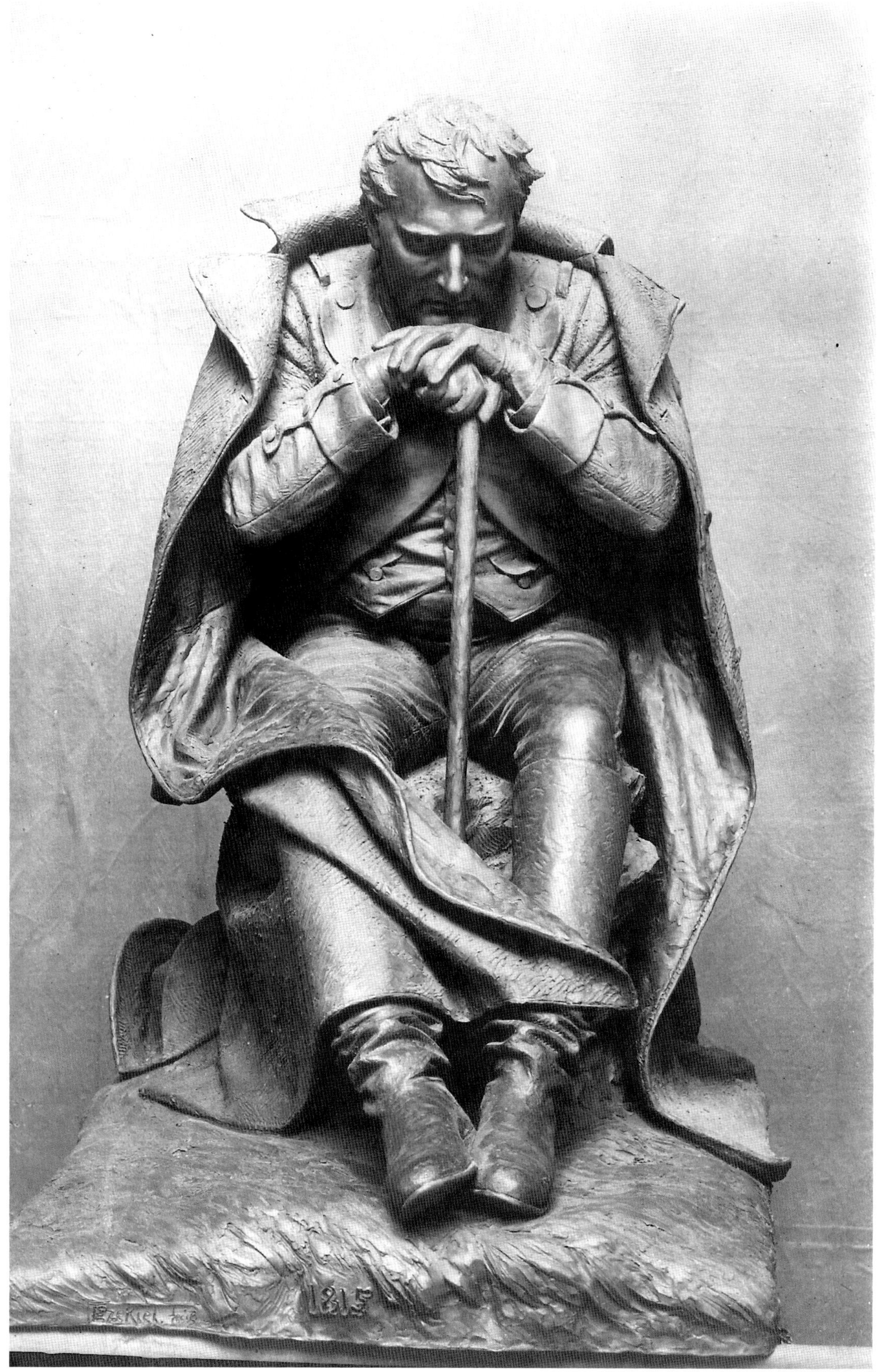
Ezekiel
1815

cost me a *great deal* more than the simple bronze statue would have done. But it allows me to carry out my artistic ideas more fully and I do not want to sacrifice them for simple profit and would not do it."[10] At least Ezekiel was long gone when, in another cruel twist, the Seligman memorial went missing, either lost when the Asylum closed in 1941 or destroyed when the building was razed in the mid-1950s. Tragically, Ezekiel's estate had donated the artist's autograph album—a treasure trove of "who's who"—to the Asylum in 1931, which has been lost as well.[11] The Seligman memorial sums up many errors of Ezekiel's career: too much allegory, too much classicism, too much storytelling, too many recycled themes, and then the sculpture's demise. How thrilled Ezekiel was to gain this commission from a beneficent Jewish institution in his homeland and to memorialize an esteemed fellow coreligionist. How distraught he would have been to know it is gone.

Napoleon, the making of which was frequently covered by the press, did not fare any better (fig. 97). Experiencing a lull in orders in 1906, Ezekiel set his sights on "one which I had always hoped to be able to do," and thus began crafting a life-size Napoleon, another sculpture injudiciously derived from his private passions.[12] Recall that Ezekiel considered "Moses, Christ, and Napoleon the three greatest men that had ever lived."[13] The two conceptions of Napoleon, a bronze bust in addition to a life-size sculpture fashioned first in marble and then bronze, stemmed from "great admiration of the Hero" since his childhood, because of his military prowess.[14] Based on a death mask purchased in Paris, the sculpture shows the former emperor sitting on a rock at St. Helena, deeply contemplative, his head bent and chin resting on his cane. His uniform was specially made for a model who posed in Napoleon's guise, chosen based on his close size resemblance to the former emperor. Ezekiel took great care to model the folds of the mantle and the creases in Napoleon's vest, trousers, and boots. Wind dramatically blows the overcoat—"an unexpected addition," as per Ezekiel.[15] That cloak sits heavily on Napoleon's shoulders as he reflects on his fate since being exiled after his defeat at Waterloo, so signified by the date "1815" carved into the base.

FIG. 97 Moses Jacob Ezekiel, *Napoleon*, circa 1910. Bronze, life-size. Lost. Photo: Virginia Military Institute Archives, Lexington.

Critics and visitors to Ezekiel's atelier lauded the potency of the sculpture. One Italian critic observed that the general appeared "not as a man of victory, thirsting for war, seeking after the dominion of the world, but rather with the true skill of the artist he has represented Napoleon after the struggle with Olympic severity."[16] "An eminent American" viewing the lone figure, remarked, as quoted in the *New York Times*, "There is a tragedy in that stick."[17] A special correspondent from Rome movingly wrote about the "great Emperor . . . at St. Helena, sitting, and leaning on a cane. His sword is his no longer."[18] The stark cane on which Napoleon rests his weary head is effective for its simplicity, a conception nearly ruined by Ezekiel's predilection for overornamentation. In 1909, critic Luigi Callani of *Il popolo romano* described *Napoleon* clasping a crucifix for strength instead of his scepter.[19] Wisely, Ezekiel removed that superfluous touch, which points to his penchant for revision, in part because of his own uncertainty. J. P. Morgan expressed interest in the bronze version while visiting the studio but didn't bite in the end; on that same trip, the two men traveled to Centocelle, outside

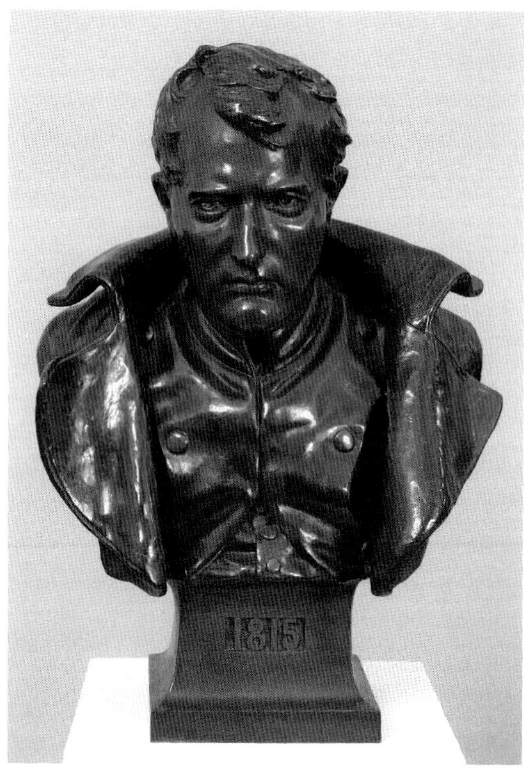

FIG. 98 Moses Jacob Ezekiel, *Napoleon*, 1908. Bronze, 25 in. Virginia Military Institute Museum, Lexington. Photo: Virginia Military Institute Museum, Lexington.

Rome, to view the Wright brothers' demonstration flights.[20] Erskine Ross of Los Angeles, a New Market veteran who later served as a circuit and district judge, purchased the bronze full-scale *Napoleon* around 1914. Somehow, both massive sculptures in marble and bronze have disappeared.

President Teddy Roosevelt's sister Corinne Robinson was also impressed with *Napoleon.* (Ezekiel would lunch with her when in the United States.) During her outing at the Baths, she asked Ezekiel for a marble bust portrait of the emperor, which is either lost or was never made; only a twenty-five-inch-tall bronze bust remains (1908; fig. 98).[21] John Woodruff Simpson, who commissioned Ezekiel to make the busts of great artists, originally asked him for a bust of Napoleon, but whether he ever purchased a *Napoleon* is unknown.[22] The bust comprises Napoleon's upper torso and accents his military uniform. He stares off into the distance, not downward as in the full-length sculpture. Napoleon holds his head up, but his exhaustion is palpable, the man more pathetic than powerful. Ezekiel wrote that novelist Francis Marion Crawford (son of sculptor Thomas Crawford) proclaimed the sculpture "not a bust. It is the history of Napoleon himself."[23] Regardless of whether Crawford actually said this, Ezekiel saw his *Napoleon* sculptures as among his most compelling, and those words might be his own characteristically flamboyant estimation.

Excitement about Ezekiel's life-size *Napoleon* reached King Victor Emmanuel III from his mother, Queen Margherita, who earlier came to see the in-progress statue at the Tower of Belisarius. News accounts reported that Ezekiel would once again "be honored by a royal visit to his studio in 1909," when the king visited.[24] The *Richmond Times-Dispatch* proudly relayed that the king, so impressed, would confer the title "Officer of the Crown of Italy" on Ezekiel.[25] Soon after, the sculpture, which he labored on for almost three years, was chiseled in marble and intended for exhibition at the Paris Salon. No records indicate that it was exhibited there. Visitors came to see *Napoleon* for years. In 1913, *Napoleon* still made the news. High-ranking politician and Southerner Oscar Straus and his wife visited Ezekiel, where they spent over an hour admiring *New South* and "the cast of his famous Napoleon," as per the *New York Times.*[26]

This last stage of Ezekiel's career shows him at his most ambitious and impractical. (Remember that the year before he died, Ezekiel embarked on an equestrian portrait of Stonewall Jackson, only in clay, as proof of his skill for posterity; chapter 6.) His unrealistic, uncommissioned, massive *Napoleon* confirms anew his idealistic belief in an outmoded moment in art, especially when it came to his passion projects, often concerning military figures. Indeed, enamored by uniforms and the military, and always hopeful to secure a major monument commission in Europe, Ezekiel sculpted evermore on speculation and subjects of dwindling interest for future patrons. Other highly ambitious unrealized monuments to European leaders are knowable only through a handful of photographs showing large clay models, for which dating is fairly uncertain. A vivid equestrian portrait of *Victor Emmanuel II*, fashioned after Donatello's 1453 *Equestrian Portrait of Gattamelata* (Erasmo da Narni) in Padua, presents the king calmly commanding his energetic horse, in the vein of Ezekiel's equestrian submission of Robert E. Lee atop his steed. Ezekiel strategically created the monument to coincide with the fiftieth anniversary celebration, in 1911, of the unification of Italy. He was unquestionably hoping that the king's son would purchase the sculpture in his father's honor (the same hope he had for Queen Margherita purchasing the sculpture he made of her, on view in his studio during one of her social calls). Additionally, Ezekiel's interest in Emmanuel II connects to his reverence for Rome and his desire to sculpt like his exemplar, Donatello. This was not the only time that Ezekiel conceived a pie-in-the sky monument to a European leader.

Worthy of brief mention are two more imprudent statues made, Ezekiel hoped, to ensure his place as a great monument maker. Journeyman *Marco Polo* (after 1900) is designed in a style closely resembling *Judah Maccabee*. *Polo* stands similarly erect, in uniform, head gazing upward over his left shoulder, with his right arm in motion. A second monument, of the highly influential but excommunicated seventeenth-century Jewish philosopher, *Baruch Spinoza* (after 1900), revives the subject of the bronze statuette he made in the 1880s but with an altogether new design and at an ambitious scale. Expelled from Amsterdam's Jewish community for his public and heterodox theological-political ideas, Spinoza sits pensively on a sparsely blocked-out step, his left hand placed on a book. Ezekiel's focus on a Jewish subject that would have been wholly unfamiliar to most non-Jews also reflects the artist's desire to revisit his roots and the Jewish subjects of his younger days. Neither sculpture was realized.

Relocation, Removal, and Ezekiel's Modern-Day Invisibility Revisited

While I was writing this book, part and parcel with the removal of Confederate monuments, statues of Christopher Columbus were swiftly dismantled because of the explorer's ties to colonialism and Native American genocide. Among them was one by Ezekiel, erroneously described in past scholarship as made for display at the Italian Pavilion of the 1893 World's Columbian Exposition in Chicago—a celebration of the four-hundredth anniversary of Columbus's landing on American soil. As described in Ezekiel's memoir, that nine-foot statue of *Christopher Columbus* (fig. 99) was commissioned in 1892 by Chicago businessman Henry J. Furber for his new building, to be known as the Columbus.[27] Ezekiel's monument, much like dozens of Columbus statues across the country,

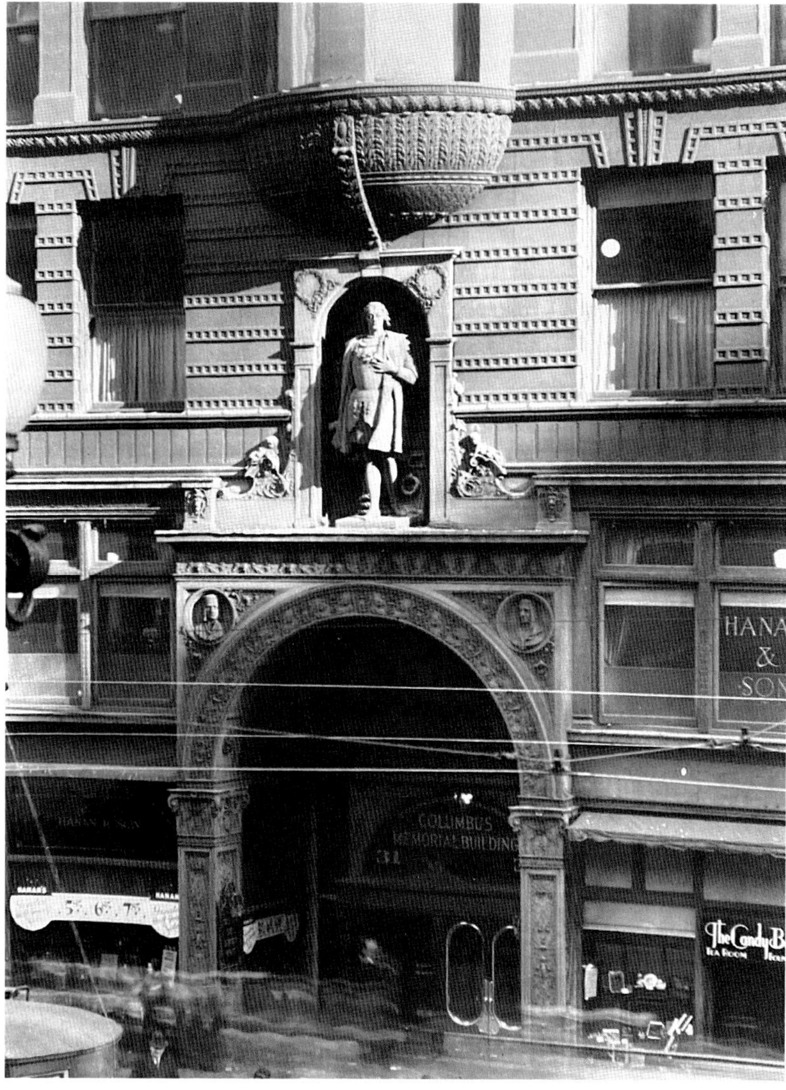

FIG. 99 Moses Jacob Ezekiel, *Christopher Columbus*, 1893. Bronze, 9 ft. Facade of Columbus Memorial Building, 1932. Photo: Courtesy of Chicago Historical Society.

FIG. 100 (OPPOSITE) Moses Jacob Ezekiel, *Peace*, 1901. Marble, 35 1/2 in. Private collection. Photo: Meyer Fine Art of Virginia.

has suffered a fate that one would expect for his still-standing monuments such as West Virginia's *Stonewall Jackson* or Virginia's *John Warwick Daniel*. Striving for historical accuracy according to, Ezekiel attested, "the only historical record we have," he depicted the explorer in armor, as he had read in a description by Columbus's contemporary voyager Bartolomé de las Casas.[28] That costume is as awkward and inelegant as the barrel-chested sculpture. The historical accuracy that Ezekiel so craved—and well used for *Dürer* at the Corcoran Gallery, *Stonewall Jackson*, *Napoleon*, and a host of other monuments—was ill served in this case.

Columbus stood in the second-story niche of the Columbus Memorial Building until the edifice's razing in 1958. The statue was then relegated to a lumberyard, until it was briefly brought to light for the city's 1966 Columbus Day parade. After improbable stints in the yard of a car service shop and the city's Department of Urban Renewal, *Columbus* found a new home in Chicago's Arrigo Park (formerly Vernon Park) at the center of a fountain.[29] With the insistent social and political ruptures during the country's reckoning with race relations of the past and present, in 2020 city officials removed *Columbus* from the park under the cover of darkness and placed him in storage, citing concerns about public safety.[30] Incensed by the decision, Chicago's Italian American community argued that the city breached a fifty-year contract with the Joint Civic Committee of Italian Americans. Briefly pacified after securing permission to clean the statue of graffiti, the Italian American community celebrated by showing off the polished sculpture a few hours after the Columbus Day parade, before returning it to storage.[31] No doubt, Ezekiel would have been bewildered by the controversies around his art, let alone its relocation and removal—and just as aggrieved that not once was his name mentioned as sculptor of the monument.

Ezekiel was also spared knowing the posthumous misfortune of his statue of *Peace*, although this thirty-five-inch-tall marble work found a happier ending (1901; fig. 100). In 2004, gallerist Michael Meyer purchased *Peace*, which presents a woman draped in classical robes and holding roses, from a dealer in Connecticut, where for years she had decorated his property. At some point, the sculpture was spray-painted black, thereby obscuring the signature. When Meyer acquired *Peace*, which he admired for its technical chops even though he did not know the sculptor's name and believed it was unsigned, he had the work restored. A signature, filled in by the black paint, revealed the statue to be by Ezekiel.[32] *Peace* is now

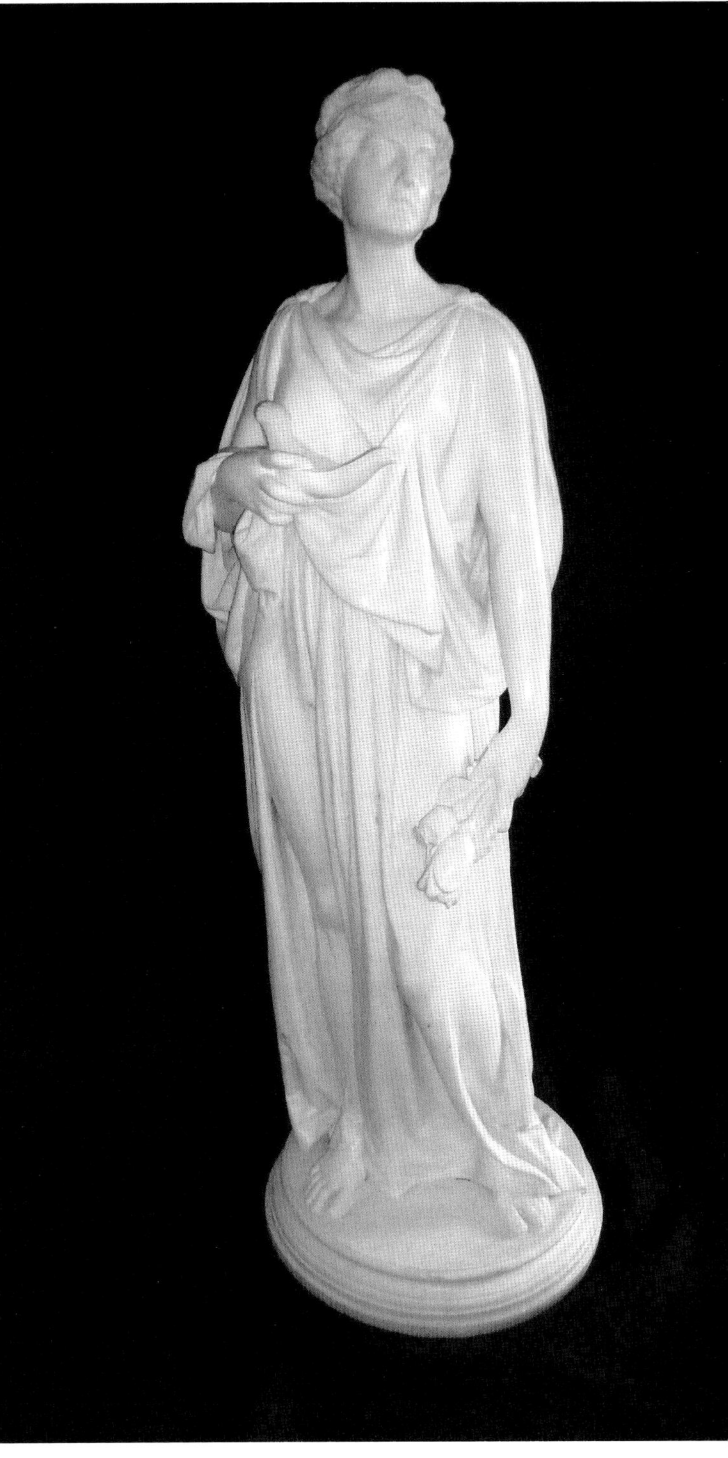

safely sheltered indoors in a private Pennsylvania collection.

Ezekiel's Final Roll Call

The mobility of Ezekiel's body presaged the mobility of his sculptures. Exhausted from volunteer work by day for the American Red Cross coordinating supplies to Italian soldiers during World War I, he would return to the Tower of Belisarius at night, which was damp due to a lack of coal during the hostilities. It all was too much for the seventy-two-year-old artist, who succumbed to pneumonia in March 1917.[33] His close friend and supporter Thomas Nelson Page found an envelope marked "To be opened after my death" among Ezekiel's papers, with a request to be buried at the base of his Confederate monument in Arlington. Page honored this wish and made the necessary arrangements from Rome, however belatedly.[34] Delayed by the war and diplomatic negotiations, his body was temporarily housed in the de Bosis family crypt in Rome, which Ezekiel had designed with three small bronze reliefs (1902; now missing), until it could be transferred to the United States four years later. In March 1921, Ezekiel was buried at the base of *New South* in one of four spots of honor, with special permission from Congress because existing laws only allowed for Confederate veterans residing in Washington, DC, or the vicinity to be interred in the Confederate section.[35] His grave marker does not flaunt his honorifics—"Sculptor," "Sir," or "Cavaliere"—but more modestly reads, "Moses J. Ezekiel, Sergeant of Company C, Battalion of Cadets of the Virginia Military Institute." Ezekiel's funeral service was the first ever held at Arlington's Memorial Amphitheater.

The elaborate pageantry of the ceremony and service was a grand affair, orchestrated just as Ezekiel would have wanted.[36] His casket, guarded by six uniformed VMI cadets, was covered by a cornucopia of flowers atop an American flag, and he was buried with full military honors. Fittingly, the Marine Band played Franz Liszt's "Liebestraum No. 3." Rabbi David Philipson of Cincinnati paid tribute and recited the Mourner's Kaddish. Secretary of War John Weeks delivered a lengthy principal address.[37] Carefully chosen pallbearers offered a cross-section of Ezekiel's life: the president of the University of Virginia (who shepherded *Jefferson* and the *Homer Group* to the school); one of his New Market comrades, the former assistant secretary of war, and the presidents of the Southern Society of New York and Washington; the editor of *Art and Archaeology*, the president of the Smithsonian Institution, and the directors of the Corcoran Gallery of Art and National Gallery of Art; as well as members of Congress. The Italian ambassador along with members of Congress and the Cabinet sat in boxes of honor near Ezekiel's bedecked casket. It all began when President Harding's eulogy, quoted widely by the press and in this book's introduction, lionized the sculptor "a great Virginian, a great artist, a great American and a great citizen of world fame."[38] If that were not enough, an evening service arranged by the Arlington Confederate Monument Association remembered the sculptor as well. Led by a different rabbi, the service showcased Ezekiel's Jewish, artistic, Southern, and expatriate identities. Sculptor Henry K. Bush-Brown remembered him with the eulogy, "Sir Moses Ezekiel as a Sculptor." Colonel Robert E. Lee, the son of General Robert E. Lee, spoke to "Sir Moses Ezekiel as an American and as Southerner." Lastly, the ambassador of Italy,

Senator Vittorio Rolandi-Ricci, paid tribute to "Sir Moses Ezekiel as an adopted son of Italy.[39]

Ezekiel's death resonated around the Western world, in 1917 and 1921. Dozens of obituaries from both sides of the ocean mourned his passing and described his art and life in varying degrees of depth.[40] As at his funeral and memorial service, obituaries typically highlighted one of Ezekiel's identities with a nod to his other endeavors. Art periodicals broadly lauded his sculpture: "By his own genius [Ezekiel] has gained the recognition of the world and the love of many friends," wrote Bush-Brown in *Art and Archaeology*.[41] Southern papers praised his war service and Confederate monuments: *Confederate Veteran* noted his "service to his country when as a boy of seventeen he served with the V.M.I. cadets and helped make history on the field of New Market," and his "matchless bronze memorial, his South with laurel extended, whose brow the first rays of the rising sun light up with dazzling brilliancy."[42] Jewish papers underscored his religion and contributions to Jewish culture, especially *Religious Liberty*: "He presented in his life and work the highest type of the artist and the Jew," wrote the *Hebrew Standard*, and a comprehensive obituary in the *American Jewish Year Book* characterized Ezekiel as "so vitally a Jew that he could not help projecting his own nature into the creations of his brain and his hand."[43]

Had Ezekiel written his own obituary (and considering his prolific writings and desire to control his public image, he likely did at some point), he might have kept it simple, akin to the epitaph on his headstone. But I doubt that. Even in the end, defining himself by the exhilaration and trauma of his military service, Ezekiel would have boasted in long form—he was ever insecure and reveled in acclaim. Or maybe he would not have hesitated to lament his travails, as he often did, but with a melodramatic caveat. Ezekiel once wrote of "bear[ing] the cross of my own art," while immodestly adding that he always remained "a little in doubt whether the bestowal of genius is a divine bounty or not. After all, it is something like showing the sky to a bird and then clipping his wings."[44] And so, with the last words of this excavation of Ezekiel's art and life, I will write my own simple epitaph for an unrepentant rebel who otherwise lived a cosmopolitan life in Europe as a friend of the elite, a feted sculptor, and a practicing Jew—who alternately enriched and transgressed on American art and history:

> Moses Jacob Ezekiel
>
> Jewish, Confederate, Expatriate Sculptor

EPILOGUE

Ezekiel and Me, the Final Controversy

Soon before hitting the "send" button to deliver this manuscript to press, I became enmeshed in yet another Ezekiel controversy, when the lives of a nineteenth-century Jewish American sculptor and a twenty-first-century historian of Jewish American art collided once again. I received an email from the Society for the Preservation of Jewish Civil War history containing a petition to save the "Ezekiel Monument in Arlington Cemetery." The email, from July 1, 2023, was addressed to prominent academics in Jewish studies along with figures in the Jewish communal world. It read:

All,

Good morning. Hope everyone is well.

We are making progress in our fight to save the Ezekiel Monument in Arlington. Congressman Bob Good and Senator Tom Cotton have both agreed to offer amendments to the National Defense Authorization Act (NDAA) defunding any legislation authorizing removal of the memorial. As respected members of the Jewish Community and renowned historians and academicians would you be willing to sign on to this letter in support of this effort? Please respond with your name and title.

Kindest regards
Jack Schewel

The Honorable Kevin McCarthy, Speaker
The Honorable Mike Rogers, HASC Chair
The Honorable Jack Reed, Chairman Senate Armed Services Committee
The Honorable Roger Wicker, Ranking Member, Senate Armed Services Committee

Dear Speaker McCarthy, Chairmen Reed and Rogers and Senator Wicker,

The Society for the Preservation of Jewish Civil War History is deeply troubled by Secretary of Defense Lloyd

Austin's acceptance of the Congressional Naming Commission's recommendation to remove the historic Moses Ezekiel Memorial in Arlington National Cemetery. The directive is based on a highly controversial interpretation of legislation passed by the 117th Congress, since enacted as Public Law 116-283, which has far-reaching implications for the Jewish Community, the Memorial itself, Arlington National Cemetery, and our nation.

We express grave concern for the impact of this decision which undermines the integrity and significance of Arlington National Cemetery, which is our nation's most iconic military cemetery, and includes burials of Jewish veterans from both sides of America's most costly war.

But more importantly, this memorial is the opus work of arguably the world's most important Jewish Artist, from a country that welcomed Jews into the art community. We are reminded that during WWII, Jewish art was considered "degenerate" by the Nazi Party in Germany, and that the important works of Jewish artists were confiscated and destroyed by Joseph Goebbels's Ministry of Propaganda.

In today's era of heightened awareness of Antisemitism, what message does it send by removing the most significant work of American Jewish Art from our Nation's most important military cemetery? We believe it can and will be construed by many as Antisemitic.

We must remember and learn from our history, but we must not do as the Nazis did and eliminate it. Removing from Arlington National Cemetery the centerpiece of Section 16 marking the final resting place of its Jewish sculptor must be halted.

If you have any questions or require additional information, please do not hesitate to contact Rabbi Eric Wisnia, at spjcwh@gmail.com

We urge all Americans to join us in the fight to overturn this directive and protect Jewish military history at Arlington National Cemetery.

Furthermore, we, the undersigned, strenuously object to the desecration of the Moses Ezekiel memorial at Arlington National Cemetery.

Signed
Your Name Here

I was stunned and swiftly responded (after which I soon received vicious "hate emails" in reply):

Dear all,

Some of you know me and some do not. For those who don't, a brief introduction: I am a professor of art history who has been writing a book about Moses Jacob Ezekiel, funded by the National Endowment for the Humanities. The book is almost complete, save for the introduction, and the manuscript will be submitted to my press at the end of August. The book is heavily dependent on archives and is a reconstruction of MJE's working practice, life, and body of work, including—for your interests here—combing of his cadet file at VMI.

I feel compelled to send this email because your petition is off base.

Let me begin by making clear: I'm somewhat sympathetic to keeping *New South* (not "the Ezekiel Memorial") at Arlington for several reasons but none that you cite. And I am sympathetic to Ezekiel as an artist, man, and Jew. But your petition misstates crucial facts.

1. To reiterate from above: It's not the "Moses Ezekiel Memorial in Arlington National Cemetery." It's the nation's Confederate monument, titled *New South*, by Ezekiel.

2. The petition states: "This memorial is the opus work of arguably the world's most important Jewish Artist."

New South is not his opus work. And MJE is not even close to the world's most important Jewish artist across borders and over time. He's not even in the top 50% (I am an expert in modern Jewish art). MJE is indeed very important for other reasons.

3. The petition states: "In today's era of heightened awareness of Antisemitism, what message does it send by removing the most significant work of American Jewish Art from our Nation's most important military cemetery? We believe it can and will be construed by many as Antisemitic."

New South is NOT a work of Jewish American art (MJE did make several important works that can be deemed "Jewish American art"). Moreover, *New South* isn't the "most significant work of American Jewish art," even if you made the argument that it's Jewish American art. First, the term we use is Jewish American art. Second, I could name dozens of essential works of Jewish American art (including 2 by Ezekiel). I would never name *New South* as Jewish American nor in the top 100 if I did (the monument is fraught with problems aside from the racist iconography). Valuing it at this level of importance is an affront to Jewish American art and the many much more important artists and their pivotal works.

Not only are your characterizations inaccurate across the board, but they also connect Jews to the Confederacy in a way that is not well-advised. Removing the work has nothing to do with antisemitism. Very few even know the monument was made by a Jew. Trying to keep the monument standing by crying antisemitism is a false construct and a weak argument. It's embarrassing.

I could continue but I imagine you see the points I'm making, whether you agree with me or not. I'm also not trying to offend anyone. I'm just trying to make clear—as an Ezekiel scholar and a trained historian of modern Jewish art—why this petition is misstated and perpetuates falsehoods.

I urge you to halt this petition as it stands.

Respectfully,
Samantha Baskind

Moses Jacob Ezekiel has been lost to history and—at least in this misguided petition—resurrected for all the wrong reasons. A Jewish American artist in many respects, but not at all for those reasons that he is now, on occasion, mentioned (or rather sometimes *used* for partisan reasons). A Jewish, Confederate, expatriate sculptor whose separate identities infused his art, as considered in this study. A late nineteenth-century celebrity monument maker whose life and oeuvre importantly connect to the broad concerns of his era and ours. In the complex twenty-first century, where oppositional lines are meticulously drawn and zealous judgments are broadly cast about what is good and what is bad, historians face significant risk in their statements and research. Metal should often be melted, but ideas not so much. Recovery should always be vital to historians' work. And it bears repeating: Recovery does not necessarily mean acceptance.

NOTES

Preface

1. This sixty-four-inch-tall marble version of *Faith* (1877) was owned by the closed Peabody Art Collection, now managed by the Maryland State Archives, and is currently displayed in a building on Johns Hopkins University's campus.
2. Shimron, "Princeton University Scraps Exhibit."
3. Shimron, "Princeton University Scraps Exhibit."
4. Blake, "Firestone Exhibition of Jewish American Artists."
5. For example, Lapin, "Outrage as Jewish Art Exhibit at Princeton Is Canceled." Among local Jewish newspapers were the *Cleveland Jewish News*, the *Jewish Exponent* (Philadelphia), the *Pittsburgh Jewish Chronicle*, and the *St. Louis Light*.
6. Spencer, "Where the Buck Stops"; Hoffman, "Exhibit at Princeton Is Canceled."
7. "Art Exhibition CANCELED at Princeton."
8. Soave, "Art Curator Accuses Princeton."

Introduction

1. "Who Are the Ten Greatest Virginians?," clipping in Moses Ezekiel papers (hereafter Ezekiel papers), MS collection 44, box 2, folder 2, American Jewish Archives, Cincinnati, OH (hereafter AJA).
2. "American Sculptor, Moses Ezekiel, Dies." Following the special cable from Rome announcing his death, the *Times* printed its own very lengthy obituary, listing many sculptures and accolades.
3. Eulogy sent from Warren Harding to Marion Butler (March 30, 1921), Moses Jacob Ezekiel papers, MS-0010, Virginia Military Institute Archives, Preston Library, Lexington, VA (hereafter VMI Archives). Butler, vice president of the Arlington Confederate Monument Association, read the eulogy on the president's behalf. Harding wrote in a personal note of his "deep and unfeigned regret" that he could not personally attend the service because of overwhelming presidential duties. For press accounts, see "Tribute to Ezekiel by President Harding"; and "Sir Moses Ezekiel Burial." These documents are dated 1921 rather than 1917, the year Ezekiel died, because his body could not be shipped back to the United States until after World War I.
4. For recent examples of this necessary recovery work in the field of American art, see Boylan, *Ellen Emmet Rand*; Manthorne, *Restless Enterprise*; and Dabakis, *Sisterhood of Sculptors*, a first-rate study of female neoclassical sculptors around Ezekiel's era. Recovery of African American artists includes Ater, *Remaking Race and History*; and Vendryes, *Barthé*. My own scholarship attempts to expand our understanding of artists, although sometimes central to the American canon, by parsing how their often-unknown Jewish heritage influenced their art. For example, see Baskind, *Jewish Artists and the Bible*. Note that all these uncelebrated artists, or their "other" identities, are minorities: female, African American, and Jewish.
5. Baskind, "Arlington National Cemetery's Confederate Monument"; Baskind, "Jewish Sculptor of the Confederacy"; Baskind, "Which Statues Should Fall?"
6. For early studies on neoclassicism, see especially Gerdts, *American Neo-Classic Sculpture*; and Thorp, *Literary Sculptors*, esp. 172, 189 (on Ezekiel).
7. Crane, *White Silence*. On nineteenth-century American painters' enchantment with Rome, see Vance, McGuigan, and McGuigan, *America's Rome*.
8. "Moses Ezekiel Home Again" (*The Cadet*), 2, Virginia Military Institute Archives, Preston Library, Lexington (hereafter VMI Archives). Repeated verbatim in "Sir Moses Ezekiel Home Again" (*Hebrew Standard*), 7.
9. Ezekiel, *Memoirs*, 399, 400.
10. Moses Jacob Ezekiel, "Memories of the Baths of Diocletian / Memories of a Southern Veteran," undated, Archives of American Art, Smithsonian Institution, Washington, DC (hereafter Ezekiel, "Memories," AAA), 507–8. Mislabeled as "Memoirs" not "Memories" in the archival listing.

11. Ezekiel, "Memories," AAA, 194; Ezekiel, *Memoirs*, 179.
12. Ezekiel, *Memoirs*, 215.
13. Vance, *America's Rome*, 189; Brooks, *Dream of Arcadia*, 100–103.
14. See esp. Corn, *Georgia O'Keeffe*.
15. Will and testament of Moses Jacob Ezekiel, Ezekiel papers, box 1, folder, 5, AJA.
16. Among other sources, descriptions of the studio can be found in Bosis, "Baths of Diocletian"; Wrenshall, "American Sculptor in Rome," 12256; and Collman, "October Anniversary," 4. The "anniversary" in the latter title likely referred to Ezekiel's birthday, October 28.
17. "Ezekiel Refuses to Move."
18. Didier, "American Authors and Artists," 491.
19. Baedeker, *Handbook for Travelers*, 116.
20. "Unveiling of the Bronze Homeric Group," 232. On American cultural tourism, see Stowe, *Going Abroad*; and Gerdts, "Celebrities of the Grand Tour."
21. "Ezekiel Refuses to Move."
22. "Mrs. Alsop Has Hard Trip."
23. Mason, *Spell of Italy*, 151.
24. Mason, *Spell of Italy*, 152.
25. Ezekiel, *Memoirs*, 124.
26. Ezekiel papers, box 1, folder 2, AJA.
27. "Among the Sculptors" (December 1899), 686.
28. Brooks, *Dream of Arcadia*, 259.
29. Craven, *Sculpture in America*, 268, 312, 337–38, 377.
30. For an excellent essay on Ezekiel's style and insights into some of his work, see Tarbell, "Moses Jacob Ezekiel's Sculpture and Aesthetic." The essay appeared in a short catalog accompanying a 1985 solo exhibition of Ezekiel's art. See also Cohen and Gibson, *Moses Ezekiel*, an indispensable primer to Ezekiel; and Nash, *Life and Times*. This last contribution is well-intentioned but flawed. Written by a family member, the book largely consists of quotes from the artist's autobiography and very rarely discusses the art (only three works are reproduced). See also Soria, "Moses Ezekiel's Studio in Rome." In some of these publications, dates and facts are a little off, which I have rectified in this study.
31. Ezekiel, *Memoirs*. Editors Gutmann and Chyet's extensive introduction and tremendous efforts to locate his sculptures are the backbone of Ezekiel research.
32. "Americans Write Memoirs in Rome."
33. Ezekiel, "Memories," AAA.
34. Sturrock, "Theory Versus Autobiography," 24.
35. Philipson mentions the lengthy article in his autobiography, *My Life as an American Jew*, 178, 295, with a short discussion of Ezekiel's death and funeral (293–95).
36. "List of Works of Sir Moses Ezekiel," Ezekiel papers, box 2, folder 1, AJA.
37. For example, *Catalogue of Mr. Henry C. Ezekiel's Private Collection*, 12. An astounding number of commissioned portrait busts are described in his unedited memoir. See Ezekiel, "Memories," AAA.
38. Two unsubstantiated assertions about Ezekiel not in the scope of this book deserve mention: that he fathered a child with an enslaved woman in his household when he was fourteen years old, and that he was homosexual. Most likely, it cannot be both ways. Even so, the former is based on a single mention in a 1954 book, and the latter on supposition because he never married, and traveled with a male friend, the painter Fedor Encke. On Ezekiel's rumored daughter, see Buckler, *Doctor Dan*, 148–49. His sexuality is a running theme through Nash, *Life and Times*. Gutmann and Chyet also point out the circumstantial evidence for Ezekiel's offspring in their introduction (Ezekiel, *Memoirs*, 65).
39. Ezekiel, *Memoirs*, 256.
40. Ezekiel, *Memoirs*, 256–57.
41. Ezekiel, "Memories," AAA, 303–4.
42. "Hospital in Royal Palace."
43. Bush-Brown, "Sir Moses Ezekiel," 234.

Chapter 1

1. Wolf, "B'nai B'rith." This memorial volume gathered Wolf's addresses and papers, focusing on topics of Jewish interest save for one address delivered on the anniversary of Friedrich Schiller's death, which relates to Wolf's preoccupation with democratic liberty.
2. "Israelites Centennial Monument, to the Officers and Members of the Union of American Hebrew Congregations," misdated "Cleveland, July 14–16, 1873," B'nai B'rith records, MS-900, box D4-18/8, folder 8 (Statue of Religious Liberty, 1873–1989), American Jewish Archives, Cincinnati, OH (hereafter Religious Liberty folder, AJA). The resolution

should be dated 1874. The *American Israelite* urged representatives from congregations to attend a meeting of the Council of the Union of American Hebrew Congregations in Cleveland (as well as to join, if not yet a member) of that year. Undoubtedly this is accurate, considering the resolution for the sculpture was not passed until January 1874. See *American Israelite*, July 17, 1874, 1.

3. Ezekiel, *Memoirs*, 164.
4. Ezekiel, *Memoirs*, 167. The story of *Religious Liberty*'s making is largely derived from descriptions peppered throughout the first half of Ezekiel's *Memoirs*.
5. Measurements for the sculpture vary in newspaper accounts. These measurements were taken during an assessment of the sculpture in 2009. Institutional files, archives of the Weitzman National Museum of American Jewish History, Philadelphia, PA (hereafter WNMAJH archives).
6. In addition to *Faith* held by the Maryland State Archives in Annapolis (formerly in the Peabody Institute's art collection), a different sculpture titled *Faith* was made for a Roman Jewish patron in a public space. This *Faith* was conceived as an allegorical female figure for the Massarani family tomb in Rome (lost).
7. Ezekiel, *Memoirs*, 185.
8. Ezekiel, *Memoirs*, 185.
9. Ezekiel, *Memoirs*, 185.
10. For a comprehensive account of the dedication ceremony and other details about the B'nai B'rith Centennial Committee's problems acquiring payment for Ezekiel, see *Report of the Executive Committee*.
11. Quoted in Philipson, "Moses Jacob Ezekiel," 15.
12. Quoted in Clement and Hutton, *Artists of the Nineteenth Century*, 243.
13. The entire review, by correspondent Leopold Julius of *Leipziger Zeitschrift für Bildende Kunst*, was reprinted in the *Richmond Daily Dispatch* on June 5, 1876. The *Dispatch* titles the review "Religious Liberty: A Criticism of M. Ezekiel's Group by Dr. Leopold Julius—a Great Compliment to a Former Citizen of Richmond." One of Ezekiel's friends, unnamed, made a drawing of the sculpture for the original review.
14. Philipson, "Moses Jacob Ezekiel," 14.
15. Ezekiel, *Memoirs*, 188.
16. Ezekiel, *Memoirs*, 180–81.
17. On early manifestations of allegorical women in both American paintings and material culture, see Taylor, "America as Symbol."
18. Agulhon, *Marianne into Battle*, 18–22.
19. The first two editions, unillustrated, were published in Italy in 1593 and 1602. An enlarged third edition (1603) contained illustrations as did subsequent versions. Ripa, *Baroque and Rococo Pictorial Imagery: The 1758–60 Hertel Edition*, set a standard for illustrations.
20. On changing personifications of America, see Fleming, "From Indian Princess to Greek Goddess." On the transformation of Liberty's headpiece, see Korshak, "Liberty Cap as a Revolutionary Symbol."
21. On the evolution of Crawford's sculpture and Liberty imagery, see Fryd, *Art and Empire*, 177–208; and Crane, *White Silence*, 382–84.
22. Ezekiel, *Memoirs*, 171, 172.
23. Fryd, *Art and Empire*, 187–88. Still described in 1927 as Liberty in Fairman, *Art and Artists*, 129.
24. Ezekiel, *Memoirs*, 168.
25. There exist two identical busts of *Mercury*, the Roman god of commerce, shown as a pudgy boy wearing his winged cap: the Centennial version at the Virginia Military Institute and a later version at the Virginia Museum of Fine Arts (1901, incised "Paris" on the back).
26. Ground plans of Memorial Hall and the Art Annex in United States Centennial Commission, *International Exhibition, 1876*, 136, 138. For a description of the history of the exposition and buildings erected in Fairmount Park, see, among others in this chapter's endnotes, Scharf and Westcott, *History of Philadelphia*.
27. Ingram, *Centennial Exposition*, 611.
28. Moses Ezekiel to Edward Valentine, May 1, 1876, The Valentine Archives, Richmond, VA (hereafter Valentine Archives).
29. "Statue to Religious Liberty" (September 29, 1876), translated in full by the *Jewish Record*, clipping in an extensive scrapbook made by State Senator Horatio Gates Jones (hereafter Jones scrapbook), 1998.33.1, gift of Garry G. Greenstein, WNMAJH archives. Recognized for his commitment to religious equality, the non-Jewish Jones spoke at the sculpture's installation ceremony. For his making of the statue, Jones dubbed Ezekiel a "hero, whose name will go down to posterity." Jones's speech

is reprinted in *Report of the Executive Committee of the Constitution Grand Lodge*, 27, B'nai B'rith International Archives, Washington, DC.

30. Quoted in "Triumph in Art," clipping in Ezekiel papers, box 2, folder 2, AJA. In an otherwise valuable study of sketches made by leading American sculptors, the author erroneously identifies a clay model for the female figure atop Ezekiel's Arlington Cemetery Confederate monument as *Religious Liberty*. See Rogers, *Sketches and Bozzetti*, 62.
31. Lippincott, *Visitor's Guide to the Centennial Exhibition*, 23.
32. Magee, *Magee's Illustrated Guide*, 148. This misinterpretation is repeated in Scharf and Westcott, *History of Philadelphia*, 1875.
33. Magee, *Magee's Illustrated Guide*, 178, 185.
34. Ingram, *Centennial Exposition*, 611.
35. Ezekiel, *Memoirs*, 190–91.
36. Quoted in "Religious Liberty" (December 1, 1876). The unveiling was covered by several newspapers, including the *Jewish Record*, the *Public Ledger and Transcript*, and the *New York Herald*; see clippings in Jones scrapbook, WNMAJH archives. See also *Richmond Daily Dispatch*, December 2, 1876, 1.
37. "Statue to Religious Liberty" (December 1, 1876), clipping in Jones scrapbook, WNMAJH archives.
38. "Constitution of the Independent Order B'nai B'rith," 1868, unpaged, B'nai B'rith International Archives, MS-900, box B1a-37, folder 2, AJA. An earlier, less expansive version, from 1860, referred instead to "the highest interests of Judaism." See also Grusd, *B'nai B'rith*, 47, 61–62, an important history of the Order. The emphasis in the founding 1843 preamble was also broad, aiming to unite "Israelites in the work of promoting their highest interests and those of humanity" (48), indicating shifts within the Order's goals. Subtle differences manifest in revised preambles to the Order's constitution throughout the 1800s. For an excellent account of B'nai B'rith's evolving purposes over time, see Moore, *B'nai B'rith*.
39. Wolf, "Day of Atonement Address," 258. The well-connected Wolf published a volume containing papers about his interactions with US presidents, titled *The Presidents I Have Known*.
40. Wolf, *American Jew*, 10. Wolf provides a list of Jewish soldiers by name, rank, company, and regiment, separated by states (Ezekiel is listed on p. 390).
41. Smith, "New Light on the Jewish Question," 137, 141.
42. Smith, "England's Abandonment," 618.
43. Richardson, *Diseases of Modern Life*, 98.
44. Quoted in Singerman, "Jew as Racial Alien," 109.
45. Quoted in White, *Renoir*, 211.
46. Adler, "Can Jews Be Patriots?," 637.
47. Straus, introduction to Peters, *Jew as a Patriot*, x. More broadly, with repetition, see Peters, *Justice to the Jew*. These publications were followed by Peters's *The Jews in America*, written in commemoration of the 250th anniversary of Jewish settlement in America. Peters concludes the preface by writing, "If what he has written will remove prejudice, and lead to justice, the author will feel well repaid for the labor involved in this refined study of history" (7).
48. Straus, introduction to Peters, *Jew as a Patriot*, xxix.
49. Simon Wolf to President Ulysses S. Grant, June 26, 1876, and President Ulysses S. Grant to Simon Wolf, June 28, 1876, reproduced in Wolf, "B'nai B'rith and the Philadelphia Statue of Religious Liberty," 278.
50. "Statue to Religious Liberty" (December 1, 1876), clipping in Jones scrapbook, WNMAJH archives.
51. Magee, *Magee's Illustrated Guide*, 148.
52. Kirshenblatt-Gimblett, *Destination Culture*, 86–88. For a full-length study of the Centennial's American artistic program, see Orcutt, *Power and Posterity*. More broadly, see Giberti, *Designing the Centennial*; as well as the primary sources Magee, *Magee's Illustrated Guide*; and Norton, *Frank Leslie's Historical Register*.
53. Gallagher, *Catholic Centennial Fountain*.
54. "Amending the Constitution."
55. Exod. 27:20–21 (Jewish Publication Society of America Version of the Tanakh; hereafter JPS).
56. Bartholdi wrote an account of the sculpture, in part to raise money for the American Pedestal Fund; see Bartholdi, *Statue of Liberty*.
57. Num. 6:24–27 (JPS).
58. "Centennial Monument of Religious Liberty," clipping in Ezekiel papers, box 1, folder 5, AJA. Italics and capitalization in original.
59. Ezekiel, *Memoirs*, 322.
60. Exod. 13:9 (JPS).
61. Bogart, *Public Sculpture and the Civic Ideal*, esp. 227–31.

62. Letters reprinted in Zola and Dollinger, *American Jewish History*, 73–74. Jacob Ezekiel published several articles about Jewish history, including "Jews of Richmond" and "Persecutions of the Jews in 1840."
63. Moses Ezekiel to Marjorie Taylor, July 22, 1886, Valentine Archives. Ezekiel repeats the exact phrase, "tragedy of my life," in *Memoirs*, 190. He sculpted Taylor's hand in marble (ca. 1880s, The Valentine Museum, Richmond, VA).
64. Memo from the Constitution Grand Lodge, IOBB Centennial Committee, New York, January 1875, B'nai B'rith International Archives, Washington, DC.
65. Full address in "B'nai B'rith Annual Convention I.O.B.B." For a listing of disbursements and debts to date for *Religious Liberty*, see *Report of the Executive Committee*, 35–36.
66. Louis, "Letter to the Editor."
67. "Letter from Hon. Simon Wolf," clipping in Jones scrapbook, WNMAJH archives.
68. *Proceedings of the General Convention*, 29. See also "The Unpaid Statue" (May 11, 1877, and May 25, 1877), clippings in Jones scrapbook, WNMAJH archives. Despite these financial difficulties, District 3 paid all the dedication expenses plus a dinner after the unveiling. See Grusd, *B'nai B'rith*, 81. From 1875, when the monument was commissioned, to 1878, with Ezekiel still awaiting payment, B'nai B'rith's brotherhood grew from 17,800 members to 21,480 (ibid., 80).
69. "Statue to Religious Liberty" (December 1, 1876), clipping in Jones scrapbook, WNMAJH archives.
70. Ezekiel, *Memoirs*, 192.
71. A short book reviewing B'nai B'rith's history includes two photographs of *Religious Liberty* (31, 73), and the author asserts that the Order sees the sculpture "as one of its proudest accomplishments" (33). See Bisgyer, *This Is B'nai B'rith*. Bisgyer was secretary of B'nai B'rith as well as executive vice president for twenty years.
72. Grusd, "B'nai B'rith Rededicates 'Liberty.'" For a transcript of the ceremony in stapled booklet form, accompanied by two dozen letters offering good wishes (including from President Franklin Roosevelt), see "Roger Williams' Celebration (Re-Dedication of Statue of Religious Liberty) Under Auspices of B'nai B'rith," Religious Liberty folder, AJA.
73. Blumberg, "On Celebrating Ourselves," clipping in Religious Liberty folder, AJA.
74. Wolf, "Patriotism and Religion," 240.
75. Press release, "B'nai B'rith International and National Museum of American Jewish History, 'Statue of Religious Liberty,' Joint Venture," January 22, 1985, institutional files, WNMAJH archives.
76. National Museum of American Jewish History mission statement, institutional files, WNMAJH archives.
77. *Everyone Comes to America with a Dream*, n.p., in the author's possession.
78. Wolf, "Convention of 1874," 9.

Chapter 2

1. Ezekiel, *Memoirs*, 84.
2. Near the end of the twentieth century, scholarship began to illuminate the role of religion in American art, although most often Judaism plays a small role in these discussions. Key sources include Promey's comprehensive article "'Return' of Religion in the Scholarship of American Art"; Promey and Morgan, *Visual Culture of American Religions*; and Schwain, "Visual Culture and American Religions."
3. The *Hebrew Standard*, a weekly based in New York City, announced that *David* was presented by the recently dissolved Cincinnati Club to Hebrew Union College. See "Items of Interest in the Jewish World" (July 5, 1912). The bust eventually made its way to the Skirball Cultural Center in Los Angeles.
4. Moses A. Waterman to VMI Superintendent Francis H. Smith, August 21, 1862; and Moses A. Waterman to VMI Superintendent Francis H. Smith, April 10, 1864, both in VMI Archives.
5. Moses Ezekiel to Catherine Ezekiel, August 27, 1869, in Ezekiel, *Memoirs*, 456. Ezekiel's first marble reliefs, modeled during his first trip home after studying in Germany, were portraits of his mother and father (1874; Skirball Cultural Center, Los Angeles).
6. Ezekiel, *Memoirs*, 76.
7. Ezekiel, *Memoirs*, 80–81.
8. Ezekiel, *Memoirs*, 281.
9. Letters from Virginia Vacca, née de Bosis (daughter of Adolfo de Bosis), to Zebulon Hooker, January 1,

1950, and February 10, 1950, Ezekiel papers, box 1, folder 6, AJA. Ezekiel was so close to the de Bosis family that he took a teenaged Virginia to America during his 1914 trip home. He made a small, under-life-size marble relief of Virginia (1908–9; lost). Virginia Vacca, née de Bosis, to Joseph Gutmann, February 13, 1971, Ezekiel papers, box 1, folder 7, AJA.

10. Moses Ezekiel to Jacob Ezekiel, January 1899, in Philipson, "Moses Jacob Ezekiel," 44–45.
11. Lilian de Bosis to Hannah Workum, April 4, 1917, Ezekiel papers, box 1, folder 2, AJA.
12. Taylor, "Personal Appreciation," 335.
13. *Landscape* (1860) and *Gypsy Bride* (1861) are in the collection of the Virginia Military Institute Museum, Lexington. Ezekiel mentions *The Prisoner's Wife* (1870; lost), made for Mary Custis Lee, in his memoir.
14. Ezekiel, *Memoirs*, 102. In a book-length study, Bland shows that idolatry, not visual art, was forbidden in Jewish tradition in *Artless Jew*. On the misconception that Jews are aniconic, see also Olin, *Nation Without Art*.
15. Ezekiel, *Memoirs*, 124, 127, 130.
16. Klein and Sarna, *Jews of Cincinnati*, 6, 181.
17. A 1995 retrospective exhibition mounted by the Skirball Cultural Center in Los Angeles, reconstructed Mosler's oeuvre and life, resurrecting him from near obscurity; see Gilbert, *Henry Mosler Rediscovered*. For the pioneering work on early Jewish American artists, see Gutmann, "Jewish Participation in the Visual Arts"; and, more recently, Baskind, "Jewish Artists Begin."
18. Ezekiel, *Memoirs*, 129–30.
19. Gardner, *Yankee Stonecutters*, 67–68.
20. Ezekiel, *Memoirs*, 130.
21. Ezekiel, *Memoirs*, 130.
22. "Two Israelites in Cincinnati"; "Ezekiel-Mosler."
23. Ezekiel's early years are described in some depth in Hooker, "Moses Jacob Ezekiel"; and Chyet, "Moses Jacob Ezekiel" (March 1973).
24. Ezekiel, "Memories," AAA, 168.
25. Ezekiel, *Memoirs*, 181. That visitor, Princess Carolyne Sayn-Wittgenstein, would later become a good friend and supporter (as well as the lover of Franz Liszt, one of Ezekiel's closest friends).
26. Kasson, *Marble Queens*, 173–83; Wunder, *Hiram Powers*, 1:134–44.
27. Ezekiel, *Memoirs*, 179.
28. Moses Ezekiel to Edward Valentine, May 1, 1876, Valentine Archives.
29. Ezekiel, *Memoirs*, 179.
30. Ezekiel, *Memoirs*, 179.
31. Gen. 3:8 (JPS); italics added.
32. Fisher, "Entitling," 298.
33. Wunder, *Hiram Powers*, 1:182, 305–6.
34. Ezekiel, *Memoirs*, 261.
35. Moses Ezekiel to Henry Ezekiel, July 11, 1903, in Philipson, "Moses Jacob Ezekiel," 27.
36. Quoted in Philipson, "Moses Jacob Ezekiel," 9–10.
37. Ezekiel to Valentine, May 1, 1876, Valentine Archives.
38. Ives, Kurtz, and Zolnay, *Illustrations of Selected Works*, xlv.
39. *Catalogue of Mr. Henry C. Ezekiel's Private Collection*, 13; "Art Notes." Harjes earlier contracted Ezekiel to produce a bronze torso of himself (1881; Virginia Military Institute, Lexington).
40. The marble was a little less than four feet tall, in comparison to the bronze at 4 1/2 feet. Silke Kiesant, curator, Prussian Palaces and Gardens Foundation, Berlin-Brandenburg, personal communication with author, February 9, 2021.
41. "Sir Moses Ezekiel" (November 30, 1913).
42. Small statuette mentioned in *Catalogue of Mr. Henry C. Ezekiel's Private Collection*, 13. Gift to Sella discussed in Ezekiel, *Memoirs*, 419.
43. Tincker, *Jewel in the Lotos*, 216.
44. Vosmaer, *Amazon*, 69.
45. *Eve Hearing the Voice*, 1997.152, curatorial files, Cincinnati Art Museum files, Cincinnati, OH (hereafter CAM files).
46. Quoted in Sachar, *History of the Jews in America*, 75.
47. Quoted in Berman, *Richmond's Jewry*, 185. For more on antisemitism in Richmond during this period, see 186–88, 247–48.
48. Ezekiel, *Memoirs*, 75.
49. Quoted in Philipson, "Moses Jacob Ezekiel," 9.
50. *Wagner on Music and Drama*, 51–59.
51. Peters, "Peters Praises the Jews." At more length, on Jewish contributions with a litany of names, see Peters, "Jews in America"; and Peters, *Justice to the Jew*. The book came out in heavily revised editions to correct factual errors, including one from a Jewish press.
52. Cohen, "Wrong Praise for the Jew," 6.

53. Peters, "Dr. Peters on the Jew." Peters similarly describes Jewish contributions, where he cites Ezekiel, Mosler, and Mark Antokolsky in a book-length discussion; see Peters, *Jew as a Patriot*, 187.
54. Kertzer, *Popes Against the Jews.*
55. Ezekiel, "Impressive Were the Ceremonies."
56. Ezekiel, *Memoirs*, 307.
57. As reported in Taylor, "Personal Appreciation," 335.
58. For coverage by journalists in France, Germany, Russia, and Austria-Hungary, and the stubborn antisemitism it initiated, see Brennan, *Reflection of the Dreyfus Affair.*
59. Quoted in Kertzer, *Popes Against the Jews*, 184.
60. Quoted in Kertzer, *Popes Against the Jews*, 184.
61. Quoted in Kertzer, *Popes Against the Jews*, 184.
62. Quoted in Kertzer, *Popes Against the Jews*, 211.
63. Read, *Dreyfus Affair.*
64. Nochlin, "Degas and the Dreyfus Affair," 96.
65. White, *Renoir*, 211.
66. White, *Renoir*, 121. For more antisemitic remarks, see 124, 133, 213.
67. Edgar Degas to Henri Rouart, July 7, 1901 (letter 889), in *Letters of Edgar Degas*, 3:249. In Degas to Albert Bartholemé, August 10, 1897 (letter 743), he writes of looking forward to time with a friend "for some anti-Semitic reading and conversation" (3:217). See also Degas to Hortense Valpinçon, September 24, 1904 (letter 997), 3:271.
68. Quoted in Shikes and Harper, *Pissarro*, 307.
69. Taylor, "Personal Appreciation," 338.
70. Taylor, "Personal Appreciation," 335.
71. Enamored with Shakespeare's tragedy, Ezekiel chiseled a marble bust of *Jessica* (1880), Shylock's daughter. In its day, *Jessica* was bought by a patron in Paris for his music salon, and it is now in the collection of the Smithsonian American Art Museum. See Moses Ezekiel to "Sir" (most likely William MacLeod), April 1, 1881 (letter 2129), COR0002.0-RG series 1 subseries 1, box RG2-2008.004, folder 38, Corcoran Gallery of Art and Corcoran College of Art and Design, Corcoran Gallery of Art directors' records, Special Collections Research Center, George Washington University, Washington, DC (hereafter CGA Director's Records).
72. Moses Ezekiel to Edward Valentine, July 23, 1875, Valentine Archives.
73. Didier, "American Authors and Artists," 492.
74. I have assigned this date based on its description as a new work in "Ezekiel Refuses to Move." There is no evidence the maquette was ever enlarged or bronzed.
75. Jth. 8:32 (New Revised Standard Version).
76. In addition to *Judith*, Ezekiel exhibited five other works at the French Salon: a five-foot-tall *Faith* (1880, plaster), an unnamed portrait bust (1880, marble), a bust of a young boy (1881, bronze), a bust of *Franz Liszt* (1882, bronze; see chapter 4), and a marble bust of *Friedrich "Frederick" Hassaurek* (1884), a Cincinnati-based journalist and ambassador to Ecuador. The *Hassaurek* bust is in Cincinnati's Spring Grove Cemetery, and a later marble (1887) at the Cincinnati Art Museum. See Fink, *American Art*, 341.
77. Ezekiel, *Memoirs*, 213. Later in the memoir, Ezekiel alleged that *Judith* was considered in his day, not just by himself but others, as "one of the best pieces of modern sculpture" (301). See also 271.
78. Bosis, "Baths of Diocletian."
79. Ezekiel, *Memoirs*, 282–83.
80. Ezekiel, *Memoirs*, 331–32.
81. Ezekiel, *Memoirs*, 194.
82. Lowe, *Stieglitz*, 90.
83. Lowe, *Stieglitz*, 88, 129. Robinson erroneously refers to Edward Stieglitz's marble as a plaster cast in *Georgia O'Keeffe*, 211, 300.
84. *Judith* (National Gallery of Art, Washington, DC) in Greenough, *Alfred Stieglitz*, 1:469. Stieglitz took another photograph of *Judith* in the wooden cart: *Georgia O'Keeffe, Fred and Ella Varnum, and Bly* (1920; National Gallery of Art, Washington, DC) in Greenough, *Alfred Stieglitz*, 2:933. The photograph shows O'Keeffe and three others, one the gardener at Lake George, posing mockingly with Ezekiel's sculpture.
85. Lowe, *Stieglitz*, 237–38.
86. Stieglitz to Herbert Seligmann, September 4, 1922, quoted in Greenough, *Alfred Stieglitz*, 1:469.
87. Lowe, *Stieglitz*, 238; Robinson, *Georgia O'Keeffe*, 300.
88. Ezekiel, *Memoirs*, 301.
89. Countess Hugo quoted in Philipson, "Moses Jacob Ezekiel," 28.
90. Ezekiel, *Memoirs*, 459, app. E.
91. Amishai-Maisels, "Jewish Jesus."
92. Ezekiel, *Memoirs*, 301.

93. Bosis, "Baths of Diocletian."
94. Ezekiel's *The Dying Alexander* was listed at auction for $500 in 1930, with the buyer unknown. See *Catalogue of Mr. Henry C. Ezekiel's Private Collection*, 15. *David Singing his Song of Glory* is documented to have been in the private collection of Rabbi Victor Reichert and his wife, Louise, as late as 1987, but it is now lost.
95. "List of Works of Sir Moses Ezekiel," Ezekiel papers, box 2, folder 1, AJA; Ezekiel, *Memoirs*, 321.
96. *The Martyr* was purchased by an individual named John McCoy, of Baltimore. Mentioned in a letter from Moses Ezekiel to "Sir" (most likely William MacLeod), April 1, 1881 (letter 2129). It eventually found a home in the historic Old Cathedral of Baltimore, when an art dealer was asked to appraise it for the Archdiocese of Baltimore in 2003. (The sculpture was in the archbishop's residence.) One can surmise that McCoy donated *The Martyr*, because no records exist about how it ended up in the cathedral. Robert Simon, appraiser of sculpture, Robert Simon Fine Art, personal communication with author, May 9, 2022.
97. *El diritto*, September 2, 1876, quoted in Clement and Hutton, *Artists of the Nineteenth Century*, 243.
98. Taft, *History of American Sculpture*, 263.
99. Wrenshall, "American Sculptor in Rome," 12257.
100. Ezekiel, *Memoirs*, 178. On Antokolsky, see Glants, *Where Is My Home?*; and Litvak, "Rome and Jerusalem." When in Paris in 1893 to model some portrait busts, Ezekiel also visited Antokolsky in his studio there.
101. Amishai-Maisels, "Origins of the Jewish Jesus," 55–62. The first substantial numbers of Jews to become professional fine artists in Europe were well surveyed in a Jewish Museum exhibition on nineteenth-century Jewish painters, with an accompanying catalog; see Goodman, *Emergence of Jewish Artists*, which includes artists from Germany, France, England, Italy, the Netherlands, Austria, the Pale of Settlement, modern Poland, Ukraine, and Russia.
102. Wunder, *Hiram Powers*, 2:180.
103. Tuckerman, *Memorial of Horatio Greenough*, 33; Moll, "Sculpture and Spectacle," 216–26.
104. "Jewish Painter's Idea of Jesus" (*New Era*).
105. "Of Interest to Jewish Readers," 652.
106. "Jewish Painter's Idea of Jesus" (*New Era*), 75, 76. Rosenthal's painting gained such notice that *Literary Digest*, a general interest weekly, partly reprinted the article with the same title.
107. Quoted in "Jewish Painter's Idea of Jesus" (*New Era*), 76.
108. "Men and Matters" (October 13, 1896). Ezekiel personally couriered the bust to the United States during his 1896 trip, gifting the sculpture to his younger sister Esther Samuels. The article mentions that Samuels was considering donating the bust to the Cincinnati Art Museum, but she opted not to do so. The next mention of the sculpture dates to 1902, when the *Cincinnati Enquirer* ran an article noting the piece, there titled *The Christ* and which Ezekiel called "Man of Sorrow," had been sold to an unnamed buyer. See "Ezekiel's Famous Bronze Bust." The buyers can be discerned, but it is unknown whether Samuels was the seller. According to museum records, Harry W. Levy and George W. Harris donated the bust that same year. *Ecce Homo*, 1902.6, curatorial files, CAM files.
109. Ezekiel, *Memoirs*, 178, 298.
110. Ezekiel, *Memoirs*, 298.
111. Ezekiel, *Memoirs*, 276.
112. Ezekiel, *Memoirs*, 275.
113. Ezekiel, *Memoirs*, 282.
114. Bosis, "Baths of Diocletian."
115. Ezekiel, *Memoirs*, 246. Among others, Ezekiel mentions a visit from Isabella Stewart Gardner, who saw the piece (338).
116. Stiles, *New Footprints in Old Places*, 78–79.
117. Wrenshall, "American Sculptor in Rome," 12257.
118. Whiting, *Italy*, 97.
119. Wrenshall, "American Sculptor in Rome," 12257.
120. Cubitt, "Martyrs of Charity."
121. Virginia Vacca, née de Bosis, to Joseph Gutmann, February 13, 1971, Ezekiel papers, box 1, folder 7, AJA.
122. "Study Daringly Original."
123. Virginia Vacca, née de Bosis, to Joseph Gutmann, October 24, 1971, Ezekiel papers, box 1, folder 7, AJA.

Chapter 3

1. Gutmann, "Jewish Themes," 32. On rabbinical portraiture, see Cohen, *Jewish Icons*.

2. "Bust of the Venerable Isaac M. Wise"; letter from Selma Wise to President and Members of the Board of Governors of the Hebrew Union College, June 26, 1899, Bust of I. M. Wise file, curatorial files, Skirball Museum, Cincinnati, Ohio.
3. For the standard biography on Wise, see Temkin, *Isaac Mayer Wise.*
4. Ezekiel, *Memoirs*, 392.
5. Moses Ezekiel to Catherine Ezekiel, August 27, 1869, in Ezekiel, *Memoirs*, 456.
6. Wise, "Sculptor and the Rabbi," 5.
7. Wise, "Editorial."
8. Ezekiel, *Memoirs*, 392–93.
9. Wise, "Sculptor and the Rabbi," 5.
10. Morris Goldstein, a cantor in Cincinnati, painted a large, three-quarter-length, seated portrait of Wise holding a book, his arm resting on an end table, on which sits a copy of the *Israelite*. The painting was gifted by Hebrew Union College to the National Portrait Gallery in Washington, DC, in 1977. The gallery dates this painting to 1881, but based on Wise's appearance, close to that of Ezekiel's sculpture and photographs of the rabbi around that time, it was painted closer to his death. After sitting in storage for decades, the painting was finally hung on the museum's walls in 2022.
11. Wise, "Sculptor and the Rabbi." The *Cincinnati Enquirer* also reported that Wise was pleased with the sculpture in process, which he invited visitors to see at his home before it was shipped to Rome. See "Bust of the Venerable Isaac M. Wise."
12. "Bust of I. M. Wise."
13. "Men and Matters" (April 28, 1900).
14. "Sculpture," 396. The same magazine featured Ezekiel in a complimentary profile a year earlier, nodding to recent projects such as *Religious Liberty* and his biblical conceptions, alongside reporting that he had been busy for several weeks modeling the bust of Wise. "Among the Sculptors" (December 1899).
15. On Beer's short life with a brief mention of the prize, see Kahn, "Michael Beer." More extensively on the prize, see Bertz, "Dreaming of Raphael."
16. Dimmick, "Mythic Proportion"; Gerdts, "Neoclassic Relief."
17. March 9, 1903, letter reprinted in the *American Israelite* as "Israel: A Symbolical Work" (June 23, 1904); earlier reprinted in the *Jewish Exponent* (May 1, 1903). Also in the *New York Herald* (May 1904), clipping in Ezekiel papers, box 2, folder 2, AJA.
18. "Israel: A Symbolical Work" (June 23, 1904).
19. Moses Ezekiel to an unknown recipient, May 22, 1873, in Philipson, "Moses Jacob Ezekiel," 7.
20. "Israel: A Symbolical Work" (June 23, 1904) ; "Success of a Cincinnati Artist."
21. See Amishai-Maisels, "Origins of the Jewish Jesus," 55–62, for a detailed discussion of the differences between Ezekiel's two conceptions of *Israel*, to which I am indebted. My argument advances her observation: "The large muscular resurgent Israel on the right . . . reflects the artist's Zionist views on settling Russian Jews in Palestine and restoring the Jewish nation" (73).
22. Moses Ezekiel to Jacob Ezekiel, March 26, 1873, in Philipson, "Moses Jacob Ezekiel," 7.
23. Edelmann, "Ahasuerus."
24. See especially Anderson's classic *Legend of the Wandering Jew.*
25. For one of many editions with and without the accompanying poem, see Doré, *Legend of the Wandering Jew*. Cohen looks at visual transformations vis-à-vis the historical time and place in his essential article "'Wandering Jew.'"
26. Gregorovius, *Ghetto and the Jews of Rome.*
27. Ezekiel, "Ghetto and the Jews in Rome," clipping in Ezekiel papers, box 1, folder 3, AJA.
28. Ezekiel, *Memoirs*, 232. On the ceremony, see Brandfon, *Intimate Strangers.*
29. Moses Ezekiel to Jacob Ezekiel, July 7, 1891, in Philipson, "Moses Jacob Ezekiel," 52.
30. Moses Ezekiel to Jacob Ezekiel, July 7, 1891, in Philipson, "Moses Jacob Ezekiel," 53. Later, at the First Zionist Congress of 1897, the same goal, to foster "the settlement of Palestine with farmers, laborers, and artisans," was set out. See Epstein, *Dream of Zion*, 84.
31. Moses Ezekiel to Jacob Ezekiel, July 7, 1891, in Philipson, "Moses Jacob Ezekiel," 52.
32. Moses Ezekiel to Jacob Ezekiel, July 7, 1891, in Philipson, "Moses Jacob Ezekiel," 52–53.
33. On the Star of David as a Jewish symbol over time, see Scholem, "Star of David." For its emergence in the United States, see Sarna, *American Judaism*, 106–7.

34. "Israel: A Symbolical Work" (June 23, 1904).
35. Hermann, "Moses Ezekiel," 809. On the journal's goal to underscore pride and commonalities among European Jews, notably through Jewish culture, see Brenner, *Marketing Identities*.
36. *Ost und West* 1 (January 1901): 5–6.
37. Ezekiel, *Memoirs*, 392. Regardless of whether the conversation took place as Ezekiel described, the artist's thoughts on the subject come through, and his characterization of Wise's views are confirmed by primary documents and subsequent scholarly literature.
38. Ezekiel, *Memoirs*, 392, 393.
39. Wise, *American Israelite* (July 14, 1882). For more on Wise's perspective about this subject, see Weinman, "Attitude of Isaac Mayer Wise."
40. Cohen, "Reaction of Reform Judaism," esp. 361–65; Greenstein, *Turning Point*; Meyer, "American Reform Judaism and Zionism"; Urofsky, *American Zionism*, esp. 81–116.
41. Reprinted in Meyer, *Response to Modernity*, 387–88.
42. For a general history of Zionism and its various philosophies, see Laqueur, *History of Zionism*.
43. Hess, *Rome and Jerusalem*, 117.
44. Moses Ezekiel to Jacob Ezekiel, July 7, 1891, in Philipson, "Moses Jacob Ezekiel," 53.
45. Pensler, *Theodor Herzl*, 67–69.
46. Herzl, *Jewish State*.
47. Quoted in Berkowitz, *Jewish Self-Image in the West*, 55.
48. Ezekiel, *Memoirs*, 393.
49. Moses Ezekiel to an unknown recipient, May 22, 1873, in Philipson, "Moses Jacob Ezekiel," 7–8.
50. Isa. 49:15 (JPS).
51. Isa. 54:1–2 (JPS).
52. Isa. 40:1–2 (JPS).
53. "Art Bas-Relief."
54. "Art Bas-Relief."
55. "Israel: A Symbolical Work" (June 23, 1904).
56. Ezekiel, *Memoirs*, 431, 433.
57. Letter from Selma Wise to President and Members of the Board of Governors of the Hebrew Union College, June 26, 1899, Bust of I. M. Wise file, curatorial files, Skirball Museum, Cincinnati, Ohio. In June 1956, Wise's son, Rabbi Jonah Wise, donated the bronze to the Union of American Hebrew Congregations, at the time representative of 530 Reform Congregations. See "Isaac Mayer Wise Is Honored."
58. The synagogue does not have documentation about the provenance of the bust, but administrators believe it was donated by Ochs. Personal communication with author, January 18, 2023.
59. Sarna, "Touro Monument Controversy."
60. Wise quoted in Sarna, "Touro Monument Controversy," 85.
61. D. P., "Jews in Art."
62. D. P., "Jews in Art."
63. On the visual imagery of first-generation European Zionists, see Berkowitz, *Zionist Culture*.
64. See, for example, *Herzl in Profile*.
65. "Opening Address by President Wise," xii.
66. Isa. 11:6 (JPS).
67. Moses Ezekiel to Joseph Krauskopf, July 13, 1889, reprinted in Peixotto, *Menorah*, 220.
68. On a century of Jewish journalism in America, see *People in Print*. For the Bloch publishing house, see Singerman, "Bloch and Company."
69. Moses Ezekiel to Joseph Krauskopf, July 13, 1889, reprinted in Peixotto, *Menorah*, 219–20.
70. Moses Ezekiel to Philip Cowen, November 4, 1892, Ezekiel papers, box 1, folder 1, AJA.
71. Moses Ezekiel to Philip Cowen, November 4, 1892, Ezekiel papers, box 1, folder 1, AJA.
72. Moses Ezekiel to Joseph Krauskopf, July 13, 1889, reprinted in Peixotto, *Menorah*, 220.
73. Sarna, *JPS*, 366.
74. "Announcement: The Jewish Publication Society of America," dated November 8, 1888, reprinted in the definitive study on the topic, Sarna, *JPS*, 355. See also a short but important intermediary article in the *Jewish Book Annual*, published from 1942 to 1999 and chronicling Jewish literature yearly across genres, further reflecting the importance Jewish Americans placed on publication efforts: Jacobs, "Two Generations of Jewish Literary Labor." Jacobs briefly mentions Ezekiel's seal (92).
75. Krauskopf, "Need of the Hour," in *Sunday Discourses Before the Reform Congregation Keneseth Israel: Series I*, 7, Keneseth Israel archives, Elkins Park, PA (hereafter KI archives).
76. Isa. 42:6 (JPS).
77. Krauskopf, "Need of the Hour," in *Sunday Discourses Before the Reform Congregation Keneseth Israel: Series I*, 7, KI archives.

78. Gal, "Mission Motif."
79. Prov. 3:17–18 (JPS).
80. *Jewish Publication Society*, 173.
81. "Jewish Churches in Big Convention"; "Isaac M. Wise Memorial Window." For advance coverage, see "Union of American Hebrew Congregations."
82. Program for unveiling and consecration of Isaac M. Wise memorial window, January 21, 1909, Moses Jacob Ezekiel files, box 1, folder 13, Beth Ahabah Museum and Archives, Richmond, VA.
83. "Jewish Churches in Big Convention."
84. Mark, "Isaac Mayer Wise Memorial Window," 54, KI archives.
85. Philipson, "Moses Jacob Ezekiel," 47.
86. Krauskopf, "Consecration," in *Sunday Discourses Before the Reform Congregation Keneseth Israel: Series XXII*, 5, KI archives. The 1908–9 issue of Krauskopf's sermons featured Ezekiel's sketch of the Wise window as its frontispiece.
87. Pinsker, *Auto-Emancipation*, 16, 9. Note that *Auto-Emancipation* was printed in the United States by the Maccabaean Publishing Company, as was a 1904 edition of Herzl's *The Jewish State*.
88. Zalmona, *Boris Schatz*; Ofrat, *One Hundred Years of Art in Israel*, 23.
89. *Ost und West* 3, no. 5 (May 1903): 293.
90. Mark, "Isaac Mayer Wise Memorial Window," 54.
91. Moses Ezekiel to Henry Ezekiel, December 6, 1908, Ezekiel papers, box 1, folder 2, AJA.
92. Krauskopf, "Consecration," in *Sunday Discourses Before the Reform Congregation Keneseth Israel: Series XXII*, 5, KI archives.
93. Krauskopf's speech confirms that this design element appeared in the final window.
94. Moses Ezekiel to Henry Ezekiel, December 6, 1908, Ezekiel papers, box 1, folder 2, AJA.
95. Mitchell, "'Devastating.'"
96. Krauskopf, "Consecration," in *Sunday Discourses Before the Reform Congregation Keneseth Israel: Series XXII*, 5, KI archives.
97. Ezekiel, *Memoirs*, 274–75, 336–37, 364, 384–90.
98. Ezekiel, *Memoirs*, 411, 435. On the popularity of spiritualism and the occult in their time, see Wallace, *Scientific Aspect*. An avowed spiritualist, Sherlock Holmes author Arthur Conan Doyle wrote *The History of Spiritualism*.

Chapter 4

1. The medallion was based on a profile photograph of Corcoran mailed to Ezekiel in Rome. The profile sketch sent to the States dissatisfied the collector: "The general expression amounting to a scowl is neither what my friends or myself desire." Another photograph generated a second sketch by Ezekiel, which was approved. Corcoran quoted in Robertson, *American Louvre*, 62. Ezekiel originally suggested a bust of Minerva for the medallion. See William MacLeod, Curator's journal, May 12, 1881, vol. 4, 1881, series 1 subseries 4, box 196, vol. 9, CGA Director's Records. MacLeod's journals are invaluable records about the daily activities of the gallery and Corcoran's thoughts on various matters.
2. Ezekiel was paid $2,000 for the pediment and $1,800 apiece for the allegorical sculptures on the top of the columns (still in place). A note from May 8, 1882 (no. 2554, series 1 subseries 1, RG2-2008.005, folder 26, CGA Director's Records), indicates a payment total to date of $6,709.
3. "Art in Washington."
4. "Art Immortals Removed."
5. Robertson, *American Louvre*, 47–48, 53; Tank, "Dedicated to Art."
6. Moses Ezekiel to William Corcoran, April 7, 1877 (letter 1064), series 1 subseries 1, box RG2-2008.002, folder 26, CGA Director's Records.
7. Moses Ezekiel to William MacLeod, April 11, 1877 (letter 1064.5), series 1 subseries 1, box RG2-2008.002, folder 26, CGA Director's Records. This letter is also numbered 1064 in the archive, but it is a different letter from that of April 7, misattributed in the cataloging. I have assigned it my own number, 1064.5, for clarification.
8. Moses Ezekiel to William Corcoran, April 7, 1877 (letter 1064).
9. Moses Ezekiel to William MacLeod, April 11, 1877 (letter 1064.5).
10. Moses Ezekiel to George Washington Riggs (Corcoran's former banking partner), June 12, 1878 (letter 1392), series 1 subseries 1, box RG2-2008.003, folder 2, CGA Director's Records.
11. Moses Ezekiel to William MacLeod, March 8, 1878 (misattributed in archive as March 18) (letter 1321), series 1 subseries 1, box RG2-2008.002, folder 52, CGA Director's Records.

12. Moses Ezekiel to William Corcoran, April 7, 1877 (letter 1064).
13. MacLeod, Curator's journal, September 7, 1878, vol. 2, 1878, series 1 subseries 4, box 196, vol. 8; and April 6, 1880, vol. 3, 1879–1880, series 1 subseries 4, box 198, box 2, vol. 1, CGA Director's Records.
14. MacLeod, Curator's journal, January 24, 1880, and January 26, 1880, vol. 3, 1879–1880, series 1 subseries 4, box 198, box 2, vol. 1, CGA Director's Records.
15. Moses Ezekiel to William MacLeod, May 31, 1880 (letter 1878) (misattributed in archive as May 29), series 1 subseries 1, box RG2-2008.004, folder 13, CGA Director's Records. Ezekiel also asks for additional funds because he needed money to pay for materials for the next statues in line to be made. Ezekiel briefly mentions working on *Homer* and a bust in the Paris Salon, and confides that he has no other commissions pending. Clearly, Ezekiel was hoping for some work from Corcoran.
16. MacLeod, Curator's journal, November 6, 1879, vol. 3, 1879–1880, series 1 subseries 4, box 198, box 2, vol. 1, CGA Director's Records.
17. MacLeod, Curator's journal, September 27, 1880, and October 12, 1880, vol. 3, 1879–1880, series 1 subseries 4, box 198, box 2, vol. 1, CGA Director's Records.
18. Moses Ezekiel to William Corcoran, October 23, 1880 (letter 2060), series 1 subseries 1, box RG2-2008.004, folder 31, CGA Director's Records.
19. Kitschen, *Als Kunstgeschichte populär wurde*.
20. Moses Ezekiel to George Riggs, November 2, 1880 (letter 1959), series 1 subseries 1, box RG2-2008.004, folder 21, CGA Director's Records, accepting the commission for the other seven sculptures.
21. MacLeod, Curator's journal, November 17, 1880, vol. 3, 1879–1880, series 1 subseries 4, box 198, box 2, vol. 1, CGA Director's Records. MacLeod indicates that the art committee had to pick one American subject; see Curator's journal, November 22, 1880, vol. 3, 1879–1880, series 1 subseries 4, box 198, box 2, vol. 1, CGA Director's Records.
22. Quoted in Sarah Cash's excellent essay on the Corcoran's American art collection; see "'Encouraging American Genius,'" 24.
23. Robertson, *American Louvre*, 58.
24. Cash, "'Encouraging American Genius,'" 23.
25. Tank, "Dedicated to Art," 35–36, 44.
26. Wallach, "William Wilson Corcoran's Failed National Gallery," 32, 35. More broadly, on the inception of American art institutions in the 1870s, notably the Corcoran, the Metropolitan Museum of Art, and Boston's Museum of Fine Arts, see Wallach, "Birth of the American Art Museum."
27. On the Met's architecture and a brief discussion of the facade sculpture, see Heckscher, "Metropolitan Museum of Art."
28. "'Friendship' Auction.'"
29. "Crawford Figure Retrieved," clipping in Ezekiel papers, box 2, folder 2, AJA.
30. "Recluse Now Greeter," clipping in Ezekiel papers, box 2, folder 2, AJA.
31. Woodliff, "Two Well-Traveled Ezekiels Added to Botanical Garden," clipping in VMI Archives.
32. Polson, "Carry Me Back to Ole Virginny," and Polson, "Last Ezekiel Statues in Place at Gardens," clippings in Ezekiel papers, box 2, folder 2, AJA; Julian H. Hirst, Norfolk city manager, to David W. Steadman, Chrysler Museum director, August 27, 1985, MSS 2015-044, Norfolk Botanical Garden Records, Sargeant Memorial Collection, Norfolk Public Library, Norfolk, VA (hereafter NBGR); Friddell, "An Ashtray Desperado by Accident," clipping in Ezekiel papers, box 2, folder 2, AJA.
33. Robert O. Matthews, superintendent, Botanical Gardens, to Shurl Montgomery, Norfolk director of parks and recreation, August 9, 1985, NBGR.
34. David W. Steadman, Chrysler Museum director, to Julian H. Hirst, Norfolk city manager, July 26, 1985, NBGR.
35. Strahan, *Art Treasures of America*, 3.
36. Henderson, *Art Treasures of Washington*, 39, 40.
37. Ezekiel, *Memoirs*, 215.
38. Didier, "American Authors and Artists," 492; Walker, *Franz Liszt*, 396. The bust does not appear to have gone to what is now known as the Franz Liszt Academy of Music in Budapest. Ezekiel indicates that it ended up in the Los Angeles home of VMI classmate Judge Erskine Ross. Ezekiel's *Napoleon* was purchased by Ross as well (conclusion). Ezekiel, *Memoirs*, 254.
39. Ezekiel, *Memoirs*, 241.
40. Franz Liszt to Marie zu Sayn-Wittgenstein, November 24, 1882, in *Letters of Franz Liszt*, 261.
41. Fink, *American Art*, 341. Ezekiel made an unknown number of undated smaller bronze miniatures

of *Liszt* (two are known: private collection and Congregation Beth Ahabah, Richmond, VA). One miniature, seven-inch bust of *Anthony Drexel* (1903; Congregation Beth Ahabah, Richmond, VA), plated in silver, derives from Ezekiel's marble busts at Drexel University: A forty-three-inch marble bust of *Drexel* (1904) is positioned in his eponymous university's main building in Philadelphia, and a twenty-eight-inch marble bust (1903) is also owned by the university.

42. Bellinzoni, *Popolo romano*, March 30, 1886, quoted in *Catalogue of Mr. Henry C. Ezekiel's Private Collection*, 14.
43. In a May 4, 1951, letter to Zebulon Hooker, Virginia Volterra (a close Jewish friend of Ezekiel's in Rome, along with her celebrated mathematician husband, Vito) wrote that she had a marble version (likely Ezekiel's or that owned by Cardinal Prince Gustav von Hohenlohe-Schillingsfürst); see Ezekiel papers, box 1, folder 6, AJA. Two later Volterra family members owned the sculpture until its very recent 2020 acquisition by the Virginia Museum of Fine Arts. Moses Jacob Ezekiel file, Virginia Museum of Fine Arts, Richmond.
44. Franz Liszt to Marie zu Sayn-Wittgenstein, November 24, 1882, in *Letters of Franz Liszt*, 260.
45. *Catalogue of Mr. Henry C. Ezekiel's Private Collection*, 14.
46. Hilmes, *Franz Liszt*, 393–94.
47. Coffin, *Villa d'Este at Tivoli*, 123.
48. Coffin, *Villa d'Este at Tivoli*, 123.
49. Franz Liszt to Olga van Meyendorff, January 7, 1881, in *Letters to Olga Von Meyendorff*, 393–94. In that same letter, Liszt mentions several works in Ezekiel's studio, including *Blind Homer and Young Guide*, and the Corcoran statues, singling out *Michelangelo*, *Raphael*, *Dürer*, and *Rembrandt*.
50. "Among the Sculptors" (December 1899).
51. Ezekiel, "Memories," AAA, 264.
52. Ezekiel, "Memories," AAA, 275.
53. On the company Ezekiel kept and his fascination with celebrity, see Chyet, "Moses Jacob Ezekiel: Art and Celebrity."
54. Ezekiel, *Memoirs*, 263.
55. Ezekiel, *Memoirs*, 263.Years later, the *New York Times* reported on the project to turn the villa into an Austrian Academy of Fine Arts, underscoring that Ezekiel lived there for months with Liszt and the cardinal. See "Fine Frescoes Recovered."
56. Ezekiel, "Memories," AAA, 328–29; "Sir Moses Ezekiel" (November 30, 1913). This long biographical article reveals that several busts of the cardinal were produced.
57. "Sir Moses Ezekiel Home Again," 3; J. W. W., "Ezekiel Bronzes," 189.
58. M. J. P., "European Estimate of an American Sculptor," clipping in Ezekiel papers, box 2, folder 2, AJA.
59. Moses Ezekiel to Jacob Ezekiel, July 7, 1891, in Philipson, "Moses Jacob Ezekiel," 52.
60. Bush-Brown, "Sir Moses Ezekiel," 234.
61. "Order of Commencement Services" program, March 30, 1921, Ezekiel papers, box 1, folder 4, AJA.
62. Bosis, "Baths of Diocletian."
63. Moses Ezekiel to "Sir" (most likely William MacLeod), April 1, 1881 (letter 2129).
64. Ezekiel, *Memoirs*, 83.
65. "Morgan Declines $100,000 Painting."
66. "Ezekiel Refuses to Move."
67. Ezekiel, *Memoirs*, 301.
68. Ezekiel, *Memoirs*, 321–22.
69. Ezekiel, *Memoirs*, 322.
70. Moses Ezekiel to "Sir" (most likely MacLeod), April 1, 1881 (letter 2129).
71. Moses Ezekiel to William Corcoran, February 15, 1883 (letter 2843), series 1 subseries 1, box RG2-2008.006, folder 13; Moses Ezekiel to William Corcoran, December 12, 1882 (letter 2756), series 1 subseries 1, box RG2-2008.006, folder 4; Moses Ezekiel to William Corcoran, June 7, 1884 (letter 3287), series 1 subseries 1, box RG2-2008.007, folder 14, all in CGA Director's Records.
72. Moses Ezekiel to William Corcoran, March 5, 1880 (letter 1799), series 1 subseries 1, box RG2-2008.004, folder 5, CGA Director's Records.
73. Collman, "October Anniversary," 4.
74. Moses Ezekiel to William Corcoran, March 5, 1880 (letter 1799).
75. Ezekiel, *Memoirs*, 279–80.
76. J. W. W., "Ezekiel Bronzes," 190.
77. "Unveiling of the Bronze Homeric Group," 235.
78. Ezekiel, *Memoirs*, 425.
79. Alderman's telegram quoted in Ezekiel, *Memoirs*, 425. Ezekiel's cablegram quoted in "Unveiling of the Bronze Homeric Group," 244.

80. "Unveiling of the Bronze Homeric Group," 232, 233.
81. Moses Ezekiel to Henry Ezekiel, June 22, 1866, in Philipson, "Moses Jacob Ezekiel," 3.
82. Ezekiel, *Memoirs*, 399.
83. Simpson family collection, photo albums, 1902–3 NY, pp. 1–3, John Woodruff Simpson Memorial Library, East Craftsbury, VT.
84. Although much more modest, Ezekiel's association of children with nature can also be seen in his portrait bust of Margaret Friend (1895; Cincinnati Art Museum), where she appears to emerge from the petals of her blouse.
85. Le Normand-Romain and Buley-Uribe, "1885–1915," 86. That generous donation includes twenty-eight sculptures, eight drawings, and three drypoint prints. See Dickerson, "Sculpture at the National Gallery," 188–89.
86. Le Normand Romain and Buley-Uribe, "1885–1915," 85; Butler and Lindsay, *European Sculpture*, 372–76.
87. Ezekiel, *Memoirs*, 102, 272.
88. Mrs. Schmidlapp letter to Alfred Goshorn, director of CAM, March 27, 1888, 1889.516, CAM files.
89. Moses Jacob Ezekiel, *Henry Wadsworth Longfellow*, 1889.516, CAM files.
90. "Longfellow in Marble," clipping in CAM files.
91. Buick, *Child of the Fire*, 88; Wunder, *Hiram Powers*, 2:65.
92. "Longfellow in Marble," clipping in CAM files.
93. Shelley, "Defence of Poetry," 85.
94. "Unveiling of the Bronze Homeric Group," 232.
95. Shelley, "Defence of Poetry," 112.
96. Percy Bysshe Shelley to T. L. Peacock, November 16, 1818, in *Essays and Letters*, 246; Shelley, *Selected Poems and Prose*, 429.
97. Hawthorne, *Marble Faun*, 93.
98. Dabakis, *Sisterhood of Sculptors*, 72, 96–97.
99. Byer, "Words, Monuments, Beholders," 163.
100. Ezekiel, *Memoirs*, 319. Ezekiel would visit with the Leavitts in New York, too. See Ezekiel, *Memoirs*, 395. The *New York Times* noted one of those visits in 1910: "Historic Tower as Studio." This is likely the *Shelley* currently at the University of Cincinnati, but provenance is uncertain.
101. Ezekiel, "Keats-Shelley Memorial."
102. Hawthorne, *Marble Faun*, 134.
103. Clars Auction Gallery, personal communication with author, January 24, 2022.
104. Ezekiel, *Memoirs*, 404, 406.
105. Ezekiel, *Memoirs*, 396, 390.
106. Vance, *America's Rome*, 187–88.
107. Dimmick, "Veiled Memories," 177.
108. Moses Jacob Ezekiel file, Virginia Museum of Fine Arts files, Richmond.
109. Ezekiel, *Memoirs*, 420. Sella's portrait bust was in the collection of the University of Rome until 1961; see G. Chiarotti to Sarah Grossman, April 15, 1971, Ezekiel papers, box 1, folder 7, AJA.
110. "Baltimore." In general, Ezekiel was favorably covered by *American Art News*. His *Anthony Drexel* monument, for instance, was given notice, with details of its progress and commission. See "Philadelphia Art News."
111. "Ezekiel's 'Poe' Burned" (December 28, 1913); "Ezekiel's 'Poe' Burned" (January 2, 1914).
112. "Ezekiel's Bronze Poe Unveiled at Last." The article mentions several other works by Ezekiel, among them *Blind Homer and Young Guide* and "scores of busts and reliefs in various countries."
113. Krainick, "Sir Moses Ezekiel Statue," 48–57.
114. "Ezekiel Must Move"; "Ezekiel Refuses to Move."
115. Ezekiel, *Memoirs*, 433–34.
116. "Historic Tower as Studio." Ezekiel wrote of the labors to turn the tower into a studio: adding flooring, removing walls of brick, and putting in a marble stairway to lead to the upper story. Ezekiel, *Memoirs*, 437.
117. Ezekiel, *Memoirs*, 442.
118. Ezekiel, *Memoirs*, 313.
119. Ezekiel, *Memoirs*, 280–81.
120. On artists' fascination with the antique, see Haskell and Penny, *Taste and the Antique*.
121. MacLeod, Curator's journal, May 1, 1882, vol. 5, 1882, series 1 subseries 4, box 196, vol. 10, CGA Director's Records.
122. Moses Ezekiel to William Corcoran, May 23, 1882 (letter 2577), series 1 subseries 1, box RG2-2008.005, folder 28, CGA Director's Records. The letter was sent from Paris, where Ezekiel was staying for two months working on some commissions. With characteristic braggadocio, Ezekiel wrote of *Liszt*, "My portrait is considered by his pupils, relatives and friends as the most truthful and lifelike that has been yet made."
123. MacLeod, Curator's journal, March 26, 1878, vol. 2, 1878, series 1 subseries 4, box 196, vol. 8, CGA Director's Records.

124. MacLeod, Curator's journal, October 13, 1879, vol. 3, 1879–1880, series 1 subseries 4, box 198, box 2, vol. 1, CGA Director's Records.
125. MacLeod, Curator's journal, December 24, 1883, vol. 6, 1883, series 1 subseries 4, box 196, vol. 11, CGA Director's Records.

Chapter 5

1. Ezekiel provides this date in a letter to William MacLeod, January 25, 1880 (letter 1769), series 1 subseries 1, box RG2-2008.004, folder 2, CGA Director's Records. An archived photocopy shows "Washington" in capital letters inscribed at the bottom. Moses Jacob Ezekiel files, CAM files.
2. Doss, *Memorial Mania*, 20.
3. Moses Ezekiel to William MacLeod, January 25, 1880 (letter 1769).
4. Ezekiel's brother Henry, always a steadfast and usually reliable supporter who assisted him stateside whenever possible, wrote to McLeod ten months later, but to no avail. Henry Ezekiel to William MacLeod, November 14, 1880 (letter 1972), series 1 subseries 1, box RG2-2008.004, folder 23, CGA Director's Records.
5. Moses Jacob Ezekiel file, CAM files. The head of Washington, held by the Cincinnati Art Museum, is mentioned in a *Richmond News* article from 1901 as "among the best specimens of his art" (*Religious Liberty* is signaled, too). See "Sir Moses Ezekiel's Prospective Visit," clipping in Ezekiel papers, box 2, folder 2, AJA.
6. Crane, *White Silence*, 60–85; Rand, *Horatio Greenough and the Form Majestic.*
7. Ezekiel, *Memoirs*, 178–79.
8. Quoted in Hirschfeld, *George Washington and the Jews*, 24, 25–26. In different versions, capitalization and grammar changes slightly. Here, I follow the source cited.
9. Marcus, *Jew in the American World*, 108, 109. A 1956 exhibition held at the dedication of B'nai Brith's new building in Washington, DC, displayed the original letter (lent by its then-private owner) and the Library of Congress loaned Jefferson's Virginia Statute for Religious Freedom. See Bisgyer, *This Is B'nai B'rith*. Simon Wolf included these four exchanges in *American Jew as Patriot, Soldier and Citizen*, 53–57. An analogous sentiment was extended to Washington in a 1790 joint address of the Hebrew congregations in the cities of Philadelphia, New York, Richmond, and Charleston, which merited a reply from the new president as well. See ibid., 57–59.
10. Joint Committee on the Library, extracts in substance, from minutes of May 20, 1886, *Thomas Jefferson* by Moses Jacob Ezekiel object file, catalog number 22.00002.000, Office of Senate Curator, United States Senate, Washington, DC (hereafter TJ object file).
11. Moses Ezekiel to Edward Clark, June 6, 1886, TJ object file.
12. Moses Ezekiel to Edward Clark, July 21, 1886, TJ object file.
13. Moses Ezekiel to Edward Clark, September 12, 1888, TJ object file.
14. "Form No. 155, Declaration as to the Works of Art," TJ object file.
15. Poulet et al., *Jean-Antoine Houdon*, 269–73.
16. Moses Ezekiel to Edward Clark, March 23, 1889, TJ object file.
17. Moses Ezekiel to William M. Evarts, March 23, 1889, TJ object file.
18. Moses Ezekiel to Anson G. McCook, March 23, 1889, TJ object file.
19. "Proposed Statue of President."
20. Ezekiel, *Memoirs*, 375.
21. Moses Ezekiel to Jacob Ezekiel, March 26, 1973, in Philipson, "Moses Jacob Ezekiel," 5.
22. Moses Ezekiel to Hannah Waterman, March 21, 1886, in Philipson, "Moses Jacob Ezekiel," 6.
23. Ezekiel, "Memories," AAA, 323–24.
24. A portion of this history is indebted to Isaac Wolfe Bernheim's memoir *The Story of the Bernheim Family*. Part 1 covers his family history from 1772, beginning with his grandfather's birth and discussing their life in Germany, Judaism, and Bernheim's immigrant success story. Details about the commission and gifting of the *Jefferson* monument form part 2, pp. 100–122.
25. Letter from the Bernheims, the park commissioners' written response, and adopted resolution reprinted in "Munificent."
26. Jefferson County Courthouse file, Louisville Metro Hall, Louisville, KY; "Thomas Jefferson Monument."
27. Wrenshall, "American Sculptor in Rome," 12256.

28. Wunder, *Hiram Powers*, 2:180–81.
29. Thomas Jefferson to Margaret Bayard Smith, August 6, 1816, quoted in *Jefferson's Extracts*, 376.
30. A similar quotation from the Virginia Statute for Religious Freedom was later carved on the interior walls of the Jefferson Memorial in Washington, DC (1939–43), as was the passage from the Declaration of Independence. Words from Jefferson's letter to Benjamin Rush likewise appear on the Jefferson Memorial, in a frieze below the dome.
31. Ezekiel, *Memoirs*, 184.
32. "Rome to Have New American Officials."
33. "At the Quarries," 636.
34. Alden, "London Literary Letter."
35. "Jefferson Statue Shipped"; "Tunnels Too Small."
36. Moses Ezekiel to Henry Ezekiel, September 16, 1897, in Philipson, "Moses Jacob Ezekiel," 40.
37. "Thomas Jefferson Monument."
38. All spellings conform with Ezekiel's written on the tablet.
39. Moses Ezekiel to Henry Ezekiel, September 16, 1897, in Philipson, "Moses Jacob Ezekiel," 41.
40. Moses Ezekiel to Jacob Ezekiel, January 27, 1899, in Philipson, "Moses Jacob Ezekiel," 43.
41. Bernheim, *Story of the Bernheim Family*, 118–19.
42. Ezekiel, *Memoirs*, 128, 198. For the authoritative study of General Orders No. 11, see Sarna, *When General Grant Expelled the Jews*.
43. Quoted in Sarna, *When General Grant Expelled the Jews*, 68; Ezekiel, *Memoirs*, 198.
44. Quoted in Korn, *American Jewry and the Civil War*, 134.
45. Moses Ezekiel to "My dear comrade and friend," July 23, 1904, VMI Archives.
46. Ezekiel, *Memoirs*, 128.
47. Ezekiel, *Memoirs*, 199.
48. Ezekiel, *Memoirs*, 398.
49. Ezekiel, *Memoirs*, 440.
50. "Unveiled." Two-thirds of the front page was taken up with news about the unveiling, Ezekiel, and the Bernheim brothers. The dedication was covered widely. For example, see "Ezekiel's Statue of Thomas Jefferson," clipping in Ezekiel papers, box 2, folder 2, AJA.
51. "Unveiled."
52. Bernheim, *Story of the Bernheim Family*; Bernheim, *Closing Chapters*.
53. Bernheim, *Story of the Bernheim Family*, 92, 94.
54. Bernheim, *Story of the Bernheim Family*, 92.
55. Bernheim, *Story of the Bernheim Family*, 95.
56. Cobb, *Rise of Religious Liberty*, vii; see also, more recently, Ragosta, *Religious Freedom*.
57. Taylor, "Personal Appreciation," 336.
58. Andrew White to the Bernheim brothers, June 12, 1900, in Philipson, "Moses Jacob Ezekiel," 42.
59. Ezekiel, *Memoirs*, 409.
60. "List of Gifts to the University," 155.
61. Bruce, *History of the University of Virginia*, 319–20. Listed anonymously as "A Friend, in memory of Gratz Cohen, $500," in "List of Gifts to the University," 156.
62. J. W. W., "Ezekiel Bronzes," 191; "Ezekiel Statue to Be Unveiled" and "Statue of Jefferson Presented to University of Virginia," clippings in Ezekiel papers, box 2, folder 2, AJA.
63. "List of Gifts to the University," 155–58. Gifts earmarked for the Jefferson monument take up four pages.
64. Craven, *Sculpture in America*, 205–6.
65. Dennis, *Karl Bitter*.
66. "Ezekiel, Sculptor, Arrives." The paper erroneously quoted Ezekiel as saying three years when it had been five.
67. "Unveiling of Ezekiel's Statue," 366. The frontispiece of UVA's alumni magazine displayed a photograph of the monument, while the issue included a full-page signed photo of the artist and all speeches from the unveiling.
68. "Unveiling of Ezekiel's Statue," 367.
69. "Unveiling of Ezekiel's Statue," 369.
70. In a biography of his brother, Rosewell Page mentions that Ezekiel presented a "beautiful" bronze model of Jefferson to T. Page. See *Thomas Nelson Page*, 160.
71. "Unveiling of the Bronze Homeric Group," 238. For the entirety of the lengthy speech, see ibid., 236–39.
72. Uriah Levy's military accomplishments and commitment to Judaism were acknowledged in 1959 when the navy's oldest Jewish chapel, located in Norfolk, Virginia, was renamed in his honor. In December 2011, a statue of Levy was erected outside of Philadelphia's Congregation Mikveh Israel, so chosen because his bar mitzvah was held there in 1805. Earlier, Levy's epaulets were displayed at the

opening exhibition for B'nai B'rith's new building in 1956, as was a portrait of him in uniform. See Bisgyer, *This Is B'nai B'rith*, 13, 19.

73. Somma, "'Lost in America.'" In addition to statues, d'Angers was known for his bronze portrait medallions, of which he made approximately five hundred; one represents Uriah Levy (1833). See Reinis, *Portrait Medallions*, 292–93.
74. Reprinted in Marcus, *Memoirs of American Jews*, 84. For Levy's full autobiographical statement, see 78–116.
75. Mays and Small, "Jefferson Statue Will Be Removed."
76. Uriah Levy to John Coulter, November 1832, quoted in Fitzpatrick and Saphire, *Navy Maverick*, 128.
77. Uriah Levy to John Coulter, November 1832, quoted in Fitzpatrick and Saphire, *Navy Maverick*, 128.
78. Leepson, *Saving Monticello*; Urofsky, *Levy Family and Monticello*.
79. Ezekiel, *Memoirs*, 396.
80. Ezekiel, *Memoirs*, 272.
81. Ezekiel, *Memoirs*, 103.
82. Ezekiel, *Memoirs*, 128.
83. Wolf, *Presidents I Have Known*, 24, 29.
84. Urofsky, *Levy Family and Monticello*, 83.
85. Myers was especially supportive of the Hebrew Technical Institute for Girls, not only providing monies but acting as president. The school erected a bronze sculpture titled *Torch of Wisdom* (ca. 1923) in his memory.
86. Ezekiel, *Memoirs*, 365.
87. Ezekiel, *Memoirs*, 365.
88. "Unpublished Bust of Lincoln by Sir Moses Jacob Ezekiel," clipping in VMI Archives.
89. Marcus, *Jew in the American World*, 200.
90. For an early published instance of this exchange, see Markens, *Abraham Lincoln and the Jews*, 12.
91. Sarna and Shapell, *Lincoln and the Jews*, 84–118.
92. Cohen and Gibson date the bronze to 1880, but my research indicates that the marble came first. After a conversation with Gibson, he agreed with this revised assessment. Cohen and Gibson, *Moses Ezekiel*, 140; Keith Gibson, personal communication with author, June 29, 2020.
93. Orcutt, *John Rogers*, 167.
94. "Bronze Bust May Adorn Public Site." Another known copy of the bust resides in the University of Cincinnati Public Library. In 1927, one of Ezekiel's Lincoln busts was publicly displayed in a window by the Cincinnati-based Loring Andrews Company in observance of Lincoln's birthday. The *Cincinnati Times-Star* was quick to praise the sculpture and Ezekiel, deceased for a decade. The article judged the bust "a distinguished bronze" and "a wonderful composite portrait of his subject, which is particularly rare and valuable on that account, apart from being the work of one of America's greatest sculptors." "Ezekiel Bust of Lincoln on Exhibition in Cincinnati," clipping in Moses Jacob Ezekiel file, CAM files.
95. "Proposed Monuments."
96. Governor Augustus E. Willson to Isaac and Bernard Bernheim, May 30, 1910, reprinted in Bernheim, *Story of the Bernheim Family*, 145.
97. Taft, *History of American Sculpture*, 263.

Chapter 6

This chapter was started before Ezekiel's Confederate monuments were subject to censure and the large-scale removal of such monuments from public spaces. Accordingly, the chapter was reworked several times as I was chasing the news. After the book went to copyediting, *New South* was dismantled, crated, and put in storage as of December 22, 2023. I changed the chapter's language to indicate that the statue no longer stands, but I was not able to add additional material about the final fight to halt the removal. Virginia Governor Glenn Youngkin has publicly expressed his desire for the monument to be reassembled at New Market Battlefield State Historical Park where Ezekiel's VMI copy of Stonewall Jackson was transferred in 2020. Negotiations with the Department of the Army to arrange a transfer of the statue from federal to state ownership are ongoing. Undoubtedly, there will have been further developments since the book's publication.

1. One notable exception is Sarah Beetham, who privileges artists' identities vis-à-vis lone soldier monuments in "Sculpting the Citizen Soldier." Since the mid-2010s, books as well as hundreds of articles in the mainstream press discuss the pros and cons of removing Confederate sculptures and the history of their making. For a lucid discussion of the most

recent developments as this book goes to press, see Cox, *No Common Ground*; and Beetham's excellent article, "From Spray Cans to Minivans."

2. Davis, *Battle of New Market*. Partly informed by Ezekiel's autobiography, the 2014 film *Field of Lost Shoes*, directed by Sean McNamara, features Josh Zuckerman playing the future sculptor as a VMI cadet.
3. Quoted in Berman, *Richmond's Jewry*, 239.
4. Ezekiel, *Memoirs*, 112.
5. Ezekiel, *Memoirs*, 105–12.
6. See, for example, a twelve-page letter with details on many matters: Moses Ezekiel to "My dear comrade and friend," July 23, 1904, VMI Archives; "Fighter, Too"; and Moses Ezekiel to Sallie, September 3, 1904, reprinted in Couper, *One Hundred Years at V.M.I*, 328–29. The following description of Ezekiel's experience at New Market derives primarily from these accounts, as well as sources in later notes.
7. Ezekiel, *Memoirs*, 107.
8. Moses Ezekiel to "My dear comrade and friend," July 23, 1904, VMI Archives.
9. Howard, "Recollections of New Market," 59.
10. See Wise, "West Point of the Confederacy," 468, 469, 471, with a detailed description of the trek to New Market and action.
11. Wise, "West Point of the Confederacy," 470. Of Jacqueline Beverly Stanard, he remembered, "His body was still warm and his last messages had been words of love. Poor Jack! Playmate, roommate, friend—farewell."
12. Davis, *Battle of New Market*, 160; Ezekiel, *Memoirs*, 109–11.
13. Cox, "Confederate Monument," 158; Doss, *Memorial Mania*, 11.
14. Moses Ezekiel to General and Superintendent Francis H. Smith, December 2, 1886, VMI Archives.
15. Moses Ezekiel to Greenlee Letcher, February 10, 1900, VMI Archives.
16. "Cadet's Monument."
17. Ezekiel, *Memoirs*, 112–13. Ezekiel donated a three-quarter-size bronze replica of the statue to the Museum of the Confederacy in Richmond (now the American Civil War Museum) in 1914. Moses Ezekiel to Mrs. Silliman, June 27, 1914, Ezekiel papers, box 1, folder 1, AJA. See also "Joan of Arc Statue." A nine-inch bronze replica of *Virginia Mourning Her Dead* tops the Jonathan Myrick Daniels Humanitarian Award, established by VMI's Board of Visitors in 1997 to honor Class of 1961 valedictorian Jonathan Daniels, gunned down while trying to save the life of a young Black girl during a Civil Rights voter registration drive in Alabama. According to VMI records, the award "recognizes individuals who have made significant personal sacrifices to protect or improve the lives of others."
18. Cablegram from Moses Ezekiel to VMI, June 23, 1903, VMI Archives. Original Latin: "Adsum atque illustris complexus limina portae et memor et fidus gratulor."
19. Dean, *Shook over Hell*, 70, 115.
20. "Fighter, Too."
21. Faust, *Republic of Suffering*, 209.
22. Chapman, *Ten Months in the "Orphan Brigade,"* 38.
23. Bierce, "What I Saw of Shiloh," 110; "sentenced to life" quoted in Morris, *Ambrose Bierce*, 205.
24. *Walt Whitman: The Correspondence*, 127n92.
25. Ezekiel's medal is housed at the VMI Museum, engraved on the reverse, "VMI Alumni Ass'n to M. Ezekiel." In 1914, he designed a bronze medal for the Society of the Cincinnati in Virginia. That medal, with an armored Virtus on the front holding a spear near the cadet barracks and the eagle of Cincinnati on the back, was annually awarded to a graduating VMI cadet who embodied character and leadership.
26. Moses Ezekiel to "My dear comrade and friend," July 23, 1904, VMI Archives.
27. Historian Edward A. Pollard coined the term the "Lost Cause" in his book of the same name. On the history of the Lost Cause over time, see Foster, *Ghosts of the Confederacy*; and Wilson, *Baptized in Blood*.
28. Keith Gibson, personal communication with author, October 15, 2020.
29. Keith Gibson, personal communication with author, August 24, 2022.
30. Harris, "Heroism of V.M.I. Cadets at New Market," clipping in Ezekiel papers, box 2, folder 2, AJA.
31. Moses Ezekiel to Marjorie Taylor, June 17, 1886, Valentine Archives. On Ezekiel's accounting of the Lee competitions, see also *Memoirs*, 212–13, 214.
32. This discussion of the Lee competitions relies on "Monument to General Robert E. Lee," especially

195, 198; and Driggs, Wilson, and Winthrop, *Richmond's Monument Avenue*, 38–55.

33. Moses Ezekiel to William MacLeod, June 3, 1886 (letter 3795), series 1 subseries 1, box RG2-2008.009, folder 21, CGA Director's Records.
34. Ezekiel, *Memoirs*, 212.
35. Prov. 16:32 (JPS).
36. Savage, *Standing Soldiers*, 142.
37. Savage, *Standing Soldiers*, 134–35, 140–42.
38. Ezekiel, "Memories," AAA, 132; Ezekiel, *Memoirs*, 152.
39. Moses Ezekiel to Joe, November 2, 1916, VMI Archives.
40. MacLeod, Curator's journal, entries on June 5, 7, 12, 1886, vol. 8, 1886, series 1 subseries 4, box 198, vol. 2, CGA Director's Records.
41. Moses Ezekiel to Marjorie Taylor, June 17, 1886, Valentine Archives. A month later, Ezekiel once again laments being overlooked for the Lee monument in a letter to Taylor, showing his unwillingness to let go of his animosity. See Moses Ezekiel to Marjorie Taylor, July 22, 1886, Valentine Archives.
42. Moses Ezekiel to Superintendent and General Scott Shipp, September 2, 1897, VMI Archives.
43. Ezekiel, *Memoirs*, 278.
44. Ezekiel, *Memoirs*, 279.
45. "Libby Prison Statue"; "Ezekiel's Models Not Liked"; "Ezekiel's Models and Letters"; "Among the Sculptors" (December 1892).
46. Ezekiel, "To the Editor of the *Dispatch*," December 15, 1892 (letter in response to November 8, 1892, article), clipping in Ezekiel papers, box 2, folder 2, AJA.
47. Moses Ezekiel to Esther Davis (his great niece), March 19, 1916, Ezekiel papers, box 1, folder 2, AJA.
48. Moses Ezekiel to Esther Davis, March 19, 1916, Ezekiel papers, box 1, folder 2, AJA.
49. On the arch, see Sharp, "Smith Memorial."
50. Sharp, "Smith Memorial," 171–72.
51. Dabakis, *Sisterhood of Sculptors*, 207–11.
52. Ezekiel, *Memoirs*, 165.
53. Ezekiel, "Memories," AAA, 522–24.
54. Ezekiel, *Memoirs*, 426.
55. Moses Ezekiel to Captain Henry Wise, July 10, 1909, VMI Archives. Wise was commander of one of the New Market cadet battalions. Ezekiel revisits the battle at length in this letter.
56. Moses Ezekiel to Leonora Levy, May 10, 1866, Ezekiel papers, box 1, folder 1, AJA.
57. On women's groups and the commissioning of Confederate monuments, see Janney, *Burying the Dead*; and Cox, *Dixie's Daughters*.
58. Fink, *American Art*, 387.
59. Dryfhout, *Work of Augustus Saint-Gaudens*, 28–29, 110–15.
60. Moses Ezekiel to Edward Valentine, November 10, 1908, Valentine Archives.
61. Moses Ezekiel to Isabel Maury, November 10, 1908, Ezekiel papers, box 1, folder 2, AJA.
62. "Ezekiel, Sculptor, Arrives"; "Charleston Trip," clipping in VMI Archives; "Statue of 'Stonewall Jackson.'"
63. Moses Ezekiel to Edward W. Nichols, August 23, 1910, VMI Archives.
64. See, for example, a four-page letter about the inscription and other matters from Moses Ezekiel to Superintendent and General Edward W. Nichols, April 14, 1911, VMI Archives.
65. Moses Ezekiel to Superintendent and General Edward W. Nichols, March 5, 1912, VMI Archives.
66. Quoted in Cohen and Gibson, *Moses Ezekiel*, 115.
67. Shapira, "VMI Removes Statue."
68. Keith Gibson, personal communication with author, January 15, 2021.
69. Kabler, "Capitol Building Commission Again Stonewalls."
70. "Monument to John W. Daniel." Subscriptions were requested in June 1911, and Ezekiel was immediately named as the sculptor. Its making was covered by *American Art News*, along with Ezekiel's work on *Poe*. See "Art and Artists."
71. *Proceedings Connected with the Unveiling*, 13.
72. Brevard, "History of a Memorial Gateway."
73. On Confederate soldier monuments, see Beetham, "From Spray Cans to Minivans"; and Savage, *Standing Soldiers*, esp. 162–86.
74. "Unveil Monument at Johnson's Island," clipping in Johnson's Island Preservation Society archives, Sandusky, Ohio.
75. Schonfeld, "Robert E. Lee's Direct Descendant." On Lee's desire to move past civil strife and reembrace allegiance to the Union, see correspondence quoted in Pryor, *Reading the Man*, 434–35.
76. Schonfeld, "Robert E. Lee's Direct Descendant."

77. Shapiro, "Descendants of Rebel Sculptor."
78. This discussion relies in part on a key source published three months after the monument's debut: Herbert, *History of the Arlington Confederate Monument*, 75–79. Herbert, who served as master of ceremonies at the unveiling, chronicled the commission, creation, and dedication in the seventy-nine-page document. See also "Monument in Arlington."
79. The only sustained discussions of *New South*'s artistic program are Jacob, *Testament to Union*, 164–71; and Cox's fundamental essay that proved crucial to my thinking, "Confederate Monument."
80. Ezekiel, *Memoirs*, 111.
81. "Week in Art"; Moses Ezekiel to Greenlee Letcher, chair of the VMI Alumni Association, late summer 1899, VMI Archives.
82. The entire biblical passage: "And He shall judge between the nations, and shall decide for many peoples; and they shall beat their swords into plowshares, and their spears into pruninghooks; nation shall not lift up sword against nation, neither shall they learn war any more" (Isa. 2:4; JPS).
83. Herbert, *History of the Arlington Confederate Monument*, 77.
84. Moses Ezekiel to Mammy Keziah, July 23, 1875, Ezekiel papers, box 1, folder 1, AJA.
85. On the appropriation of the "mammy" motif across time, see McElya, *Clinging to Mammy*.
86. Brown, "Muted South," 767–68.
87. Ezekiel, *Memoirs*, 93, 96.
88. Ezekiel, *Memoirs*, 168, 169–70.
89. Quoted in Korn, *American Jewry and the Civil War*, 15.
90. On the number of Jews in the Confederate military, see Rosen, "Jewish Confederates," 118. The Weitzman National Museum of American Jewish History indicates seven thousand Union soldiers and three thousand Confederate soldiers on its wall signage. On population numbers, see Rosen's comprehensive study, *Jewish Confederates*, 25. On Union soldiers, see Mendelsohn, *Jewish Soldiers in the Civil War*.
91. Evans, *Judah P. Benjamin*, 97.
92. Quoted in Rosen, *Jewish Confederates*, 37.
93. Quoted in Korn, *American Jewry and the Civil War*, 17.
94. Rosen, *Jewish Confederates*, 16, 211.
95. Rosen, *Jewish Confederates*, 77.
96. Ezekiel, *Memoirs*, 118.
97. Straus, *Under Four Administrations*, 12.
98. Straus, *Under Four Administrations*, 12.
99. Around 1897, Ezekiel mentions finishing a marble bust of Mr. Straus, which might have been Oscar but could also well have been Isidor. Ezekiel, "Memories," AAA, 539. In Straus's own memoir, he refers to Ezekiel as "our distinguished American sculptor." *Under Four Administrations*, 158.
100. Bernheim, *Story of the Bernheim Family*, 90–91.
101. Rosen, *Jewish Confederates*, 338–39; Stollman, *Daughters of Israel*, 221–22.
102. Wolf, *American Jew*.
103. Krowl, "'In the Spirit of Fraternity.'"
104. On the history of the Confederate section with a few words on the statue, see Blair, *Cities of the Dead*, 179–93, 201–7.
105. Ezekiel, *Memoirs*, 439.
106. Speech reproduced in Herbert, *History of the Arlington Confederate Monument*, 19, 20.
107. See "Monument over Southern Soldiers," with a list of known names of those buried in the cemetery. See also "Heroes of the Stars and Bars."
108. Ezekiel, *Memoirs*, 440. On reconciliation across time, with an eye toward the reality of racism over the sentimentalizing of heroism, see Blight, *Race and Reunion*.
109. Eulogy sent from Warren Harding to Marion Butler, March 30, 1921, VMI Archives.
110. "Forget the Past." Speech also printed in Herbert, *History of the Arlington Confederate Monument*, 70, 71. For further coverage of the dedication, see "Gray and Blue Join."
111. Ezekiel, *Memoirs*, 124.
112. Ezekiel, *Memoirs*, 418.
113. Herbert, *History of the Arlington Confederate Monument*, 44.
114. Herbert, *History of the Arlington Confederate Monument*, 56.
115. Stolberg, "'They Answered the Call.'"
116. "Women's National Confederate Memorial."
117. Grady, "New South."
118. President Woodrow Wilson, speech at the unveiling; see Herbert, *History of the Arlington Confederate Monument*, 70.

119. Moses Ezekiel to General and Superintendent Francis H. Smith, December 2, 1886, VMI Archives.
120. Ezekiel, *Memoirs*, 61.
121. Ezekiel, *Memoirs*, 112.
122. He also dedicated the memoir to Thomas Nelson Page: "Dedicated to my friend the Southern author Thomas Nelson Page, American Ambassador in Rome." Ezekiel, "Memories," AAA.

Conclusion

1. Documentation differs on the height of the sculpture. Philipson's biographical article says the sculpture stands ten feet tall, but a *New York Times* article covering the unveiling, also written by Philipson and likely more accurate, states the height as twelve feet. Philipson, "Moses Jacob Ezekiel," 37; Philipson, "Jesse Seligman Memorial."
2. Seligman's reach was wide: He founded the better-known Society for Ethical Culture; Grant offered him the position of secretary of treasury, which he declined; and his firm helped manage the monies for the Civil War. See *In Memoriam*. On the Asylum, see Bogen, *Luckiest Orphans*.
3. "Ezekiel, the Celebrated Sculptor"; Philipson, "Jesse Seligman Memorial."
4. "Help the Orphans." Jozef Israëls, one of the foremost artists in nineteenth-century Holland, also Jewish, donated a work and two autograph letters. This constitutes the only evidence that the two men knew each other and presents an intriguing connection that deserves further exploration.
5. The meaning of the monument is described in a flyer: "The Jesse Seligman Memorial," possibly distributed at its dedication in 1896, Ezekiel papers, box 2, folder 5, AJA. See also Philipson, "Jesse Seligman Memorial," with variations on the colors of the marble; and an article from the Roman newspaper *Popolo romano* (February 22, 1896), quoted in full in Philipson, "Moses Jacob Ezekiel," 37.
6. Seligman's memorial book relates that Ezekiel made a death mask, while the sculptor's memoir indicates that he never did, despite efforts to do so. Considering the tribute volume's much closer proximity to Seligman's death—plus the fact that Ezekiel was fortuitously in New York when Seligman died—most probably he made a death mask and misremembered. See *In Memoriam*, 134.
7. Ezekiel crafted an unknown number of statuettes of the girl, one of which survives (1896, Virginia Military Institute).
8. Philipson, "Jesse Seligman Memorial."
9. Moses Ezekiel to Jacob Ezekiel, January 22, 1895, in Philipson, "Moses Jacob Ezekiel," 38.
10. Moses Ezekiel to Jacob Ezekiel, undated (ca. 1894–95), in Philipson, "Moses Jacob Ezekiel," 38.
11. "Hebrew Orphan Home."
12. Ezekiel, *Memoirs*, 411.
13. Ezekiel, *Memoirs*, 282.
14. Moses Ezekiel to Thomas Nelson Page, January 5, 1907, Thomas Nelson Page Papers, box 5. David M. Rubenstein Rare Book and Manuscript Library, Duke University, Durham, North Carolina.
15. Ezekiel, *Memoirs*, 413.
16. Translation of *Il popolo romano* article in "Critics Praise Statue of Jackson," clipping in VMI Archives.
17. "Statue for Virginia" (November 22, 1908).
18. "Statue for Virginia" (November 22, 1908).
19. *Il popolo romano* in "Critics Praise Statue of Jackson." For the longest description of the sculpture in its day, see Wrenshall, "American Sculptor in Rome," 12258.
20. Ezekiel, *Memoirs*, 425, 433.
21. "Statue for Virginia" (November 28, 1908), noting that the full-scale *Napoleon* "is treated originally."
22. Ezekiel, *Memoirs*, 399.
23. Ezekiel, *Memoirs*, 411.
24. "Rome to Have New American Officials."
25. "More Honors for Ezekiel," clipping in Ezekiel papers, box 2, folder 2, AJA.
26. "Rome Is Still Chilly."
27. Ezekiel, *Memoirs*, 317. There is no mention of Ezekiel's sculpture in the comprehensive four-volume record of the Fair sponsored by its board of directors, Johnson, *History of the World's Columbian Exposition*. I am indebted to conversations with Keith Gibson about this matter and his own research into the misunderstanding. Gibson generously shared his unpublished research note, "Which Columbus Statue Was Exhibited at the Chicago World's Fair?" In sum, the timing of the sculpture's arrival in the United States has caused confusion, especially with another *Columbus*

sculpture commissioned for the fair by Gorham Manufacturing as a display of its craftsmanship. That one, made in silver by Auguste Bartholdi—creator of the Statue of Liberty—was later melted down.

28. Moses Ezekiel to Henry Ezekiel, February 22, 1892, quoted in Philipson, "Moses Jacob Ezekiel," 35.
29. Wolfe, "Long Journey Home to End for Columbus"; program for Columbus Plaza dedication, October 12, 1966, VMI Archives.
30. Pratt et al., "Seeking to 'Protect Public Safety.'"
31. Ramos, "Italian American Group." Ezekiel's miniature bronze of *Columbus* (lost) was exhibited at a January 1913 exposition at the Jewish Settlement House in Cincinnati.
32. Michael Meyer, personal communication with author, September 5, 2020, and December 28, 2021.
33. A six-page typed letter from Lilian de Bosis to Ezekiel's sister describes his last days of illness, the love he received, and his funeral. Lilian de Bosis to Hannah Workum, April 4, 1917, Ezekiel papers, box 1, folder 2, AJA.
34. "Sculptor to Be Buried"; Lilian de Bosis to Hannah Workum, April 4, 1917, Ezekiel papers, box 1, folder 2, AJA.
35. "Arlington Grave Asked by Ezekiel."
36. "Order of Commencement Services," program in VMI Archives.
37. "Address of Hon. John Weeks, Secretary of War, the Funeral Services of Sir Moses Ezekiel," March 30, 1921 (six manuscript pages), Ezekiel papers, box 1, folder 4, AJA.
38. "Sir Moses Ezekiel Burial."
39. "Memorial Service, in Honor of the Late Sir Moses Ezekiel," program in VMI Archives.
40. Among others in Europe, see "Well-Known Sculptor," clipping in VMI Archives. *La tribuna* was one of several Italian papers lamenting Ezekiel's passing and reporting details about his funeral at the Tower of Belisarius. His death made the front page of newspapers in the two American cities where he once lived: "Sir Moses Ezekiel, Native of Richmond"; and "Famed Cincinnati Sculptor Expires." The *Cincinnati Enquirer* covered Ezekiel's death and later the plans for his funeral at Arlington a handful of times. See, for example, in great depth, "Ezekiel, Famous Sculptor, Dies in Rome."
41. Bush-Brown, "Sir Moses Ezekiel," 227. Ezekiel's obituary in *American Art News* included a laundry list of his sculptures; see "Obituary." His notice ran next to Albert Pinkham Ryder's, who died the following day. The magazine ran another notice when Ezekiel was interred at Arlington: "The body of Sir Moses Ezekiel, a sculptor of international fame . . . was removed to the Arlington National Cemetery, March 30, and buried with becoming honors." "Sir Moses Ezekiel" (April 9, 1921).
42. Odenheimer et al., "Sir Moses Ezekiel." *Confederate Veteran* published a different lengthy obituary two months earlier: "Sir Moses Ezekiel" (May 1917). The longer obituary did not shy away from his Jewish origins.
43. *Hebrew Standard*, April 6, 1917, 12. Four years later, the paper briefly noted that his body would soon be buried at Arlington. See also "Items of Interest in the Jewish World" (March 25, 1921); and Oppenheim, "Moses Jacob Ezekiel," 229.
44. Ezekiel, *Memoirs*, 374.

BIBLIOGRAPHY

Archives and Museum Files

Unpublished items from archival sources are fully cited in the endnotes and excluded from the bibliography.

Archives of American Art, Smithsonian Institution, Washington, DC (AAA)
Beth Ahabah Museum and Archives, Richmond, VA
B'nai B'rith International Archives, Washington, DC
Cincinnati Museum of Art files, Cincinnati, OH (CAM files)
Corcoran Gallery of Art and Corcoran College of Art and Design, Corcoran Gallery of Art, Special Collections Research Center, George Washington University, Washington, DC (CGA Director's Records)
David M. Rubenstein Rare Book and Manuscript Library, Duke University, Durham, NC
Folsom Historical Center archives, Louisville, KY
Jacob Rader Marcus Center of the American Jewish Archives, Cincinnati, OH (AJA)
Johnson's Island Preservation Society, Sandusky, OH
John Woodruff Simpson Memorial Library, East Craftsbury, VT
Keneseth Israel archives, Elkins Park, PA (KI archives)
Louisville Metro Hall, Louisville, KY
Norfolk Botanical Garden Records, Sargeant Memorial Collection, Norfolk Public Library, Norfolk, VA (NBGR)
Office of Senate Curator, United States Senate, Washington, DC
Skirball Museum files, Cincinnati, OH
The Valentine Archives, Richmond, VA (Valentine Archives)
Virginia Military Institute Archives, Preston Library, Lexington, VA (VMI Archives)
Virginia Museum of Fine Arts files, Richmond, VA
Weitzman National Museum of American Jewish History archives, Philadelphia, PA (WNMAJH archives)

Period Newspapers, Journals, and Magazines

Alexandria Gazette and Virginia Advertiser
Alumni Bulletin (University of Virginia)
American Art News
American Israelite
B'nai B'rith Magazine
B'nai B'rith News
The Cadet (Virginia Military Institute)
Century Magazine
Charleston Gazette-Mail
Chicago Tribune
Cincinnati Enquirer
Cincinnati Times
Cincinnati Times-Star
Commercial Tribune (Cincinnati)
Confederate Veteran
Contemporary Review
Courier-Journal (Louisville, KY)
Frank Leslie's Illustrated Newspaper
Hebrew Standard
Israelite
Jewish Exponent
Jewish Record
Jewish Telegraph Agency
Jewish Voice (St. Louis)
Ledger-Star (Norfolk, VA)
Life
Literary Digest
The Menorah: A Monthly Magazine
Monumental News
New Era Illustrated Magazine
News and Advance (Lynchburg, VA)
New York Herald
New York Times
Ost und West
Philadelphia Inquirer
Publications of the American Jewish Historical Society
Richmond Daily Dispatch
Richmond News Leader
Richmond Times

Richmond Times-Dispatch
Richmond Virginian
Richmond Whig
Sandusky (OH) *Daily Register*
Southern Historical Society Papers
The State (Richmond, VA)
Sunday Magazine of the Evening Star (Washington, DC)
Union Home Study Magazine
Virginian-Pilot (Hampton Roads)
Washington Post
Washington Times
The World's Work: A History of Our Time

Primary Sources

Adler, Hermann. "Can Jews Be Patriots?" *Nineteenth Century* 3, no. 14 (April 1878): 637–46.

Alden, William L. "London Literary Letter." *New York Times*, June 16, 1900, 24.

"Amending the Constitution." *New York Times*, February 28, 1873, 8.

"American Sculptor, Moses Ezekiel, Dies." *New York Times*, March 28, 1917, 13.

"Americans Write Memoirs in Rome: Archbishop Seton and Moses Ezekiel, the Sculptor, Setting Down Their Reminiscences." *New York Times*, January 4, 1914, 27.

"Among the Sculptors." *Monumental News: An Illustrated Monthly Monumental Art Journal* 4, no. 12 (December 1892): 462.

"Among the Sculptors." *Monumental News* 11, no. 12 (December 1899): 686.

"Arlington Grave Asked by Ezekiel." *Washington Times*, March 30, 1917, 2.

"Art and Artists." *American Art News* 12, no. 30 (May 2, 1914): 3.

"Art Bas-Relief: Done by Sculptor Ezekiel for B'ne B'rith Arrived Safely in New York." *Cincinnati Enquirer*, June 17, 1904, 12.

"Art Exhibition CANCELED at Princeton, Woke Left Takeover on Campuses?" *The Hill*, April 5, 2022. https://www.youtube.com/watch?v=22887d-UnlI.

"Art Immortals Removed." *Washington Post*, June 23, 1899, 4.

"Art in Washington: The Corcoran Gallery." *New York Times*, January 20, 1874, 3.

"Art Notes." *New York Times*, April 19, 1903, 8.

"At the Quarries." *Monumental News: The Granite News* 3, no. 35 (November 1900): 634–38.

Baedeker, K. *Italy: Handbook for Travelers: Central Italy and Rome*. 10th ed. Leipsic: Karl Baedeker, 1890.

"Baltimore." *American Art News* 10, no. 22 (March 9, 1912): 4.

Bartholdi, Frederic Auguste. *The Statue of Liberty Enlightening the World*. New York: North American Review, 1885.

Bernheim, Isaac W. *The Closing Chapters of a Busy Life*. Denver: Welch-Haffner, 1929.

———. *The Story of the Bernheim Family*. Louisville, KY: John P. Morton, 1910.

Bierce, Ambrose. "What I Saw of Shiloh." In *Phantoms of a Blood-Stained Period: The Complete Civil War Writings of Ambrose Bierce*, edited by Russell Duncan and David J. Klooster, 93–110. Amherst: University of Massachusetts Press, 2002.

Bisgyer, Maurice, ed. *This Is B'nai B'rith*. 14th ed. Washington, DC: Supreme Lodge of B'nai B'rith, circa 1956–58.

Blake, Kalena. "Firestone Exhibition of Jewish American Artists Featuring Works from Confederate Soldiers Canceled." *Daily Princetonian*, March 27, 2022. https://www.dailyprincetonian.com/article/2022/03/princeton-milberg-ezekiel-confederate-firestone-library-exhibition.

Blumberg, David M. "On Celebrating Ourselves: A Bicentennial Round-Up." *National Jewish Monthly*, 1976, 4.

"B'nai B'rith Annual Convention I.O.B.B." *Cincinnati Enquirer*, January 22, 1877, 7.

Bosis, Lilian Vernon de. "The Baths of Diocletian: Sculptor's Ideal Studio." *Cincinnati Enquirer*, September 19, 1909, C7.

Brevard, Marie. "History of a Memorial Gateway." *Confederate Veteran* 22, no. 1 (January 1914): 38–39.

"Bronze Bust May Adorn Public Site in Louisville, Lincoln the Subject." *Courier-Journal* (Louisville, KY), August 4, 1900, 7.

Bruce, Philip Alexander. *History of the University of Virginia, 1819–1919: The Lengthened Shadow of One Man*. Vol. 5. New York: Macmillan, 1922.

Bush-Brown, Henry K. "Sir Moses Ezekiel: American Sculptor." *Art and Archaeology: The Arts Through the Ages* 11, no. 6 (June 1921): 227–34.

"Bust of I. M. Wise: Present from His Congregation Soon to Be in Cincinnati." *New York Times*, May 9, 1900, 6.

"Bust of the Venerable Isaac M. Wise Completed in Clay by Ezekiel the Sculptor." *Cincinnati Enquirer*, August 28, 1899, 10.

"Cadet's Monument." *Alexandria Gazette and Virginia Advertiser*, June 21, 1899, 1.

Catalogue of Mr. Henry C. Ezekiel's Private Collection of Sculptures and Pictures. Cincinnati: Traxel Art, 1930.

"Centennial Monument of Religious Liberty." *Jewish Record*, January 21, 1876.

Chapman, Conrad Wise. *Ten Months in the "Orphan Brigade": Conrad Wise Chapman's Civil War Memoir*. Edited by Ben L. Bassham. Kent, OH: Kent State University Press, 1999.

"The Charleston Trip." *The Cadet* (Virginia Military Institute) 4, no. 1 (September 23, 1910): 1.

Clement, Clara Erskine, and Laurence Hutton. *Artists of the Nineteenth Century and Their Works: A Handbook*. Vol. 1. Rev. ed. Boston: Houghton, Mifflin, 1883.

Cobb, Sanford H. *The Rise of Religious Liberty in America: A History*. New York: Macmillan, 1902.

Cohen, Lionel de R. "Wrong Praise for the Jew." *New York Times*, April 25, 1899, 6.

Collman, Sophie. "An October Anniversary: Sir Moses Ezekiel." *Union Home Study Magazine* 13, no. 2 (October 1920): 4–5.

"Crawford Figure Retrieved: Museum Gets Statue of Sculptor." *Richmond News Leader*, October 23, 1952, 21.

"Critics Praise Statue of Jackson: Sculptor Has Also Completed Master Figure of the First Napoleon." *Richmond Times-Dispatch*, April 8, 1909.

Degas, Edward. *The Letters of Edgar Degas*. Edited by Theodore Reff. 3 vols. New York: Wildenstein Plattner Institute, 2020. Distributed by Pennsylvania State University Press.

Didier, Eugene L. "American Authors and Artists in Rome." *Lippincott's Magazine of Popular Literature and Science* 34 (November 1884): 491–95.

Doré, Gustave. *The Legend of the Wandering Jew: A Series of Twelve Designs*. Philadelphia: George Gebbie, 1873.

Doyle, Arthur Conan. *The History of Spiritualism*. New York: Doran, 1926.

D. P. "The Jews in Art." *American Israelite*, June 14, 1900, 4.

Everyone Comes to America with a Dream: What's Yours? Philadelphia: National Museum of American Jewish History, n.d. Brochure.

"Ezekiel Bust of Lincoln on Exhibition in Cincinnati." *Cincinnati Times-Star*, February 12, 1927.

"Ezekiel, Famous Sculptor, Dies in Rome." *Cincinnati Enquirer*, March 28, 1917, 9.

Ezekiel, Jacob. "The Jews of Richmond." *Publications of the American Jewish Historical Society* 4 (1896): 21–27.

———. "Persecutions of the Jews in 1840." *Publications of the American Jewish Historical Society* 8 (1900): 141–45.

Ezekiel, Moses. "The Ghetto and the Jews in Rome." *Jewish Record*, September 8, 1876.

———. "Impressive Were the Ceremonies." *Cincinnati Enquirer*, July 14, 1901, 8.

———. "Keats-Shelley Memorial." *New York Times*, April 17, 1909, 245.

———. *Moses Jacob Ezekiel: Memoirs from the Baths of Diocletian*. Edited by Joseph Gutmann and Stanley F. Chyet. Detroit: Wayne State University Press, 1975.

———. "To the Editor of the *Dispatch*." *Richmond Times-Dispatch*, letter dated December 15, 1892. [Publication date of letter unknown.]

"Ezekiel-Mosler: Two Famous Cincinnatians." *American Israelite*, March 31, 1898, 8.

"Ezekiel Must Move." *American Art News* 8, no. 20 (February 26, 1910): 5.

"Ezekiel Refuses to Move." *New York Times*, January 30, 1910, 18.

"Ezekiel's Bronze Poe Unveiled at Last." *American Art News* 20, no. 3 (October 29, 1921): 3.

"Ezekiel, Sculptor, Arrives: Here to Attend Unveiling of His Statue of Jefferson in Charlottesville." *New York Times*, May 25, 1910, 9.

"Ezekiel's Famous Bronze Bust, 'The Christ,' Sold to Unknown Purchaser." *Cincinnati Enquirer*, July 18, 1902, 12.

"Ezekiel's Models and Letters to the Committee Not Entirely Satisfactory." *News and Advance* (Lynchburg, VA), November 10, 1892, 4.

"Ezekiel's Models Not Liked: Why the Virginia Committee Will Select Another Sculptor." *New York Times*, November 10, 1892, 6.

"Ezekiel's 'Poe' Burned." *American Art News* 12, no. 13 (January 2, 1914): 5.

"Ezekiel's 'Poe' Burned." *New York Times*, December 28, 1913, C4.

"Ezekiel's Statue of Thomas Jefferson: Splendid Specimen of Art Unveiled Last Week." *Richmond Times*, November 17, 1901.

"Ezekiel Statue to Be Unveiled." *Richmond Times-Dispatch*, June 8, 1910.

"Ezekiel, the Celebrated Sculptor." *Cincinnati Enquirer*, March 30, 1896, 4.

"Famed Cincinnati Sculptor Expires in Italian Capital." *Commercial Tribune* (Cincinnati), March 28, 1917, 1.

"Fighter, Too: Sir Moses Ezekiel Tells a War Story." *Courier-Journal* (Louisville, KY), November 8, 1901, 10.

"Fine Frescoes Recovered." *New York Times*, February 4, 1912, 31.

"Forget the Past, Wilson Bids South." *New York Times*, June 5, 1914, 2.

Friddell, Guy. "An Ashtray Desperado by Accident." *Virginian-Pilot* (Hampton Roads), August 9, 1974.

"'Friendship' Auction: It Writes Ironic Finis to the McLean Legend." *Life* 24, no. 20 (May 17, 1948): 44–45.

Gallagher, Daniel J. *The Catholic Centennial Fountain Illustrated: A Tribute of the Catholics of America to the Centennial of the Nation's Birth*. Philadelphia: Daniel J. Gallagher, 1877.

Grady, Henry W. "The New South." In *The Speeches of Henry W. Grady, with a Biographical Sketch of His Life*, 9–20. Atlanta: Chas. P. Byrd, 1895.

"Gray and Blue Join: Unite in Unveiling Great Confederate Monument." *Washington Post*, June 5, 1914, 3.

Gregorovius, Ferdinand. *The Ghetto and the Jews of Rome*. Translated by Moses Hades. 1853. Reprint, New York: Schocken Books, 1948.

Grusd, Edward E. "B'nai B'rith Rededicates 'Liberty.'" *B'nai B'rith Magazine*, November 1936, 46–47.

Harris, Walter Edward. "Heroism of V.M.I. Cadets at New Market Will Be Commemorated in Enduring Bronze." *Richmond Times-Dispatch*, June 21, 1903.

Hawthorne, Nathaniel. *The Marble Faun*. New York: Hurst, 1860.

"Hebrew Orphan Home Gets Ezekiel's Studio Register." *Jewish Telegraph Agency*, July 10, 1931. https://www.jta.org/archive/hebrew-orphan-home-gets-ezekiels-studio-register.

Hebrew Standard, April 6, 1917, 12. [Author and title unknown.]

"Help the Orphans: By Buying Fine and Artistic Drawings." *Cincinnati Enquirer*, May 4, 1882, 4.

Henderson, Helen W. *The Art Treasures of Washington*. Boston: L. C. Page, 1912.

Herbert, Hilary A. *History of the Arlington Confederate Monument*. Washington, DC: n.p., 1914.

Hermann, Georg. "Moses Ezekiel." *Ost und West* 3 (December 1903): 805–14.

"Heroes of the Stars and Bars Will Have Memory Perpetuated on Johnson's Island." *Cincinnati Enquirer*, June 8, 1910, 9.

Herzl, Theodor. *The Jewish State*. Translated by Sylvie d'Avigdor. 1896. Reprint, Garden City, NY: Dover Publications, 1988.

Hess, Moses. *Rome and Jerusalem: A Study in Jewish Nationalism*. Translated with an introduction by Meyer Waxman. 1918. Reprint, New York: Bloch, 1943.

"Historic Tower as Studio: Italy Gives Moses Ezekiel Belisarius Tower in Aurelian Wall." *New York Times*, May 22, 1910, 23.

Hoffman, A. R. "Exhibit at Princeton Is Canceled over Demands That Two Jewish Artists from Dixie Be Removed." *New York Sun*, April 4, 2022. https://www.nysun.com/article/exhibit-at-princeton-is-canceled-over-demands-that-two-jewish-artists-from-dixie-be-removed.

"Hospital in Royal Palace." *New York Times*, January 19, 1915, 6.

Howard, John Clarke. "Recollections of New Market." *Confederate Veteran* 34, no. 2 (February 1926): 57–59.

Ingram, J. S. *The Centennial Exposition, Described and Illustrated*. Philadelphia: Hubbard Bros., 1876.

In Memoriam: Jesse Seligman. New York: Press of Philip Cowen, 1894.

"Isaac Mayer Wise Is Honored by Son." *New York Times*, June 17, 1956, 49.

"Isaac M. Wise Memorial Window." *American Israelite*, January 21, 1909, 4.

"Israel: A Symbolical Work Modelled After the Crucifixion." *American Israelite*, June 23, 1904, 3.

"Israel: A Symbolical Work Modelled After the Crucifixion." *Jewish Exponent*, May 1, 1904, 8, 10.

"Israel: A Symbolical Work Modelled After the Crucifixion." *New York Herald*. May 1904.

"Items of Interest in the Jewish World." *Hebrew Standard*, July 5, 1912, 4.

"Items of Interest in the Jewish World." *Hebrew Standard*, March 25, 1921, 4.

Ives, Halsey C., Charles M. Kurtz, and George Julian Zolnay. *Illustrations of Selected Works in the Various National Sections of the Department of Art with Complete List of Awards by the International Jury, Universal Exposition St. Louis, 1904*. St. Louis: Louisiana Purchase Exposition Company, 1904.

"Jefferson Statue Shipped." *Courier-Journal* (Louisville, KY), May 8, 1900, 3.

Jefferson, Thomas. *Jefferson's Extracts from the Gospels: "The Philosophy of Jesus" and "The Life and Morals of Jesus."* Edited by Dickinson W. Adams. Princeton, NJ: Princeton University Press, 1983.

"Jewish Churches in Big Convention." *New York Times*, January 17, 1909, 8.

"A Jewish Painter's Idea of Jesus." *Literary Digest* 29, no. 2 (1904): 51–52.

"A Jewish Painter's Idea of Jesus." *New Era Illustrated Magazine* 5, no. 1 (1904): 75–76.

The Jewish Publication Society: Twenty-Fifth Anniversary. Philadelphia: Jewish Publication Society of America, 1913.

"Joan of Arc Statue." *American Art News* 13, no. 1 (October 10, 1914): 5.

Johnson, Rossiter, ed. *A History of the World's Columbian Exposition*, 4 vols. New York: D. Appleton, 1897–98.

J. W. W. "The Ezekiel Bronzes." *Bulletins of the University of Virginia: Alumni Bulletin*, n.s., 7, no. 2 (April 1907): 188–92.

Kabler, Phil. "Capitol Building Commission Again Stonewalls on Stonewall Statue, Approves Flooring." *Charleston Gazette-Mail*, July 14, 2021. https://www.wvgazettemail.com/news/capitol-building-commission-again-stonewalls-on-stonewall-statue-approves-flooring/article_82ee9114-4cb8-5fba-82c0-a84ec117f4e3.html.

Krauskopf, Joseph. "Consecration of the Isaac M. Wise Memorial Window." *Jewish Voice* (St. Louis), January 29, 1909, 5.

———. *Sunday Discourses Before the Reform Congregation Keneseth Israel: Series I, 1887–88*. Philadelphia: Oscar Klonower, 1888.

———. *Sunday Discourses Before the Reform Congregation Keneseth Israel: Series XXII, 1908–1909*. Philadelphia: Oscar Klonower, 1909.

Lapin, Andrew. "Outrage as Jewish Art Exhibit at Princeton Is Canceled over Ties to the Confederacy." *Jerusalem Post*, March 30, 2022. https://www.timesofisrael.com/outrage-as-jewish-art-exhibit-at-princeton-is-canceled-over-ties-to-the-confederacy.

"Letter from Hon. Simon Wolf." *Jewish Record*, February 21, 1877.

"The Libby Prison Statue." *Richmond Times-Dispatch*, November 10, 1892, 2.

Lippincott, J. B. *Visitor's Guide to the Centennial Exhibition and Philadelphia*. Philadelphia: J. B. Lippincott, 1876.

"List of Gifts to the University." *Alumni Bulletin* (University of Virginia), 3rd ser., 5, no. 2 (April 1912): 150–77.

Liszt, Franz. *The Letters of Franz Liszt to Marie zu Sayn-Wittgenstein*. Edited and translated by Howard E. Hugo. Cambridge, MA: Harvard University Press, 1953.

———. *Letters to Olga Von Meyendorff, 1871–1886*. Cambridge, MA: Harvard University Press, 1979.

"Longfellow in Marble: A Heroic Reminder of the Famous in Antique." *Cincinnati Times*, 1890, 70.

Louis, Charles. "Letter to the Editor." *American Israelite*, February 23, 1877, 80.

Magee, Richard. *Magee's Illustrated Guide of Philadelphia and the Centennial Exhibition: A Guide and Description to All Places of Interest in or About Philadelphia, to the Centennial Grounds and Buildings, and Fairmount Park*. 2nd ed. Philadelphia: Richard Magee and Son, 1876.

Mark, A. S. "Isaac Mayer Wise Memorial Window." In *Reform Congregation Keneseth Israel Year Book XXI, 1909–1910*, 54–55. Philadelphia: S. W. Goodman, 1910.

Mason, Caroline Atwater. *The Spell of Italy*. Boston: L. C. Page, 1909.
Mays, Jeffrey C., and Zachary Small. "Jefferson Statue Will Be Removed from N.Y.C. Council Chambers." *New York Times*, October 18, 2021. https://www.nytimes.com/2021/10/18/nyregion/thomas-jefferson-statue-ny-city-council.html.
"Men and Matters." *Cincinnati Enquirer*, October 13, 1896, 4.
"Men and Matters." *Cincinnati Enquirer*, April 28, 1900, 5.
Mitchell, Madeline. "'Devastating.' Hebrew Union College Closes 147-Year Residential Rabbinical Program in Cincinnati." *Cincinnati Enquirer*, April 11, 2022. https://www.cincinnati.com/story/news/2022/04/11/hebrew-union-college-closes-rabbinical-program-in-cincinnati/7283324001.
M. J. P. "A European Estimate of an American Sculptor," *The State* (Richmond, VA), July 7, 1886.
"The Monument in Arlington." *Confederate Veteran* 22, no. 7 (July 1914): 292–99.
"Monument over Southern Soldiers Buried on Johnson's Island, in Historic Hudson Bay." *Cincinnati Enquirer*, May 22, 1910, 17.
"The Monument to General Robert E. Lee: History of the Movement for Its Erection." *Southern Historical Society Papers* 17 (1889): 187–335.
"Monument to John W. Daniel." *Alexandria Gazette and Virginia Advertiser*, June 27, 1911, 1.
"More Honors for Ezekiel." *Richmond Times-Dispatch*, 1909. [Month and day unknown.]
"Morgan Declines $100,000 Painting." *New York Times*, April 12, 1908, 18.
"Moses Ezekiel Home Again." *The Cadet* (Virginia Military Institute) 3, no. 25 (June 13, 1910): 2.
"Mrs. Alsop Has Hard Trip: Reaches Rome in Downpour at Night—Entertained by Ezekiel." *New York Times*, February 27, 1910, 20.
"Munificent: Gift of Messrs. Bernheim to the City." *Courier-Journal* (Louisville, KY), September 21, 1899, 1.
Norton, Frank H., ed. *Frank Leslie's Historical Register of the United States Centennial Exposition, 1876*. New York: Frank Leslie's, 1877.
"Obituary: Sir Moses Ezekiel." *American Art News* 15, no. 25 (March 31, 1917): 4.
Odenheimer, Cordelia Powell, Elizabeth B. Bashinsky, Lutie Hailey Walcott, Mrs. Eugene Little, Mrs. J. Norment Powell, Elizabeth T. Sells, Mrs. Frank A. Walke, and Maude E. Merchant. "Sir Moses Ezekiel." *Confederate Veteran* 25, no. 7 (July 1917): 329.
"Of Interest to Jewish Readers." *New Era Illustrated Magazine* 5, no. 6 (1904): 652.
"Opening Address by President Wise." *Year Book of the Central Conference of American Rabbis* 7 (1897–98): vi–xiii.
Oppenheim, Samson D. "Moses Jacob Ezekiel." *American Jewish Year Book* 19 (1917): 227–32.
Page, Rosewell. *Thomas Nelson Page: A Memoir of a Virginia Gentleman*. New York: Charles Scribner's Sons, 1923.
Peixotto, Benjamin F., ed. *The Menorah: A Monthly Magazine, Official Organ of the B'nai B'rith* 7 (July–December 1889): 219–20.
Peters, Madison C. "Dr. Peters on the Jew." *New York Times*, April 27, 1899, 6.
———. *The Jew as a Patriot*. Introduction by Oscar S. Straus. New York: Baker and Taylor, 1902.
———. "Jews in America." *Sunday Magazine of the Evening Star* (Washington, DC), July 30, 1904, 5–6, 19.
———. *The Jews in America: A Short Story of Their Part in the Building of the Republic*. Philadelphia: John C. Winston, 1905.
———. *Justice to the Jew: The Story of What He Has Done for the World*. London: Tennyson Neely, 1899.
———. "Peters Praises the Jews." *New York Times*, March 9, 1899, 4.
"Philadelphia Art News." *American Art News* 3, no. 72 (March 25, 1905): 7.
Philipson, David. "Jesse Seligman Memorial." *New York Times*, April 24, 1896, 10.
———. "Moses Jacob Ezekiel." *Publications of the American Jewish Historical Society* 28 (1922): 1–62.
———. *My Life as an American Jew*. Cincinnati: John G. Kidd and Son, 1941.
Pinsker, Leo. *Auto-Emancipation*. Translated by D. S. Blondheim. 1882. Reprint, New York: Maccabaean, 1906.
Pollard, Edward A. *The Lost Cause: A New Southern History of the War of the Confederates*. New York: E. B. Treat, 1866.
Polson, Beth. "Carry Me Back to Ole Virginny." *Washington Post*, February 17, 1974, E1, E3.

———. "Last Ezekiel Statues in Place at Gardens." *Ledger-Star* (Norfolk, VA), August 8, 1974, A8.

Pratt, Gregory, Kori Rumore, Sophie Sherry, and Gregory Royal Pratt. "Seeking to 'Protect Public Safety,' Mayor Lori Lightfoot Removes Christopher Columbus Statues Overnight from Chicago Parks 'Until Further Notice.'" *Chicago Tribune*, July 24, 2020. https://www.chicagotribune.com/politics/ct-chicago-christopher-columbus-statue-grant-park-lori-lightfoot-20200724-2hsbobbt7ndmpmkgyh6vfl7cvq-story.html.

Proceedings Connected with the Unveiling of the Statue of Senator John Warwick Daniel. Lynchburg, VA: n.p., 1915.

Proceedings of the General Convention of the Independent Order of B'nai B'rith, Philadelphia, January 26–30, 1879. New York: G. Van der Potendyk and W. Cahn Printers, 1879.

"Proposed Monuments: Louisville, KY." *Monumental News: The Granite News* 3, no. 33 (September 1900): 514.

"The Proposed Statue of President William Henry Harrison." *Frank Leslie's Illustrated Newspaper*, October 22, 1887, 157.

Ramos, Manny. "Italian American Group was Allowed to Borrow Columbus Statue to Clean It." *Chicago Sun Times*, October 21, 2021. https://chicago.suntimes.com/news/2021/10/12/22723167/italian-american-group-returns-columbus-statue-chicago-park-district-cleanup-graffiti.

"Recluse Now Greeter." *Richmond News Leader*, June 15, 1960.

"Religious Liberty: A Criticism of M. Ezekiel's Group by Dr. Leopold Julius––a Great Compliment to a Former Citizen of Richmond." *Richmond Daily Dispatch*, June 5, 1876, 1.

"Religious Liberty." *Philadelphia Inquirer*, December 1, 1876.

Report of the Executive Committee of the Constitution Grand Lodge, I.O.B.B., 1875–1876. New York: M. Thalmessinger, Stationer and Printer, 1877.

Richardson, Benjamin Ward. *Diseases of Modern Life*. New York: Bermingham, 1882.

Ripa, Cesare. *Baroque and Rococo Pictorial Imagery: The 1758–60 Hertel Edition of Ripa's "Iconologia" with 20 Engraved Illustrations*. Translated with an introduction and commentaries by Edward A. Maser. New York: Dover Publications, 1971.

"Rome Is Still Chilly." *New York Times*, May 11, 1913, 34.

"Rome to Have New American Officials." *New York Times*, June 19, 1909, 2.

Scharf, J. Thomas, and Thompson Westcott. *History of Philadelphia, 1609–1884*. Vol. 3. Philadelphia: L. H. Everts, 1884.

Schonfeld, Zach. "Robert E. Lee's Direct Descendant Denounces Charlottesville White Nationalists: 'There's No Place For that Hate.'" *Newsweek*, August 15, 2017. https://www.newsweek.com/robert-e-lee-statue-charlottesville-donald-trump-white-nationalists-651208.

"Sculptor to Be Buried." *Cincinnati Enquirer*, April 3, 1918, 3.

"Sculpture." *Monumental News* 12, no. 7 (July 1900): 396.

Shapira, Ian. "VMI Removes Statue of Confederate Gen. Stonewall Jackson After Long Resistance." *Washington Post*, December 7, 2020. https://www.washingtonpost.com/local/vmi-stonewall-jackson-statue-removed/2020/12/07/a4721c98-3891-11eb-9276-ae0ca72729be_story.html.

Shapiro, T. Rees. "Descendants of Rebel Sculptor: Remove Confederate Memorial from Arlington Cemetery." *Washington Post*, August 18, 2017. https://www.washingtonpost.com/local/virginia-politics/descendants-of-rebel-sculptor-remove-confederate-memorial-from-arlington-national-cemetery/2017/08/18/d4da6a3e-842b-11e7-ab27-1a21a8e006ab_story.html.

Shelley, Percy Bysshe. "A Defence of Poetry." In *Selected Prose Works of Shelley*, 75–118. London: Watts, 1915.

———. *Essays and Letters*. Edited with an introduction by Ernest Rhys. 1886. Reprint, Freeport, NY: Books for Libraries Press, 1971.

———. *Selected Poems and Prose*. Edited by Jack Donovan and Cian Duffy. New York: Penguin, 2016.

Shimron, Yonat. "Princeton University Scraps Exhibit of Jewish American Artists with Confederate Ties." *Religion News Service*, February 10, 2022. https://religionnews .com /2022 /02 /10 /princeton-university-scraps-exhibit-of -jewish-american-artists-with-confederate-ties.

"Sir Moses Ezekiel." *American Art News* 19, no. 26 (April 9, 1921): 6.

"Sir Moses Ezekiel." *Cincinnati Enquirer*, November 30, 1913, B8.

"Sir Moses Ezekiel." *Confederate Veteran* 25, no. 5 (May 1917): 235–36.
"Sir Moses Ezekiel Burial." *New York Times*, March 31, 1921, 12.
"Sir Moses Ezekiel Home Again." *Hebrew Standard* 55, no. 23 (June 4, 1910): 3, 7.
"Sir Moses Ezekiel, Native of Richmond, Passes Away in Rome." *Richmond Times-Dispatch*, March 28, 1917, 1.
"Sir Moses Ezekiel's Prospective Visit." *Richmond News*, September 21, 1901.
Smith, Goldwin. "England's Abandonment of the Protectorate of Turkey." *Contemporary Review* 31 (February 1878): 603–19.
———. "New Light on the Jewish Question." *North American Review* 153, no. 417 (August 1891): 129–43.
Soave, Robby. "Art Curator Accuses Princeton of 'Anti-Intellectual Surrender to Cancel Culture.'" *Reason*, April 5, 2022. https://reason.com/2022/04/05/princeton-university-jewish-art-cancel-culture-confederacy.
Spencer, Leslie. "Where the Buck Stops." *Princetonians for Free Speech*, June 27, 2022. https://princetoniansforfreespeech.org/blogs/news/where-the-buck-stops.
"Statue for Virginia." *American Art News* 7, no. 7 (November 28, 1908): 2.
"Statue for Virginia." *New York Times*, November 22, 1908, 20.
"Statue of Jefferson Presented to University of Virginia." *Richmond Virginian*, June 15, 1910.
"Statue of 'Stonewall Jackson.'" *Cincinnati Enquirer*, September 28, 1910, 4.
"Statue to Religious Liberty." *Jewish Record*, September 29, 1876.
"Statue to Religious Liberty: The Gift of the Israelites of America to the Nation." *Jewish Record*, December 1, 1876.
Stiles, Pauline. *New Footprints in Old Places*. San Francisco: Paul Elder, 1917.
Stolberg, Sheryl Gay. "'They Answered the Call,' Obama Says of Veterans." *New York Times*, May 25, 2009. https://www.nytimes.com/2009/05/26/us/politics/26wreath.html.
Strahan, Edward, ed. *The Art Treasures of America*. Vol. 1. Philadelphia: George Barrie, 1879.
Straus, Oscar S. *Under Four Administrations: From Cleveland to Taft*. Boston: Houghton Mifflin, 1922.
"Study Daringly Original, Says Rabbi Philipson of Ezekiel's Conception of Deity." *Cincinnati Enquirer*, March 28, 1921, 12.
"Success of a Cincinnati Artist." *Israelite*, September 12, 1873, 6.
Taft, Lorado. *The History of American Sculpture*. New York: Macmillan, 1903.
Taylor, Mary Argyle. "A Personal Appreciation of Sir Moses Jacob Ezekiel." *Alumni Bulletin* (University of Virginia) 10, no. 4–5 (August–October 1917): 327–38.
"Thomas Jefferson Monument, Louisville, KY: Sir Moses Ezekiel, Sculptor." *Monumental News: A Monthly Journal of Monumental Art* 14, no. 1 (January 1902): 19.
Tincker, Mary Agnes. *The Jewel in the Lotos*. London: W. H. Allen, 1884.
"Tribute to Ezekiel by President Harding Is Received by Sculptor's Brother." *Cincinnati Enquirer*, April 24, 1921, A20.
"Triumph in Art: Ezekiel's Great Work for the Centennial—What a Foreign Journal Says of It." *Richmond Whig*, November 26, 1875.
Tuckerman, Henry T. *A Memorial of Horatio Greenough*. New York: Putnam, 1853.
"Tunnels Too Small: Jefferson Monument is Delayed in New York." *Courier-Journal* (Louisville, KY), June 4, 1900, 5.
"Two Israelites in Cincinnati Have Recently Attained High Distinction in Fine Arts." *American Israelite*, August 1, 1879, 6.
"Union of American Hebrew Congregations: Two Great Events at the Philadelphia Convention." *American Israelite*, December 24, 1908, 4.
United States Centennial Commission. *International Exhibition, 1876: Report of the Director-General*. Vol. 1. Washington, DC: Government Printing Office, 1880.
"The Unpaid Statue." *Jewish Record*, May 11, 1877.
"The Unpaid Statue." *Jewish Record*, May 25, 1877.
"Unpublished Bust of Lincoln by Sir Moses Jacob Ezekiel." *New York Times*, February 8, 1919.
"Unveiled: Ezekiel Statue of Thomas Jefferson." *Courier-Journal* (Louisville, KY), November 10, 1901, C1–2.

"Unveiling of Ezekiel's Statue of Jefferson." *Alumni Bulletin* (University of Virginia), 3rd ser., 3, no. 4 (August 1910): 363–78.
"Unveiling of the Bronze Homeric Group." *Alumni Bulletin* (University of Virginia), n.s., 7, no. 3 (July 1907): 230–45.
"Unveil Monument at Johnson's Island: Sculptor Sir Moses Ezekiel." *Sandusky (OH) Daily Register*, June 8, 1910.
Vosmaer, Carl. *The Amazon*. Translated by Elizabeth Jane Irving. New York: William S. Gottsberger, 1884.
Wagner, Richard. *Wagner on Music and Drama*. Edited by Albert Goldman and Evert Sprinchor. Translated by H. Ashton Ellis. New York: Da Capo Press, 1988.
Wallace, Alfred Russel. *The Scientific Aspect of the Supernatural*. London: F. Farrah, 1866.
"The Week in Art." *New York Times*, October 28, 1899, 22.
"Well-Known Sculptor: Death of Mr. Moses Ezekiel." *Paris Daily Rail*, March 31, 1917.
White, Barbara Ehrlich. *Renoir: His Life, Art, and Letters*. New York: Harry N. Abrams, 1984.
Whiting, Lilian. *Italy: The Magic Land*. Boston: Little, Brown, 1907.
"Who Are the Ten Greatest Virginians?" *Richmond Times-Dispatch*, March 22, 1931.
Wise, Isaac Mayer. *American Israelite*, July 14, 1882, 12. [Title unknown.]
———. "Editorial." *American Israelite*, June 8, 1899, 1.
Wise, Isidor. "The Sculptor and the Rabbi." *Union Home Study Magazine* 13, no. 2 (October 1920): 5.
Wise, John S. "The West Point of the Confederacy: Boys in Battle at New Market, Virginia, May 15, 1864." *Century Magazine* 37, no. 3 (January 1889): 461–71.
Wolf, Simon. *The American Jew as Patriot, Soldier and Citizen*. Philadelphia: Levytype, 1895.
———. "The B'nai B'rith and the Philadelphia Statue of Religious Liberty." In *Selected Addresses and Papers of Simon Wolf*, 277–80. Cincinnati: Union of American Hebrew Congregations, 1926.
———. "The Convention of 1874 and the Statue of Religious Liberty." *B'nai B'rith News* 13, no. 9 (May 1921): 9.
———. "Day of Atonement Address." In *Selected Addresses and Papers of Simon Wolf*, 247–59. Cincinnati: Union of American Hebrew Congregations, 1926.
———. "Patriotism and Religion." In *Selected Addresses and Papers of Simon Wolf*, 240–46. Cincinnati: Union of American Hebrew Congregations, 1926.
———. *The Presidents I Have Known, from 1860–1918*. Washington, DC: Press of Byron S. Adams, 1918.
Wolfe, Sheila. "Long Journey Home to End for Columbus." *Chicago Tribune*, May 15, 1966.
"Women's National Confederate Memorial." *Monumental News* 27, no. 8 (August 1915): 451.
Woodliff, Wayne. "Two Well-Traveled Ezekiels Added to Botanical Garden." *Ledger-Star* (Norfolk, VA), July 4, 1962.
Wrenshall, Katherine H. "An American Sculptor in Rome." *World's Work: A History of Our Time* 19 (November 1909–April 1910): 12255–64.

Secondary Sources

Agulhon, Maurice. *Marianne into Battle: Republican Imagery and Symbolism in France, 1789–1880*. Cambridge: Cambridge University Press, 1981.
Amishai-Maisels, Ziva. "The Jewish Jesus." *Journal of Jewish Art* 9 (1982): 84–104.
———. "Origins of the Jewish Jesus." In *Complex Identities: Jewish Consciousness and Modern Art*, edited by Matthew Baigell and Milly Heyd, 51–86. New Brunswick, NJ: Rutgers University Press, 2001.
Anderson, George K. *The Legend of the Wandering Jew*. Providence, RI: Brown University Press, 1965.
Ater, Renée. *Remaking Race and History: The Sculpture of Meta Warrick Fuller*. Berkeley: University of California Press, 2011.
Baskind, Samantha. "Arlington National Cemetery's Confederate Monument Has a Troubling History." *Washington Post*, October 7, 2022. https://www.washingtonpost.com/made-by-history/2022/10/07/arlington-national-cemetary-confederate-monument.
———. *Jewish Artists and the Bible in Twentieth-Century America*. University Park: Pennsylvania State University Press, 2014.
———. "Jewish Artists Begin to Make Their Mark." In *Yearning to Breathe Free: Jews in Gilded Age America*, edited by Adam D. Mendelsohn and

Jonathan D. Sarna, 109–56. Princeton, NJ: Princeton University Press, 2022.

———. "The Jewish Sculptor of the Confederacy." *Tablet Magazine*, January 21, 2021. https://www.tabletmag.com/sections/arts-letters/articles/stonewall-jackson-moses-jacob-ezekiel-vmi.

———. "Which Statues Should Fall?" *Jewish Renaissance*, October 2020, 13–15.

Beetham, Sarah. "From Spray Cans to Minivans: Contesting the Legacy of Confederate Soldier Monuments in the Era of 'Black Lives Matter.'" *Public Art Dialogue* 6, no. 1 (2016): 9–33.

———. "Sculpting the Citizen Soldier: Reproduction and National Memory, 1865–1917." PhD diss., University of Delaware, 2014.

Berkowitz, Michael. *The Jewish Self-Image in the West*. New York: New York University Press, 2000.

———. *Zionist Culture and West European Jewry Before the First World War*. Cambridge: Cambridge University Press, 1993.

Berman, Myron. *Richmond's Jewry, 1769–1976*. Charlottesville: University of Virginia Press, 1979.

Bertz, Inka. "Dreaming of Raphael: The Politics and Aesthetics of the *Michael-Beer-Stiftung* for Jewish Artists." *Ars Judaica* 16 (2020): 69–94.

Blair, William A. *Cities of the Dead*. Chapel Hill: University of North Carolina Press, 2004.

Bland, Kalman. *The Artless Jew: Medieval and Modern Affirmations and Denials of the Visual*. Princeton, NJ: Princeton University Press, 2000.

Blight, David W. *Race and Reunion: The Civil War in American Memory*. Cambridge, MA: Belknap Press of Harvard University Press, 2001.

Bogart, Michele H. *Public Sculpture and the Civic Ideal in New York City, 1890–1930*. Chicago: University of Chicago Press, 1989.

Bogen, Hyman. *The Luckiest Orphans: A History of the Hebrew Orphan Asylum of New York*. Urbana: University of Illinois Press, 1992.

Boylan, Alexis L., ed. *Ellen Emmet Rand: Gender, Art, and Business*. London: Bloomsbury Visual Arts, 2020.

Brandfon, Frederic. *Intimate Strangers: A History of Jews and Catholics in the City of Rome*. Philadelphia: Jewish Publication Society; Lincoln: University of Nebraska Press, 2023.

Brennan, James F. *The Reflection of the Dreyfus Affair in the European Press, 1897–1899*. New York: Peter Lang, 1998.

Brenner, David A. *Marketing Identities: The Invention of Jewish Ethnicity in "Ost und West."* Detroit: Wayne State University Press, 1998.

Brooks, Van Wyck. *The Dream of Arcadia: American Writers and Artists in Italy, 1760–1915*. New York: E. P. Dutton, 1958.

Brown, Sterling A. "The Muted South." *Callaloo* 21, no. 4 (Fall 1998): 767–78. [Originally published in 1945.]

Buckler, Helen. *Doctor Dan: Pioneer in American Surgery*. Boston: Little, Brown, 1954.

Buick, Kirsten Pai. *Child of the Fire: Mary Edmonia Lewis and the Problem of Art History's Black and Indian Subject*. Durham, NC: Duke University Press, 2010.

Butler, Ruth, and Suzanne Glover Lindsay, with Alison Luchs, Douglas Lewis, Cynthia J. Mills, and Jeffrey Weidman. *European Sculpture of the Nineteenth Century*. Washington, DC: National Gallery of Art; New York: Oxford University Press, 2000.

Byer, Robert H. "Words, Monuments, Beholders: The Visual Arts in Hawthorne's *The Marble Faun*." In *American Iconology: New Approaches to Nineteenth-Century Art and Literature*, edited by David C. Miller, 163–85. New Haven, CT: Yale University Press, 1993.

Cash, Sarah. "'Encouraging American Genius': Collecting American Art at the Corcoran Gallery of Art." In *Corcoran Gallery of Art: American Paintings to 1945*, edited by Sarah Cash, 15–37. Manchester: Hudson Hills Press, 2011.

Chyet, Stanley F. "Moses Jacob Ezekiel: A Childhood in Richmond." *American Jewish Historical Quarterly* 62, no. 3 (March 1973): 286–94.

———. "Moses Jacob Ezekiel: Art and Celebrity." *American Jewish Archives* 35, no. 1 (April 1983): 40–51.

Coffin, David R. *The Villa d'Este at Tivoli*. Princeton, NJ: Princeton University Press, 1960.

Cohen, Naomi Wiener. "The Reaction of Reform Judaism in America to Political Zionism (1897–1922)." *Publications of the American Jewish Historical Society* 40, no. 4 (June 1951): 361–94.

Cohen, Richard I. *Jewish Icons*. Berkeley: University of California Press, 1998.

———. "The 'Wandering Jew' from Medieval Legend to Modern Metaphor." In *The Art of Being Jewish in Modern Times*, edited by Barbara Kirshenblatt-Gimblett and Jonathan Karp, 147–75. Philadelphia: University of Pennsylvania Press, 2008.

Cohen, Stan, and Keith Gibson. *Moses Ezekiel: Civil War Soldier, Renowned Sculptor*. Missoula, MT: Pictorial Histories, 2007.

Corn, Wanda M. *Georgia O'Keeffe: Living Modern*. New York: Delmonico Books / Prestel, 2017. Exhibition catalog.

Couper, William. *One Hundred Years at V.M.I.* Vol. 2. Richmond, VA: Garrett and Massie, 1939.

Cox, Karen L. "The Confederate Monument: A Token of Reconciliation." In *Monuments to the Lost Cause: Women, Art, and the Landscapes of Southern Memory*, edited by Cynthia J. Mills and Pamela H. Simpson, 148–62. Knoxville: University of Tennessee Press, 2003.

———. *Dixie's Daughters: The United Daughters of the Confederacy and the Preservation of Confederate Culture*. Gainesville: University Press of Florida, 2003.

———. *No Common Ground: Confederate Monuments and the Ongoing Fight for Racial Justice*. Chapel Hill: University of North Carolina Press, 2021.

Crane, Sylvia E. *White Silence: Greenough, Powers, and Crawford, American Sculptors in Nineteenth-Century Italy*. Coral Gables: University of Miami Press, 1972.

Craven, Wayne. *Sculpture in America*. New York: Thomas Y. Crowell, 1968.

Cubitt, Geoffrey. "Martyrs of Charity, Heroes of Solidarity: Catholic and Republican Responses to the Fire at the Bazar de la Charité, Paris, 1897." *French History* 21, no. 3 (2007): 331–52.

Dabakis, Melissa. *A Sisterhood of Sculptors: American Artists in Nineteenth-Century Rome*. University Park: Pennsylvania State University Press, 2014.

Davis, William C. *The Battle of New Market*. Garden City, NY: Doubleday, 1975.

Dean, Eric T., Jr. *Shook over Hell: Post-Traumatic Stress, Vietnam, and the Civil War*. Cambridge, MA: Harvard University Press, 1997.

Dennis, James M. *Karl Bitter: Architectural Sculptor, 1867–1915*. Madison: University of Wisconsin Press, 1967.

Dickerson, C. D., III. "Sculpture at the National Gallery of Art: From Andrew W. Mellon to Katherine Seney Simpson to Today." In *Rodin in the United States: Confronting the Modern*, edited by Antoinette Le Normand-Romain, 185–91. Williamstown, MA: Clark Art Institute; New Haven, CT: Yale University Press, 2022. Exhibition catalog.

Dimmick, Lauretta. "Mythic Proportion: Bertel Thorvaldsen's Influence in America." In *Thorvaldsen: L'ambiente, l'influsso, il mito*, edited by Patrick Kragelund and Mogens Nykjar, 169–91. Rome: L'Erma di Bretschneider, 1991.

———. "Veiled Memories, or, Thomas Crawford in Rome." In *The Italian Presence in American Art, 1760–1860*, edited by Irma B. Jaffe, 176–93. New York: Fordham University Press, 1989.

Doss, Erika. *Memorial Mania: Public Feeling in America*. Chicago: University of Chicago Press, 2010.

Driggs, Sarah Shields, Richard Guy Wilson, and Robert P. Winthrop. *Richmond's Monument Avenue*. Chapel Hill: University of North Carolina Press, 2001.

Dryfhout, John H. *The Work of Augustus Saint-Gaudens*. Hanover, NH: University Press of New England, 1982.

Edelmann, R. "Ahasuerus, the Wandering Jew: Origin and Background." In *The Wandering Jew: Essays in the Interpretation of a Christian Legend*, edited by Galit Hasan-Rokem and Alan Dundes, 1–10. Bloomington: Indiana University Press, 1986.

Epstein, Lawrence J. *The Dream of Zion: The Story of the First Zionist Congress*. Lanham, MD: Rowman and Littlefield, 2016.

Evans, Eli N. *Judah P. Benjamin: The Jewish Confederate*. New York: Free Press, 1988.

Fairman, Charles E. *Art and Artists of the Capitol of the United States of America*. Washington, DC: Government Printing Office, 1927.

Faust, Drew Gilpin. *This Republic of Suffering: Death and the American Civil War*. 2008. Reprint, New York: Vintage Books, 2009.

Fink, Lois Marie. *American Art at the Nineteenth-Century Paris Salons*. Cambridge: Cambridge University Press, 1990.

Fisher, John. "Entitling." *Critical Inquiry* 11, no. 2 (December 1984): 286–98.

Fitzpatrick, Donovan, and Saul Saphire. *Navy Maverick: Uriah Phillips Levy*. Garden City, NY: Doubleday, 1963.

Fleming, E. McClung. "From Indian Princess to Greek Goddess: The American Image, 1783–1815." *Winterthur Portfolio* 3 (1967): 37–66.

Foster, Gaines M. *Ghosts of the Confederacy: Defeat, the Lost Cause, and the Emergence of the New South, 1865–1913*. New York: Oxford University Press, 1987.

Fryd, Vivien Green. *Art and Empire: The Politics of Ethnicity in the U.S. Capitol, 1815–1860*. New Haven, CT: Yale University Press, 1992.

Gal, Allon. "The Mission Motif in American Zionism (1898–1948)." *American Jewish History* 75, no. 4 (June 1986): 363–85.

Gardner, Albert TenEyck. *Yankee Stonecutters: The First American School of Sculpture, 1800–1850*. Freeport, NY: Books for Libraries Press, 1945.

Gerdts, William H. *American Neo-Classic Sculpture: The Marble Resurrection*. New York: Viking Press, 1973.

———. "Celebrities of the Grand Tour: The American Sculptors in Florence and Rome." In *The Lure of Italy: American Artists and the Italian Experience, 1760–1914*, edited by Theodore E. Stebbins Jr., 66–93. Boston: Boston Museum of Fine Arts; New York: Harry N. Abrams, 1992. Exhibition catalog.

———. "The Neoclassic Relief." In *Perspectives on American Sculpture Before 1925*, edited by Thayer Tolles, 2–23. New York: Metropolitan Museum of Art; New Haven, CT: Yale University Press, 2003.

Giberti, Bruno. *Designing the Centennial: A History of the 1876 International Exhibition in Philadelphia*. Lexington: University Press of Kentucky, 2002.

Gilbert, Barbara C. *Henry Mosler Rediscovered: A Nineteenth-Century American-Jewish Artist*. Los Angeles: Skirball Museum, 1995. Exhibition catalog.

Glants, Musya. *Where Is My Home? The Art and Life of the Russian Jewish Sculptor Mark Antokolsky, 1843–1902*. Lanham, MD: Rowman and Littlefield, 2010.

Goodman, Susan Tumarkin, ed. *The Emergence of Jewish Artists in Nineteenth-Century Europe*. New York: Merrell, 2001. Exhibition catalog.

Greenough, Sarah. *Alfred Stieglitz: The Key Set*. 2 vols. New York: Harry N. Abrams, 2002.

Greenstein, Howard. *Turning Point: Zionism and Reform Judaism*. Chico, CA: Scholars Press, 1981.

Greenwald, Alice M., ed. *Ezekiel's Vision: Moses Jacob Ezekiel and the Classical Tradition*. Philadelphia: National Museum of American Jewish History, 1985. Exhibition catalog.

Grusd, Edward E. *B'nai B'rith: The Story of a Covenant*. New York: Appleton-Century, 1966.

Gutmann, Joseph. "Jewish Participation in the Visual Arts of Eighteenth- and Nineteenth-Century America." *American Jewish Archives* 15, no. 1 (April 1963): 21–57.

———. "Jewish Themes in the Art of Moses Jacob Ezekiel." In *Ezekiel's Vision: Moses Jacob Ezekiel and the Classical Tradition*, edited by Alice M. Greenwald, 27–33. Philadelphia: National Museum of American Jewish History, 1985. Exhibition catalog.

Haskell, Francis, and Nicolas Penny. *Taste and the Antique: The Lure of Classical Sculpture, 1500–1900*. New Haven, CT: Yale University Press, 1981.

Heckscher, Morrison H. "The Metropolitan Museum of Art: An Architectural History." *Metropolitan Museum of Art Journal*, n.s., 53, no. 1 (Summer 1995): 1–80.

Herzl in Profile: Herzl's Image in the Applied Arts. Tel Aviv: Tel Aviv Museum, 1978. Exhibition catalog.

Hilmes, Oliver. *Franz Liszt: Musician, Celebrity, and Superstar*. Translated by Stewart Spencer. New Haven, CT: Yale University Press, 2016.

Hirschfeld, Fritz. *George Washington and the Jews*. Newark: University of Delaware Press, 2005.

Hooker, Zebulon Vance. "Moses Jacob Ezekiel: The Formative Years." *Virginia Magazine of History and Biography* 60, no. 2 (April 1952): 241–54.

Jacob, Kathryn Allamong. *Testament to Union: Civil War Monuments in Washington, D.C.* Photographs by Edwin Harlan Remsberg. Baltimore: Johns Hopkins University Press, 1998.

Jacobs, Maurice. "Two Generations of Jewish Literary Labor: Sixty Years of the Jewish Publication

Society of America." *Jewish Book Annual* 7 (1948–49): 89–100.

Janney, Caroline E. *Burying the Dead but Not the Past: Ladies' Memorial Associations and the Lost Cause*. Chapel Hill: University of North Carolina, 2008.

Kahn, Lothar. "Michael Beer (1800–1833)." In *Leo Baeck Institute Yearbook* 12, 149–60. London: East and West Library, 1967.

Kasson, Joy S. *Marble Queens and Captives: Women in Nineteenth-Century American Sculpture*. New Haven, CT: Yale University Press, 1990.

Kertzer, David I. *The Popes Against the Jews: The Vatican's Role in the Rise of Modern Anti-Semitism*. New York: Alfred A. Knopf, 2001.

Kirshenblatt-Gimblett, Barbara. *Destination Culture: Tourism, Museums, and Heritage*. Berkeley: University of California Press, 1988.

Kitschen, Friederike. *Als Kunstgeschichte populär wurde: Illustrierte Kunstbuchserien 1860–1960 und der Kanon der westlichen Kunst*. Berlin: Deutscher Verlag für Kunstwissenschaft, 2021.

Klein, Nancy H., and Jonathan Sarna, eds. *The Jews of Cincinnati*. Cincinnati: Center for the Study of the American Jewish Experience, 1989.

Korn, Bertram W. *American Jewry and the Civil War*. 1951. Reprint, Marietta, GA: R. Bemis, 1995.

Korshak, Yvonne. "The Liberty Cap as a Revolutionary Symbol in America and France." *Smithsonian Studies in American Art* 1, no. 2 (1987): 52–69.

Krainick, Clifford. "The Sir Moses Ezekiel Statue of Edgar Allan Poe in Baltimore." In *Myths and Realities: The Mysterious Mr. Poe*, edited by Benjamin Franklin Fisher, 48–57. Baltimore: Edgar Allan Poe Society, 1985.

Krowl, Michelle A. "'In the Spirit of Fraternity': The United States Government and the Burial of Confederate Dead at Arlington National Cemetery." *Virginia Magazine of History and Biography* 111, no. 2 (2003): 151–86.

Laqueur, Walter. *A History of Zionism*. New York: Schocken Books, 2003.

Leepson, Marc. *Saving Monticello: The Levy Family's Epic Quest to Rescue the House That Jefferson Built*. Charlottesville: University of Virginia Press, 2001.

Le Normand-Romain, Antoinette, and Christina Buley-Uribe. "1885–1915: The Era of Collectors." In *Rodin in the United States: Confronting the Modern*, edited by Antoinette Le Normand-Romain, 68–115. Williamstown, MA: Clark Art Institute; New Haven, CT: Yale University Press, 2022. Exhibition catalog.

Litvak, Olga. "Rome and Jerusalem: The Figure of Jesus in the Creation of Mark Antokol'skii." In *The Art of Being Jewish in Modern Times*, edited by Barbara Kirshenblatt-Gimblett and Jonathan Karp, 228–53. Philadelphia: University of Pennsylvania Press, 2008.

Lowe, Sue Davidson. *Stieglitz: A Memoir/Biography*. New York: Farrar, Straus and Giroux, 1983.

Manthorne, Katherine. *Restless Enterprise: The Art and Life of Eliza Pratt Greatorex*. Oakland: University of California Press, 2020.

Marcus, Jacob Rader, ed. *The Jew in the American World: A Source Book*. Detroit: Wayne State University Press, 1996.

———, ed. *Memoirs of American Jews, 1775–1865*. Vol. 1. Philadelphia: Jewish Publication Society of America.

Markens, Isaac. *Abraham Lincoln and the Jews*. New York: Printed for Isaac Markens, 1909.

McElya, Micki. *Clinging to Mammy: The Faithful Slave in Twentieth-Century America*. Cambridge, MA: Harvard University Press, 2007.

McNamara, Sean, dir. *Field of Lost Shoes*. Manhattan Beach, CA: Brookwell McNamara Entertainment, 2015.

Mendelsohn, Adam D. *Jewish Soldiers in the Civil War: The Union Army*. New York: New York University Press, 2022.

Meyer, Michael A. "American Reform Judaism and Zionism: Early Efforts at Rapprochement." *Studies in Zionism* 7 (Spring 1983): 49–64.

———. *Response to Modernity: A History of the Reform Movement in Judaism*. New York: Oxford University Press, 1988.

Moll, Jeffrey Richmond. "Sculpture and Spectacle: Horatio Greenough's *Christ* and *Lucifer*." *Winterthur Portfolio* 50, no. 4 (2016): 209–47.

Moore, Deborah Dash. *B'nai B'rith and the Challenge of Ethnic Leadership*. Albany: State University of New York Press, 1981.

Morris, Roy, Jr. *Ambrose Bierce: Alone in Bad Company*. New York: Crown, 1995.

Nash, Peter Adam. *The Life and Times of Moses Jacob Ezekiel: American Sculptor, Arcadian Knight.* Madison, NJ: Fairleigh Dickinson University Press, 2014.

Nochlin, Linda. "Degas and the Dreyfus Affair: A Portrait of the Artist as Anti-Semite." In *The Dreyfus Affair: Art, Truth, and Justice*, edited by Norman L. Kleeblatt, 96–116. Berkeley: University of California Press, 1987. Exhibition catalog.

Ofrat, Gideon. *One Hundred Years of Art in Israel.* Translated by Peretz Kidron. Boulder, CO: Westview Press, 1998.

Olin, Margaret. *The Nation Without Art: Examining Modern Discourses on Jewish Art.* Lincoln: University of Nebraska Press, 2001.

Orcutt, Kimberly, ed. *John Rogers: American Stories.* New York: New-York Historical Society, 2010. Exhibition catalog.

———. *Power and Posterity: American Art at Philadelphia's 1876 Centennial Exhibition.* University Park: Pennsylvania State University Press, 2017.

Pensler, Derek. *Theodor Herzl: The Charismatic Leader.* New Haven, CT: Yale University Press, 2020.

A People in Print: Jewish Journalism in America. Philadelphia: National Museum of American Jewish History, 1987. Exhibition catalog.

Poulet, Anne L., with Guilhem Scherf, Ulrike D. Mathies, Christoph Frank, Claude Vandalle, Dean Walker, and Monique Barbier. *Jean-Antoine Houdon: Sculptor of the Enlightenment.* Washington, DC: National Gallery of Art; Chicago: University of Chicago Press, 2003. Exhibition catalog.

Promey, Sally. "The 'Return' of Religion in the Scholarship of American Art." *Art Bulletin* 85, no. 3 (September 2003): 581–603.

Promey, Sally, and David Morgan, eds. *The Visual Culture of American Religions.* Berkeley: University of California Press, 2001.

Pryor, Elizabeth Brown. *Reading the Man: A Portrait of Robert E. Lee Through His Private Letters.* New York: Viking Press, 2007.

Ragosta, John A. *Religious Freedom: Jefferson's Legacy, America's Creed.* Charlottesville: University of Virginia Press, 2013.

Rand, Harry. *Horatio Greenough and the Form Majestic: The Biography of the Nation's First Washington Monument.* Washington, DC: Smithsonian Institution, 2020.

Read, Piers Paul. *The Dreyfus Affair: The Scandal That Tore France in Two.* New York: Bloomsbury, 2012.

Reinis, J. G. *The Portrait Medallions of David d'Angers: An Illustrated Catalogue of David's Contemporary and Retrospective Portraits in Bronze.* New York: Polymath Press, 1999.

Robertson, Charles J. *American Louvre: A History of the Renwick Gallery Building.* Washington, DC: Smithsonian American Art Museum; London: D Giles Limited, 2015.

Robinson, Roxana. *Georgia O'Keeffe: A Life.* Hanover, NH: University Press of New England, 1989.

Rogers, Millard F., Jr. *Sketches and Bozzetti by American Sculptors, 1880–1950.* Cincinnati: Cincinnati Art Museum, 1987.

Rosen, Robert N. "Jewish Confederates." In *Jewish Roots in Southern Soil: A New History*, edited by Marcie Cohen Ferris and Mark I. Greenberg, 109–33. Lebanon, NH: University Press of New England, 2006.

———. *The Jewish Confederates.* Columbia: University of South Carolina Press, 2000.

Sachar, Howard M. *A History of the Jews in America.* New York: Vintage Books, 1993.

Sarna, Jonathan D. *American Judaism: A History.* 2nd ed. New Haven, CT: Yale University Press, 2019.

———. *JPS: The Americanization of Jewish Culture, 1888–1988.* Philadelphia: Jewish Publication Society, 1989.

———. "The Touro Monument Controversy: Aniconism vs. Anti-Idolatry in a Mid-Nineteenth-Century American Jewish Religious Dispute." In *Between Jewish Tradition and Modernity: Rethinking an Old Opposition*, edited by Michael A. Meyer and David N. Myers, 80–95. Detroit: Wayne State University Press, 2014.

———. *When General Grant Expelled the Jews.* New York: Schocken Books, 2012.

Sarna, Jonathan D., and Benjamin Shapell. *Lincoln and the Jews: A History.* New York: Thomas Dunne Books, 2015.

Savage, Kirk. *Standing Soldiers, Kneeling Slaves: Race, War, and Monument in Nineteenth-Century*

America. Princeton, NJ: Princeton University Press, 1999.
Scholem, Gershom. "The Star of David: History of a Symbol." In *The Messianic Idea in Judaism, and Other Essays on Jewish Spirituality*, 257–81. New York: Schocken Books, 1971.
Schwain, Kristin. "Visual Culture and American Religions." *Religion Compass* 4, no. 3 (2010): 190–201.
Sharp, Lewis. "The Smith Memorial." In *Sculpture of a City: Philadelphia's Treasures in Bronze and Stone*, edited by Nicholas B. Wainwright, 168–79. New York: Walker, 1974.
Shikes, Ralph E., and Paula Harper. *Pissarro: His Life and Artwork*. New York: Horizon Press, 1980.
Singerman, Robert. "Bloch and Company: Pioneer Publishing House in the West." *Jewish Book Annual* 52 (1994–95): 110–30.
———. "The Jew as Racial Alien: The Genetic Component of American Anti-Semitism." In *Anti-Semitism in American History*, edited by David A. Gerber, 103–28. Urbana: University of Illinois Press, 1986.
Somma, Thomas P. "'Lost in America': David D'Angers's Bronze Statue of Thomas Jefferson, 1832–1833." In *American Pantheon: Sculptural and Artistic Decoration of the United States Capitol*, edited by Donald R. Kennon and Thomas P. Somma, 90–110. Athens: Ohio University Press, 2004.
Soria, Regina. "Moses Ezekiel's Studio in Rome." *Journal of the Archives of American Art* 4, no. 2 (April 1964): 6–9.
Stollman, Jennifer A. *Daughters of Israel, Daughters of the South: Southern Jewish Women and Identity in the Antebellum and Civil War South*. Boston: Academic Studies Press, 2013.
Stowe, William W. *Going Abroad: European Travel in Nineteenth-Century American Culture*. Princeton, NJ: Princeton University Press, 1994.
Sturrock, John. "Theory Versus Autobiography." In *The Culture of Autobiography: Constructions of Self-Representation*, edited by Robert Folkenflik, 21–37. Stanford, CA: Stanford University Press, 1993.
Tank, Holly. "Dedicated to Art: William Corcoran and the Founding of His Gallery." *Washington History*, Fall–Winter 2005, 26–51.
Tarbell, Roberta K. "Moses Jacob Ezekiel's Sculpture and Aesthetics in the Context of Nineteenth-Century Art and Philosophy." In *Ezekiel's Vision: Moses Jacob Ezekiel and the Classical Tradition*, edited by Alice M. Greenwald, 11–21. Philadelphia: National Museum of American Jewish History, 1985. Exhibition catalog.
Taylor, Joshua C. "America as Symbol." In *America as Art*, 3–35. Washington, DC: Smithsonian Institution Press, 1976.
Temkin, Sefton D. *Isaac Mayer Wise: Shaping American Judaism*. Oxford: Oxford University Press, 1992.
Thorp, Margaret Farrand. *The Literary Sculptors*. Durham, NC: Duke University Press, 1965.
Urofsky, Melvin I. *American Zionism from Herzl to the Holocaust*. Garden City, NY: Anchor Press / Doubleday, 1975.
———. *The Levy Family and Monticello, 1834–1923: Saving Thomas Jefferson's House*. Charlottesville, VA: Thomas Jefferson Foundation, 2001.
Vance, William L. *America's Rome: Catholic and Contemporary Rome*. Vol. 2. New Haven, CT: Yale University Press, 1989.
Vance, William L., Mary K. McGuigan, and John F. McGuigan Jr. *America's Rome: Artists in the Eternal City, 1800–1900*. Cooperstown, NY: Fennimore Art Museum, 2009. Exhibition catalog.
Vendryes, Margaret Rose. *Barthé: A Life in Sculpture*. Foreword by Jeffrey Stewart. Jackson: University Press of Mississippi, 2008.
Walker, Alan. *Franz Liszt: The Final Years, 1861–1886*. Vol. 3. Ithaca, NY: Cornell University Press, 1996.
Wallach, Alan. "The Birth of the American Art Museum." In *The American Bourgeoisie: Distinction and Identity in the Nineteenth Century*, edited by Sven Beckert and Julia B. Rosenbaum, 242–56. New York: Palgrave Macmillan, 2010.
———. "William Wilson Corcoran's Failed National Gallery." In *Exhibiting Contradiction: Essays on the Art Museum in the United States*, 22–37. Amherst: University of Massachusetts Press, 1998.
Weinman, Melvin. "The Attitude of Isaac Mayer Wise Toward Zionism and Palestine." *American Jewish Archives* 3, no. 2 (January 1951): 3–23.

Whitman, Walt. *Walt Whitman: The Correspondence.* Vol. 1, *1842–1867*. Edited by Edwin Haviland Miller. New York: New York University Press, 1961.

Wilson, Charles Reagan. *Baptized in Blood: The Religion of the Lost Cause, 1865–1920*. Athens: University of Georgia Press, 1980.

Wunder, Richard P. *Hiram Powers: Vermont Sculptor, 1805–1873*. 2 vols. Newark: University of Delaware Press, 1991.

Zalmona, Yigal. *Boris Schatz: The Father of Israeli Art.* Jerusalem: Israel Museum, 2006. Exhibition catalog.

Zola, Gary Phillip, and Marc Dollinger, eds. *American Jewish History: A Primary Source Reader.* Waltham, MA: Brandeis University Press, 2014.

INDEX

Works of art and books are indexed by artist (if known) or author. Page numbers in italics refer to illustrations. Art by Ezekiel unless indicated otherwise. "Ezekiel" refers to Moses Jacob Ezekiel; family members are named in full.